Homes of British
Speedway

ROBERT BAMFORD & JOHN JARVIS

TEMPUS

First published 2001

PUBLISHED IN THE UNITED KINGDOM BY:

Tempus Publishing Ltd
The Mill, Brimscombe Port
Stroud, Gloucestershire GL5 2QG

PUBLISHED IN THE UNITED STATES OF AMERICA BY:

Tempus Publishing Inc.
2A Cumberland Street
Charleston, SC 29401

Tempus books are available in France and Germany from the following addresses:

Tempus Publishing Group
21 Avenue de la République
37300 Joué-lès-Tours
FRANCE

Tempus Publishing Group
Gustav-Adolf-Straße 3
99084 Erfurt
GERMANY

British Library Cataloguing in Publication Data.
A catalogue record for this book is available from the British Library.

ISBN 0 7524 2210 3

Typesetting and origination by Tempus Publishing.
PRINTED AND BOUND IN GREAT BRITAIN.

CONTENTS

Acknowledgements   6

Introduction   7

The Homes of British Speedway   9

Beach Venues   281

Grass Speedway Tracks   285

ACKNOWLEDGEMENTS

This book is dedicated to Rosemary, for enduring thirty years of speedway research and endless visits to track sites.

The authors would like to thank a whole host of people, who over the years, have helped to unearth various pieces of information that have contributed to the production of this book. These include:

Michael Allen, Les Aubrey, Nick Barber, Roger Beaman, Tommy Bryce, Derek Carruthers, Max Connor, the late Revd Wilf Curtis, Trevor Delaney, Keith Farman, Graham Fraser, Colin Goddard, Les Hawkins, Bryan Horsnell, Roger Hulbert, Ted Humphrey, Mike Hunter, Jim Henry, Jeremy Jackson, Matt Jackson, Tony Jackson, Dave James, Trevor James, Dick Jarvs, Alan Jones, Howard Jones, Roger Last, Tony Lethbridge, Peter Lipscomb, Charles McKay, Trevor Miles, Peter Morrish, Ian Moultray, Bob Norman, Peter Oakes, Colin Parker, Geoff Parker, Fred Paul, Adrian Pavey, Robin Playsted, Bryan Seery, Glynn Shailes, John Smart, Dave Stallworthy, Ian Steel, Barry Stephenson, Norrie Tait, Steve Thorn, Bryan Tungate, Dave Twydell, Barry Wallace, Eric Watson, Bob Wayte.

INTRODUCTION

Speedway, like most sports today, has undergone many changes over the years, and historians Robert Bamford and John Jarvis, ever mindful of those changes have in this, their latest book, sought to chronicle them for the speedway connoisseur.

The book represents countless hours of work for both men. John has, over a number of years, built up a fine collection of track details, which now form a library of slides and a card index system. To this, Robert has added further information regarding the dates on which tracks opened and closed, and in a number of cases, happily reopened again, along with details of the various men who promoted the sport at each particular venue.

The book seeks to provide not only a summarised history, but a useful guide to supporters, and there are many who enjoy the hobby of programme collecting. It is a fine reference work that will be a welcome addition to the bookshelf of the speedway fan.

I was privileged to be asked to assist with researching some of the information on behalf of both Robert and John and ,whilst it was hard work, it was both interesting and informative. Of the few circuits that I was asked to help with, I learned much that I didn't know, and I have no doubt that you, the reader, will feel the same.

With regard to programme collecting, the book details all tracks, and as far as one can tell, programmes were always issued; some race-day programmes are very rare and extremely valuable. The rarity and value of the 1961 World Final programme, held at Malmo Stadium in Sweden, is well known within speedway, and now the reader will doubtless find more details of old venues, where now very scarce programmes were issued.

I am happy to commend the book to all speedway enthusiasts, as a welcome addition to their memorabilia collections. Do enjoy an excellent read.

Glynn Shailes
September 2001

A

ALDERSHOT

ADDRESS: Aldershot Sports Stadium, Boxall's Lane, Aldershot, Hampshire
YEARS OF OPERATION: 1929 Open
FIRST MEETING: 3 July 1929
TRACK LENGTH: 440 yards

An advert in May 1929, stated: 'The concern of the Aldershot Sports Stadium Ltd, which is shortly to open a speedway just outside Aldershot, wishes to secure the services of a racing manager. Applications should be addressed to E. Greenfell, Imperial Hotel, Aldershot.' A crowd of just 500 turned up for the opening meeting on 3 July 1929, when Stan Lemon won the Golden Armlet, but numbers did increase at subsequent meetings. The fastest recorded time was 94.8 seconds,

for 4 laps of the almost circular track. The stadium was almost devoid of any terracing or stands. This was a short-lived dirt-track operation, staging just eight meetings, with the final one going ahead on 5 August 1929, when the Golden Armlet was again raced for. The stadium site was subsequently redeveloped as a reservoir surrounded by housing.

ALDERSHOT

ADDRESS: Aldershot Stadium, Oxenden Road, Tongham, near Farnham, Hampshire
YEARS OF OPERATION: 1950-51 National League Division 3; 1952 Southern League; 1953 Open Licence; 1954 Southern Area League; 1957 Southern Area League; 1958 Open Licence; 1959 Southern Area League; 1960 Open Licence
FIRST MEETING: 10 April 1950
TRACK LENGTH: 302 yards (1950-58); 300 yards (1959-60)

Aldershot Stadium, Tongham, Hampshire.

A

NICKNAME: 'Shots' (1950-53 & 1959-60); 'Poppies' (1957)

There are suggestions that the track was used for training around 1930, but this may have been on a grass circuit at the time. Dicky Southouse was in charge of the track preparations in 1949, when the track was originally planned to be 285 yards in length. The shape of the track was one of the oddest in speedway history, being best described as 'pear-like'. The first trials on the track were held in February 1950. The track subsequently opened on 10 April 1950, when Basil Harris won the Easter Trophy. The Shots became members of the National League Division 3 in 1950, under the promotion of Bob Netcott and E. Netcott. Aldershot remained in Division 3 in 1951, prior to becoming members of the Southern League in 1952. However, that '52 season was marred by tragedy, when Goran Andersson died following a track crash at Aldershot Stadium. After a year of open licence events in 1953, Aldershot joined the Southern Area League in '54, only to withdraw having completed ten meetings. The final home match was against Brafield (Lost 41-42) in the league on 12 June. The track remained silent until 22 April 1957, when a Best Pairs event was staged. The track was subsequently used by California that season for their Southern Area League fixtures, riding under the name of Aldershot Poppies (and promoted by N.E. Cartlidge). Just two open licence meetings were staged at the stadium in 1958: 7/4 Easter Trophy; 10/5 Oxford Juniors. The Shots were back in business in 1959, again partaking in the Southern Area League, prior to a short season of open licence events in 1960, under the promotion of John Pilblad. The last scheduled meeting at the venue was versus a Young Overseas side on 13 August 1960, but unfortunately it was rained off. Upon the cessation of speedway at the venue, the track was eventually covered with tarmac and used for stock-car racing, under the auspices of the Spedeworth International Ltd. A final stock-car meeting was staged at the venue on 21 November 1992, after which the stadium closed down.

ALEXANDRA PALACE
ADDRESS: Roller Skating Arena, Alexandra Palace, Wood Green, London
YEARS OF OPERATION: 1937 Indoor Speedway Exhibition

In 1937, Phil Bishop attempted to race his speedway machine against a famous roller-skating champion at Alexandra Palace Roller Skating Arena!

AMMANFORD
ADDRESS: Ty-Gwaith Pony Trotting Track, nr Bryn Amman, South Wales
YEARS OF OPERATION: 1970 Open
FIRST MEETING: 12 September 1970
TRACK LENGTH: 440 yards

The one and only meeting at the venue was promoted by the Carmarthen Club at the Ammanford Trotting track on 12 September 1970, when Tig Perry won the 500cc Final. The competitors in the meeting were mainly grass-track riders, both solo and sidecar. Although the track was said to be made of cinders, the event was advertised as 'track racing'.

ARENA-ESSEX
ADDRESS: Arena-Essex Raceway, A1306 Arterial Road, Purfleet, Essex
YEARS OF OPERATION: 1984-90 National

League; 1991 British League Division 2; 1992-94 British League Division 1; 1995 British Premier League; 1996 British Conference League; 1997-2000 British Premier League

FIRST MEETING: 5 April 1984

TRACK LENGTH: 253 metres (1984-90); 252½ metres (1991-94); 285 metres (1995-2000)

NICKNAME: 'Hammers'

LEAGUE CHAMPIONS: 1991

KNOCK-OUT CUP WINNERS: 1991

Arena-Essex was the brain-child of Chick Woodroffe, who staged his first stock-car meeting at the venue on 1 May 1978. National League speedway arrived at the stadium, situated close to the Dartford Tunnel in 1984, when Chick Woodroffe and Wally Mawdsley became co-promoters. The opening meeting took place on 5 April 1984, when Bob Garrad won the Essex Radio Championship. The track was originally inside a tarmac car circuit, with no speedway safety fence. The outside line was marked by white flags and on many occasions riders were excluded for leaving the track. The outside post of the starting gate was taken down and carried to the centre-green during the first lap of a race. Peter Thorogood replaced Wally Mawdsley as co-promoter in 1986. Upon the amalgamation of the British and National Leagues, Arena-Essex became members of the new Division 2 in 1991, under the promotion of Terry Russell and Ivan Henry. That year, the track was made more conventional with the introduction of a proper safety fence in time for the start of the season. Having won the British League Division 2 Championship, the Hammers gained promotion to Division 1, and top-flight speedway arrived at the track in 1992. With the reopening of Hackney, promoters Terry Russell and Ivan Henry switched to the

Arena-Essex Raceway, Purfleet.

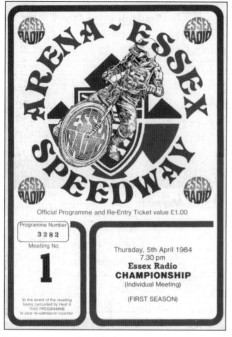

The programme from the first-ever meeting at Arena Essex, 1984.

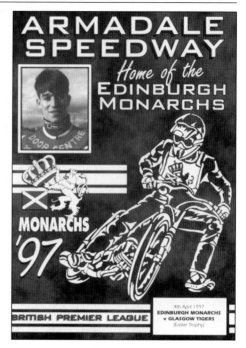

The opening meeting programme from Armadale Stadium, 1997.

Waterden Road venue, leaving Chick Woodroffe and Peter Thorogood to take up the reigns again at Arena, with a season of Conference League racing. In 1997, the Hammers joined the British Premier League, which was the equivalent of Division 2. On 14 June 1997, the BBC cameras were at Arena to film scenes for *Eastenders*, which featured soap character Ricky Butcher as a rider for the fictitious 'Walford Lions'. Actor Sid Owen was replaced by Hammer Troy Pratt for the actual race scenes. In 2000, Chick Woodroffe sold the speedway promotion, due to ill-health, with a consortium under the banner of Arena Speedway 2000 Ltd, taking over. The new promoters were headed by Colin Brine, with Peter Thorogood still on board as co-promoter. The year 2000 ended in great sadness on 3 December, with the death of the stadium owner, a man regarded by many as 'Mr Arena-Essex', Chick Woodroffe.

ARMADALE
ADDRESS: Armadale Stadium, Bathgate Road, Armadale, West Lothian
YEARS OF OPERATION: 1997-2000 British Premier League
FIRST MEETING: 4 April 1997
TRACK LENGTH: 280 metres
NICKNAME: 'Monarchs'
KNOCK-OUT CUP WINNERS: 1997, 1999
PREMIERSHIP WINNERS: 1998

Situated some twenty miles from Edinburgh, on the way to Glasgow, Armadale was a former stock car and greyhound racing circuit. Armadale became home to Edinburgh Monarchs in 1997, after they had been forced out of their Powderhall home at the end of the

Armadale Stadium, West Lothian.

1995 season. In 1996, they rode as the Scottish Monarchs at Shawfield Stadium in Glasgow. The initial practice session at Armadale saw Blair Scott become the first rider to set a wheel on the track. The opening meeting at Armadale was staged on 4 April 1997, when Edinburgh lost 43-47 to old rivals Glasgow in the Spring Trophy. The Monarchs have been promoted throughout their four years at the venue by Edinburgh Speedway (1986) Ltd (John Campbell and Alex Harkess).

ASHINGTON
ADDRESS: Portland Park Stadium, Ashington, Northumberland
YEARS OF OPERATION: 1972 Open Licence
FIRST MEETING: 5 April 1972
TRACK LENGTH: 400 yards
NICKNAME: Arrows

Ashington Football Club first played at Portland Park in 1909. The ground was sub-let from the Duke of Portland, who within three years had provided a grandstand and renamed the venue. Just twelve years later, Ashington were in the Football League, having terraced the ground on three sides and provided a thousand seats in an improved stand. Their stay in the League lasted for just eight seasons though, from 1921/22 to 1928/29 inclusively. A first greyhound meeting was staged at the venue on 3 October 1936. After the Second World War, Portland Park changed dramatically, with part of the terracing being removed and the pitch pushed northwards to make way for a larger track. A second grandstand lasted until 1971, when it was destroyed by a massive fire. It was eventually replaced by a more modest structure. The covered terrace opposite the grandstand was in place until 1990, when it was found to contain asbestos

Portland Park Stadium, Ashington.

and the roof was removed. Greyhound racing closed in 1964, but reopened again on 17 August 1984. Jeff Brownhut promoted car events at the stadium in 1971. He, along with Geoff Penikett, was the man responsible for bringing speedway to the venue in 1972, with the opening meeting being staged on 5 April, when Ashington lost 33-45 to Birmingham in a challenge match. It was a short-lived venture, however, as the second, and last meeting, was held on 17 May 1972, when Phil Crump won the Northumberland Open Championship.

ASPATRIA
ADDRESS: Brayton Domain Speedway, Aspatria, Cumbria
YEARS OF OPERATION: 1971 Training

Organised by Bessemer Speedway Club, this training track was situated twenty miles from Workington and run on Forestry Commission land. The club was known as Brayton Domain Speedway and its chief instructor was Lou Sansom.

AUDENSHAW
ADDRESS: Ashton Old Road, Audenshaw, Manchester
YEARS OF OPERATION: 1928-31 Open
FIRST MEETING: 3 March 1928
TRACK LENGTH: 880 yards

The venue was a converted trotting track, known locally as 'The Snipe'. As the track had been used for trotting, it was feared that there was a danger of tetanus if any of the riders fell! It was first thought that the ACU would only licence the track for clockwise racing, although normal racing was subsequently permitted. The opening meeting on 3 March 1928, was promoted by the South Manchester Club and attracted a crowd of some 15,000. H. Mitchell was the surprise winner of the

Unlimited Final, as the meeting had an all-star field, which included Ginger Lees and Billy Galloway. A total of seven meetings were staged in that initial season of track action. In 1929, meetings were promoted by Stalybridge Motor Club, an organisation not recognised by speedway's governing body, so riders were banned from racing at the circuit by the Northern Dirt-Track Owners Association. However, many riders did take part under false names and wore masks. This problem was eventually overcome when a new company, Northern Motor Sports Ltd, was formed to take over the running in association with the South Manchester Club. They were given associate membership of the Northern Dirt-Track Owners Association and, as such, were then approved to run meetings by the ACU. Due to the lack of a safety fence in certain parts of the track, the authorities began to take a closer look at the venue. Heaps of coal slag had been used as a buffer between the track and the outside perimeter in some areas where there was no fence, and this was obviously dangerous for the riders. After the racing was 'blacked', the crowds turned up in even greater numbers to see riders appear from properly licensed tracks. As had happened before at the venue, all the riders wore masks to conceal their identity and rode under false names like 'Dan De Lyon', 'The Red Terror' and 'The Thriller'. Twenty-eight-year-old George Rowlands was killed at the circuit in June 1929. In March 1930, the stadium went up for sale in lots, as housing had sprung up all around the immediate area – however, racing carried on throughout the summer, although the meetings continued to be run without a licence. On 29 June 1930, more than 12,000 spectators paid

for admission, with another 5,000 obtaining free entry when barriers were broken down. On 30 August 1930, William Owens from Widnes received fatal injuries in a crash at the track and had died within two hours. On 2 August 1931, James Kenny died from injuries received in another accident at the track. Due to the track having no licence, Kenny had been riding under the name of Jack Smith. Later on in August 1931, Billy Brown became the fourth rider to die after crashing at the venue. The Brown incident finally brought the curtain down on the track, when a court injunction was enforced. The fifteenth and final meeting of that 1931 season was held on 16 August, when Riskit Riley was victorious in the Audenshaw Cap. Several attempts were made to reopen the doors to speedway, but to no avail. A first greyhound meeting took place at the stadium on 15 March 1932. Prior to the Second World War, the site had gone for good, having become a housing estate.

AVIEMORE
ADDRESS: Aviemore Ice Rink, Aviemore, Highlands
YEARS OF OPERATION: 1972 Indoor Ice Speedway
FIRST MEETING: 8 April 1972

Indoor ice speedway was popular in 1972, with meetings also taking place at Kirkcaldy, Murrayfield and Solihull. Just one meeting was staged at the Aviemore Ice Rink, on 8 April 1972, when Allan Forbes and Pete Bremner won the Best Pairs event. As was the case at Kirkcaldy and Murrayfield, the meeting at Aviemore was promoted by Trevor Hay.

AYCLIFFE
ADDRESS: Aycliffe Stadium, Aycliffe

Aycliffe Stadium, County Durham.

Trading Estate, nr Darlington, County Durham
YEARS OF OPERATION: 1948 Practice; 1952 Training and Open
TRACK LENGTH: 370 yards

The idea of a dog track in Aycliffe was formulated in 1946 by a group of local businessmen. In 1948, Mr Arthur Moody, one of the directors, was keen to incorporate a cinder track with the project. The turfed dog track was already laid and it worked out that a speedway track of 340-350 yards could be put down inside, although the bends would be tight, with long straights. A number of riders took their bikes to the site and rode a considerable number of laps on the grass infield, in order to convince the directors that speedway was practical. During 1949, little progress was made, due to difficulties over construction licences. Work eventually started in 1951, with a voluntary labour force of amateurs and enthusiastic juniors laying an ash surface over a base of hard clinker. The ash was donated by the nearby Darlington Power Station. A tarmac starting area was laid and a portable safety fence erected on springs and tension wire. In little more than a year, a bare field with a dog track had become a floodlit stadium, with a grandstand and regulation size speedway track. During 1952, the track was used by novice riders for training on Sunday afternoons, with their performances monitored by Freddie Fewsdale. Mr Fewsdale resigned as manager later in 1952, to be replaced by Margaret Kent, who freely admitted that she knew nothing about speedway. However, she did state that she would be running the Aycliffe Swallows the following Easter. She went on: 'We're already negotiating for some London riders and ran a series of trials earlier this year that attracted about 200 riders, including ex-Newcastle and Middlesbrough men'. Sadly though, her plans never came to fruition. The site was used extensively for stock car racing from 1956 onwards. Greyhound racing ceased at the venue in the 1960s.

AYR
ADDRESS: Dam Park, Ayr
YEARS OF OPERATION: 1937 Open
FIRST MEETING: 19 July 1937

Dirt-track meetings were promoted by Maurice and Roland Stobart, after a cinder track had been laid, a safety fence erected and starting gate installed. Clerk of the course was Jimmie Guthrie, winner of the Isle of Man TT race in 1937. The opening meeting, held on 19 July 1937, attracted a crowd of 5,000 people, who saw Steve Langton triumph in the Provost Wills Trophy. Admission charges were 1/- and 2/6 for terracing and grandstand respectively. Two days after the first meeting, a team match was staged between Workington and

Lancaster, which Workington won 18-10. Sadly, this was another short-lived dirt-track venue though, with just the two meetings taking place. The stadium closed to greyhound racing in 1972, having staged the sport for thirty-nine years. The venue was refurbished as an athletics stadium in the mid-1980s.

B

BALLYMENA
ADDRESS: Showgrounds, Ballymena, County Antrim
YEARS OF OPERATION: 1982 Open
FIRST MEETING: 13 July 1982
TRACK LENGTH: 440 yards

This was a stock car and hot-rod circuit, run under the promotion of Robert Mathers. There was an estimated crowd of 5,000 in attendance for the one and

Dam Park, Ayr.

only speedway meeting, on 13 July 1982, when Cradley Heath beat an Ivan Mauger Select 40-38, in a challenge match. For the purpose of the meeting, the tarmac track had been covered in a shale and sand surface, while a special wooden safety fence was also erected.

BARNET

ADDRESS: Mays Lane, Barnet, Greater London
YEARS OF OPERATION: 1929-37 Open
FIRST MEETING: 27 July 1929

Mr A. Goody from Stoke Newington, opened negotiations for the purchase of land to be used for dirt-track racing in March 1928. Racing was staged at the site that year on 17 August but, to all intents and purposes, it was the grass-track variety. The circuit was situated at the bottom of Barnet Hill, two miles from the Great North Road and racing was promoted by Barnet Speedway Ltd. The directors of the company were Messrs Banister, Botten and de Cort, motor dealers from Highbury Corner. The track was 'D' shaped, with one very short straight, two sharp turns and one long bend. The long bend had an upward slope, while the more acute of the sharp turns had a pronounced downward sweep. The opening dirt-track meeting at the circuit took place on 27 July 1929. A handful of meetings were run that year, on Sundays with a 3.30 p.m. start. George Wilks is known to have ridden at Barnet in 1929, using a V-twin Speedway James. Gordon Parkins first saw speedway when he went to Barnet in 1935.

BARNSLEY

ADDRESS: Lundwood, Barnsley, South Yorkshire
YEARS OF OPERATION: 1928 Open; 1929 English Dirt-track League; 1930 Northern League
FIRST MEETING: 29 May 1928
TRACK LENGTH: 380 yards

The track was built on a hillside, with turf piled up to a height of three feet around the track to form a safety fence. Things were very basic, as there were no pits or stands. The opening meeting, held on 29 May 1928, was promoted by Barnsley Motorcycle and Car Club. The opening meeting of the 1929 season saw Bob Allen establish a new track record of 1 minute 29.0 seconds. Allen was also victorious in the Silver Sash and All-Star Scratch Race. Lundwood was actually the very first track in Britain to stage a league match, when Barnsley entertained Leeds on 29 March 1929. In 1930, Barnsley resigned from the Northern League and it was announced that the closure was because attendance figures had seldom reached the 2,000 mark. The final meeting at the venue was a staging of the Golden Helmet on 5 July. During the Second World War, the track was used for Home Guard and Army exercises. There were suggestions that the track could be used for training in 1949, but nothing ever came to fruition.

BARROW

ADDRESS: Holker Street, Barrow-in-Furness, Lancashire
YEARS OF OPERATION: 1930 Open; 1972 Open Licence and British League Division Two; 1973-74 British League Division Two
FIRST MEETING: 21 June 1930
TRACK LENGTH: 415 yards (1972-73); 370 yards (1974)
NICKNAME: 'Happy Faces' (1972); 'Bombers' (1973-74)

Lundwood, Barnsley.

Holker Street had been the home of Barrow Football Club since 1909. It was a traditional four-sided ground until the early 1970s. On the North side was the main stand, which held 1,500 spectators and ran for three-quarters of the pitch length with a paddock at the front. Opposite the main stand was covered terracing, known as the 'Popular Side'. Barrow FC originally became members of the Football League in 1921/22, but lost their League status at the end of the 1971/72 campaign, when they were replaced by Hereford United. The original track consisted of cinders laid on top of the grass, running around the outside of the football pitch, with a two-foot-high safety fence made of corrugated sheets with sharp points at the top! The opening grass speedway meeting at the venue took place on 12 June 1930, when Eric Airey won the Senior Final. This was quickly followed nine days later, by an opening dirt-track meeting on 21 June when G. Skerron won the Senior Final. Claude Rye was successful in Golden Helmet meetings staged at the venue on 14 July and 21 July 1930. Frank Charles is known to have won the Golden Armlet meeting staged on 28 July 1930. That was the final meeting to be staged at the venue until speedway was resurrected there in 1972. The reason given for the closure later, in August 1930, was that the ground was being made ready for the new football season. Ground alterations had to be made in 1972, in order to allow the return of speedway, under the promotion of Wally Mawdsley, Ivan Mauger and Peter Oakes. This meant demolishing terracing at the end of the ground to let the pitch be moved West. This allowed the track to be widened and the return of speedway saw John Harrhy win a World Championship qualifying round on 27 April 1972. Having started with open

Holker Street, Barrow-in-Furness.

licence meetings, Barrow later became participants in the British League Division Two, when they took over the licence and fixtures of West Ham. George Graham was promoter at the venue from 1973-74, but after three seasons of racing, the track was lost to the sport, when Mr Graham was unable reach an agreement over rent with the football club. The final meeting at Holker Street was held on 24 September 1974, when Barrow beat Workington 43-35 in a challenge match. In 1979, the undeveloped part of the stadium was considerably improved when squash courts, a bar and leisure centre were built.

BARROW
ADDRESS: Little Park, Roose, Barrow-in-Furness, Lancashire
YEARS OF OPERATION: 1931 Open
FIRST MEETING: 1 June 1931
TRACK LENGTH: 350 yards

Little Park was the home of Barrow Football Club, prior to their move to Holker Street in 1909. The site of the track was on the old rugby football ground, which was situated 3 miles from the town centre. Barrow Rugby League Club had used the ground from 1914 to 1931. During the 1920/21 season, the Rugby Committee agreed to purchase the ground from Lord Richard Cavendish for £3,000. A new 66 yard long stand was subsequently opened on 3 September 1921. A record crowd of 12,214 turned up on 17 March 1923 for a third round Challenge Cup tie versus Oldham. In 1924, another stand, which seated 500 people and had standing room for 4,000 was erected. In 1928/29, the Rugby Committee decided to seek a move into the centre of town, which resulted in the opening of Craven Park on 29 August 1931. The main stand and wooden shelters, along with 92,000 turfs, were moved from Little Park to create the new venue. Amongst the stars booked for the opening dirt-track meeting on 1 June 1931, were Frank Varey, Frank Charles, Wally Hull, Max Grosskreutz, Indian Allen and Tommy Simpson. Frank Varey was the first rider to set a wheel on the track, but it was Frank Charles who was victorious in the main Handicap Final. A report on the following weeks meeting stated: 'The racing at the second meeting on 8 June 1931, fell much below the standard of the previous week. The majority of the visitors appearing to have adopted the 'safety first' motto on the bumpy surface.' Following a third meeting on 15 June, the next event planned for 22 June was cancelled, pending an ACU inspection, because previous meeting reports had suggested the track to be very bumpy. After receiving approval from the ACU, the track reopened on 24 August that year, for what was the venue's fourth and final meeting. Greyhound racing was also staged at Little Park, but ceased in 1932, when the stadium was sold. The stadium site is now lost to housing, although the nearby Ship Inn, which acted as the club's changing rooms, still remains. The present Roose Amateur Rugby League Club play on the adjacent recreation ground, off Leece Lane.

BARROW

ADDRESS: Barrow-in-Furness, Lancashire
YEARS OF OPERATION: 1952 Training

It was reported in 1950 that a small, but enthusiastic group of Dalton-in-Furness businessmen, headed by Mr C.A. Hindle, were working hard to bring speedway to the area. They had acquired a small practice track and were encouraging several local riders to also travel to Sheffield and Wigan for further experience. Information on this venue is sketchy, but training sessions were definitely run in 1952.

BARROW

ADDRESS: Park Road Stadium, Park Road, Barrow-in-Furness, Cumbria
YEARS OF OPERATION: 1977 Open; 1978 National League; 1981 National League; 1983 Training; 1984 Open; 1985 National League and Open Licence
FIRST MEETING: 16 August 1977
TRACK LENGTH: 300 yards (1977-78); 306 yards (1984-85)
NICKNAME: 'Furness Flyers' (1977-78); 'Blackhawks' (1984-85)

This was a council-owned site, with the track and stadium constructed by locally-based Cliff Hindle. Cliff Hindle and Chris Roynon were amongst those involved in noise level tests in July 1976. Four machines were used whilst environmental health officers measured the noise. The track opened on 16 August 1977, when Barrow defeated Glasgow 44-34, in the first of a series of open licence challenge matches, under the promotion of the aforementioned Cliff Hindle. Barrow joined the National League in 1978, but the track closed at the end of the season, following a year of poor on-track results. The final meeting was staged on 3 October when the Furness Flyers defeated Teesside 43-35 in a challenge match. The homeless Berwick side used the venue in 1981, between 18 April and 6 June, when they staged six meetings, while another two were postponed. The track was used for training in 1983, under the guidance of Chris Roynon, but apparently only two youngsters turned up for the initial session! Under the promotion of Chris Roynon, speedway returned to the venue

Park Road Stadium, Barrow-in-Furness.

Opening meeting programme from Park Road, 1977.

on 17 July 1984, when Barrow beat Stoke 40-38 in a challenge match. Following a successful series of open licence events in 1984, the renamed Blackhawks joined the National League in 1985, but they were forced to withdraw due to the weakness of their team. At the time of their withdrawal, they had ridden just three league matches, but they continued to run with an open licence for the remainder of the year. The final speedway meeting to be staged at Park Road was held on 10 September 1985, when the Blackhawks defeated Workington 41-37, in a challenge match. By 1987, a sand-based greyhound circuit had been installed, with Chris Roynon as the owner and racing manager.

BASINGSTOKE
ADDRESS: Ice Rink, Westfield Lido, West Ham Park, West Ham, Basingstoke, Hampshire

YEARS OF OPERATION: 1991 Ice Racing Demonstration
FIRST MEETING: October 1991

The rink was opened in 1988, with an ice size of 197 x 98 feet, while the arena had a spectator capacity of 2,000. Graham Drury raced four laps on his own against the clock, before ice speed skater Paul Johnson, beat the former speedway rider's time by a couple of seconds. This challenge formed part of the TV show *You Bet*, and was screened on Friday 1 November 1991. The Quad Oval Racing Association ran a four-team meeting at the venue on 4 December 1994, with the result being Reading 23 Swindon 21 Basingstoke 16 Coventry 16. A second quad meeting was staged at the rink on 8 January 1995.

BELFAST
ADDRESS: Windsor Park, Belfast
YEARS OF OPERATION: 1928 Open
FIRST MEETING: 29 September 1928

The track was situated around the Linfield Football Club pitch. The Ulster Centre of the Motorcycle Union of Ireland raised objections about the racing and refused to issue a permit. Promoted by the British Dirt-Track Racing Association, the one and only meeting at the venue was staged on 29 September 1928, when Stewie St George won the Golden Helmet. After the meeting, however, the Ulster Centre sought an explanation from the riders who took part. The participants were subsequently suspended from taking part in unauthorised meetings at Windsor Park, and were each fined £1. Discussions were held in 1929, regarding the reopening of the track, and although agreement was reached, subject to the compliance with all

the necessary regulations, racing was never staged at the venue again.

BELFAST
ADDRESS: Gibson Park, Belfast
YEARS OF OPERATION: 1947 Open; 1949 Training
TRACK LENGTH: 440 yards

Racing in 1947 was organised by Henry Robinson and Norman Railton, whose company was known as The Irish Recreation Company. The track surface was laid by a helpful bunch of would-be spectators. A picket safety fence was installed and held in place by sandbags. Four teams are known to have raced at the venue on a twice weekly basis in 1947: Antrim Aces, Tyrone Typhoons, Down Bucaneers, Cregagh Panthers. The track record was held by Billie McCrea, who clocked 100.8 seconds. In 1949, it was reported that 'In preparation for the opening of Dunmore Park Speedway, practice meetings are being held at the other Belfast track, Gibson Park, three times a week, with admission to the public at the price of 1/9 each Friday night. Already, members of the Improvement Committee of Belfast Corporation have had to visit Gibson Park to see if local residents complaints about noise are fully justified.'

BELFAST
ADDRESS: Dunmore Park, Alexandra Park Avenue, Antrim Road, Belfast
YEARS OF OPERATION: 1950 Open; 1968 Open
FIRST MEETING: 20 May 1950
TRACK LENGTH: 316 yards
NICKNAME: 'Bees'

Greyhound racing was first staged at the

venue on 6 September 1928. The original 1950 speedway track had 18-inch banking, with a top dressing of red kiln dust on a clay base, with crushed granite. Promoted by Dunmore Speedway Co. Ltd, the opening meeting at the venue took place on 20 May 1950, when Tommy Turnham won the Dunmore Trophy. A team was formed in that initial year, and rode under the name of Belfast Bees, and was promoted by Dunmore Speedway Co. Ltd. Average attendances for a series of thirteen open licence meetings in 1950 were reportedly around the 5,000 mark but, in spite of that, the track closed at the end of the year. Under the promotion of Nason Promotions Ltd, the track reopened for speedway on 3 June 1968, when Bob Kilby was victorious in an individual event. Two further meetings are known to have been staged that year, on 10 June and 15 June.

BELLE VUE

ADDRESS: Greyhound Stadium, Kirkmanshulme Lane, Gorton, Manchester
YEARS OF OPERATION: 1928 Open; 1988-90 British League; 1991-94 British League Division One; 1995-96 British Premier League; 1997 British Elite League and British Amateur League; 1998-2000 British Elite League
FIRST MEETING: 28 July 1928
TRACK LENGTH: 440 yards (1928); 285 metres (1988-2000)
NICKNAME: 'Aces' (The Amateur League side of 1997, were known as 'Colts')
LEAGUE CHAMPIONS: 1993

The greyhound track at Kirky Lane was the first to open in Britain when, on 24 July 1927, some 1,700 enthusiasts witnessed a dog called Mistley win the very first race. A grass-track meeting took place at the venue on 5 May 1928, with Syd Jackson emerging as the winner. The dirt track was originally stated to be similar in size and shape to Wimbledon and Harringay, with the first meeting going ahead on 28 July 1928, when Frank Arthur won the Golden Helmet. A total of thirteen meetings were staged at the Greyhound Stadium in that initial year, promoted under the banner of International Speedways Ltd. The last meeting of 1928 was held on 18 September, when Oliver Langton won the Silver Armlet, after which the dirt-track racing moved to the Zoological Gardens in Hyde Road. When the stadium at Hyde Road was sold to British Car Auctions in 1987, the world-famous Aces moved back to the Greyhound Stadium, under the promotion of Peter Collins, John Perrin and Don Bowes. The opening meeting of the new era at Kirky Lane was held on 1 April 1988, and saw Belle Vue take on Bradford in the Frank Varey Northern Trophy. However, the match was abandoned after just two heats, with the Aces leading 7-5. Due to other business commitments, Peter Collins resigned from his promotional position in June 1989, leaving John Perrin and Don Bowes in charge of the tracks affairs. With the amalgamation of the two leagues, Belle Vue became members of the British League Division One in 1991. A management change saw George Carswell link with John Perrin and Don Bowes as co-promoter in 1994. Both divisions of the British League joined together to form a twenty-one team Premier League in 1995, with Belle Vue becoming founder members. A further change on the promoting side that year saw John Hall take the place of Don Bowes, to link up with John Perrin and George Carswell. The

Belle Vue Greyhound Stadium, Manchester.

Premier League broke in two at the end of 1996, with the Aces becoming members of the new Elite League, where they have remained right up to the present day. In 1997, two teams operated at the venue, with the Aces participating in the British Elite League, while the Colts partook in the British Amateur League. The Colts' opening fixture took place following an Elite League match versus Ipswich on 2 May and saw the home side win 39-30, versus the Anglian Angels. The meeting was abandoned after twelve heats, but the result was allowed to stand. Due to fixture congestion, the Colts were forced to hold their last three home matches of the one-year operation at Buxton. The final Colts league match at Kirky Lane was held on 5 September after an Elite League match between Belle Vue and Bradford, and saw the Colts lose 26-46 to Mildenhall. Again, the meeting was abandoned after twelve heats, with the result standing.

BELLE VUE
ADDRESS: Zoological Gardens, Hyde Road, Manchester
YEARS OF OPERATION: 1929 English Dirt-track League; 1930 Northern League; 1931 Northern League and Southern League; 1932-33 National League; 1934 National League and Reserve League; 1935-36 National League; 1937 National League and Provincial League; 1938 National League Division One; 1939 National League Division One and Division Two; 1940-45 Open; 1946 National League; 1947-56 National League Division One; 1957-64 National League; 1965-67 British League; 1968-69 British League Division One and Division Two; 1970-74 British League Division One; 1975-87 British League
FIRST MEETING: 23 March 1929
TRACK LENGTH: 418 yards (1929-46 and

1954-87); 423 yards (1947-53)

NICKNAME: 'Aces' (The Reserve League team of 1934 were known as 'Goats'; The Provincial League team of 1937 were known as 'Merseysiders'; The Division Two side of 1968-69 were called the 'Colts')

LEAGUE CHAMPIONS: 1930, 1931, 1933, 1934, 1935, 1936, 1963, 1970, 1971, 1972, 1982 (The Division Two side also won their league in 1968 and 1969!)

KNOCK-OUT CUP WINNERS: 1931, 1972, 1973, 1975 (The Division Two side also won their Knock-out Cup in 1969)

NATIONAL TROPHY WINNERS: 1933, 1934, 1935, 1936, 1937, 1946, 1947, 1949, 1958

ACU CUP WINNERS: 1934, 1935, 1936, 1937, 1946

BRITISH SPEEDWAY CUP WINNERS: 1939

BRITANNIA SHIELD WINNERS: 1957, 1958, 1960

INTER-LEAGUE KNOCK-OUT CUP WINNERS: 1975

PREMIERSHIP WINNERS: 1983

LEAGUE CUP WINNERS: 1983

The stadium had a capacity of 40,000, and was built around an existing athletics and cycling track, which was originally used by Salford Harriers in 1888. It is alleged that Britain's first open grass-track event took place at the venue on 25 February 1928, when a six-hour programme was held on a smooth grass surface third-of-a-mile circuit, with all events being run over ten laps. The meeting attracted a crowd of 12,000 people and started at 2 p.m., with an hour interval after four events. During the interval, forty acetylene flares were lit around the stadium, along with a searchlight, creating quite a spectacle. Oliver Langton won the 500cc Solo Final, while Syd Jackson took the 350cc Solo Final. Darfield and District Motorcycle & Light Car Club are known to have staged a grass-track meeting at Belle Vue on 28 May 1928. Later, with the grass gone, it was claimed to be the first purpose-built dirt-track in Britain, with a wire-mesh fence mounted on coil springs, augmented by a special tensional strainer wire. Foundations, composed mainly of clinker, had been laid at the start of the previous winter and had been allowed to settle for nearly six months. The top dressing of cinders was three inches deep. Racing was opened under the auspices of the North Manchester Motor Club in conjunction with International Speedway Ltd, the trading company of legendary supremo E.O. (Eric) Spence. The opening dirt-track meeting at the stadium was staged on 23 March 1929, when Arthur Franklyn won the Golden Helmet. The stadium was also used by Manchester Central Football Club, who played in the Cheshire League until they disbanded. It was reported in 1929 that, during the interval of a soccer match between Manchester Central and Buxton, Arthur Franklyn and Wilfie McClure treated the spectators to a few quick laps of the dirt-track. McClure was handicapped by a tight engine, so after four laps, he toured into the pits and downed tools. Belle Vue resigned from the English Dirt-track League in July 1929, stating that league racing was not popular enough, although by the following year, the club was in the Northern League. In 1931, Belle Vue Reserves took over Harringay's fixtures, after they had withdrawn from the Southern League. That meant the Manchester club had a side operating in both the Northern

North Manchester Motor Club

PRESIDENT: J. HENRY ILES, Esq.

PROGRAMME

BELLE VUE SPEEDWAY

Saturday, March 23rd, 1929.

At 7-0 p.m.

The Management reserve the right to alter or vary this Programme without notice.

Held under the General Competition and Special Track Rules of the Auto Cycle Union, together with the Supplementary Regulations of the Club.

Track Licence No. 318.

Prize Money and Appearance Fees in accordance with the Scales authorised by the Northern Dirt Track Owners' Association.

Extract from Supplementary Regulations :—" If, in the opinion of the Clerk-of-the-Course, a fallen rider lies on the Track to the danger of other riders, and by his having fallen, definitely jeopardises the chances of a following competitor, the race will be stopped by the display of the Red Track Lights, and immediately re-run."

OFFICIALS.

CLERK-OF-THE-COURSE - -	E. O. SPENCE, ESQ.
JUDGE - - - - -	A. S. MORGAN, ESQ.
STARTER - - - -	J. W. CAMPBELL, ESQ.
TIMEKEEPER - - - -	H. S. WHEELDON, ESQ.
PIT STEWARD - - - -	R. BOYES, ESQ.
MECHANICAL SUPERINTENDENT	M. GAVSON, ESQ.
TREASURER - - - -	S. CHESTER, ESQ.
TRACK MANAGER - - -	B. L. BROOK, ESQ.

Opening Demonstration

Franklyn's Mystery Riders

IN FOUR-LAP RACE.

WHO ARE THEY ?

The very rare programme from the first-ever meeting at Belle Vue's famous Hyde Road Stadium.

Belle Vue's Golden Jubilee programme, 1978.

League and the Southern League that year. On 12 September 1931, Jimmy 'Indian' Allan died, three days after crashing at Belle Vue. In 1932, Belle Vue also took part in the National Speedway Association Trophy, which was held prior to the National League Championship. After a trial game on 20 August 1933, the first rugby match between Belle Vue Rangers and Warrington took place two weeks later, on 2 September at Hyde Road. The playing surface was among the best in the league, with thousands standing on the speedway track for the big matches. Rangers were served with notice to quit in June 1955. Belle Vue again operated two teams in 1934, one in the National League and the other, known as the Goats, in the Reserve League (which was also sometimes referred to as the National League Division Two). Liverpool transferred their Provincial League operation to Belle Vue in 1937, so again, Belle Vue operated a team in both leagues and

even adopted the Merseysiders' moniker. The first home match ridden as the Merseysiders took place on 19 August, when the home team beat Southampton 49-35. Also that year, the control tower on the centre green was replaced by a box on top of the stand at the end of the season. Aside from speedway, the track was used for midget car racing in 1938, under the direction of The Association of Speedway Car Racing Circuits. In 1939, Belle Vue Reserves took over the National League Division Two fixtures of Stoke, who withdrew after eight meetings, so yet again two sides operated from Hyde Road that year. The reserve side also partook in the Northern Section of the Union Cup that season, along with Edinburgh, Glasgow, Newcastle and Sheffield. Belle Vue ran a staggering total of 176 meetings (including two in September 1939) during the war years, which were attended by 2,816,000 people in total. The winners of the war-time British Individual Championships were: 1940 Eric Chitty, 1941 Eric Chitty, 1942 Eric Chitty, 1943 Ron Clarke, 1944 Frank Varey, 1945 Bill Kitchen. The 1940 season opened on 22 March and a total of twenty-nine meetings were staged that year. Hyde Road opened for business on 11 April 1941, and a total of twenty-nine meetings were again held that year. The track opened on 4 April in 1942, staging twenty-seven meetings that season. E.O. Spence had run the show right from the start but, from 22 May 1943, Alice Hart became promoter at the track. A total of twenty-four meetings were held that year, the first of which was on 24 April. Twenty-six meetings were staged in 1944, including the opener on 8 April. In 1945, the track opened on 31 March and an amazing total of thirty-nine meetings were staged throughout the year, including six novice meetings, which were held on Wednesdays. Sadly though, Maurice Butler died the day after crashing at Belle Vue on 22 August that year. After the war, team racing resumed, with the Aces taking their place in the 1946 National League, and subsequently Division One the following year. There was sadness on 13 September 1947 however, when legendary supremo E.O. Spence died. The effervescent Johnnie Hoskins took over from Alice Hart as promoter in 1953. With so few tracks left running, the Aces found themselves in the eleven-team National League in 1957. A further change on the promotional side occurred in 1960, when Ken Sharples took charge. Harold Jackson took over as general speedway manager in 1964, prior to the Aces becoming founder members of the British League in 1965. Dent Oliver became speedway manager in 1967, and remained in position until 1973. The 1968 season saw the stadium housing two teams (again), with Belle Vue Colts partaking in the newly-formed British League Division Two. The Colts' opening meeting was held at Hyde Road on 8 May when they beat Canterbury 55-23, in the very first match of the new league. The Colts venture lasted for two seasons, with the final match being staged on 24 September 1969, when the home side beat Crewe 55-23, in the Knock-out Cup final. The following season, Belle Vue moved their Division Two operation to Rochdale. Frank Varey took over as speedway manager in 1974, before long-time Belle Vue Zoo Park director Jack Feranley took up the promoting reigns in 1975. In 1982, former stock car world champion Stuart Bamforth became pro-moter, having purchased the stadium from the then owners, Trust House Forte. The famous Hyde Road circuit was then also used for stock car racing right up to its closure in 1987. Following the announcement that Stuart Bamford had sold the stadium for redevelopment, the last speedway meeting was staged on 1 November 1987, when a double-header took place. Firstly, Belle Vue defeated Coventry 40-38, in a replay of the League Cup final, before losing 37-41 to Cradley Heath in a British League match. The site is now covered by the ADT Car Auctions showroom, which was opened on 13 June 1989.

BELLE VUE
ADDRESS: Zoological Gardens Car Park, Hyde Road, Manchester
YEARS OF OPERATION: 1950-51 Training

During the winter of 1950/51, Bob Harrison is known to have run a training track in the Belle Vue car park.

BERWICK
ADDRESS: Shielfield Park, Tweedmouth, Berwick-upon-Tweed, Northumberland
YEARS OF OPERATION: 1968-74 British League Division Two; 1975-80 National League; 1995 Demonstration; 1996 Conference League; 1997 British Premier League and British Amateur League; 1998-2000 British Premier League
FIRST MEETING: 18 May 1968
TRACK LENGTH: 405 metres (1968); 402 metres (1969-80); 368 metres (1996-2000)
NICKNAME: 'Bandits' (The Amateur League team of 1997 were known as 'Border Raiders').
KNOCK-OUT CUP WINNERS: 1980

Shielfield Park, Berwick-upon-Tweed.

The original owner of the land in 1890 was a butcher by the name of Shiel Dods. Berwick Rangers first played at the site in 1890, but were forced to move to Meadow Field following an argument in 1902. The football club returned to Shielfield Park in 1919. The original pitch was next to the current one, which opened in September 1954, with a match versus Aston Villa. Constructed almost entirely by volunteers, the new Shielfield Park was set out with a wide track and sea turf from Goswick. The centrepiece was the former Midland Road stand from Valley Parade, Bradford. Work started on the adjacent site in 1951, and prior to the official opening in 1954, an outer track was used by a motorcycle stunt team. The operating of speedway at the stadium was the brain-child of Andrew Taylor (known as Danny), with the track being opened by Mayor J.H. Thomson on 18 May 1968, when Berwick lost 37-41 to Newcastle

Colts in a challenge match before a crowd of 3,000 fans. Berwick subsequently joined the British League Division Two, but sadly, Danny Taylor died at the end of that initial season in October 1968, with his wife, Elizabeth, and son, Ken, taking over the running of the track. Mrs T. and Ken subsequently took the Bandits into the New National League upon its formation in 1975. The stadium landlords Berwick Rangers FC, gave the Bandits notice to quit in 1980, and speedway ceased at the venue following a double-header on 6 September that year, when the Bandits defeated Peterborough 49-29 in a National League match, prior to beating Mildenhall 52-26, in a Knock-out Cup semi-final tie. The Bandits' premature departure from Shielfield Park forced them to stage two outstanding league fixtures, plus their 'home' leg of the Knock-out Cup final at Newcastle's Brough Park. During 1981, the homeless

Berwick team staged meetings at Craighead Park (Glasgow), Brough Park (Newcastle), Derwent Park (Workington) and Park Road (Barrow) in an effort to maintain their place in the National League, while they got their new track ready at Berrington Lough. In mid-September, however, they withdrew from the league with their record being expunged. They did continue in the Knock-out Cup though and, despite having to ride all their matches away from home, made it to the final, only to lose to Edinburgh. Greyhound racing was introduced to Shielfield Park in 1991. Promoter Mike Hope was behind plans for the return of speedway to the venue in 1996. Prior to this, Kevin Little, David Meldrum, Anthony Barlow and Paul Gould had taken part in formal noise level tests at the stadium in July 1995. The track reopened for speedway on 17 August 1996, when the Bandits beat Owlerton Prowlers 49-29 in a British Conference League fixture. In 1997, Berwick were admitted to the British Premier League, with John Robertson joining Mike Hope as co-promoter. The promoters ran two sides at the track that year, with Berwick Border Raiders also partaking in the British Amateur League, which had replaced the Conference League. Having completed their 1997 fixtures, however, the Border Raiders opted out of the Amateur League and what turned out to be their last home match was held on 4 October that year, when they defeated Oxford 52-26. Subsequently, speedway continued to run at the Northumberland venue, but with just the senior Berwick side partaking in the Premier League. A change of promoter in 1999 saw Peter Waite take over the running of the track,

with the Bandits continuing on into 2000 (the club's thirty-third consecutive season) and beyond.

BERWICK

ADDRESS: Berrington Lough Stadium, Nr Ancroft, Northumberland

YEARS OF OPERATION: 1982-90 National League; 1991 British League Division One; 1992 British League Division Two; 1993 Open; 1994 British League Division Three; 1995 British Academy League

FIRST MEETING: 24 April 1982

TRACK LENGTH: 250 metres (1982-84); 242 metres (1985-86); 253 metres (1987-95)

NICKNAME: 'Bandits'

KNOCK-OUT CUP WINNERS: 1989, 1995

GOLD CUP WINNERS: 1991

LEAGUE CHAMPIONS: 1994, 1995

Planning permission for the track at Berrington Lough was granted on 11 June 1981. It was hoped to be ready for opening in July or August that year, but plans were delayed until the start of the 1982 season, when the Bandits rejoined the National League. The opening meeting at the new track was staged on 24 April 1982, when Berwick beat Edinburgh 56-40 in a challenge match. The club was still under the promotion of Elizabeth Taylor, but a number of other directors had joined the board by then, including Davie Fairbairn, Ian Graham and Peter Waite. During 1984, Davie Fairbairn took up the promoting reigns, and he was to remain in charge until the end of 1989. There was sad news for the Bandits supporters in June 1986, at the announcement of the death of former promoter Elizabeth Taylor, aged sixty-six.

Berrington Lough Stadium, near Ancroft, Northumberland.

The 1989 campaign was marred by the death of Ian Graham on 23 August. Ian had done so much for Berwick speedway over the years, as a supporter, accountant and director. Terry Lindon became promoter in 1990, and the following year made the bold decision to take the Bandits into the British League Division One. However, one season in the higher echelons of British speedway ended with the club being asked to resign from Division One amid mounting financial problems. Terry Lindon carried on in 1992, with Dave Younghusband as co-promoter, as the Bandits reverted to the British League Division Two. With continuing financial difficulties, Terry Lindon departed at the end of the season and the future of the track was thrown into serious doubt. Mike Hope and John Campbell resurrected the track late in 1993, stag-

ing just two meetings before the end of the season: 2 October featured The Rose *v*. The Thistle, and 16 October the Stars of Tomorrow. In 1994, Mike Hope took Berwick into the newly-formed British League Division Three, and continued on the following year, when that became the British Academy League. Later on, in 1995, promoter Mike Hope revealed plans to take the Bandits back to their original home at Shielfield Park in 1996. The final meeting staged at Berrington Lough saw the Bandits defeat Stoke 63-42, in the British Academy League Knock-out Cup final on 21 October 1995.

BERWICK
ADDRESS: Berwick Training Track, Berrington Lough, Nr Ancroft, Northumberland
YEARS OF OPERATION: 1989-91

Training; 1993 Training
TRACK LENGTH: 120 metres

It was reported in 1986 that Berwick were due to start work on their new training track at Berrington Lough. The man behind the venture was Mark Courtney, and it was hoped to form a junior club when it was finished. Work was delayed, but eventually the mini-track was completed in time for the 1989 season. The training track was adjacent to Berwick's main circuit, situated behind the back straight. In 1991, Chris Morton was on hand to offer advice, coaching and tuition, although the mini-track was restricted to machines with an engine capacity of 250cc or less. 125cc meetings were run at the venue in the summer of 1993, for which programmes were apparently produced.

BETHERSDEN

ADDRESS: Bethersden, Nr Ashford, Kent
YEARS OF OPERATION: 1968-71 Training
TRACK LENGTH: 320 yards

It was reported in August 1968, that Reg Luckhurst planned to open his own training school in the grounds of his pig farm. He constructed his track on farmland situated off the A28 Ashford to Tenterden Road. The cost of training was £1 per day on the ash-surfaced circuit, with riders using a cowshed as a changing room. Barry Thomas and Dave Jessup are known to have trained on the private track prior to the 1969 season. Alan Sage came to the fore while training at the track in January 1970. Graham Banks and Ted Hubbard are known to have used the facilities in 1971. The track closed following complaints about noise later in 1971, although it was later rumoured, in January 1974, that Reg Luckhurst had planned to use the track to try out a Weslake prior to the up-coming season.

BIRMINGHAM

ADDRESS: Alexander Sports Stadium, Perry Barr, Birmingham, West Midlands
YEARS OF OPERATION: 1928 Open; 1946 Northern League; 1947-48 National League Division Two; 1949-56 National League Division One; 1957 National League; 1960 Open
FIRST MEETING: 12 July 1928
TRACK LENGTH: 380 yards (1928); 402 yards (1946-60)
NICKNAME: 'Brummies'.
ANNIVERSARY CUP (DIVISION TWO) WINNERS: 1948

The Alexander Sports Stadium is the long-time home of Birchfield Harriers Athletics Club. Dirt-track racing was promoted in 1928 by Sutton Coldfield and North Birmingham Automobile Club. A crowd of 6,000 turned up for the opening meeting on 12 July 1928, when Gordon Baxter won the Scratch Race. Twelve meetings were held that year, the last of which went ahead on 1 September, but there was to be no more of the cinder sport at the venue until 1946. During wartime, the stadium was occupied by Italian prisoners of war. Promoter Les Marshall resurrected the track after the war, with the reopening meeting taking place on 4 May 1946, when the Brummies beat Norwich 56-48 in a National Trophy tie. The Brummies partook in the Northern League that year, but the season was marred by the death of thirty-three-

Alexander Sports Stadium, Perry Barr, Birmingham.

Re-opening meeting programme, 1960.

year-old Canadian Charlie Appleby in a crash at Newcastle on 7 October. And as if that wasn't enough, twenty-five-year-old Hugh Watkinson died following a crash while practising at the Alexander Stadium in November. Birmingham joined the National League Division Two in 1947, before achieving promotion to Division One in 1949. With the sport going through a rough time, and tracks closing up and down the country, the Brummies found themselves in the eleven-team National League in 1957. It was still something of a shock though, when Les Marshall announced Birmingham's withdrawal after their 66-30 National League victory over Swindon on 27 July that year. The team fulfilled one further away match at Belle Vue, but at the time of their closure, Birmingham had completed just nine matches of their league programme, with Bradford subsequently taking over their remaining fixtures. Under the promotion of Phil Hart and Doug Ellis, the track reopened on 20 May 1960, when Arne Pander won the Alan Hunt Memorial Trophy. Just nine meetings were staged that year and they were the last to be staged at the track. The final meeting of the nine was held on 23 September, when the Brummies lost 41-49 to London in a challenge match. Planning permission was sought for speedway to return to the venue in 1985, but nothing came to fruition. The stadium has continued to be used for major athletics events, which are often screened on television.

BIRMINGHAM

ADDRESS: Hall Green Greyhound Stadium, York Road, Hall Green, Edgbaston, Birmingham, West Midlands
YEARS OF OPERATION: 1928 Open; 1929-30 Southern League; 1931 Open; 1934 National League and Reserve League; 1937 Provincial League; 1938 National League Division Two
FIRST MEETING: 3 August 1928
TRACK LENGTH: 339 yards (1928-30); 340 yards (1931-34); 302 yards (1937-38)
NICKNAME: 'Blues' (1928-34); 'Bulldogs' (1937-38)

The track opened for greyhound racing on 24 August 1927, in front of 20,000. Dirt-track racing was promoted by International Speedways in 1928, with the black cinder track being constructed inside the existing dog track. The opening dirt-track meeting was staged at the stadium on 3 August 1928, when Eric Spencer won the Golden Helmet. With the start of league racing in 1929, a side riding as Hall Green entered the Southern League, only to resign after completing just seven of their fixtures;

however, the track did continue to run with an open licence. Hall Green rejoined the Southern League in 1930, but had the misfortune of the grandstand burning down in July – the cause of the fire was believed to be a dropped cigarette end. Nine open licence fixtures followed in 1931, with the final one taking place on 12 June when the home side beat West Ham 30-23 in a challenge match. Following that, the track remained closed for two full seasons. Reopening in 1934, Hall Green operated two teams, one in the National League and the other in the Reserve League; however, a loss of £4,000 was recorded on the season, and the track closed again. After another two year absence, the cinder sport returned in 1937, with the renamed

A rare Birmingham (Hall Green) programme.

Hall Green Greyhound Stadium, Birmingham.

Birmingham Bulldogs operating in the Provincial League. There was tragedy that year though, when twenty-three-year-old Stan Hart died in a track crash at the stadium on 25 August. After completing a year of National League Division Two racing in 1938, a court injunction was taken out against speedway and that was the end of the sport at the venue.

BIRMINGHAM

ADDRESS: Motordrome Greet, Colebrook Road, Birmingham, West Midlands
YEARS OF OPERATION: 1928 Open
FIRST MEETING: 6 August 1928
TRACK LENGTH: 350 yards

The track cost £2,000 to construct and was created on an old rubbish dump at the rear of the BSA factory. It was built by Birmingham Motorcycle Club, whose clubroom is still in Colebrook Road, just inside the main gate of the Serck radiator factory, which now covers the site. The track was used extensively for practice purposes in 1928, prior to an opening meeting on 6 August, which saw Dennis Mansell win the three-lap Sidecar Race, while Bunny Wilcox took the honours in the 500cc Final. Only one other meeting was staged at the venue, two days after the first, on 8 August.

BIRMINGHAM

ADDRESS: Perry Barr Greyhound Stadium, Walsall Road, Birmingham, West Midlands
YEARS OF OPERATION: 1929-30

Southern League; 1971-74 British League Division Two; 1975 National League; 1976-83 British League
FIRST MEETING: 13 April 1929
TRACK LENGTH: 410 yards (1929-30); 350 yards (1971-76); 330 yards (1977-83)
NICKNAME: 'Brummies' (1971-83)
LEAGUE CHAMPIONS: 1974, 1975
KNOCK-OUT CUP WINNERS: 1974

Perry Barr Stadium opened for greyhound racing on 7 April 1928. The greyhound track stood in twenty-two acres of its own ground, with soil banking surrounding the circuit so that spectators could have a decent view. There was parking for 5,000 cars. In 1929, dirt-track meetings were promoted by Velodromes Ltd, with Fred Mockford installed as manager. Following an opening meeting on 13 April, Birmingham subse-

quently joined the Southern League. Birmingham resigned from the Southern League after a meeting on 14 May 1930. It appeared that complications had arisen between the greyhound and dirt-track interests, when the former began to press for the running of bi-weekly meetings. Dirt-track racing did continue, however, with open licence events. The greyhound management ran a dirt-track meeting on 23 August 1930, but racing was confined to Douglas machines in an effort to reproduce the shows of old. A final meeting was staged on 11 October that year, and it would be forty long years before speedway returned to the West Midlands venue. Under the promotion of Speedway Presentations (Birmingham) Ltd, Colin Barber, Joe Thurley and John Berry brought speedway back to the venue in 1971. The reopening meeting was held on 24 May,

Perry Barr Greyhound Stadium, Birmingham.

when Birmingham drew 39-39 with Long Eaton in a Knock-out Cup tie, after which, the Brummies subsequently took their place in the British League Division Two. Division Two turned into the New National League in 1975, with the Brummies taking their place in the new set-up and storming to the championship. They then applied to join the British League, and were eventually accepted in time for the 1976 campaign. Peter York became general manager at the track in 1979, before a change of promotion in 1981, when Dan McCormick and Chris Van Straaten took over, under the banner of Topshire Ltd. The stadium owners, Ladbrokes, announced during 1983 that the venue would be closing for supermarket development. A final speedway meeting was staged later that year on 10 October, when Birmingham lost 23-55 to Cradley Heath in a challenge match. The Brummies subsequently relocated to the Wheels Project at Bordesley Green. A final greyhound meeting was staged at Perry Barr on 14 April 1984.

BIRMINGHAM

ADDRESS: National Exhibition Centre, Birmingham, West Midlands
YEARS OF OPERATION: 1980 Indoor Speedway; 1984 Indoor Speedway
FIRST MEETING: 17 January 1980

Four separate indoor sessions on a latex surface were staged over the course of three days, between 17 and 19 January 1980. Jan Andersson proved to be the master of the tricky circuit, winning the Daily Mirror International Championship. The three-day event was promoted by Charles Ochiltree, Wally Mawdsley and Peter Oakes, under

the title of World Indoor Speedway Championship Presentations Ltd. In 1984, further indoor meetings were promoted at the NEC by Wally Mawdsley and Bob De Jong, the first of which saw England lose 42-52 to Europe on 21 January. The following day, Jan Andersson was victorious in the Daily Mirror Euro-Superstars Grand Prix. Later in 1984, on 17 November, a Rest of the World side defeated England 57-37 at the NEC. The following day, John Jorgensen, Jan Andersson, Hans Nielsen and Shawn McConnell partook in a Grand Prix-style event that formed part of combined programme, which also included trials and moto-cross racing.

BIRMINGHAM

ADDRESS: Birmingham Wheels Project, Bordesley Green, Birmingham, West Midlands
YEARS OF OPERATION: 1984 Open Licence; 1985-86 National League
FIRST MEETING: 2 September 1984
TRACK LENGTH: 330 metres (1984-85); 300 metres (1986)
NICKNAME: 'Brummies'

Having lost their Perry Barr home to re-development, promoter Dan McCormick moved the Brummies to the Wheels Project in the Bordesley Green district of Birmingham. The track opened on 2 September 1984, with a Junior Four Team Tournament that finished Birmingham 31, Long Eaton 27, Stoke 21, Cradley Heath 14. Birmingham joined the National League in 1985, under the promotion of Les Powell and Tom Evitts (Second City Promotions Ltd), but extensive track problems were experienced, which led to talk of a move back to the old Perry Barr circuit

Birmingham Wheels Project, Birmingham.

at the Alexander Sports Stadium. Birmingham carried on at the Wheels Centre in 1986, with Duncan Corbett replacing Tom Evitts as co-promoter in mid-season. However, Duncan Corbett stepped down after three months, leaving Les Powell in sole control of a track where crowd levels had never been good. What turned out to be the final meeting at the venue was staged on 26 September, when the Brummies crashed to a 30-48 defeat versus Eastbourne in a National League fixture. The track was subsequently covered in tarmac, and used for stock car racing.

BLACKPOOL
ADDRESS: Blackpool & Fylde Motor and Aero Club, Highfield Road Sports Ground, South Shore, Blackpool, Lancashire
YEARS OF OPERATION: 1928-30 Open

GRAND OPENING MATCH - SUNDAY, 2nd SEPTEMBER, 1984
JUNIOR 4 TEAM TOURNAMENT
Birmingham v. Long Eaton v. Cradley Heath v. Stoke
Official Programme 50 p

Birmingham Wheels Project opening programme.

FIRST MEETING: 21 April 1928
TRACK LENGTH: 880 yards

Originally constructed as a trotting track, the circuit was never actually used for this purpose. Eleven dirt-track meetings were promoted in 1928, by North Manchester Motor Club. The opening meeting was staged on 21 April when a crowd of around 4,000 saw Oliver Langton win the Unlimited Class. All the races at the early meetings were run clockwise over a distance of six laps – an amazing three miles in total! It is recorded that at the fourth Highfield Road meeting on 14 July 1928, C.E. Needham covered the six-lap distance in 3 minutes and 56 seconds. The banked track surface was apparently comprised of 75 per cent sand, and 25 per cent earth – it having being claimed that cinders or ashes were not conducive to broadsiding in a 1928 report! Open licence events continued in 1929, but just three meetings were staged at the circuit in 1930, the last being held on 21 April, after which the stadium was reported to be lying idle. By all accounts this was a superb venue, with an impressive grandstand and a paddock area that contained more than 100 well-built horse boxes, which were easily converted into pits for the dirt-track riders.

BLACKPOOL
ADDRESS: South Shore Greyhound Stadium, St Annes Road, South Shore, Blackpool, Lancashire
YEARS OF OPERATION: 1928-29 Open
FIRST MEETING: 11 September 1928

Greyhound racing was first staged at the stadium on 30 July 1927. With a circuit laid inside the greyhound course, dirt-track racing arrived at the venue in 1928. Six meetings were staged that year, promoted by the British Dirt-Track Racing Association Ltd, with the opener being held on 11 September when Ginger Lees won the Golden Gauntlet. Two seasons of open licence events were staged, before the cinder sport petered out at the venue. The stadium became home to Blackpool Borough Rugby League Club between 1954 and 1963. Due to the position of the inside hare rail, the pitch was the minimum allowed for Rugby League. When the stadium was sold for housing, Blackpool Borough RLC were given until the end of the 1962/63 season to find a new home. A final greyhound meeting took place on 30 October 1964. The stadium site was lost to housing in the late 1960s, with a road called Stadium Drive left in its memory.

BOLTON
ADDRESS: Raikes Park, Manchester Road, Bolton
YEARS OF OPERATION: 1928 Open; 1929 English Dirt-track League and Open
FIRST MEETING: 20 August 1928
TRACK LENGTH: 440 yards

A first greyhound meeting took place at Raikes Park on 10 December 1927. Seven dirt-track meetings were held at Raikes Park in 1928, on a red shale track that had been constructed inside a greyhound course. The promoters were M.F. Edwards and A. Horrocks, who were motor dealers in Bolton itself. They promoted under the title of The Lancashire Dirt-Track Racing Association Ltd. A crowd of over

Raikes Park, Bolton.

6,000 were in attendance for the opening meeting on 20 August 1928, when Norman Dawson won the Senior Cup. In 1929, W.D. Meagher, chairman of the Northern Dirt-Track Owners Association and a director at the Preston and Leeds tracks, took over complete control of the venue. A crowd of 4,000 people attended the first meeting of the 1929 season, on 23 March. A total of only four meetings were staged in 1929 (on 23/3, 29/3, 6/4 and 20/4). The final meeting of the four was Bolton's one and only English Dirt-track League match, versus Preston, which they won 36-24. Bolton subsequently resigned from the league, with their fixtures being taken over by Hanley. It was reported that Jack Gordon was anxious to obtain a licence to run speedway at the venue in 1951, but nothing came to fruition. It was also reported in 1991, that 'The Department of the Environment overturned an appeal by the stadium owners to turn the site into a retail and hotel complex. The company is now investing in the track, in a bid to attract stock-car racing.'

BOSTON
ADDRESS: Boston Sports Stadium, New Hammond Beck Road, Boston, Lincolnshire
YEARS OF OPERATION: 1970-74 British League Division Two; 1975-84 National League; 1986-87 National League
FIRST MEETING: 16 August 1970
TRACK LENGTH: 380 yards (1970-80); 363 yards (1981); 352 yards (1982-87)
NICKNAME: 'Barracudas'
LEAGUE CHAMPIONS: 1973
KNOCK-OUT CUP WINNERS: 1973

A first greyhound meeting staged at the venue was held on 1 June 1964. Promoted by Cyril Crane and Gordon

41

Parkins, under the banner of Sporting Enterprises (Boston), speedway arrived at the stadium on 16 August 1970, when Boston beat Peterborough 49-29, in the Inter-Counties Challenge Cup. Subsequently, the newly-formed Barracudas joined the British League Division Two, completing the fixtures of King's Lynn Starlets, following their withdrawal from Saddlebow Road. After winning the BL Division Two League and Knock-out Cup double in 1973, Boston were refused a licence to join the British League Division One. The Barracudas became founder members of the New National League in 1975. A slight change at the top in 1980 saw Cyril Crane become sole-promoter, although Gordon Parkins stayed on as general manager. Having completed ten successive years of National League racing, Boston did not run in 1985 – the

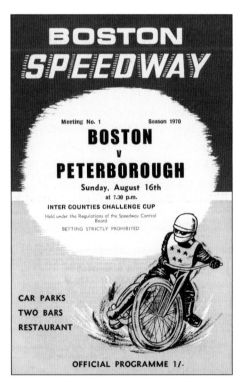

Boston's opening meeting programme, 1970.

last meeting from their first period of track action took place on 14 October 1984, when Billy Burton won the Lincolnshire Trophy. Promoter Cyril Crane citing that, due to the ninety hours a week it took to run speedway, he was neglecting his other business interests. After a year out of action, the track reopened on 6 April 1986, when Boston defeated Peterborough 44-34, in the Poacher Shield. Boston rejoined the National League that year, under the promotion of Lincolnshire Speedways Ltd, a consortium including Cyril Crane, Mike Corby and Richard Green. The track continued on into 1987, but falling crowds created a financial strain and the club were forced to withdraw from the league. The last meeting ever staged at the venue took place on 1 August, 1987, when the Barracudas lost 23-55 to Eastbourne in a National League fixture. In an effort to resurrect speedway in Boston, Stephen Lambert ran a Conference League side at King's Lynn in 2000, under the name of Boston Barracuda-Braves, while he continued his search for a suitable site in the Lincolnshire town.

BOTHWELL
ADDRESS: Bothwell Park Farm, Bothwell, Nr Glasgow
YEARS OF OPERATION: 1949-50 Open and Training; 1951 Training
FIRST MEETING: 26 November 1949
NICKNAME: 'Bulls'

A field owned by James Gibson at Bothwell Farm was set aside and a cinder track, along with safety fence, was constructed during the summer of 1949. Laid on a railway siding, the track was constructed entirely by voluntary

Boston Sports Stadium.

labour, using red shale from an adjacent pit. Allan Robertson, Ken McKinlay and Alf McIntosh were the prime movers behind the idea, which became known as Bothwell Park Training School. The school instructors were Ken Le Breton, Will Lowther and Joe Crowther. The first team match at the track was staged on 26 November 1949, when Bothwell Bulls beat Will Lowther's Select 40-39. Among the riders taking part were Ken McKinlay, Tommy Miller, Alec 'Farmer' Grant and Willie Gordon. The announcer at the meeting was Joe Crowther. The last bend became known as the 'Devil's Elbow', due to the number of falls at that particular part of the track. A report in late January 1950, stated that 'Sunday 8 January saw the Bothwell Park Motorcycle Club at practice once again. Due to inclement weather, the track was a quagmire of mud and the riders had to suffer occasional headers into the dirt!' In 1950, Gundy Harris landed in England from Australia, and received practice facilities at Bothwell. On his first outing, he looped and severely buckled his machine. A Best Pairs meeting was staged on 18 March 1950, with Tommy Miller (14 points) and Duncan Hendry (3 points) emerging as the winners. Gundy Harris and partner Fred Rowe finished fourth. A report in April 1950, stated 'By the way, Bothwell is a pukka track with starting gate, red shale surface, refreshments, grandstand, music, bikes and riders. Also it is the only track where they use a warning flag on the back railway straight, which is one of the safest factors yet devised.' During the winter of 1950/51, Bothwell lost the use of their track and made plans to move to Calderbank. The final speedway at the venue amounted to training sessions and these ceased in February 1951. Ian Hoskins proposed reopening the track in 1968, but nothing came to fruition.

BOURNEMOUTH

ADDRESS: Westover Ice Rink, Westover Road, Bournemouth, Dorset
YEARS OF OPERATION: 1933 Indoor Ice Speedway

Ice speedway on grass bikes with spiked tyres is known to have been staged at Westover Ice Rink in October 1933. The size of the ice was 120 by 80 feet, while there was a spectator capacity for 1,000.

BOURNEMOUTH

ADDRESS: Windsor Hall,
Bournemouth International Centre, Bournemouth, Dorset
YEARS OF OPERATION: 2001 Indoor Speedway
FIRST MEETING: 27 January 2001

Promoted by Jon Cook, Martin Dugard, Matthew Ford and Michael Golding, indoor speedway on a real shale surface was first staged at the BIC on Saturday 27 January 2001, when David Meldrum won the SVR and JT Commercials Shoot-Out. A further meeting was staged on the afternoon of Sunday 28 January 2001, when a four-team tournament for the Sea View Coaches Trophy finished thus: Elite-Eagles.com 44, World Champ Select 33, Poole 20, Polish Select 20. A third meeting went ahead on the evening of 28 January 2001, which saw Paul Hurry triumph in the Verwood Ford Indoor Classic.

BRADFORD

ADDRESS: Shelf Moor, Bradford, West Yorkshire
YEARS OF OPERATION: 1928 Open
FIRST MEETING: 15 April 1928
TRACK LENGTH: 880 yards

Dirt-track racing arrived at Shelf Moor on 15 April 1928, when Oliver Langton won the Solo Final. Races in the first meeting were held over two laps. Meetings were promoted by Bradford Motor Club. The track was described as being roughly oval in shape, half grass and half cinders.

BRADFORD

ADDRESS: Fronby Avenue, Bradford, West Yorkshire
YEARS OF OPERATION: 1928 Open
FIRST MEETING: 19 May 1928

Promoted by Bradford Special Constables Association, dirt-track racing was first staged at the venue on 19 May 1928, when A.G. Mitchell won the Russell Rose Challenge Trophy. The track was a mixture of soil and loose cinders.

BRADFORD

ADDRESS: Greenfield Autodrome, Dudley Hill, Bradford, West Yorkshire
YEARS OF OPERATION: 1928 Open; 1961 Open; 1962 Provincial League
FIRST MEETING: 7 July 1928
TRACK LENGTH: 335 yards
NICKNAME: 'Panthers' (1961-62)

The site was used by Bradford Northern Rugby League Club in the 1907/08 season, when it was then known as Greenfield Athletic Ground. The rugby club rented the stadium from Whitaker's Brewery for a mere £8. The six-acre field had a pear-shaped running and trotting track around it. Bradford Northern's headquarters were at the adjacent Greenfield Hotel and the brewery became the club's main sponsor. Northern lost to Huddersfield in the opening match at Greenfield on 7 September 1907, when a crowd of 7,000 was in attendance. Northern spent £302 on a grandstand, fencing and the pitch at the stadium. The first greyhound meeting at the venue was held in October 1927. Dirt-track meetings in 1928 were promoted by Bradford and District Motor Club. Just four meetings were staged in 1928, the first of which took place on 7 July when Alec Hill won the Championship Belt. Attendance figures were very poor though – only 2,000 people attended each of the first two meetings, and this dropped to 1,000 for the third, while a meagre 750 saw the fourth and last meeting on 25 July, when Oliver Langton won the scratch event. Apparently, the gate receipts did not even cover the prize money that was paid out at the four meetings. The track was described as having tight bends, with the starting gate close to the first turn. Further dirt-track action took place at the venue on 2 August 1928, when a Bike v. Greyhound event was held during a greyhound meeting. Speedway returned to Greenfield in 1961, when it was promoted by Jess Halliday. A considerable amount of work had to be done prior to any racing, with over 900 tons of earth being removed before a new track was laid. Six open meetings were staged at the venue in 1961, the first of which was a challenge match on Tuesday 15 August, when Bradford lost 30-47 to Sheffield. In 1962 the track operated in the Provincial League, with Mike Parker taking over as promoter mid-way through the campaign. It was, however, not a successful venture, as support was never good and the side ended up bottom of the league. The track closed at the end of that year, with the final meeting being staged on 9 October when a Provincial League double-header saw the Panthers draw 39-39 with Sheffield, before defeating Leicester 49-28. Greyhound racing was staged at the venue until March 1969. The former site of the Greenfield Stadium and hotel is now covered by industrial warehousing.

BRADFORD

ADDRESS: Odsal Stadium, Odsal Top, Bradford, West Yorkshire

YEARS OF OPERATION: 1945 Open; 1946 National League; 1947-56 National League Division One; 1957 Open and National League; 1959 Open; 1960 Provincial League; 1970-74 British League Division Two; 1975 National League; 1984 Demonstration; 1985 Open; 1986-90 British League; 1991-94 British League Division One; 1995-96 British Premier League; 1997 British Elite League

FIRST MEETING: 23 June 1945

TRACK LENGTH: 382 yards (1945-46); 370 yards (1947-54); 376 yards (1955-57); 386 yards (1959-60); 380 yards (1970-72); 375 yards (1973-74); 370 yards (1985-95); 374 yards (1996-97)

NICKNAME: 'Boomerangs' (1946-49); 'Tudors' (1950-57); 'Panthers' (1960); 'Northern' (1970-73); 'Barons' (1974-75); 'Dukes' (1986-97)

GOLD CUP WINNERS: 1990

BSPA CUP WINNERS: 1991

KNOCK-OUT CUP WINNERS: 1991, 1992, 1993, 1995

PREMIERSHIP WINNERS: 1994

LEAGUE CHAMPIONS: 1997

The speedway track was constructed around the pitch belonging to Bradford Northern Rugby League Club, who had had control of the ground since

Odsal Stadium, Bradford.

1 January 1934. The stadium was officially opened on 1 September 1934, when Bradford lost 16-31 to Huddersfield. Rugby club director Harry Hornby linked up with promoter Johnnie Hoskins to bring speedway to the stadium in 1945. The track was opened by Lord Mayor Alderman Cecil Barnett on 23 June 1945, when a crowd of 20,000 watched Wilf Jay win the A.J. Elvin Cup. After a season of open licence events in 1945, Odsal joined the National League in 1946, when attendance figures averaged an amazing 31,000. Thirty-two-year-old Albert Rosenfeld lost his life ten days after crashing at Odsal on 6 July 1946. A Test Match between England and Australia attracted a crowd of 47,050 on 5 July 1947. The team went under the name of Odsal between 1946 and 1956, but thereafter they were called Bradford –

although they used no fewer than six different nicknames over their track history. A concrete starting grid was laid in 1948, measuring three feet in width (it was the first of its kind in the country). Johnnie Hoskins stepped down at the end of the 1948 campaign, with Bruce Booth reaching agreement with Harry Hornby to take over as promoter. Joe Abbott was killed at Odsal Stadium on 1 July 1950, in a match against West Ham. Known as the 'Iron Man', he was forty-seven-years old when he died. During the 1950s, it was discovered that the Odsal Stadium had been situated in a deep channel that was gouged out during the fourth ice age, some 10,000 years previously. On 26 May 1954, the stadium hosted the first stock car meeting in Britain to be held outside London. In 1957, Bradford ran open licence meetings, but joined the

National League upon Birmingham's closure, taking over the Brummies remaining fixtures. The track closed at the end of the season, however, with the last meeting being against Oxford (won 58-37) in the league on 28 September. In 1959, four pirate meetings were staged at the venue by Mike Parker, who had been refused a licence by the Speedway Control Board. Composite meetings were staged, which included midget car racing, with some of the riders using false names for fear of suspension. The first of these pirate meetings was a Cavalcade of Speedway event staged on 6 June, while further meetings included a challenge match versus Liverpool, another track which was running without a licence at the time. Under the promotion of Jess Halliday, Bradford competed in the Provincial League in 1960, but the rugby club refused permission for further meetings to be staged after the end of the season. The final meeting had seen the home team lose 31-41 to Rayleigh in a league encounter on 13 August. Promoter Jess Halliday subsequently reintroduced speedway to Bradford's Greenfield Autodrome in 1961. Under the promotion of Mike Parker and Les Whaley, speedway returned to Odsal on 24 June 1970, when Bradford defeated Eastbourne 44-34 in a British League Division Two fixture. The side had taken over the fixtures of Nelson, who had closed after completing eight league meetings. Bill Bridgett joined the promotional team of Mike Parker and Les Whaley in 1971, before a further change mid-way through 1973 saw former rider Alan Knapkin take over the running of the track. Bradford became founder members of the New National League in 1975, when more changes on the promotional side saw Jim Streets take over, under the banner of Motor Sport Promotions (Bradford) Ltd. The track again closed at the end of the 1975 campaign, however, following a National League double-header on 1 October when Bradford defeated both Stoke (45-33) and Mildenhall (51-27). In September 1984, Chris Morton, Peter Collins and Larry Ross took part in a demonstration at Odsal, with every move scrutinised by FIM officials with a view to the return of speedway to the venue in 1985, for World Championship events. The reopening meeting took place on 12 May 1985, when a World Team Cup qualifying round was staged. The result of the meeting was: England 42, Australia 21, New Zealand 17, Finland 16. The final of the World Individual Championship was held at Odsal on 31 August 1985, when Erik Gundersen retained the title he had won the previous year in Gothenburg. Under the promotion of Eric Boothroyd, British League racing began at Odsal in 1986, following the closure of Halifax at the end of the 1985 season. Eric Boothroyd was joined by Bobby and Allan Ham on the promotional side in 1990. That same year, a second World Final was staged at the venue on 1 September, when Sweden's Per Jonsson took the title. Upon the merger of the British League with the National League in 1991, Bradford became members of the new Division One, with Bobby and Allan Ham taking over full control of the track. Further changes to the sport saw Bradford become part of the twenty-one-team British Premier League in 1995. With the splitting up of the Premier League, the

Dukes joined the new British Elite League in 1997 but, despite winning the championship, it was the last season of action at the track. The final meeting was held on 11 October that year, when Greg Hancock won the Elite League Riders' Championship. In 2000, the remaining shale was lifted from Odsal and used in the construction of a new track at Oak Tree Arena, Highbridge in Somerset.

BRADFORD

ADDRESS: Training Track, Bradford, West Yorkshire
YEARS OF OPERATION: 1948 Training
TRACK LENGTH: 240 yards

It was reported in November 1948, that 'Odsal's novice riders have their own winter training track. A pit hill on the outskirts of the city has taken new shape and every weekend, riders are to be seen tearing around the 240-yard track'.

BRAFIELD

ADDRESS: Brafield Sports Stadium, Brafield-on-the-Green, Nr Northampton, Northamptonshire
YEARS OF OPERATION: 1951 Training; 1953 Open and Training; 1954-55 Southern Area League; 1966-67 Open Licence; 1968 Training; 1971 Training
TRACK LENGTH: 420 yards (1951-53); 430 yards (1954-55); 335 yards (1966-67)
NICKNAME: 'Flying Foxes' (1954-55); 'Badgers' (1966-67)

The stadium was originally built in 1947, for the presentation of midget car racing, although the first such meeting wasn't held until 10 September 1949. A local baker, Dave Hughes, was the man behind the venture. Jim Wright introduced a training school at Brafield in 1951, with the track being available for practice every Sunday. Midget car training sessions were staged at Brafield in 1952. Speedway training in 1953 was under the direction of Paddy Mills, costing 15/9 per day. The first meeting proper at the stadium was held on 2 May 1954, when Brafield defeated Eastbourne 50-33 in a Southern Area League match. Later in 1954, Brafield were served with an injunction to prevent Sunday racing. This was, however, successfully defended, but Paddy Mills did transfer his training school operation to Long Eaton, where he ran three pirate meetings. Crowds were poor in 1955, and Brafield closed to speedway following a qualifying round of the Southern Area League Riders' Championship on 21 August, which was won by Colin Gooddy. The speedway track was subsequently covered in tarmac to allow stock car racing, which first took place on 14 August 1955. Speedway returned in 1966, under the control of John La Trobe, with the reconstructed track being situated inside the stock car circuit. The reopening meeting in 1966 took place on 14 August, when Ian Champion won the Midland Junior Riders Championship. That was the first of six open licence meetings to be staged that year. The last speedway meeting at the venue took place on 21 May 1967, when Brafield drew 48-48 with a Hackney 'B' team. That was the final meeting of six open licence events staged at the stadium that year. Malcolm Shakespeare is known to have used the circuit for training purposes in 1968. In 1971, Frank Smith used the Brafield circuit for practice purposes.

Brafield Sports Stadium, Northamptonshire.

BRAINTREE
ADDRESS: Towerlands Equestrian Centre, Braintree, Essex
YEARS OF OPERATION: 1982 Demonstration

The Towerlands indoor centre was owned by millionaire horse owner Tom Hunnable. The all-seater stadium had a capacity for 1,200 people. The indoor surface had a base layer of wood shavings, some nine inches deep. On top of that, there was four solid inches of soil, which itself was covered in a four-inch loose mixture of wood shavings and soil. Original speedway tests were carried out by Alan Johns and some Eastbourne juniors in March 1982. Terry Russell held further trials at the venue on 29 November 1982. Several riders were involved, including Barry Thomas, Alan Sage, Paul Bosley and Alan Johns. Sage was the first rider to try out the surface, which quickly cut up badly. Following discussions, the top layer was removed, and although the harder base proved better, it soon became glazed, which would cause problems for horse-jumping events. A North *v*. South meeting was proposed for 30 January 1983, but it never came to fruition.

BREICH
ADDRESS: Westwood Bing, Breich, Nr Whitburn, West Lothian
YEARS OF OPERATION: 1966 Training

In November 1966, local riders raced on an improvised track constructed on the site of an old ash tip, situated in a field that was owned by a local farmer. The track was surrounded with hillocks, which were ideal for any spectators to view from.

BRIGHTON

ADDRESS: Hove Stadium, Neville Road, Hove, East Sussex
YEARS OF OPERATION: 1928 Open
FIRST MEETING: 23 June 1928

The stadium was situated on high ground in Hove, giving excellent views of the sea. Greyhound racing was first held at the venue on 2 June 1928. Dirt-track racing was promoted in 1928, by Associated Southern Speedways (Brighton) Ltd, under the direction of Johnnie Hoskins, with the track being built inside the 525-yard dog circuit. Practice sessions were staged during the three weeks leading up to the opening meeting. The promotion only ran the one meeting, on Saturday 23 June, which was considered a flop, despite featuring riders of the calibre of Lionel Wills, Charlie Datson and Ron Johnson.

Charlie Datson won the £40 Brighton Scratch, while H. Miller was triumphant in the £50 Hove Handicap. A further three meetings are confirmed to have been held in July 1928, probably promoted by the stadium owners, with the last one taking place on 21 July. Following the final meeting, the management continued to stage midweek practice sessions in a search for new talent. These continued into August, when the organisers decided to stop until the completion of the installation of stadium lighting. Rumours of possible dirt-track activity at the stadium in 1929, have as yet proved to be without any solid confirmation. A licence to run open meetings at the venue in 1947 was refused, although it is known that midget-car racing was staged that year. In 1948, another plan to run speedway met with a refusal from the Council to

Hove Stadium, East Sussex.

grant a licence. The stadium hosted a further midget-car meeting on the August Bank Holiday in 1950, and although the crowd enjoyed the spectacle and it was hoped to stage further such events, it seems likely that no others were actually held. A possible return to the stadium by speedway has been proposed on several other occasions (in 1955, 1966 and 1977), with nothing ever coming to fruition. The 1977 plan to re-introduce speedway was vetoed on noise grounds.

BRIGHTON

ADDRESS: Brighton Centre, Brighton, East Sussex
YEARS OF OPERATION: 1997-2000 Indoor Speedway
FIRST MEETING: 14 December 1997
TRACK LENGTH: 120 metres

This was an amazing concept of real indoor speedway racing on a shale surface, promoted by Jon Cook and Martin Dugard. Two meetings were staged on the day of the event – one at 3 p.m., with the other starting at 7.30 p.m. The first meeting at the Brighton Centre was held on the afternoon of 14 December 1997, when the Brighton Tigers defeated Greg Hancock's World Select 62-51. The evening Brighton Bonanza Individual Championship was won by Paul Hurry. The 1998 event was staged on 13 December and saw England defeat a Rest of the World side 70-42, before Brent Werner took the Brighton Bonanza Championship. A third meeting was held on 12 December 1999, which saw Mark Loram and Craig Boyce win the Millennium Pairs Championship, prior to Paul Hurry taking the honours in the Brighton Bonanza Championship. A fourth successful meeting, held on 10 December 2000, saw Shawn McConnell and Bobby Schwartz win the Pairs Championship, before Martin Dugard took the Brighton Bonanza Championship.

BRISTOL

ADDRESS: Knowle Stadium, Wells Road, Bristol
YEARS OF OPERATION: 1928-30 Open; 1936-37 Provincial League; 1938 National League Division One; 1939 National League Division Two; 1946 Open; 1947-49 National League Division Two; 1950-53 National League Division One; 1954-55 National League Division Two; 1959 Open; 1960 Provincial League
FIRST MEETING: 25 August 1928
TRACK LENGTH: 344 yards (1928-30); 290 yards (1936-60)
NICKNAME: 'Bulldogs'
LEAGUE CHAMPIONS: 1937, 1948, 1949, 1954
KNOCK-OUT CUP WINNERS: 1960

Knowle Stadium opened on 23 July 1927, with a greyhound meeting. The winner of the very-first race was a dog called 'Plunger'. The first dirt-track meeting was held on 25 August 1928, when the track was opened by Deputy Lord Mayor Alderman Frank Moore. The man who was to reign supreme at Knowle in the opening era, Len Parker, won the Bristol Golden Helmet in that opening event. Meetings were promoted by the British Dirt-track racing Association Ltd. The initial period of track action lasted for three years, with the final meeting being staged on 23 September 1930, when Len Parker won the Evening Times Track Championship. Speedway returned to the stadium on 8 May 1936, when Bristol defeated Southampton 38-32 in a Provincial League fixture. Meetings were then promoted by Knowle Greyhound Stadium and managed locally by Ronnie Greene. The nickname 'Bulldogs' was acquired on 7 August 1936, following a suggestion from a member of the Supporters' Club. Under the auspices of The Bristol Motor Sports Ltd, Ronnie Greene and Fred Mockford took over as promoters in 1937. Bristol took over the licence of National League side Hackney in 1938, and this allowed them to move up from the Provincial League into Division One. After a disastrous year in the top-flight, Bristol exchanged their licence with Southampton in order to return to Division Two racing for the 1939 season. The Bulldogs also partook in the Southern Section of the Union Cup that year, along with Norwich and Hackney. The Second World War spelt the end for speedway in 1939, with the last meeting going ahead on 25 August when Bristol beat Sheffield 47-37 in a National League Division Two match. Following the war, speedway resumed at Knowle with an open licence, under the promotion of Reg Witcomb and Bob Steel. The reopening meeting saw Jeff Lloyd and Syd Littlewood triumph in a Junior Best Pairs event on 19 July 1946. The Bulldogs subsequently joined the National League Division Two in 1947, before gaining promotion to Division One in 1950. Promotional changes had seen Reg Witcomb assume sole control in 1948, prior to George Allan taking over in 1949 (upon Witcomb leaving to help with the opening of Swindon at Blunsdon). In 1954, Bristol were relegated back into the National League Division Two, before resigning the following season. Their last meeting was staged on 17 June 1955, when the Bulldogs beat Rayleigh 50-46 in a league encounter. For a third time, speedway

reopened at Knowle on 15 May 1959, when Ronnie Moore was victorious in the Bristol Challenge Bowl. Promoters Jack Knott, Eric Salmon and Bill Hamblin staged open licence events that season, prior to Bristol joining the Provincial League in 1960. The last-ever meeting at Knowle was held on Friday 23 September 1960, when Bristol beat Rayleigh 59-37 in the second leg of the Provincial Cup final. It was a winning finale, as that gave the Bulldogs an aggregate victory of 100-89. One further individual meeting, for the Bristol Cup was scheduled for 30 September, but fell foul of inclement weather and was never re-staged. A final greyhound meeting took place at Knowle on 28 January 1961. The stadium site was sold for £132,000 in 1961, and is now covered with housing.

BRISTOL
ADDRESS: Eastville Stadium, Stapleton Road, Eastville, Bristol
YEARS OF OPERATION: 1977-78 British League
FIRST MEETING: 29 April 1977
TRACK LENGTH: 390 metres
NICKNAME: 'Bulldogs'

Bristol Rovers Football Club originally bought the site that was to become Eastville Stadium for £150 in 1896, prior to playing their first match at the ground the following year. A first greyhound meeting was run at the stadium on Saturday 16 June 1928 – the first race was appropriately named the Rover Stakes. In 1940, Bristol Rovers sold the stadium to the greyhound company for £12,000, but continued to lease the ground for matches. Speedway arrived at Eastville in 1977, courtesy of pro-

Bristol programme cover illustration, 1954.

moters Pat Tapson, Wally Mawdsley and John Richards, who took the Bulldogs straight into the higher echelons of the British League. No foundations were ever laid for the speedway track, however; instead the circuit was cut into the turf of the greyhound circuit. Bristol Rovers' soccer pitch had to be narrowed and the enclosure terracing reduced in order to accommodate the track. The safety fence was made from marine ply-board, with wire mesh on the straights. The first eight speedway meetings were run on a dual-purpose surface, however; from the ninth meeting onwards, sand was lifted from the greyhound track beforehand. The second bend was reshaped after the initial meeting on 29 April, which was watched by a massive attendance of over 14,000 people – who witnessed Ole Olsen triumph in the Daily Mirror Open Tournament. The greyhounds subsequently moved from Thursday nights to Wednesday evenings in mid-August, to allow extra time for the removal of sand from the track. Meetings were run throughout 1977 without Council planning approval. The Council had sought High Court action to stop the venture on noise and nuisance grounds prior to its opening. The Court found in favour of the stadium, but imposed limitations on its use – only one meeting per week, with racing to be finished by 10.00 p.m. and track maintenance completed by 10.30 p.m. Despite the fact that huge crowds turned up to watch meetings, an injunction was issued in December 1978, and speedway was never again staged at Eastville. What turned out to be the final meeting had been held on 27 October 1978, when a double-header saw Scott Autrey and Vaclav Verner win the Daily Mirror Invitation

Eastville Stadium, Bristol.

Pairs Trophy, before Bristol were held to a 21-21 draw by a Daily Mirror Select side. Bristol Rovers played their final match at Eastville on 26 April 1986, prior to moving into Twerton Park, home of Bath City FC. Greyhound racing continued at the stadium for some years after Rovers' departure, while large retail outlets were built up around the immediate area. The stadium itself was eventually sold for redevelopment and the site is now covered by an Ikea superstore.

BRISTOL

ADDRESS: Redwick Farm, New Passage, Bristol
YEARS OF OPERATION: 1986
Demonstration

In 1986, Steve Bishop took his bike along to Redwick Farm for a brief test of noise levels – riding around the area and warming up his machine.

BROXBURN

ADDRESS: Sports Park, Greendykes Road, Broxburn, Nr Livingston, Lothian
YEARS OF OPERATION: 1928-29 Training and Trials
TRACK LENGTH: 434 yards

George McKenzie was involved with the design of the track, which was constructed around the pitch of Broxburn United Football Club, who had ceased activities by the end of the 1927/28 season. The venue was within sight of the main Edinburgh-to-Glasgow road. The 434 yard track, with its wooden fence, was built using a mixture of shale from nearby tips, mixed with waste oil, rather than cinders. A practice-cum-trial was run on Wednesday 12 September 1928,

but only three-quarters of the circuit was used. Following the trial, suggested changes to the curves were carried out by the end of the month. The Midland Dirt-Track Racing Club held a sports day on 20 October 1928, with both professional and amateur runners partaking, in order to raise funds for the club. The Pedestrian Gala, as it was called, attracted a large crowd to the sports park. Trials are known to have been held on 16 November 1928, when fourteen riders and a crowd of between 400 and 500 turned up. Mr Cowie from Mid-Calder recorded the fastest time of 1 minute 51 seconds for four laps. The track was used for a match race between Sam Reid and Drew McQueen during a motorcycle gymkhana in 1929. The race lasted for only half the distance though, with Reid falling on the second lap. The site is now covered by a sports centre and car park.

BURNLEY

ADDRESS: Towneley Stadium, Todmorden Road, Towneley Holmes, Lancashire
YEARS OF OPERATION: 1929 English Dirt-track League
FIRST MEETING: 30 March 1929

A first greyhound meeting at Towneley Stadium took place on 3 September 1927. Dirt-track racing arrived in 1929, with the opening Golden Helmet meeting being won by Arthur Franklyn on 30 March. After four open meetings, Burnley joined the English Dirt-track League, boasting a side containing three superstars in Ginger Lees, Joe Abbott and Frank Charles. A crowd of 10,000 spectators saw Burnley defeat Salford 41-22 on 11 May 1929, in their first home league

Buxton Stadium.

match. Soon after this meeting, however, the promotion decided to call it a day, due to a loss of capital. The track was put up for sale, and was taken over by Percy Platt, managing director of Rochdale Speedway. Burnley reopened on 29 June 1929, with a league match versus Leicester, but unfortunately, the meeting was abandoned after three heats, due to excessive dust – a local drought meant there was no water available to use on the track. Following a Golden Helmet meeting on 6 July which was won by Joe Abbott, Burnley withdrew from the league – they had completed just five fixtures at the time of their withdrawal, with the aforementioned clash with Salford being the only one staged at home. A final greyhound meeting was staged at the venue in 1933. The site of the track is now an open space, partly covered by a municipal golf course.

BUXTON
ADDRESS: Buxton Stadium, off A53 Leek-to-Buxton Road, Buxton, Derbyshire
YEARS OF OPERATION: 1994 British League Division Three; 1995 British Academy League
FIRST MEETING: 28 August, 1994
TRACK LENGTH: 230 metres
NICKNAME: 'Hi-Edge Hitmen'

Barry Watson, the stock-car promoter at Buxton Stadium, along with ex-speedway rider Chris Morton, were the men behind the venture to bring speedway to the venue. Work began on constructing a shale track inside the existing tarmac stock-car circuit in November 1993. Chris Morton oversaw the installation of the track, which was designed with safety in mind, giving plenty of room on the bends. The track eventually opened on 28 August 1994, when Buxton and Stoke drew 39-39 in the Peak/Potteries Challenge Trophy. Buxton subsequently became founder members of the new British League Division Three, joining Berwick, Cleve-land, Iwade, Linlithgow, Mildenhall and Stoke. In 1995, Buxton took their place in the renamed British Academy League, with Chris Morton as the sole promoter. Later in 1995, having encountered problems in combining speedway with the 'figure-of-eight' stock-car track, Buxton obtained permission to construct their own track on land adjacent to the stadium. The last speedway meeting at Buxton Stadium took place on 21 October 1995, when the Hi-Edge

Hitmen defeated Sittingbourne 62-34 in the British Academy League.

BUXTON
ADDRESS: Buxton Raceway, off A53 Leek-to-Buxton Road, Buxton, Derbyshire
YEARS OF OPERATION: 1996 British Conference League; 1997 British Amateur League; 1998-2000 British Conference League
FIRST MEETING: 19 May 1996
TRACK LENGTH: 240 metres
NICKNAME: 'Hitmen'

With Buxton moving home in 1996, their new track was constructed on land adjacent to Buxton Stadium by Ken and Richard Moss. The track has a superb safety fence design, while the straights are at different elevations,

Buxton Raceway.

with a small drop down around the first and second turns, and a rise up the third and fourth bends. As well as the change of track, the promotional team was slightly different too, with Ken Moss and Bernard Loftus linking up with Chris Morton as co-promoters. A practice session was staged at the venue a week prior to the opening, which took place on 19 May when the Hitmen beat Mildenhall 47-31 in a British Conference League fixture. With a renamed set-up in 1997, Buxton then found themselves competing in the British Amateur League. Later in 1997, due to fixture congestion at Kirkmanshulme Lane, Belle Vue Colts staged three of their Amateur League fixtures at Buxton Raceway. Ken Moss became sole promoter in 1998, when the league reverted back to being called the British Conference League. Thankfully, there have been no further changes to

Buxton's first-ever meeting programme, 1994.

the title of the league since 1998, and Buxton have continued to unearth raw talent at their superb little Peak District venue.

C

CAERPHILLY
ADDRESS: The Stadium, Virginia Park, Caerphilly, Mid Glamorgan
YEARS OF OPERATION: 1931-32 Open
FIRST MEETING: 6 April 1931
TRACK LENGTH: 587 yards

A crowd of several thousand braved the elements to witness the opening meeting on 6 April 1931, when dirt-track racing was staged on one of Britain's biggest ever circuits. The main event at the first meeting was the Virginia Park Scratch Race, which saw Champ Upham emerge as the winner. Greyhound racing was first staged at the venue on 23 May 1931. Somewhat surprisingly, no further dirt-track meetings were held in 1931, but five were staged in 1932. The first meeting of the 1932 season took place on 16 May when T. Crocker was triumphant in the Caerphilly Handicap. An innovation at this meeting was tote betting on a number of the events. At the second meeting on 4 June 1932, there was tote betting on all the events. The stadium hosted its final meeting on 16 July 1932, with the highlights of the meeting being the July Handicap and the County Handicap, but unfortunately no results are known. The site known, locally as Virginia Park, forms part of the grounds used by Caerphilly Rugby Club.

CALDERBANK

ADDRESS: Calderbank Training Track, Main Street, Calderbank, Nr Airdrie, Lanarkshire
YEARS OF OPERATION: 1951-52 Training
TRACK LENGTH: 275 yards

Built in an old steel works as a replacement for the training track at Bothwell, the oval-shaped Calderbank circuit was situated on the 'crusher' part of the works. The track was sometimes known as Airdrie, rather than Calderbank. Training sessions were still being held at the venue late on in 1952, with Jimmy Nichol, Alex Roy, Tammy Woods and Tommy Bryce, among others, known to have been in action.

CALIFORNIA

ADDRESS: Longmoor Speedway, Little California-in-England, Nine Mile Ride, Nr Wokingham, Berkshire
YEARS OF OPERATION: 1933-39 Open; 1948-53 Open; 1954-56 Southern Area League; 1957 Open; 1958 Training
FIRST MEETING: 28 May 1933
TRACK LENGTH: 310 yards (1933-53); 334 yards (1954-58)
NICKNAME: 'Poppies' (1954-56)

Before any speedway took place at the site, it had been used for motorcycle scrambles. Longmoor Speedway was the title used for the track prior to the Second World War, after which it was known simply as California. The track surface was described as sandy, with Sunday afternoon meetings being staged on the primitive side. Meetings in 1933 are known to have been promoted by South Reading Motorcycle Club, with G. Keene triumphant in the 350cc class race at the opening event on 28 May. Lloyd Goffe started his speedway career at Longmoor in 1934, using an old big-port AJS machine. A change of promotion in 1934, saw Reading and District Motorcycle Club running the show. The second meeting of 1936, held on 3 May, included among other things, a single-heat challenge match between Reading and London. Longmoor staged its final pre-war meeting on 20 August 1939, when Bill Newell won the California Cup. A further meeting scheduled for 3 September was subsequently cancelled due to the outbreak of hostilities. Speedway resumed at the track on 8 August 1948. Midget-car racing took place at the venue in 1951. Under the promotion of California Motorcycle Club, California joined the Southern Area League in 1954, and in Jimmy Gleed, Peter Mould and Gil Goldfinch, they boasted the best heat-leader trio in the league. In 1956, a homeless side known as Southern Rovers used a variety of venues for their Southern Area League fixtures, with California staging their match on 8 April. Due to the call for Sunday observance, new California promoter N.E. Cartlidge moved the Poppies to Tongham Stadium, Aldershot for the 1957 season of Southern Area League action. The last proper meeting ever staged at California took place on 5 August 1957, when Eric Hockaday won the California Championship. That was, in fact, the only meeting staged at the venue that year, with the track being occupied by campers for much of the season. The caravans and campers were cleared from the track in 1958, and training sessions are known to have taken place. The site of the track is now overgrown with trees and bushes, hidden away within a leisure area.

C

CAMBERLEY

ADDRESS: Heatherside Corner, Bagshot Heath, Camberley, Surrey
YEARS OF OPERATION: 1927 Open
FIRST MEETING: 7 May 1927

To all intents and purposes, this amounted to sand-track racing, held on heath land overlooked by the Military College. Meetings were organised by Camberley and District Motor Club. C. Harman was dominant at the opening meeting on 7 May 1927, winning the 350cc class, the 500cc class and the sidecar events. Fay Taylour was amongst the competitors and she won the unlimited class event. A report later on in May 1927 stated: 'A series of experimental speedways over a triangular course in the Gibbet Lane were tried, before a quarter-mile circuit at Heatherside Corner on the fringe of Bagshot Heath was used for the 7 May meeting'. The racing was conducted in a clockwise manner, but nonetheless was described as the first British dirt-track meeting in *Motor Cycling* magazine. A second meeting took place at the venue in July 1927, but the circuit had been altered to a distance of 1,056 yards, with races being held over two laps. Several years later, a review of the opening meeting stated: 'The sand was too loose and deep, and the competitors rode the wrong way round – in the end, they made a party of it by having pillion races'. In the mid-1950s, an article said: 'If you turn left over the railway bridge at the Jolly Farmers (public House), you can still see the site, about a couple of miles down the road towards Blackdown. A large open tract of loose sand, since used as a tank testing ground.'

CANTERBURY

ADDRESS: Kingsmead Stadium, Kingsmead Road, Canterbury, Kent
YEARS OF OPERATION: 1968-74 British League Division Two; 1975-87 National League
FIRST MEETING: 18 May 1968
TRACK LENGTH: 390 yards (1968-77); 385 yards (1978); 389 yards (1979); 422 yards (1980-86); 438 yards (1987)
NICKNAME: 'Crusaders'
LEAGUE CHAMPIONS: 1970, 1978
KNOCK-OUT CUP WINNERS: 1968

Situated on the site of an old rubbish dump, the stadium originally took two years to build and was home to Canterbury City Football Club. Their first match at Kingsmead Stadium was played on 30 August 1958, versus Ashford Town, with the official opening one week later being performed by Sir Stanley Rous. The record football attendance was for a schoolboy match between England and Wales in March 1960, when 4,100 people turned up to watch. Speedway was introduced to the stadium, under the auspices of Canterbury Speedway Ltd, better known as Johnnie Hoskins. The track was constructed on what was originally a running track for Canterbury Athletic Club. A crowd of over 7,000 people witnessed the first-ever meeting at the venue on 18 May 1968, with many more thought to have got in without paying. That first meeting saw Canterbury lose 38-39 to Belle Vue in a British League Division Two encounter. Canterbury became founder members of the New National League in 1975, prior to a change on the promotional front the following season, which saw Wally Mawdsley team up with Johnnie Hoskins as co-promoter, under the banner of W. Mawdsley Promotions. In both 1977 and 1978, the promoters had to go to court in order to keep the track running, following complaints over noise from local residents. Maurice Morley, who had been general manager since 1976, joined the promoting team of Wally Mawdsley and Johnnie Hoskins in 1979. Chris Galvin and Terry Waller, under the title of Christel Leisure took over the running of the track during the 1986 campaign, with Wally Mawdsley taking a position on the administrative side of Kingsmead Stadium. Canterbury City Council decided against renewing the Crusaders' lease in 1988, and so what turned out to be the last meeting of a 'twenty-year crusade', took place at Kingsmead Stadium on 31 October 1987, when Canterbury beat Rye House 49-29, in the Kent/Herts Trophy. Following the final meeting, the track was redeveloped as a new greyhound circuit. Greyhound racing ceased after a final meeting on 30 October 1999.

CARDIFF
ADDRESS: White City Stadium, Sloper Road, Grangetown, Cardiff, South Glamorgan
YEARS OF OPERATION: 1928-30 Open; 1934 Open; 1935 Open; 1936 Provincial League; 1937 Open
FIRST MEETING: 26 December 1928
TRACK LENGTH: 396 yards

A first greyhound meeting at the stadium was held on 7 April 1928. The first ever rugby league match to be played in Cardiff took place at Sloper Road on 14 November 1928, when Wales took on England in front of 70,000 spectators. The first dirt-track meeting at the venue was staged on Boxing Day 1928, when Champ Upham won the Cardiff City Trophy in

Kingsmead Stadium, Canterbury.

front of 25,000 spectators. A second dirt-track meeting was staged on 12 January 1929, under the promotion of Provincial Dirt-Tracks (Cardiff) Ltd, who staged an amazing total of fifty-five meetings throughout that year. For the purpose of track grading, a contraption like an outsize brush was harnessed to a horse to pull around the circuit. Jack Lyons of the South Wales Riders' Union was appointed general manager and secretary of Cardiff in 1930, but only open licence meetings were staged that year. For three full years, the track remained dirt-track racing free until just one meeting was staged in 1934 – a charity event on 4 October with 3,000 spectators in attendance. The meeting was staged for the benefit of the Cardiff Royal Infirmary, with Len Parker victori-

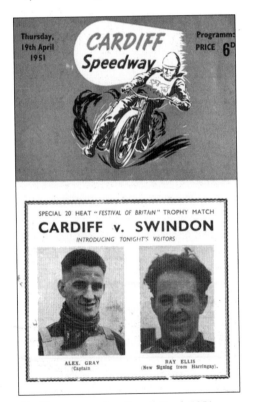

Cardiff programme from Penarth Road, 1951.

ous in the ROP Scratch Race, while D.T. Morgan won the Hospital Handicap Race. Open licence meetings were staged in 1935, and it was reported that a handsome profit had been made from the meetings. The owners, The Greyhound Racing Association of South Wales, then decided to go in for the sport in a big way, widening the track and adding banking to a height of 2 feet 6 inches from the inner to the outer edge. Sadly, that optimism was soon to disappear after only a handful of meetings, as Cardiff resigned from the Provincial League midway through the 1936 season. The last meeting at the stadium was a National Provincial Trophy event versus West Ham Hawks on 1 June, which the home side won 43-28. It was subsequently reported in the *South Wales Echo* of 6 June that 'It has been decided not to run any further speedway meetings for the time being at the White City Speedway, Sloper Road, Cardiff. This decision has been taken owing to the fact that the public response has been very poor this season and, owing to the very heavy expense incurred in league racing, the loss has been very heavy. It is possible, however, that racing will take place at this track on certain occasions at a later date.' One open style meeting was staged on 24 July 1937, and although a result is not known, it was reported that the event was not a success. In 1937, the syndicate that originally built the stadium made an unsuccessful application to join the Rugby League. The site later became Guest Keen's Sports Ground.

CARDIFF

ADDRESS: Penarth Road Stadium, Penarth Road, Cardiff, South Glamorgan

YEARS OF OPERATION: 1950 Training; 1951 National League Division Three; 1952-53 Southern League
FIRST MEETING: 5 April 1951
TRACK LENGTH: 400 yards
NICKNAME: 'Dragons'

The track was laid under the supervision of Alf Elliott, and although it was ready for racing, only training sessions were held in 1950. The first official meeting at the stadium went ahead on 5 April 1951, when Cardiff lost 52-56 to Rayleigh in a Daily Mail National Trophy encounter. The meeting was witnessed by a reported crowd of some 20,000 spectators. Meetings were promoted at the venue by Speedway Racing (Cardiff) Ltd, a company headed by Arthur McTaggart Short, Leslie Maidment and Lt Col. A.J. Lennox, among others. The Penarth Road Stadium became home to Cardiff Rugby League Club in 1951, with them leasing the venue from Speedway Racing (Cardiff) Ltd. The opening rugby game against Widnes took place on 22 August 1951, and attracted a gate of 2,500 spectators. Attendances for rugby league matches were never good, and had been known to drop as low as 199 people – which resulted in the team being voted out of the Rugby League. Their last game was a 14-59 defeat at the hands of Wigan on 26 April 1952, played out in front of 1,450 spectators. Bill Dutton replaced Leslie Maidment on the speedway management side in 1952. Following the Coronation Best Pairs meeting on 2 July 1953, Cardiff withdrew from the Southern League, citing falling attendances as the main reason. That final pairs meeting was, incidentally, won by Mick Holland and

Hugh Geddes. Speedway crowds had apparently fallen from an average of 9,000 in 1952, to just 3,000 at the time of their closure. The site of the stadium remained derelict until 1969, when it was built on. One of the new roads on the site was appropriately named Stadium Close, and this is the only lasting reminder of another former home of speedway.

CARLISLE
ADDRESS: Harraby Park Stadium, Holme, Carlisle, Cumbria
YEARS OF OPERATION: 1928 Training

Greyhound racing was first staged at Harraby Park on 9 June 1928. A press report in 1928, stated 'With the object of discussing the possibility of holding dirt-track racing, motorcycle, football and gymkhanas on the ground of the Carlisle Greyhound Racing and Sports Co. Ltd, the Cumberland County Motorcycle Club met a representative of the company recently, but no definite settlement was arrived at. The company has, however, placed a piece of ground at the club's disposal for purposes of practising.' A first grass speedway meeting is known to have been held on 21 July 1928, but the only pukka dirt-track racing at the site was on the practice area. Carlisle City Rugby League Club played their one and only season (1928/29) at Harraby Park Stadium, with their first home match versus Wigan Highfield taking place on 25 August 1928.

CARLISLE
ADDRESS: Moorville Park, Kingmoor, Carlisle, Cumbria
YEARS OF OPERATION: 1937 Open
FIRST MEETING: 18 September 1937

This track was built amidst local opposition by the Stobart Brothers, on the site of the former Kingmoor Brickworks. Just one meeting was staged at Moorville Park, when a crowd of around 650 spectators saw Liverpool's Tommy Price win the scratch race on the afternoon of 18 September 1937. Following the afternoon meeting at Moorville Park, the riders went on to a further meeting at Lonsdale Park, Workington in the evening. It had been hoped that the initial meeting would be the prelude for a Carlisle team to enter the Provincial League, but nothing more came of it. The site was redeveloped for housing after the Second World War.

CASTLEFORD

ADDRESS: Whitwood Stadium, Altofts Lane, Whitwood, Nr Castleford, West Yorkshire
YEARS OF OPERATION: 1979-80 Open
FIRST MEETING: 12 June 1979

Castleford's opening meeting programme, 1979.

TRACK LENGTH: 202 yards
NICKNAME: 'Kings'

Speedway at Whitwood Stadium was promoted by Jim Streets, who had a 9.30 p.m. deadline on evening meetings. The small 202-yard track hosted its first meeting on 12 June 1979, when Rod Hunter was victorious in the Daily Mirror Kings Cavalcade. A total of eleven open licence meetings were staged at the tiny venue in that initial season of racing. In 1980, just five open licence fixtures were held at the venue, the last of which saw Castleford defeat Felton 43-35 on 24 June. A further meeting (the West Yorkshire Pairs) was scheduled for 1 July 1980, but although a programme was produced, the meeting was never staged.

CATFORD

ADDRESS: Catford Cricket Ground, Penerley Road, Catford, South London
YEARS OF OPERATION: 1932 Open

Dirt-track racing was apparently tried out at the cricket ground in 1932, prior to the venture at the greyhound stadium two years later, but details are very sketchy.

CATFORD

ADDRESS: Catford Greyhound Stadium, Adenmore Road, Catford, South London
YEARS OF OPERATION: 1934 Open
FIRST MEETING: 1 September 1934
TRACK LENGTH: 280 yards

The stadium first staged greyhound racing on 30 July 1932. The dirt-track circuit was subsequently constructed inside the existing greyhound track. The first dirt-track meeting staged at the superb floodlit

Whitwood Stadium, Castleford.

venue on 1 September 1934, featured midget-car racing in the second-half of the programme. Meetings were promoted by Tom Bradbury-Pratt, who advertised the track as 'The Sandown of Speedway Racing'. Permission to reintroduce speedway at the venue was refused in 1949.

CAXTON
ADDRESS: Caxton, Nr Cambridge, Cambridgeshire
YEARS OF OPERATION: 1931 Open

Not much is known about this venue, except that amateur dirt-track events were run on Sunday afternoons in 1931, under the promotion of Newmarket Motorcycle Club.

CHALTON
ADDRESS: Chalton, Nr Horndean, Hampshire
YEARS OF OPERATION: 1928 Practice and Open
FIRST MEETING: 15 July 1928
TRACK LENGTH: 440 yards

A report in June 1928 stated: 'Recently opened for practice at Chalton, we learn that the owner Mr Jones, is anxious to help local riders and Southern clubs should they wish to hold any events. The track measures approx quarter of a mile and a nominal fee of 6d per head is made.' The track was first opened for practice sessions in June 1928, with the first dirt-track meeting going ahead the following month, on 15 July. A newspaper review of that opening meeting stated that the 'lack of a programme made it difficult to follow the various heats. The Chalton Motor Racing Club, however, intend to rectify this at the second meeting on Sunday 29 July.'

CHARLTON

ADDRESS: The Valley, Floyd Road
Charlton, London
YEARS OF OPERATION: 1948 Midget-car
Racing

The Valley has been home to Charlton Athletic Football Club during three separate spells: 1920 to 1922, 1924 to 1984 and 1992 to the present day. Two midget-car meetings were run at the venue on 15 and 22 May 1948.

CHASEWATER

ADDRESS: Chasewater Stadium, Pool Road, Brownhills, West Midlands
YEARS OF OPERATION: 1977 Long-Track
FIRST MEETING: 17 April 1977
TRACK LENGTH: 800 metres

Just one long-track meeting was staged on this sandy surfaced trotting track on 17 April 1977, when the Rest of the World defeated Great Britain, 171-136. Plans were mooted to extend the track length to 1,000 metres, but nothing came to fruition.

CHESTERFIELD

ADDRESS: Glasshouse Farm, New Whittington, Nr Chesterfield, Derbyshire
YEARS OF OPERATION: 1949-53 Training
TRACK LENGTH: 231 yards

The track surface was a mixture of shale and cinders, while the safety fence was made of rubber. A starting gate was installed and the circuit also boasted a grader. Wilf Jay ran a training school at the site, which was situated on the main Eckington-to-Chesterfield road. As a sixteen-year-old, Arthur Wright took his first rides on a speedway bike at the Chesterfield track in May 1950.

CHISWICK

ADDRESS: Mortlake Road, Chiswick, London
YEARS OF OPERATION: 1957-58 Training
TRACK LENGTH: 160 yards
NICKNAME: 'Champions' (1957); 'Nomads' (1957-58)

Originally with the nickname of Champions, Chiswick were a team who only rode in away challenge matches, hence they later became better known as the Nomads. For practice purposes, they used a former cycle speedway track situated in Mortlake Road, between Chiswick Bridge and Kew Bridge. The former cycling track had, in fact, staged the National Cycle Speedway Finals in 1953. In early 1957, Ted Payne turned the site into a 160-yard, almost circular speedway track. A starting gate was erected and the surface was a mixture of cinders and ash, while the grader was towed by Mr Payne's van. Training sessions were run on Sunday afternoons, and it was generally agreed that the track wasn't wide enough for three riders, so the speedsters only went out in pairs.

COATBRIDGE

ADDRESS: Cliftonhill Stadium, Main Street, Coatbridge, Lanarkshire
YEARS OF OPERATION: 1968-69 British League Division One; 1970-71 Training; 1973 British League Division One; 1974 British League Division Two; 1975-77 National League
FIRST MEETING: 6 April 1968
TRACK LENGTH: 380 yards (1968-73); 409 yards (1974); 380 yards (1975-77)
NICKNAME: 'Monarchs' (1968-69); 'Tigers' (1973-77)

Greyhound racing first took place at

Cliftonhill Stadium, Coatbridge.

Cliftonhill Stadium on 11 December 1931. A speedway licence was first applied for in 1950, just in case one for Motherwell was refused. Greyhound racing ceased at the venue in the mid-1950s. The speedway circuit was constructed around the pitch, which belonged to Albion Rovers Football Club. The track was used by the Edinburgh promotion (Ian Hoskins) for 1968 and 1969. The Monarchs' opening meeting at the venue took place on 6 April 1968, when the homesters defeated Glasgow 54-42 in the Champagne Derby. The last meeting of the Edinburgh promotion was staged on 11 October 1969, when Coatbridge defeated Cradley Heath 42-36 in a British League Division One match. The track licence was then transferred to Wembley, enabling top-flight speedway to return to the Empire Stadium in

1970. Training sessions were staged at Coatbridge in 1970, with the first one going ahead on 5 December when thirteen juniors turned up for tuition. The training events continued at the track during 1971. The track was used by the Glasgow promotion from 1973 to 1977. The initial Tigers meeting at Coatbridge was held on 30 March 1973, when Coatbridge suffered a 38-40, defeat at the hands of Halifax in the Watson Bros Trophy'. The Tigers subsequently took up their place in Division One of the British League, under the promotion of James Wallace and James Beaton. Glasgow's Division One licence was exchanged with Hull in 1974, with Glasgow continuing in Division Two, under the promotion of James Beaton and Neil MacFarlane. Further changes on the promotional front saw James Wallace, Dave Thomson and Bill Harrold join forces with James Beaton in 1975. A further one-and-a-half seasons of racing were promoted at Cliftonhill, by Dave Thomson and James Beaton, before speedway was forced out in 1977. This was because the stadium owners wished to introduce a new greyhound track, which meant both banked bends had to be levelled. The final speedway meeting ever staged at Cliftonhill Stadium took place on 17 June 1977, when Coatbridge lost 32-46 to Eastbourne in a National League encounter. After this final meeting, the Tigers took up residence at Blantyre Sports Stadium, resuming as Glasgow Tigers. Greyhound racing subsequently returned to the new track at Cliftonhill in September 1977.

COBRIDGE

ADDRESS: Cobridge Motordrome, Waterloo Road, Cobridge, Stoke-on-Trent, Staffordshire
YEARS OF OPERATION: 1939 Midget-car Racing

The venue was also known as the Albion Greyhound Track. Midget-car racing was held at the venue in 1939, with a meeting advertised for 8 July as Cobridge Tigers versus Coventry. Among the listed drivers were: Walter Mackereth, Johnnie Young, Val Atkinson, Frank Chiswell, Cecil Heath, Les White and Stan Mills. The stadium offered refreshments, a licensed club and free car parking. Depending on where you watched from, admission was 2/- and 1/-, with women and children at half price.

COPPULL

ADDRESS: Coppull Training Track, Coppull, Nr Adlington, Lancashire
YEARS OF OPERATION: 1947-53
Training

This was a private shale-based track, run by Oliver and Ron Hart specifically for training purposes. The 'tiny bowl circuit', as it was described, was situated on farmland in Coppull. Cyril Cooper is known to have joined the Coppull school in the winter of 1946/47, before joining Wigan for the start of the 1947 season. Dick Seers spent the winter of 1948/49 at Coppull, training and building new frames. Oliver Hart and his son, Oliver junior, were often to be found going through their paces on the short circuit. In 1993, the mini-track was – rather sadly – described as being covered over and forgotten.

COVENTRY

ADDRESS: Coventry Stadium, Lythalls Lane, Foleshill, Coventry, Warwickshire
YEARS OF OPERATION: 1928 Open; 1930 Open
FIRST MEETING: 21 July 1928
TRACK LENGTH: 352 yards

Greyhound racing opened at the stadium with a meeting on 7 April 1928. The well-appointed venue boasted three large grandstands, plus refreshment rooms and was smartly finished in red tiles. A black cinder dirt-track circuit was constructed inside the existing greyhound track. The opening meeting was held on 21 July 1928, when Norman Dawson was triumphant in the Coventry Challenge Cup. Thirteen meetings were run in that initial year, promoted by Midland Speedways (Manchester) Ltd, whose manager and clerk of the course was Jack Marshall –

a former road racer who had won the Isle of Man TT race in both 1907 and 1908. The final meeting of that first season was staged on 13 October when Syd Jackson won the News of the World Championship Belt. Following a year of inactivity, the ACU inspected the track in early 1930, with new promoters Coventry Sporting Club carrying out suggested improvements to the bends in order to bring the track into line for registration. The reopening meeting went ahead on 10 June that year, when Neville Wheeler won the scratch race event. After just six meetings, the track closed in 1930, due to a lack of co-operation from Northern and Southern promoters associations. Apparently, Coventry were originally admitted as members to the Northern Association, but the decision was later reversed. The stadium hosted its last-ever meeting on 14 July when the Blues beat the Reds 51-40. A final greyhound meeting was held at the venue on 25 September 1964. The stadium site was later redeveloped for housing in the mid-1970s.

COVENTRY

ADDRESS: Brandon Stadium, Rugby Road, Brandon, Nr Coventry, Warwickshire

YEARS OF OPERATION: 1928 Open; 1929-31 Southern League; 1932-33 National League; 1934 Open; 1936 Open; 1948 National League Division Three; 1949-56 National League Division Two; 1957-64 National League; 1965-67 British League; 1968-74 British League Division One; 1975-90 British League; 1991-94 British League Division One; 1995-96 British Premier League; 1997-2000 British Elite League

FIRST MEETING: 29 September 1928

TRACK LENGTH: 352 yards (1928-31); 365 yards (1932-36); 375 yards (1948-51); 375 yards (1952); 380 yards (1953-74); 383 yards (1975-82); 366 yards (1983-97); 331 yards (1998-2000)

NICKNAME: 'Bees'

LEAGUE CHAMPIONS: 1953, 1968, 1978, 1979, 1987, 1988

KNOCK-OUT CUP WINNERS: 1967

LEAGUE CUP WINNERS: 1981, 1985, 1987

PREMIERSHIP WINNERS: 1986

CRAVEN SHIELD WINNERS: 1997, 2000

Brandon Stadium was built in 1928 by Stanley Glanfield, with the opening dirt-track meeting going ahead on 29 September that year, when Jack Lloyd won the Coventry Handicap event. Fay Taylour is known to have won the Handicap Final on 13 October 1928. In 1929, Southern League meetings were promoted by Motordromes Ltd. Although they managed to complete their league fixtures in 1930, Coventry closed due to financial difficulties. The track licence was withdrawn, while the managing director and secretary of Motordromes Ltd were suspended. Having started 1931 with open licence events, Coventry rejoined the Southern League upon the closure of Leicester in mid-May. In 1932, Coventry also partook in the National Speedway Association Trophy, which was a league-style competition that preceded the National League Championship. Birmingham businessman Harold Trimmell was responsible for running six meetings at Brandon in 1934, when it was an unaffiliated venue. Five unlicensed meetings were again run at Brandon in 1936, the last of which was held on 13 September. Midget-car racing was staged at Brandon between 1937 and 1939. The site was used by the Army during the Second World War, after which the track was altered in shape, while some of the Nissen huts left by the Army were utilised as office buildings. After the war, Charles Ochiltree and Mrs Jack Parker re-opened Brandon for speedway on 1 May 1948, when Coventry lost 48-59 to Stoke in a National Trophy fixture. The track for the re-opening consisted of decomposed granite dust of a sandy red colour. The meeting was delayed by difficulties in lighting the track. Coventry subsequently took their place in the National League Division Three, prior to joining Division Two the following year. With only eleven tracks running in 1957, Coventry found themselves in the National League, where they would remain until the merger of the National and Provincial Leagues in 1965. Having co-promoted with Mrs Jack Parker since 1948, Charles Ochiltree was in sole charge of the track from 1961 onwards. The first-ever British League match was staged at Brandon on 27 March 1965, when Coventry beat Cradley Heath 47-31. The winner of the first race of the new era for speedway was Nigel Boocock. Twenty-eight-year-old Tony O'Donnell lost his life after crashing in a practice session at the track on 6 December 1975. A first-ever greyhound meeting was staged at Brandon on 19 September 1978. The last greyhound meeting was held at the venue on 24 October 1986. With the amalgamation of the British League and the National League in 1991, Coventry were automatically members of the British League Division One. There was another change of league for the Bees when both divisions

Brandon Stadium, Coventry.

of British Speedway joined forces to form a twenty-one team Premier League in 1995. The large Premier League split up in 1997, with Coventry joining the British Elite League. Big changes in 1998 saw alterations to the track, turning it into a Grand Prix venue, with Jason Crump triumphant in the inaugural Brandon-staged British Grand Prix on 7 August that year. The promotion also altered slightly that year, with Martin Ochiltree and Colin Pratt joining Charles Ochiltree as co-promoters. Legendary supremo Charles Ochiltree died on 29 October 1998, having completed a remarkable fifty-one consecutive seasons as promoter at Brandon. Since the death of 'CO', Coventry has continued under the promotion of Martin Ochiltree and Colin Pratt. Coventry created more speedway history on 13 May 1999, when the British Elite League fixture versus Wolver-hampton (won 48-42), became the first live match screened by Sky Television. Tony Rickardsson won the second British Grand Prix to be staged at Brandon on 31 July 1999. Wild-card entry Martin Dugard became the unexpected winner of the British Grand Prix at Brandon on 29 July 2000.

COVENTRY

ADDRESS: Brandon Stadium Car Park, Rugby Road, Brandon, Nr Coventry, Warwickshire
YEARS OF OPERATION: 1948-50 Training; 1967 Training

Jack Parker constructed a training track in the Brandon car park at the close of the 1948 season. The track was designed with one bend of 50 yards, while the other was slightly bigger at 70 yards. Novices were encouraged to start on this track, before moving on to the main stadium circuit for further practice. At the end of the 1949 season, training was again staged on the car park track, under the guidance of Bob Fletcher. The impromptu circuit had the advantage of no safety fence on which any over-zealous youngsters could entangle themselves. There was also a special patch of ground set aside for broadsiding practice. John Harrhy is known to have practised on the Brandon car park in 1967.

COWDENBEATH

ADDRESS: Central Park Stadium, off Main Street, Cowdenbeath, Fife
YEARS OF OPERATION: 1965 Open; 1966 Training
FIRST MEETING: 5 May 1965
TRACK LENGTH: 380 yards
NICKNAME: 'Lions'

Central Park has been the home of the Blue Brazil (Cowdenbeath FC) since

Cowdenbeath's opening programme, 1965.

1917. Greyhound racing was first held at Central Park Stadium on 7 July 1928. Grass-track racing is known to have been held at Central Park in 1932. Under the promotion of Johnnie Hoskins, speedway was first staged at Central Park on 5 May 1965, when Fife Lions beat Colonial Tigers 44-33. On a track constructed around the perimeter of the football pitch, eight open licence meetings were staged that year, with the team riding under the name of Fife throughout. The last of the eight fixtures in 1965 was held on 17 July, when Fife defeated Rest of Scotland 42-35. Training sessions were held at the stadium in 1966, when Jim McMillan took the first steps towards his long career on the shale. The circuit is now covered in tarmac and used for stock-car meetings.

CRADLEY HEATH

ADDRESS: Dudley Wood Sports Stadium, Dudley Wood Road, Dudley, West Midlands

YEARS OF OPERATION: 1947-48 National League Division Three; 1949-52 National League Division Two; 1959 Open; 1960-64 Provincial League; 1965-67 British League; 1968-74 British League Division One; 1975-90 British League; 1991-94 British League Division One; 1995 British Premier League

FIRST MEETING: 21 June 1947

TRACK LENGTH: 367 yards (1947-80); 370 yards (1981-95)

NICKNAME: 'Heathens' (1947-72 and 1977-95); 'United' (1973-76)

KNOCK-OUT CUP WINNERS: 1961, 1963, 1979, 1980, 1982, 1983, 1986 (shared with Oxford), 1987, 1988, 1989

INTER-LEAGUE KNOCK-OUT CUP WINNERS: 1979

Central Park Stadium, Cowdenbeath.

LEAGUE CHAMPIONS: 1981, 1983
PREMIERSHIP WINNERS: 1982, 1984, 1985, 1988, 1989, 1990
LEAGUE CUP WINNERS: 1982, 1984, 1986 (shared with Oxford)

Dudley Wood Sports Stadium was built in 1947, and hosted its first speedway meeting on 21 June that year, when Cradley Heath beat Wombwell 46-36 in a National League Division Three fixture. Meetings were promoted by Cradley Sports Enterprises Ltd (B.N. Brahams, George Bridgewater, A.F. Kent, Joseph Sidaway and Thomas Searl), with Les Marshall installed as the speedway manager, who would remain in place throughout the first two seasons of racing at the venue. A first greyhound meeting was staged at the stadium in December 1947. After two seasons in Division Three, Cradley were promoted to Division Two in 1949, when Dudley Marchant took over as speedway manager. Dick Wise became speedway manager in 1950, and held on to the job all season, despite a change of promotion on 2 June when Les Marshall returned, under the banner of Auto Speedways Ltd. Under the auspices of West Midlands Speedway Ltd, Eli Sumner became promoter at Dudley Wood in 1951. However, attendances dwindled away in 1952 and, after suffering heavy losses, the track closed at the end of the season. The final meeting had been held at Dudley Wood on 3 October when the Heathens beat Poole 48-36 in a National League Division Two encounter. In a shock move, Cradley amalgamated with Wolverhampton in 1953, and there was no further speedway at Dudley Wood for six full years. Under the promotion of

The programme from the last-ever meeting at Cradley Heath, 1995.

Mike Parker, the track reopened in 1959, when just one pirate meeting was staged, with a Midlands Select side drawing 35-35 with Bradford on 29 August. Promoted by Fred Jephcott, Cradley joined the Provincial League in 1960, and would remain there until the formation of the British League in 1965. Alan Martin linked up with Fred Jephcott as co-promoter in 1962, and the partnership would guide Cradley Heath speedway on through the start of the British League, right up to the end of the 1976 campaign. A change of promotion in 1977 saw Dan McCormick and Derek Pugh take over the running of the track. Bob Wasley replaced Dan McCormick as co-promoter in 1980, and he in turn was replaced by Peter Adams in 1981. A further change on the management side occurred in 1984, when Colin Pratt linked with Derek Pugh as co-promoter at Dudley Wood. Upon the amalgamation of the British League and the National League, the Heathens found themselves in the British League Division One in 1991. The promotional side of the club altered in 1994, with Mike Gardner and Les Pottinger joining Colin Pratt as co-promoters. With both divisions joining forces to form the British Premier League in 1995, Cradley became members of the new twenty-one-team set-up. That year also saw a further change on the promoting front, with Sven Heiding replacing Mike Gardner as co-promoter alongside Colin Pratt and Les Pottinger. With plans afoot for redevelopment at the venue, what turned out to be the last speedway meeting at Dudley Wood was staged on 28 October

1995, when a challenge match between a Greg Hancock Select and a Billy Hamill Select resulted in a 48-48 draw. Without their own track, Cradley ran as Cradley & Stoke Heathens in 1996, staging their home matches at Loomer Road in Stoke. The Dudley Wood site has continued to deteriorate since 1996, due to protracted negotiations over proposed housebuilding at the former stadium.

CRAYFORD

ADDRESS: Crayford Stadium, Stadium Road, Crayford, Kent
YEARS OF OPERATION: 1931 Open; 1935-37 Open; 1968-70 British League Division Two; 1975-83 National League
TRACK LENGTH: 300 yards (1930-69); 265 yards (1970-83)
NICKNAME: 'Highwaymen' (1968-70); 'Kestrels' (1975-83)

Dudley Wood Sports Stadium, Dudley.

Crayford Stadium, Kent.

In 1930, the venue was referred to as Crayford Grass Speedway, and was situated on the junction of the London-to-Dartford and the London-to-Rochester Road. A crowd of over 1,400 people attended the opening grass speedway meeting on Easter Monday, 21 April 1930. Grass meetings in 1930 and 1931 were promoted by Bexley Heath & District Motorcycle Club. Admission to the Sunday afternoon meetings cost 6d. Results of the opening meeting are not known, but W. Henstone is known to have won the Crayford Cup on 10 May 1930. Amateur dirt-track events were held at the venue in 1931, and again from 1935 to 1937. Wilf Plant rode at Crayford in 1935, and is quoted as saying 'They ran meetings in the same place, although there were no grandstands. I can remember the railway line running past the track. I was a junior in

those days and got much of my early training at Crayford.' A report in May 1936, stated: 'The Crayford Speedway Club hold meetings every Sunday afternoon and invite attendance. But riders must bring their own equipment. The secretary Mr F. Cattell, will be glad of enquiries.' A first greyhound meeting at the venue was staged on 10 July 1937. Promoted by Bill Bridgett, the track reopened for Speedway on 12 June 1968, when Crayford Highwaymen defeated Nelson 50-27 in a British League Division Two fixture. After three seasons of speedway activity, the track closed again, with the final meeting going ahead on 28 October 1970, when the Highwaymen thrashed Bradford 52-25 in a league match. In 1975, under the promotion of Peter Thorogood, Crayford returned to action and joined the New National League (as it was called at the time), with an opening meeting on 8 April, when the newly named Kestrels beat Boston 46-30 in a league match. A change on the management side saw Terry Russell take over as promoter in 1981. The last speedway ever seen at the venue occurred on 26 October 1983, when Crayford beat Newcastle by a single-point (48-47) in a leg of the Supernational Final. The promotion transferred to Hackney at the end of 1983, as the stadium was due for redevelopment in 1984. The stadium eventually closed after the final greyhound meeting on 18 May 1985. The owners, Ladbrokes, pledged to rebuild the stadium, and on 1 September 1986 a £2.5 million venue was opened for the first greyhound meeting of the new era. It was the first purpose-built greyhound stadium in Britain for thirty years. The original stadium had occupied twenty acres, but the new complex was more compact, being constructed on a five-acre site.

CREWE

ADDRESS: British Railways Sports Ground, Earle Street, Crewe, Cheshire
YEARS OF OPERATION: 1929-32 Open; 1969-74 British League Division Two; 1975 National League; 1976-77 Open and Training; 1978-79 Training
TRACK LENGTH: 470 yards (1929-70); 430 yards (1971-73); 436 yards (1974-79)
NICKNAME: 'Kings' (1969-75); 'Locos' (1976)
LEAGUE CHAMPIONS: 1972
KNOCK-OUT CUP WINNERS: 1972

Earle Street was home to Crewe Alexandra Football Club from 1876 to 1878. In 1906, the stadium was known as the Alexandra Athletic Grounds, hav-

British Railways Sports Ground, Earle Street, Crewe.

ing been refurbished by an independent Athletic Club formed from the former Crewe Alexandra Cricket, Football, Athletic and Bicycle Club. Slider Shuttleworth was the idol at Crewe in 1929, when open licence meetings were held. The stadium hosted unlicensed meetings in 1930, borne out by the fact that Dan De Lyon won a scratch race event on 22 August. As had happened at Audenshaw in 1929, many riders rode under assumed names for fear of identification. A Warrington newspaper reported in 1930 that, 'E.C. Deakin, who was attached to the Liverpool Stanley track earlier this year, won the Crewe Handicap at the new Alexander Speedway, Crewe, and was second in the scratch race'. Frank Varey is known to have ridden at the venue in 1932. The site later belonged to British Railways and featured a cricket pitch on the infield. Promoted by Allied Presentations Ltd, and under the direction of Maury Littlechild, speedway returned to the venue some thirty-six years after the last known activity had been recorded in 1932. The Earle Street track staged its first meeting of the British League era on 19 May 1969, when Crewe Kings lost 33-45, to Rayleigh in the Allied Presentations Ltd. Trophy. Sadly, Maury Littlechild died on 12 July 1972, Ken Adams taking over as general manager at the track for the remainder of the season. Still under the banner of Allied Presentations Ltd, Len Silver became main promoter at Crewe in 1973. Dave Parry and John Adams took over as promoters in 1975, as Crewe became founder members of the New National League. Following the withdrawal of John Adams, Mrs Violet Littlechild stepped in as co-promoter in

May, thus allowing Crewe to complete their fixtures. Although the track planned to run in 1976, the licence was eventually put on ice amid rumours that the stadium owners were going to sell the site for redevelopment. What turned out to be the final official meeting at Earle Street had already been staged on 13 October 1975, when Crewe defeated Ellesmere Port 45-33 in the Cheshire Trophy. A Crewe Training Club was formed in 1976, running various types of training events with a Crewe Locos moniker. The track is known to have been used for training purposes from 1977 to 1979. Thanks to stadium promoter Jim Barry, a combined sidecar and stock-car meeting was successfully staged at the venue in 1980. The ACU later investigated the sidecar event, claiming that the circuit did not have a licence for motorcycle meetings, but was permitted to hold stock-car and midget-car racing. A final stock-car meeting was staged at Earle Street on 11 December 1993, prior to the site giving way to supermarket development in 1994.

CRYSTAL PALACE
ADDRESS: Crystal Palace Exhibition Grounds, Sydenham, South London
YEARS OF OPERATION: 1928 Open; 1929-31 Southern League; 1932-33 National League; 1936-38 Open; 1939 National League Division Two; 1940 Open
FIRST MEETING: 19 May 1928
TRACK LENGTH: 441 yards (1928); 449 yards (1929-40)
NICKNAME: 'Glaziers'

The super stadium was designed in early 1895, by W.T. Carr, the Crystal

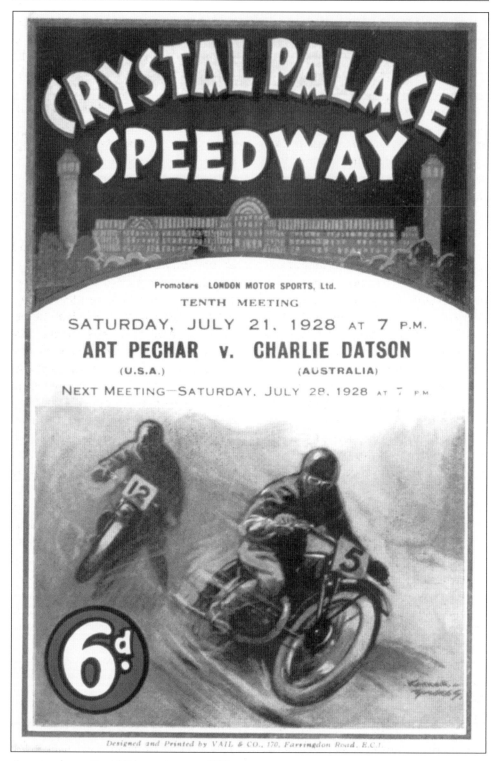

An extremely rare Crystal Palace programme, 1928.

Palace Company engineer. The North side of the ground featured multi-spanned covered seating, set back at an angle of thirty degrees on either side of the players' and committee pavilion, which had additional seating on a raised balcony. Encircling the playing area was more seating in blocks, while another uncovered stand was situated on the opposite side. FA Cup finals were held at Crystal Palace from 1895 to 1914. In 1928, promoters Fred Mockford and Cecil Smith (trading as London Motor Sports Ltd), laid a dirt-track at a cost of £5,025. A demonstration event was held on 17 May 1928, two days prior to the first official meeting. The opening meeting on 19 May was attended by a crowd of 6,000 people, but the loud speakers failed and left the promoters to keep the spectators informed with two megaphones! Roger Frogley emerged victorious from that first meeting, winning the scratch race final. A meeting staged on 15 August 1928 was described thus in a report: 'A very mixed meeting was held at the Crystal Palace last Wednesday afternoon. A number of horse races under the Galloping Association rules being interspersed between those on mechanical speed beasts. The innovation was however, not a success, and it was subsequently decided not to stage any more horse races.' In 1932, Crystal Palace partook in the National Speedway Association Trophy, which was a league-style competition that preceded the National League Championship. Due to a lack of floodlights, Crystal Palace withdrew from the National League prior to the start of the 1934 season, with the operation moving to New Cross. What turned out to

be the final meeting had already been staged on 14 October 1933, when a National League double-header had resulted in a 32-29 victory over Clapton and a 29-31 defeat at the hands of West Ham. In the absence of dirt-track racing at the venue, midget-car events were held that year. Open licence meetings resumed at the Sydenham circuit in 1936. On the evening of 30 November 1936, the wonderful glass Exhibition Hall was destroyed by fire. Despite the fire, speedway continued with open licence meetings, until the side was entered in the National League Division Two for 1939. Palace resigned from the National League in June 1939, citing falling attendances. The final home meeting that year was staged on 24 June when they defeated Stoke 56-28. One last meeting was staged at the venue on 25 March 1940, when Arthur Atkinson won the Holiday Cup. The event had been sponsored by ENSA and was laid on for the entertainment of troops. Following the meeting, the track was used by the War Department as a military tank park. In both 1948 and 1950, a group known as Croydon Speedway Ltd attempted to reopen the venue, but failed. In 1960, work commenced on a multi-purpose sports centre at the site, which was opened on 13 July 1964. To this day, you will often see the top Athletics Championships from Crystal Palace screened on television.

DAGENHAM

ADDRESS: Ripple Road, Dagenham, Essex
YEARS OF OPERATION: 1932-37 Open;

1938 Sunday Dirt-track League; 1939 Open; 1946 Open; 1947 Training
TRACK LENGTH: 320 yards
NICKNAME: 'Daggers'

From 1932 to 1935, amateur-style team matches were ridden at Ripple Road, with the home side competing under the name of Romford. In 1934, meetings were promoted by Hawk Speedways. Meetings in 1936 were promoted by the Amateur Dirt-track Riders Club. In 1938, the Sunday Dirt-track League was comprised of Dagenham, Eastbourne, Smallford, Romford and Rye House, with Romford again riding their home matches at Dagenham. Meetings that season were promoted by the Amateur Dirt-track Riders Club. The season was marred by two deaths though: firstly, Harry Rogers lost his life after crashing at the track on 19 May and then twenty-two-year-old David Jackson was killed after crashing on 11 August. Both fatal crashes occurred during training sessions at Ripple Road. That 1938 season also saw West Ham Hawks based at Dagenham for their National League Division Two fixtures. The last known pre-war meeting at the venue took place on 27 August 1939, when the Rangers beat the Hawks 47-36 in a challenge match. A further four-team tournament had been scheduled for 31 August, but it is very unlikely that this ever took place. Barking Racing Club ran open licence meetings at the venue in 1946, although some reports refer to the racing as 'dirt-cum-grass'. Greyhound racing was first held at the venue on 4 April 1939, with the final dog meeting going ahead on 23 March 1965. The site of the track was later to become a car park to Dagenham Greyhound Stadium, but it is all now part of a large cold-store complex.

DALTON-IN-FURNESS
ADDRESS: Dalton-in-Furness, Nr Barrow, Cumbria
YEARS OF OPERATION: 1972 Training
TRACK LENGTH: 350 yards

The track was constructed for the purpose of training by Cliff Hindle. The circuit was situated in a field that backed onto Hindle's Dalton-in-Furness home.

DARVEL
ADDRESS: Roundshaw, Nr Auchinleck, Ayrshire
YEARS OF OPERATION: 1980-85 Training

This was a private training track constructed by Alastair Craig on the site of an old coal mine, the main shaft of which was on the centre green. The site of the track was approximately seven miles from Darvel. The safety fence consisted of rubber sheeting, while the starting gate was the one previously used at Hampden Park. The track also had a blade grader. While continuing to use Darvel for training, Ronnie Craig, along with his brother Alastair, formed a team called Darvel Rockets, which entered the Scottish Junior League, riding their home matches at Glasgow's Blantyre Sports Stadium (1980-81) and Craighead Park (1982-84).

DONCASTER
ADDRESS: Greyhound Stadium, York Road, Doncaster, South Yorkshire
YEARS OF OPERATION: 1929 Open; 1969-70 British League Division Two; 1971 Training
FIRST MEETING: 1 September 1929

Greyhound Stadium, Doncaster.

TRACK LENGTH: 350 yards
NICKNAME: 'Stallions' (1969); 'Dragons' (1970)

The stadium first hosted greyhound racing on 14 April 1928. Dirt-track racing was first introduced to the stadium on 1 September 1929, although details of that year's activity appear to have been lost in the mists of time. Doncaster RLC were admitted to the Rugby League at a special meeting on 30 April 1951. In the opening game at York Road on 18 August 1951, they beat Wakefield Trinity. In their first season, the Supporters Club provided £300 worth of terracing at the Southern end of the stadium. At the end of their second season on, 7 May 1953, the rugby club received notice to quit, when the stadium was sold to a Sheffield businessman. Under the promotion of Mike Parker and Bill Bridgett, speedway reappeared at the greyhound stadium on 27 April 1969, when Doncaster Stallions beat Eastbourne 43-35 in a British League Division Two fixture. Under the auspices of Speedway Presentations Ltd, Joe Thurley and John Berry took over the running of the track in 1970, renaming the side with a Dragons moniker. The wheels last turned in a competitive meeting at the venue on 4 October 1970, when Doncaster defeated Bradford 43-35 in the Yorkshire Gold Cup. With disappointing crowd levels at the venue, promoters Joe Thurley and John Berry subsequently transferred their operation to Birmingham in 1971. Training sessions were staged at Doncaster during the winter of 1970/71. Greyhound racing ceased at the venue in 1986, when the stadium was effectively closed down by the Safety of Sports Grounds Act. Today the site, at the back of Regent Grove, is covered by housing.

D

DONINGTON
ADDRESS: Donington Race Circuit,
Castle Donington, Derbyshire
YEARS OF OPERATION: 1991
Demonstration

Jan O. Pedersen led a speedway demonstration on a makeshift track constructed by Barry Briggs, as part of the Save The Children Day at Donington on 27 October 1991.

DROGHEDA
ADDRESS: Lourdes Stadium, Drogheda, County Louth
YEARS OF OPERATION: 1968 Open
FIRST MEETING: 2 June 1968

The Irish Speedway Association recruited 200 members from the country grass-track riders, and negotiated for the use of the old greyhound track at Drogheda in order to stage open licence speedway meetings in the summer of 1968. Just one meeting is confirmed to have taken place at this venue, on 2 June 1968. George Fitzgerald is known to have ridden in the one 1968 meeting at Lourdes Stadium.

DROYLSDEN
ADDRESS: Moorside Stadium, Droylsden, Manchester
YEARS OF OPERATION: 1927 Open; 1929 Open
FIRST MEETING: 25 June 1927
TRACK LENGTH: 600 yards

The site of the stadium was known locally as Dodd's Farm or Doddy's Trap. Meetings were organised by Harrison Gill of the South Manchester Motor Club, with races run in an anti-clock-wise direction. The track was constructed using ciders obtained from the East Manchester Power Station. The cinders were hard-rolled on top of

Moorside Stadium, Droylsden, Manchester.

loose dirt, to form a circuit with banked bends and longish straights. Ron Cave cleaned up in the opening meeting on 25 June 1927, winning the 350cc class, the 600cc class and the sidecar events. The dirt-track reopened on 13 April 1929, in spite of an ACU ban due to the fact that the track had no safety fence. With the exception of two, all the other riders insisted on performing. However, the organisation was poor and crashes were frequent. The attendance was poor as well, with only about 400 people witnessing the event. A further meeting was staged on 20 April 1929, when another meagre attendance saw racing of a very junior nature. No programmes were issued at the meetings, but result sheets were later issued to the members of the South Manchester Club. The venue later became a trotting track. Proposals for a long-track meeting at the venue on Easter Sunday 1972 never came to fruition. In the early 1970s, a nightclub called Carriages was built next to the track, but by the end of the 1980s, this, along with the old dirt track-cum-trotting track was redeveloped as housing.

DUBLIN

ADDRESS: Harold's Cross Greyhound Grounds, Dublin
YEARS OF OPERATION: 1928 Open
FIRST MEETING: 15 September 1928
TRACK LENGTH: 440 yards

The stadium, likened to Catford, is situated about three miles from the centre of Dublin. Greyhound racing was first staged at the venue on 10 April 1928. The dirt-track circuit was constructed around the pitch belonging to Transport Football Club, who were members of the League of Ireland. Just four meetings were staged at the venue, promoted by Leinster Motorcycle and Light Car Club, the first of which saw Jack Woods win the scratch race final on 15 September 1928. Betting took place at the first two meetings, but no action was taken against the bookmakers, as they had apparently lost heavily! Stanley Woods is known to have won the handicap final held on 12 October 1928, which turned out to be the fourth and final meeting at the stadium. To this day, greyhound racing is still held at Harold's Cross. Proposals to reintroduce speedway at Harold's Cross in 1952 came to nothing.

DUBLIN

ADDRESS: Santry Greyhound Stadium, Dublin
YEARS OF OPERATION: 1948-50 Open; 1951 Training; 1968 Open
FIRST MEETING: 30 May 1948
TRACK LENGTH: 410 yards
NICKNAME: 'Saints'

In 1948, speedway was introduced to the Santry Stadium by a Mr Donohoe, who promoted meetings on Sunday afternoons. The opening meeting was held on 30 May, when Ireland defeated England 40-33 in a challenge match. Attendances for meetings in 1948 averaged 4,000. Team racing ceased in July 1950, in order to allow stadium improvements to be carried out. The final meeting on 14 July saw Santry defeat Belle Vue Starlets 44-26. For a training session on 26 November 1950, around 1,000 spectators paid a nominal admission fee to watch. However, officials of the Motorcycling Union of Ireland arrived, declared the track unlicensed and racing was immediately halted. Training sessions were held after this though, but with free admission. Later known as the Shea Stadium, it staged all of Ireland's big Athletics events. By 1968, the venue had been renamed as J.F. Kennedy Stadium. The track reopened to speedway on 28 April 1968, when Mike Broadbanks won the Individual Trophy. That opening meeting was immediately followed by a full programme of stock-car racing.

DUBLIN

ADDRESS: Shelbourne Park Greyhound Stadium, Ringsend, Dublin
YEARS OF OPERATION: 1950-54 Open; 1961 Open; 1970-71 Open
FIRST MEETING: 7 May 1950
TRACK LENGTH: 385 yards
NICKNAME: 'Tigers'

Shelbourne Park is situated in Dublin's busy docklands area. The stadium was the first to hold greyhound racing in Ireland, on 14 May 1927. The opening speedway meeting was held on 7 May 1950, when Ronnie Moore won the Shelbourne Championship. Meetings were promoted by the National Greyhound Racing Company of Ireland, who appointed Ronnie Greene as manager. No red shale was available in Ireland, so brick dust was used on the track instead. In 1951, a team of riders from California were based in Ireland, and rode as Shelbourne Park in challenge matches against visiting teams from England. The last meeting of that initial period of track action was versus Wembley on 4 July 1954, when the home side suffered a 36-42 defeat. After an absence of six years, promoters Trevor Redmond, Pat Redmond and

E. Netcott reintroduced speedway to Shelbourne Park on 2 July 1961, when the home side gained a 42-35 victory over Sheffield in a challenge match. However, after a series of open licence meetings that year, the venue was to close to speedway again for another eight long years. Under the promotion of Stuart Cosgrave, speedway returned to the venue on 5 July 1970, when Shelbourne Tigers lost 38-39 in a challenge match versus Swindon. A total of six meetings were staged at the stadium that year. Five meetings were held at Shelbourne Park in 1971, the last of which saw the homesters beat the Monarchs 41-35 in a challenge match on 20 June.

DUBLIN

ADDRESS: Chapelizod Stadium, Dublin
YEARS OF OPERATION: 1950-52 Open; 1954 Open
FIRST MEETING: 19 August 1950
TRACK LENGTH: 360 yards
NICKNAME: 'Lizods' (1950); 'Eagles' (1951-52); 'Falcons' (1954)

A crowd of 12,000 people witnessed the opening meeting on 19 August 1950, when Dublin Lizods drew 42-42 with Liverpool in a challenge match. Open licence meetings that season were promoted by Wal Morton. In 1951, promoter Geoff Woodcock staged open meetings featuring English stars and local novices, but gates were reportedly very poor. Training sessions at the track in 1952 were conducted by Des Monson. Local riders known to have attended included Dom Perry, Ginger O'Beirne, Danny O'Neill and Paddy Cullen. On 23 May 1952, Dublin beat Liverpool Chadlettes 45-26 in a challenge match. The last scheduled speedway meet-

The opening meeting programme from Chapelizod, 1950.

ing at the venue was on 20 June 1954, versus Liverpool, after which the ground was leased to a local football club. The site has now partially disappeared because of factory development.

DUNDEE
ADDRESS: Dens Park Stadium, Sandeman Street, Dundee, Tayside
YEARS OF OPERATION: 1988 Demonstration

On 8 May 1988, Edinburgh Monarchs' Scott Lamb and Ray Taaffe attended an open day at Dundee Football Club. The event was organised by sponsors Novaphone.

DUNDONALD
ADDRESS: Dundonald Ice Bowl, Dundonald, County Down
YEARS OF OPERATION: 1988 Indoor Ice Racing
FIRST MEETING: 10 March 1988

Promoted by Ian Thomas and Graham Drury, indoor ice racing was staged at Dundonald Ice Bowl over two days, starting on 10 March 1988. Andy Campbell was victorious on that first day, winning the Peugeot Talbot Ice Speedway Classic. The following day, Andy Campbell was again triumphant , winning a second meeting sponsored by the same company.

E

EARLS BARTON
ADDRESS: Greyhound Stadium, Earls Barton, Nr Northampton, Northamptonshire

YEARS OF OPERATION: 1949-50 Open; 1951-53 Training; 1957 Training
TRACK LENGTH: 280 yards

Grass-track meetings were staged at the stadium in 1947, by Wellingborough Motor Club. The mini 280-yard speedway track was subsequently constructed inside the greyhound circuit. During the 1949/50 winter, a training school was run seven days a week by Eric Irons, at a cost of £2 per day if the school machine was used, or just £1 for novices with their own equipment. The stadium hosted midget-car racing in 1951. Paddy Mills ran a training school at Earls Barton during the 1952/53 winter. The homeless Southern Rovers team used the circuit for practice sessions in April 1957. Plans to operate the track in the 1957 Southern Area League fell through, due to a dispute over the cost of providing coverings for the greyhound circuit. The site is now used as a cricket ground, with only the original grandstand left from the old venue.

EASTBOURNE

ADDRESS: Arlington Stadium, Arlington Road West, Hailsham, East Sussex

YEARS OF OPERATION: 1928-37 Open; 1938 Sunday Dirt-track League; 1939 Open; 1946 Open; 1947 National League Division Three; 1948-53 Open; 1954-57 Southern Area League; 1958 Open; 1959 Southern Area League; 1960-63 Open; 1964 Metropolitan League; 1965 Training; 1969-74 British League Division Two; 1975-78 National League; 1979-84 British League; 1985-90 National League; 1991-94 British League Division One; 1995 British Premier League; 1996 British Premier League and British Conference League; 1997-2000 British Elite League

FIRST MEETING: September 1928

TRACK LENGTH: 352 yards (1928-39); 345 yards (1946); 352 yards (1947-54); 342 yards (1955-78); 330 yards (1979-94); 301 yards (1995-96); 304 yards (1997-98); 301 yards (1999-2000)

NICKNAME: 'Eagles' (The Conference League team of 1996, had a 'Starlets' nickname).

LEAGUE CHAMPIONS: 1938, 1947, 1959, 1971, 1977, 1986, 1987, 1995, 2000

KNOCK-OUT CUP WINNERS: 1975, 1977, 1978, 1985, 1986, 1987, 1994, 1997

PREMIERSHIP WINNERS: 1995, 1996

The site of the stadium was once part of a field owned by the Duke of Devonshire, who put it up for auction. A smallholder bought it and sold a piece to the Eastbourne Motor Sports Club for £100. Although one unofficial event had been held, in September 1928, the track (then known as 'The

Arlington Stadium, Eastbourne.

Hyde') was officially opened on 5 August 1929, when Les Ashdown won the Arlington Scratch Race. Just one other meeting was staged that year, on 29 August, when Bert Hele was the winner of the same event. The original track was a rolled mixture of ash and clinker. In 1934, Charlie Dugard and Tiger Hart bought a share in the club. The Dugard family has been synonymous with the track ever since. Not many full-scale meetings were staged in the early years, with the track being used mainly for local club riders to practise on. Famous early winners of the Arlington-staged Championship of Sussex have included Rube Wilson (1933), Stan Lemon (1934), Jack Riddle (1935 and 1937), George Newton (1936) and Tiger Hart (1938). In 1938, Eastbourne were champions of the Sunday Dirt-track League, with fixtures raced against Dagenham, Smallford, Romford and Rye House. During the Second World War, the stadium site was requisitioned by the Army for training dispatch riders. The terraces had become overgrown, with the track little better than a mud bath by the end of the war. Charlie Dugard bought the track outright at the cessation of hostilities, and set about restoring the surface. Having competed in the National League Division Three in 1947, the team transferred to Hastings in 1948, with amateur open events resuming at Arlington – these included challenge matches versus Rye House and the Championship of Sussex. Thirty-three-year-old Eric Dunn died two days after a track crash at Arlington on Sunday 13 June 1948. Southern Area League racing was seen at Arlington from 1954 to 1957, but the league did not operate

in 1958, with open licence meetings resuming. The first of these saw Leo McAuliffe win the Easter Trophy on 6 April. The Southern Area League returned for one final year in 1959, with Eastbourne once again part of the set-up. The stadium hosted open licence events from 1960 to 1963, prior to Eastbourne partaking in the Metropolitan League in 1964. Bob Dugard ran training sessions at Arlington as long ago as 1965, when a youngster by the name of Phil Pratt came to the fore. The track remained unused between 1966 and 1968, but reopened on 6 April 1969 (promoted by Arlington Promotions, with Dave Lanning in position as track manager), when Eastbourne beat King's Lynn Starlets 39-37 in a British League Division Two encounter. A change on the management side saw Bob Radford installed as general manager in 1974, with Dave Lanning returning in the position the following season, when Eastbourne became founder members of the New National League. In 1976, Bob Dugard assumed the role of promoter at Arlington, with his father Charlie listed as promoter from 1979, when Eastbourne joined the British League. In 1981, Charlie Dugard was joined by Bob Dugard and Danny Dunton as co-promoters. That remained the case until 1984, when meetings were held under the direction of Oxspeed Ltd, with Bob Dugard named in the match programme as promoter. Eastbourne rejoined the National League in 1985, with Russell Lanning acting as general manager. A slight change on the running of the track saw Oxspeed Ltd still in charge in 1986, with Bob Dugard and Russell Lanning listed as promoters. Trading as G.R. Promotions, Gareth

Arlington Training Track, Eastbourne.

Rogers took over as promoter in 1988, and he was joined by Chris Galvin as co-promoter the following season. However, in 1990, Gareth Rogers again assumed the role of sole promoter. In 1991, under the direction of Don Scarff and Peter Brown, Eastbourne took over the British League Division One fixtures of Wimbledon, who had been forced to leave their Plough Lane home due to financial problems. The team rode as Eastbourne Dons for the remainder of the year, but reverted back to their more familiar Eagles nickname the following year, when promoted by Peter Brown and Trevor Geer. Len Silver and Jon Cook took over as co-promoters at Arlington in 1993. Under the promotion of Jon Cook and Bob Dugard, the Eagles became part of the twenty-one team British Premier League in 1995, when both the divisions joined forces. Two teams operated from Arlington in

1996, as Eastbourne entered a second team in the British Conference League. Riding as Eastbourne Starlets, their first home meeting was held on 12 May when the they defeated Sittingbourne 47-31. The venture only lasted the one season, with the final home meeting being staged on 15 September, the homesters losing 24-29 to Reading in a match that was curtailed after eight heats. The meeting was in fact the second part of a double-header, which was preceded by a Premier League encounter between Eastbourne and Belle Vue. When the large Premier League split in two, Eastbourne joined the top-flight racing of the British Elite League in 1997. The Arlington circuit was also used by Rye House for one British Conference League meeting on 9 May 1999. The Dugard family has continued to upgrade the stadium over the years and the impressive speedway arena now covers a large expanse. Among other sports at the venue, midget-car racing was staged in 1950, while stock cars were first seen in 1955.

EASTBOURNE
ADDRESS: Eastbourne Training Track, adjacent Arlington Stadium, Arlington Road West, Hailsham, East Sussex
YEARS OF OPERATION: 1981-82 Training; 1983-89 Open and Training; 1990-91 Training; 1993-2000 Training
TRACK LENGTH: 135 yards

The training track was built in the car park during 1981, for the development of youngsters between the ages of six and fourteen. Training school sessions were originally run by Alan Johns on Sundays from 11.30 a.m. to 2.30 p.m. Throughout the early 1980s, Martin and Paul Dugard were the leading lights on the mini-track, with Martin winning the schoolboy championship at the venue on 26 June 1983. Ben Howe was victorious in the Sussex Junior Championship in 1987. Following a year out of action, the training track reopened in 1993, thanks to a tie-up with the Government's Sportsmatch scheme. Youngsters under sixteen years of age were offered equipment, leathers and training at a cost of £15 per day. A School of Excellence was set up in 1994, through sponsorship from C. Dugard Machine Tools of Brighton, and Silver-Ski Holidays of Maidstone, along with a grant from the Institute of Sports Sponsorship. Young offenders are known to have attended a training session organised by Dean Barker, which gave them the chance to practise for themselves in an effort to re-channel their minds. The club's work with youngsters was again recognised in 1999, when Sussex Police gave the scheme a £10,000 grant, with the amount being matched by Wealdon District Council. The scheme received praise for its diversionary project, which aimed to try and keep youngsters out of trouble.

EDINBURGH
ADDRESS: Marine Gardens, Seafield Road, Portobello, Edinburgh
YEARS OF OPERATION: 1928-29 Open; 1930 Northern League; 1931 Open; 1938 Open; 1939 Open and Union Cup; 1953 Training
FIRST MEETING: 19 May 1928
TRACK LENGTH: 440 yards
NICKNAME: 'Thistles'

Marine Gardens originally opened on 31 May 1909, as a seaside attraction that included rides on the Mountain Slide and the Scenic Railway among others. A stadium was added to the pleasure complex in 1911, with the addition of a football pitch and running track. Prior to the opening dirt-track meeting in 1928, Australian Keith McKay gave an exhibition at the track on 26 March. Demonstration events were subsequently held at the venue on both 2 May (by Sprouts Elder) and 9 May (by Stewie St George). Under the direction of Jimmy Fraser, on behalf of the promoters, Scottish Dirt-track Motor Racing Club, the opening meeting took place on 19 May and attracted a crowd of over 8,000, who witnessed Stewie St George win the Gold Helmet International Race. Bookmakers were present for the first and the third meetings in 1928, before this was outlawed by the authorities. Credit for establishing the

An ultra-rare programme from Marine Gardens, 1939.

track at Marine Gardens was largely due to J.S.D. Price of the Edinburgh St George Motorcycle Club and Robert Sinclair of the Edinburgh and District Motor Club, who received active cooperation from Fred Graham-Yooll, proprietor of the complex. Edinburgh City Football Club, who played in the East of Scotland League, were based at Marine Gardens during the 1928/29 and 1929/30 seasons. Their first home match at the venue was played on 8 August 1928, when they were defeated 2-5 by Queen's Park. Just to confuse matters, Leith Athletic Football Club also played at Marine Gardens throughout the 1928/29 and 1929/30 seasons, in Scottish League Division Two. Leith's first game at the stadium took place on 18 August 1928, when

they drew 1-1 with Dunfermline. Thirty-two-year-old Walter Brown died after crashing in a consolation heat at the track on 11 May 1929, with a huge crowd of 26,000 witnessing the fatal accident. The dirt-track team withdrew from the Northern League in August 1930, having completed twelve matches. The final meeting at the Portobello venue had already taken place on 26 July when Harry Whitfield won the 500cc Marine Gardens Track Championship and £100 in prize money. The closure of the track was blamed on the high financial demands of the top riders. Remaining at the stadium, Edinburgh City FC played in the Edinburgh & District League in 1930/31, while Leith Athletic FC played in Scottish League Division One. Briefly, dirt-track racing returned in 1931 when, following a practice session at the stadium on 13 May, Alfie Williams won the Edinburgh Handicap three days later. Just one other meeting was staged that year, when Sam Aitkenhead won the Edinburgh Handicap on 20 June. That was the end of dirt-track racing at the venue until 1938. In the 1931/32 season, Leith Athletic continued to perform from Marine Gardens. Greyhound racing was first staged at the venue on 2 July 1932. Leith Athletic FC remained at the stadium for four more seasons from 1932/33, playing Scottish League Division Two football. During the 1934/35 season, Edinburgh City FC played their Scottish League 'C' Division matches at the Portobello venue. Midget-car racing was staged at Marine Gardens in 1938. Before a crowd of 15,000, speedway returned to Marine Gardens on 14 May 1938, when Ernie Price won the Scottish Silver

Torch. Further open licence events were staged that year, and in 1939, when Edinburgh also partook in the Northern Section of the Union Cup, along with Newcastle, Glasgow, Belle Vue II and Sheffield. What turned out to be the last-ever meeting at the venue was staged on 29 August, 1939, when Oliver Hart and Jack Hyland won the Best Pairs championship. During the war, the site was taken over by the armed forces, who laid concrete over the track. Harry Darling and Jack Jones are known to have trained at the venue in 1953, having found one of the straights was still there and as such, ideal for trying out starts. The site of the old track is now covered by a bus depot, which was built in 1961/62.

EDINBURGH
ADDRESS: Stenhouse Greyhound Stadium, Stenhouse, Edinburgh
YEARS OF OPERATION: 1935 Demonstration
TRACK LENGTH: 500 yards

Greyhound racing was first held at the stadium on 25 June 1932. It is known that in 1935 a speedway demonstration of just a few laps took place at the venue. Stenhouse was proposed as Edinburgh's second track to Old Meadowbank in 1949, but a licence was refused by the Speedway Control Board.

EDINBURGH
ADDRESS: Old Meadowbank Stadium, Clockmill Road, Edinburgh
YEARS OF OPERATION: 1948-54 National League Division Two; 1957 Training; 1959 Open; 1960-64 Provincial League; 1965-67 British League; 1998 Demonstration

FIRST MEETING: 17 April 1948
TRACK LENGTH: 368 yards (1948); 365 yards (1949); 363 yards (1950-67)
NICKNAME: 'Monarchs'
QUEEN'S CUP WINNERS: 1953

Old Meadowbank was used by Leith Athletic Football Club in the Scottish Football League, having previously been used by the Leith Amateur club. For four consecutive seasons, from 1936/37 to 1939/40, Scottish League Division Two matches were played at the venue, with the club inactive in 1940/41. In 1941/42, Leith played in the Scottish League North-East Division and then had a four-year gap from playing. The stadium was used by the Army as a motor transport depot during the Second World War, the ground being left in an unplayable condition by the end of the fighting. Conditions were so bad that Leith spent the 1946/47 season playing at the adjacent Corporation-owned Recreation Ground, while Old Meadowbank was renovated. The Football Club purchased the grandstand from St Bernard's Gymnasium Ground in 1947, for a fee of £2,000, and this was moved to Old Meadowbank and re-erected on the South side of the stadium. Leith resumed playing at Meadowbank in 1947/48, competing in Scottish League Division Two. An application to run speedway at Old Meadowbank was received too late for the 1947 season. Prior to staging speedway, the Scottish Football Association refused to permit the removal and relaying of the football pitch corners. In order to overcome this problem, Leith Athletic FC agreed to use a minimum-sized playing pitch. The stadium hosted its first speedway meeting on 17 April

1948, when Edinburgh lost 39-44 to Glasgow in a National League Division Two encounter. The promoting group behind the Monarchs venture included Frank Varey, Johnnie Hoskins, Bob Rae and James Mackenzie. Having finished bottom of Scottish League Division Two, Leith Athletic FC found themselves in the Scottish League 'C' Division for 1948/49. The 1949/50 season saw Leith participate in the Scottish League 'C' Division (South-East Region), before playing in the Scottish League 'C' Division (North-East Region) in 1950/51 and 1951/52. Johnnie Hoskins stepped down from the promoting company in 1950, leaving Frank Varey, Bob Rae and James Mackenzie to run the show. Monarchs great Jack Young became the first rider from a Division Two track to lift the World Championship at Wembley in 1951. Prior to the start of 1952, Jack had moved to Division One West Ham for a then world record fee of £3,750. The 1952 season also saw W.R. Young join forces with the promoting company. 1952/53 saw Leith FC playing in Scottish League 'C' Division (North-East Region), prior to just cup matches and friendlies the following season. The football club's last match at Meadowbank was played on 16 January 1954, when they drew 4-4 with Dunfermline Reserves in a friendly game. Edinburgh Monarchs resigned from the National League Division Two in 1954. The last meeting went ahead on 10 July, when Ken McKinlay won a World Championship round before a crowd of 7,000 spectators. Falling attendances and the effect of the ridiculous rate of entertainment tax imposed on speedway at the time could be levelled as the reasons for the track's premature closure. At an extra-ordinary AGM on 17 May 1955, Leith FC was wound up. A liquidator was appointed and at a meeting on 2 May 1957, it was revealed that the club had left liabilities of £12,000, while the assets amounted to only £7,300. Following the demise of Leith Athletic, the ground was used by Murrayfield Amateurs before they disappeared like their predecessors. After two full years of speedway inactivity at the stadium, locally-based junior Ian Hart contacted Edinburgh Corporation in 1957, for permission to practise at the track. Much to his surprise, this was granted for a small fee, provided he left the circuit in the same condition he found it. The only meeting staged in 1959 was promoted by The Engineering Society of Edinburgh University on 18 April. The proceeds of the meeting, which was won by Doug Templeton, went to the Edinburgh Student's Charities Appeal. On 23 April 1960, the Edinburgh Students staged a second charity meeting, which was won by Tommy Roper. Two weeks later, the Monarchs were back in action as promoter Ian Hoskins brought about the return of regular speedway. The first meeting on 7 May saw Edinburgh defeat Liverpool 39-33 in a Provincial League match. On Friday 20 September 1963, Edinburgh entertained Belle Vue in a challenge match, but the date will always be remembered as the night that legend Peter Craven was fatally injured in a heat twelve accident; Peter died in Edinburgh Hospital on Tuesday 24 September at just twenty-nine years of age. The merging of the Provincial League and the National League saw Edinburgh became founder members of the British League in 1965, with Ian Hoskins still running the show.

The Monarchs were given notice to quit in 1967, in order to accommodate the rebuilding of the stadium for the 1970 Commonwealth games. The final meeting at Old Meadowbank took place on 14 October 1967, when Wayne Briggs and Oyvind Berg won the Scottish Best Pairs Championship. Without a home, the Monarchs were forced to take up residence at Cliftonhill Stadium, Coatbridge in 1968. From 1974/75 to 1994/95 inclusive, Meadowbank Thistle Football Club were based at the stadium, playing Scottish League soccer. On 7 March 1998, Brenda Craven unveiled a plaque at Meadowbank Stadium in memory of her husband's fatal crash in 1963. The ceremony, organised by Allan Wilson, featured a parade of riders and bikes, with the highlight being the sight of Kenny McKinna broadsiding around the outside of the grass perimeter.

EDINBURGH

ADDRESS: Gyle Trotting Track, Glasgow Road, Corstorphine, Edinburgh
YEARS OF OPERATION: 1968-70 Training
TRACK LENGTH: 320 yards

The Gyle Stadium was used in the summer months for pony trotting. After passing a noise meter test in 1968, organiser Ian Beattie and a band of helpers constructed a red shale speedway circuit inside the trotting track. Bales of straw were used as a safety fence, with a caravan on site to act as a changing room. No meetings as such were ever staged, but the first training session went ahead on 14 December 1968, with Andy Meldrum looking particularly impressive on the track – which was comparable in shape to Newcastle's Brough Park. The project

opened one week later than scheduled, due to objections from local residents. In 1970, Bobby Beaton is known to have been a real thrill merchant in training sessions at Gyle. The site is now covered by the Royal Scot Hotel.

EDINBURGH

ADDRESS: Murrayfield Ice Rink, Murrayfield, Edinburgh
YEARS OF OPERATION: 1971 Trials; 1972 Indoor Ice Racing; 1987 Indoor Ice Racing
FIRST MEETING: 9 January 1972

Late in 1971, trials were held on 175cc bikes, which actually proved that speedway on ice worked. The first of five meetings took place on 9 January 1972, when Edinburgh beat Ayr 42-34 before a crowd of 4,000 spectators. Meetings were promoted by Chay Sports Ltd, whose directors were T.J. Hay and G.P. Chatham. The final meeting of the five was held on 16 April 1972. Under the promotion of Ian Thomas and Graham Drury, the roar of speedway bikes returned to the venue on 15 February 1987, when Jan Andersson won the Yugo Classic in the first part of an afternoon and evening double-header. A Four-Team Tournament was also staged as Jim McMillan's farewell meeting, with the result being England 28, Sweden 27, Denmark 23, Scotland 18.

EDINBURGH

ADDRESS: Powderhall Stadium, Beaverhall Road, Edinburgh
YEARS OF OPERATION: 1977-90 National League; 1991-94 British League Division Two; 1995 British Premier League

E

FIRST MEETING: 15 April 1977
TRACK LENGTH: 335 yards (1977-80); 339 yards (1981-87); 341 yards (1988-95)
NICKNAME: 'Monarchs'
KNOCK-OUT CUP WINNERS: 1981

Powderhall was one of the oldest stadiums in Britain, having originally been built in 1869/70 as a sports ground, and was home to the famous Powderhall Sprint. St Bernards Football Club used the stadium for friendlies and cup matches in 1889, prior to staging Scottish League Division Two matches there in 1901. St Bernards' residences at Powderhall were short-lived however, due to clashes with other sports, particularly athletics. A gold medal winner at the Paris Olympics, Eric Liddell used to train at Powderhall in the 1920s. Leith Football Club used the venue for

Opening night programme from Powderhall Stadium, 1977.

Scottish Alliance matches in 1926/27, before holding their Scottish League Division Two games there during 1927/28. Greyhound racing was first staged at the venue on 3 August 1927, when 10,000 people turned up to witness the action. Edinburgh City Football Club played their home Scottish League Division Two matches at Powderhall for three seasons, from 1931/32 to 1933/34; their first match at the venue was versus Bo'ness on 15 August 1931. An extensive programme of modernization took place at the stadium in 1970. Powderhall was mooted for speedway on several occasions, but the Greyhound Racing Association were not keen, until financial problems forced them to look to other income, with speedway finally given the go-ahead in 1977. The first official practice at Powderhall was held on Tuesday 12 April 1977, with Charlie Monk being the first rider to take to the circuit. Promoted by Mike Parker Promotions Ltd, the track opened three nights later, with a crowd of 10,000 cramming in to see Edinburgh lose 36-42 to Berwick in a challenge match. The Monarchs subsequently took their place in the nineteen-team National League. Tom Cook took over as promoter at the venue in 1982. A change on the promoting side in 1985 saw Toni Frankitti and John Campbell take up the reigns of the club. In 1986, a new promoting company was formed by the name of Edinburgh Speedway (1986) Ltd, and this saw Doug Newlands replace Toni Frankitti as co-promoter alongside John Campbell. In 1987, a new stand costing £750,000 was opened and a computer tote was installed. A further change to the pro-

Powderhall Stadium, Edinburgh.

motion in 1991 saw Alex Harkess link up with John Campbell as co-promoter. That year also saw the amalgamation of the National League and the British League, with Edinburgh becoming part of the new Division Two set-up. In 1995, the divisions joined forces to form one league of twenty-one teams, and Edinburgh became founder members of the British Premier League. The final meeting at Powderhall was staged on 6 October that year, however, when the Monarchs defeated Glasgow 62-34 in a league encounter. The stadium was sold after outline planning permission for housing and office development was granted. A final appeal against this was turned down in the autumn of 1997, after which the lovely old venue was razed to the ground.

EDMONTON
ADDRESS: Barras Sports Stadium, Edmonton, North London
YEARS OF OPERATION: 1961 Trials/Training

In 1961, Wally Mawdsley and Pete Lansdale were behind a project to introduce speedway to Barras Sports Stadium, which boasted a 440-yard cinder athletics track. A licence was refused for either Provincial League racing or training, although it was rumoured many years later that trials or training of sorts might have actually taken place.

ELLESMERE PORT
ADDRESS: The Stadium, Thornton Road, Ellesmere Port, Wirral
YEARS OF OPERATION: 1971 Demonstration; 1972-74 British League

Division Two; 1975-82 National League; 1985 National League
FIRST MEETING: 28 March 1972
TRACK LENGTH: 423 yards (1972-75); 424 yards (1976-85)
NICKNAME: 'Gunners'
LEAGUE CHAMPIONS: 1985

The Thornton Road Stadium was opened by Joe Mercer in 1968. Late in 1971, Ian Thomas staged a speedway demonstration at the venue for the benefit of Council representatives. 400 people witnessed the machines going around the edge of the football pitch, with Colin Tucker and a couple of grass-track riders going through the motions. The stadium staged its first meeting on 28 March 1972, when Ellesmere Port Gunners and Sunderland raced to a 39-39 draw in a challenge match. Under the promotion of Ian Thomas, Bill Carmen and Wally Mawdsley, the Gunners subsequently joined the British League Division Two. A change on the promoting side saw Hornets Raceways Ltd (Jim Sephton and Ron Nesbitt) take over the running of the track in 1973. More changes of promoters occurred in 1975, when Ernie Park and Joe Shaw took over at Thornton Road. That season also saw the formation of the New National League, with the Gunners taking their place as founder members. Richard Park (son of Ernie) became co-promoter in 1976, alongside Joe Shaw and Ernie Park. Twenty-year-old Stuart Shirley died after crashing while practising at the venue on 3 December 1977. Following the death of Ernie Park in February 1979, Mrs E. Park linked with son Richard and Joe Shaw on the promoting side at Thornton Road. After

The Stadium, Ellesmere Port.

competing in eleven years of track action, the track closed at the end of the 1982 season. The final meeting was against Newcastle in a leg of the Supernational Final, when the Gunners went down to a 47-49 defeat. Promoter Mervyn Porter brought speedway back to the venue for one year only in 1985. The reopening meeting went ahead on 5 April, when Ellesmere Port beat Stoke 50-28 in a challenge match. A meeting had been scheduled for the week before (on 29 March) against Long Eaton, but was postponed in the interests of safety, due to heavy rain that had left the track in a tricky state. The last-ever meeting at the circuit took place on Boxing Day 1985, when Ellesmere Port Past and Present drew 39-39 with an Inter-League Select side in the Joe Owen benefit meeting. The speedway track has since been replaced by a sand-surfaced greyhound circuit, which staged its first meeting on 29 February 1988. Rumours about a possible return for speedway started to circulate in November 2000. Noise tests were carried out at the stadium in February 2001, when local Council members met with former Long Eaton promoters Graham Drury and Tony Mole.

ELSTREE

ADDRESS: Elstree, Hertfordshire
YEARS OF OPERATION: 1947 Open
FIRST MEETING: 10 August 1947

A local farmer prepared a track by pouring oil onto a grassy field. The only covered accommodation was a canvas marquee, which also served as a dressing room. A total of nine Sunday afternoon meetings were staged and supplemented by beauty contests, side-shows and knobbly knees competitions. All nine meetings were controlled by ACU steward Arthur Humphrey.

ESSINGTON

ADDRESS: Essington Hall Farm, Essington, Nr Wednesfield, Staffordshire
YEARS OF OPERATION: 1951-52 Training

Farmers Bill and Tom Simpson built their own track and purchased a bike from Doug McLachlan for £150. Regular Sunday training sessions attracted Wolverhampton and Birmingham riders, including Derek Timms, Gundy Harris, Roy Moreton and a young Howard Cole. One side of the track was close to a duck pond, with Wilbur Nash apparently having to swim for safety on five occasions during one particular practice session!

EXETER

ADDRESS: County Ground Stadium, Church Road, St Thomas, Exeter, Devon
YEARS OF OPERATION: 1929-31 Open; 1934 Open; 1947-51 National League Division Three; 1952-53 Southern League; 1954-55 National League Division Two; 1957-58 Open; 1960 Open; 1961-64 Provincial League; 1965-67 British League; 1968-74 British League Division One; 1975-79 British League; 1980-83 National League; 1984 British League; 1985-90 National League; 1991-94 British League Division Two; 1995 British Premier League and British Academy League; 1996 British Premier League and British Conference League; 1997 British Premier League and British Amateur League; 1998-2000 British Premier League

FIRST MEETING: 9 March 1929
TRACK LENGTH: 420 yards (1929); 417 yards (1930-34); 440 yards (1947); 433 yards (1948-2000)
NICKNAME: 'Falcons' (The Academy League/Conference League team of 1995-96, was known as 'Devon Demons', while the Amateur League side of 1997, were called 'Western Warriors').
LEAGUE CHAMPIONS: 1948, 1974, 2000
NATIONAL TROPHY (DIVISION THREE) WINNERS: 1951
KNOCK-OUT CUP WINNERS: 1962, 1983
YOUNG SHIELD WINNERS: 1997

Dirt-track racing could easily have started at the venue in 1928, as terms were agreed between the promoting company and the rugby club, who owned the stadium. A draft lease was drawn up, but the necessary signatures were not forthcoming and negotiations fell through until the following year. The circuit was originally a cycling track, which was leased by Southern Speedways Ltd (Leonard Glanfield), who removed the old asphalt surface and laid a cinder surface, with lighting provided by thirty arc lamps. Prior to the opening meeting, Freddie Hore gave a four-lap demonstration after the conclusion of a rugby union match. Ron Johnson took the honours in the opening meeting on Saturday 9 March 1929, winning the Golden Helmet in front of 11,400 spectators. After the first few meetings in 1929, the wire safety fence was taken down and replaced by boards to a height of 4 feet, with a 9-inch bottom board set at an angle of 45 degrees. Southern Speedways Ltd were wound up by a County Court action brought by a local printer in 1929. Trading as County Speedways Ltd, Fred Mockford and Cecil Smith took over as promoters in 1930, but they had to overcome a long legal battle with local residents on noise grounds. Just eleven meetings were staged in 1931, before the track closed down. The final meeting was held on 22 July, when Lionel Van Praag was triumphant in the scratch race. The track remained closed in 1932 and 1933, but five amateur meetings were staged in 1934, organised by Exeter Motor Club. The first meeting of the five took place on 6 April, when Tom Whitton won the 500cc class event before a crowd of some 2,500. Falling crowds brought the venture to a close on 1 June 1934, when Devon defeated Cornwall 9-8 in a challenge match. During the Second World War, the track was occupied by the military and by the time speedway resumed in 1947, the wooden safety fence was in a state of decay and was subsequently replaced by the solid steel one that still remains at the venue. Under the promotion of Motor Sports (Exeter) Ltd, with Frank 'Buster' Buckland as speedway manager, the reopening meeting occurred on 14 April 1947, when Charlie Hayden won an individual meeting entitled The Battle For Team Places. Exeter subsequently took their place in the National League Division Three. For health reasons, 'Buster' Buckland emigrated to Australia in September 1948, with Bill Eastmond taking over the duties of speedway manager for the remainder of the season. Bert Sibley became manager at the start of the 1949 season, but he was replaced in May by W.J. 'Bill' Dutton. In 1952, Division Three

County Ground Stadium, Exeter.

became the Southern League, with the Falcons remaining in the re-titled league. In May that year, Bill Dutton moved on to Cardiff, and Bernard 'Broncho' Slade took over the duties of speedway manager at the County Ground. Australian Roy Eather was killed in a crash at the track in March 1953. With the disappearance of the Southern League in 1954, Exeter found themselves in the National League Division Two; however, the track closed again at the end of the following season. Under the promotion of Cyril Roger and Geoff Pymar, the track reopened again on 22 July 1957, when Exeter defeated Norwich 58-38 in a challenge match. The promoting duo staged open licence events that year, and a further series of six meetings in 1958. After another year's break in 1959, speedway again returned to the County Ground on 19 September 1960,

when the Falcons defeated Plymouth 38-34. That was the first of only three open licence meetings staged that year under the promotion of Wally Mawdsley and Pete Lansdale. The Falcons joined the Provincial League in 1961, prior to becoming founder members of the British League in 1965. A change on the promoting side in 1969 still saw Wally Mawdsley and Pete Lansdale running the show, but in association with John Richards and Pat Tapson. The promoters at the County Ground changed slightly in 1971, with Wally Mawdsley and John Richards looking after the Falcons' affairs, while Pete Lansdale and Pat Tapson moved on to concentrate on their other operation at Newport. When Exeter signed the legendary Ivan Mauger in 1973, a crowd of 10,500 turned up for his debut versus Poole on the Easter Monday. For financial reasons, Exeter joined the

National League in 1980, with Peter Oakes linking as co-promoter alongside Wally Mawdsley. After twenty-one years of promoting at the County Ground, Wally Mawdsley stood down in 1981, with Pam Oakes and Reg Fearman joining Peter Oakes as co-promoters. Sadly, the season was marred when thirty-year-old Tony Sanford died following a crash at the County Ground on 8 September. The Falcons rejoined the British League in 1984 but, in spite of strenuous efforts by the promotion, it proved impossible to sign the necessary heat leaders and Exeter returned to the National League the following season, when Colin Hill took over as promoter. With the amalgamation of the two leagues in 1991, Exeter continued on in the British League Division Two, which was, in effect, the equivalent of the National League. A further change to the set-up of British speedway saw the formation of the Premier League in 1995, when all the British League teams combined to form a larger league. The Falcons took their place in the new competition, with promoter Colin Hill signing future World Champion Mark Loram to bolster the side. The track was also home to Academy League racing that season, with Devon Demons running their opening meeting on 11 May when they lost 47-49 to Buxton. The Academy League became the Conference League in 1996, with Devon running what turned out to be their final meeting on 26 August, when a double-header saw them defeat Linlithgow 39-38 and Ryde 44-34. The Premier League split in two in 1997, with ten teams joining the new Elite League, while fourteen tracks (including Exeter) remained in a revamped Premier League. Exeter also joined forces with Newport in 1997 to enter a composite side, made up mainly from juniors, in the British Amateur League. Home fixtures were equally split between the two tracks, with the team riding as Western Warriors. The County Ground staged its opening Amateur League fixture on 31 March when the Warriors defeated the Shuttle Cubs 60-18. This proved to be a one-year venture though, and the track staged its final such meeting on 8 September when the Western Warriors beat Ryde 41-37. Colin Hill remains in place as promoter today, embarking on his seventeenth season at the helm, and as such is one of the longest-serving British speedway promoters of the modern era.

EXETER
ADDRESS: Exwick Fields, Nr Exeter, Devon
YEARS OF OPERATION: 1945 Open
FIRST MEETING: 21 May 1945
TRACK LENGTH: 360 yards

The site of the track was located on land owned by Bill Eastmond, behind the Thatched House Inn at Exwick Fields. Promoted by the Exeter Speedway Motor Club ('Broncho' Slade and 'Buster' Buckland), the track hosted just one meeting on 21 May 1945, when Fred Tuck took victory in the Victory Trophy, which was held as part of the Victory in Europe Day celebration. Due to adverse weather conditions, lorry-loads of sawdust were laid on the circuit, giving the effect of real dirt-track racing.

EXETER
ADDRESS: Marsh Barton Stadium,

Alphin Brook Lane, Alphington, Exeter, Devon
YEARS OF OPERATION: 1945 Open; 1948-51 Training
FIRST MEETING: 5 July 1945
TRACK LENGTH: 250 yards (1945); 333 yards (1948-51)

This track was constructed in only two weeks, on a piece of ground beside what is now Alphin Brook Lane, and was used for the initial reintroduction of speedway to Exeter following the Second World War. A 250-yard circuit was cut out, with the soil being used to build a safety fence. Cinders formed the track surface, while the brook which ran through the stadium provided washing facilities for the riders. Organised by 'Buster' Buckland, 'Broncho' Slade, Bill Eastmond and Peter Jones, the stadium hosted its first meeting on 5 July 1945, when Ron Johnson was victorious in an individual event. Just six meetings were staged at the venue that year, with the final one going ahead on 16 August, when over 7,000 people witnessed Bill Kitchen win the ACU Southern Championship. Any further racing at the stadium was precluded when the Ministry of Agriculture imposed a 'ploughing-up order' on the site, although a larger track was later used for training between 1948 and 1951. Cycle speedway was also staged at the venue in 1948. Johnny Myson and Norman Clay are known to have trained novices at the venue during the winter of 1948/49. Don Hardy was the chief training instructor at the track in 1950. Racing ceased when local housewives joined forces to complain about the dust ruining their washing. Greyhound racing also took place at the venue, with the last meeting being held in November 1957.

EXETER
ADDRESS: Peamore Circuit, Alphington, Exeter, Devon
YEARS OF OPERATION: 1950-51 Training

The track was situated at the rear of Peamore Garage, which at the time was owned by John Selleck, who later promoted at St Austell. A blue and white car sticker from the time indicated that a Peacocks nickname was used. This nickname came from the nearby Peamore House, which was well-known locally for the peacocks which lived in the grounds. During the winter of 1950/51, Don Hardy ran a training school at the circuit. Two machines, along with leathers, were available to juniors at a cost of £2 per day, plus 5/9 for insurance. Plymouth rider Brian Hitchcock was a product of the school at Peamore. A number of residents and the Local Government Planning Authority curtailed the use of the track, before training recommenced again in the 1951/52 winter.

EXETER
ADDRESS: Haldon Arena, Devon and Exeter Racecourse, Haldon Moors, Exeter, Devon
YEARS OF OPERATION: 1978-80 Long-track
FIRST MEETING: 8 October 1978
TRACK LENGTH: 880 metres

Teinbridge Council approved the scheme to construct a long-track course at Haldon on 7 November 1977, and work on the 880-metre circuit com-

Haldon Arena, Exeter.

menced the same day. Meetings were promoted by Long Track Racing Associates (John Richards, Wally Mawdsley and Peter Oakes), with the opener being held on 8 October 1978, when Reidar Eide emerged triumphant. Two further meetings were held under the Long Track Racing Associates' banner in 1979, both being won by Phil Crump. One further meeting was run at Haldon Arena, on 29 June 1980, when a national long-track competition was followed by a six-heat international long-track event.

EXETER
ADDRESS: Haldon Training Track, Haldon Arena, Devon and Exeter Racecourse, Haldon Moors, Exeter, Devon
YEARS OF OPERATION: 1978-80 Training
TRACK LENGTH: 300 metres

The training track utilised one of the bends of the 880-metre long-track, and was first opened on 29 October 1978. A large group of novices and juniors turned up for the initial session, with Vaclav Verner and Ales Dryml on hand to offer advice and tuition. Phil Crump is known to have used the track for trying out bikes in July 1979. Chris Julian used the track in 1980.

F

FARINGDON
ADDRESS: Faringdon Raceway, Wantage Road, Faringdon, Oxfordfordshire
YEARS OF OPERATION: 1985-87 Training; 1988 Open and Training
TRACK LENGTH: 250 yards

This was a training track, constructed

initially without a safety fence, inside an autograss car racing circuit. In 1985, the Speedway Control Board instructed all promoters not to allow licensed riders to race on the Faringdon Raceway, due to the fact that the organisers at the venue had allegedly been charging spectators to watch both the autograss racing and the speedway. Despite this, training sessions were held fortnightly, prior to car meetings, with the top four trainees appearing in an interval race during the autograss event. By 1986, the track was licensed by the SCB, and a 3-foot-high safety fence had been added to the bends, with the starting gate and pits moved to the opposite side to their position in 1985. A challenge match versus Iwade is known to have been planned for 9 October 1988. Ray Morse confirmed that the track did not operate into the 1990s, due to a change of heart from the local farmer, whose land the venue was constructed on.

FELTON

ADDRESS: Felton, Nr Amble, Northumberland
YEARS OF OPERATION: 1978-83 Open and Training; 1984-88 Training
TRACK LENGTH: 280 yards
NICKNAME: 'Flyers'

Ken Marshall was the man behind the project, having reached an agreement with the owners of suitable land on a derelict airfield at Felton. One of the conditions of usage was that no spectators could watch training or team events. Felton partook in the Scottish Junior League, but had to ride their home matches at Newcastle's Brough Park. Mike Hiftle was the resident tutor at the track in 1979. Eddie Ingels ran a series of training schools at the venue

Faringdon Raceway.

in 1984. Rob Grant is known to have coached Berwick juniors at Felton in 1987.

FERNDOWN
ADDRESS: New Forest Training School, St Ives Road, Ferndown, Nr Bournemouth, Hampshire
YEARS OF OPERATION: 1958-61 Training
TRACK LENGTH: 330 yards

Run by Fred Pike, the sand and soil-surfaced track was situated opposite St Ives Post Office, in a large field bordering on the St Ives Road in Ferndown. Brian Hanham was chief instructor at the site, with Norman Strachan also chipping in with advice. Ferndown rode in a second-half four-heat challenge match at Aldershot on 26 September 1959, losing 11-13. Alby Golden is known to have helped Brian Hanham with the coaching at Ferndown in 1961. There were plans to build stands and eventually gain league status, but this never came to fruition.

FLEETWOOD
ADDRESS: Highbury Avenue, Fleetwood, Lancashire
YEARS OF OPERATION: 1948-51 National League Division Two; 1952 Open
FIRST MEETING: 13 April 1948
TRACK LENGTH: 325 yards (1948); 336 yards (1949-52)
NICKNAME: 'Flyers' (1948-51); 'Knights' (1952)

In December 1936, Fleetwood Council purchased four acres of land at the Memorial Park adjoining Highbury Avenue, for the construction of a stadium for Fleetwood Football Club. The football club first used this new venue on 26 August 1939. Within a week, how-

Felton, Northumberland.

Highbury Avenue, Fleetwood.

ever, the Second World War had broken out and the ground was left to rot. The ground was reconstructed in 1946, before the team played only their second home game on 31 August that year. Following the demise of speedway at Wigan, the sport arrived at Fleetwood in 1948, when a highly-banked track was constructed around the football pitch at Highbury Avenue. This was after co-promoters Joe Waxman and Jimmy Wolfenden had obtained a seven-year tenancy from Fleetwood Town Council. The ground had a distinct slope, which made construction of the track and safety fence difficult. The fence of galvanised iron sheets was originally mounted mistakenly, with the cutting edge facing the riders! The corners of the football pitch had to be removed to allow speedway racing, and then replaced after each meeting. Prior to the opening meeting on 13 April

1948, both Stanley Matthews and Stan Mortensen did a lap on a bike, after the local mayor had declared the track open. Fleetwood's opponents, Edinburgh, had arrived early and had spent most of the afternoon getting used to the track prior to the National League Division Two encounter. The Fleetwood riders arrived an hour before the start and complained that this had been unfair – and so it proved, with the home side losing 34-49 in front of a gate of 11,000 spectators. The attraction of the sport declined badly over a few short years, with locally based ex-rider Don Potter taking over as promoter in 1952 and, despite being granted a licence to continue in the National League Division Two, he ran a series of individual and pairs meetings, plus challenge matches. In July 1952, the Control Board suspended the track licence in order to straighten out certain financial situations. This was only a temporary measure and the track soon continued with its operations. The end was nigh however, and the last meeting staged at Highbury Avenue took place on 3 September 1952, when Jeff Crawford and Harold Bottoms won the Best Pairs Trophy. It was proposed to transfer the operation to Blackpool at the end of 1952, but this never materialised. By April 1954, the track had virtually disappeared, following rebuilding work at the stadium. Now surrounded by houses, the stadium remains in position today, although it shows little sign of ever having staged speedway.

G

GLASGOW

ADDRESS: Nelson Athletic Grounds, Janefield Street, Gallowgate, Glasgow
YEARS OF OPERATION: 1928 Open; 1932 Open
FIRST MEETING: 9 April 1928
TRACK LENGTH: 486 yards

Originally called the Olympic Stadium and situated immediately North of Celtic Park, this venue became known as Glasgow Nelson after the owner's name. The stadium hosted Scotland's first-ever dirt-track meeting on Easter Monday 9 April 1928, when John Allan won the opening race in 2 minutes 37 seconds, before going on to take the final of the 350cc class. Prior to the opening meeting, practice sessions are known to have taken place on 11, 18 and 25 March and 1 April. The opening meeting attracted a crowd of 2,000

spectators, but the riders did not broadside – instead they toured around with their feet on the foot-rests. According to Norrie Isbister, who took part in the opening event, the racing was 'very amateurish'. Just five meetings were held at the venue in 1928, the last of which saw Jimmy Pinkerton win all three events (350cc, 600cc and unlimited) on 11 May. The dirt-track operation was then subsequently transferred to Carntyne. The circuit was described as being egg-shaped and had previously been used as a trotting track. Meetings were run by an amateur body known as the Glasgow Nelson Dirt-Track Motorcycling Club. Greyhound racing was first introduced to the stadium on 2 September 1930. Dirt-track racing is known to have made a fleeting return to the venue in 1932, with two meetings, the first of which saw Billy Llewellyn win the Glasgow Handicap on 17 May. The site of the stadium is now covered with a housing estate.

GLASGOW

ADDRESS: Celtic Park, London Road, Glasgow
YEARS OF OPERATION: 1928 Open
FIRST MEETING: 28 April 1928
TRACK LENGTH: 440 yards

The track was constructed around the pitch belonging to Glasgow Celtic Football Club, under the auspices of Dirt-track Speedways Ltd (G.E. Baxter). A crowd of 3,500 watched the opening meeting on 28 April 1928, when Stewie St George won both the Opening Handicap and Golden Gauntlet. The afternoon of 5 May was notable, with the dirt-track riders put on a demonstration as the half-time entertainment

Celtic Park, Glasgow.

at an Old Firm soccer match. The venture proved unpopular though, and just eleven meetings were held at the venue, with the final one going ahead on 21 July 1928, when Buzz Hibberd won the Golden Gauntlet. Afterwards, G.E. Baxter (known as Jimmy) transferred the operation to Custom House Stadium in West Ham, London. It was reported in 1963 that Trevor Redmond sought to secure the rights to use the stadium for speedway, but his attempt proved fruitless. The site of the track is now buried under the redeveloped football stadium.

GLASGOW
ADDRESS: Carntyne Greyhound Stadium, Myreside Street, Carntyne, Glasgow
YEARS OF OPERATION: 1928 Open; 1930 Open
FIRST MEETING: 25 May 1928
TRACK LENGTH: 420 yards

Greyhound racing was first seen at Carntyne on 17 September 1927. The opening dirt-track meeting took place on 25 May 1928, when Jimmy Pinkerton was triumphant in the 350cc class; however, the meeting was watched by a meagre crowd of only 600. The stadium was owned by the Scottish Greyhound Racing Co. Ltd, and their manager, Jack Nixon-Browne, had constructed the track, promoted the meetings and won the 350cc class final in the second (and what turned out to be final) meeting of 1928, on 1 June. The low level of support was cited as the reason for closure. Browne had laid the track in a pear-shaped configuration, as he considered it would be fun for the spectators. One bend was a tight hairpin, while the other followed the inside rail of the dog track. The riders didn't seem to enjoy it though, and the 420-yard circuit was described as a ploughed field with hair-

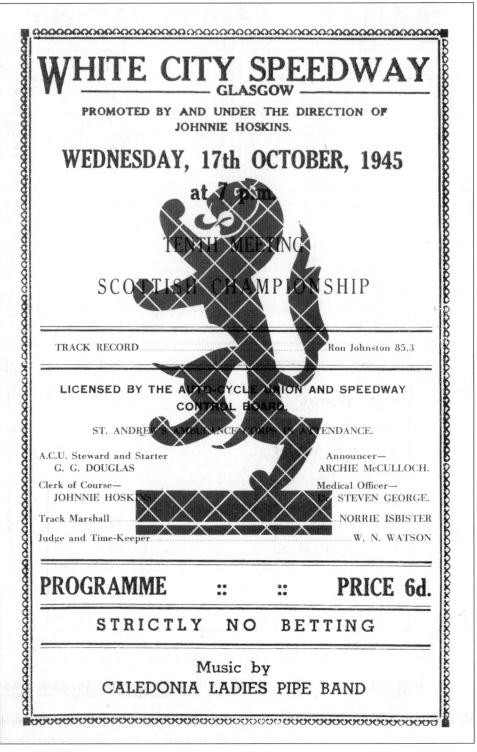

WHITE CITY SPEEDWAY
── GLASGOW ──

PROMOTED BY AND UNDER THE DIRECTION OF
JOHNNIE HOSKINS.

WEDNESDAY, 17th OCTOBER, 1945

at 7 p.m.

TENTH MEETING

SCOTTISH CHAMPIONSHIP

TRACK RECORD..Ron Johnston 85.3

LICENSED BY THE AUTO-CYCLE UNION AND SPEEDWAY
CONTROL BOARD.

ST. ANDREW'S AMBULANCE CORPS IN ATTENDANCE.

A.C.U. Steward and Starter	Announcer—
G. G. DOUGLAS	ARCHIE McCULLOCH.
Clerk of Course—	Medical Officer—
JOHNNIE HOSKINS	Dr. STEVEN GEORGE.
Track Marshall........	....NORRIE ISBISTER
Judge and Time-Keeper........................	....W. N. WATSON

PROGRAMME   ::   ::   PRICE 6d.

STRICTLY NO BETTING

Music by
CALEDONIA LADIES PIPE BAND

A very rare White City, Glasgow programme from 1945.

pin bends. Following the abortive attempt at dirt-track racing, the circuit was reconstructed as a trotting track. The new dirt-track in 1930 was originally intended to be constructed outside the greyhound circuit, with a length of 550 yards. The greyhound management, however, would not allow this, as they considered that the removal of spectators from a close proximity to the dogs would jeopardize their receipts. The cinder circuit was therefore built inside the dog track. Dirt-track racing returned on 15 May 1930, when 'Broncho' Bianchi won the Carntyne Handicap, watched by a crowd of just 1,000 spectators. At a staggering cost of £6,000, Bronco Bianchi, along with 'Buggie' Fleeman were responsible for reconstructing the track that year, but after only three further meetings, the stadium again closed to the sport. It appeared that a dispute had occurred between the venue's owners and the dirt-track concern, with the final meeting being held just a week-and-a-half after the first on 24 May, when Charles Sanderson won the Carntyne Handicap. Rumours of speedway's return to Carntyne circulated in both 1947 and 1950, but nothing came to fruition. Greyhound racing ceased at the venue in 1967. Jack Nixon-Browne, incidentally, later became the Right Honourable Lord Craighton, after serving as a Member of Parliament and then in the House of Lords.

GLASGOW
ADDRESS: White City Stadium, Paisley Road West, Ibrox, Glasgow
YEARS OF OPERATION: 1928-29 Open; 1930-31 Northern League; 1939 Union Cup; 1940 Open; 1945 Open; 1946 Northern League; 1947-53 National League Division Two; 1954 Northern Shield; 1956 Open; 1964 Provincial League; 1965-67 British League; 1968 British League Division One
FIRST MEETING: 29 June 1928
TRACK LENGTH: 430 yards
NICKNAME: 'Lions' (1939-40); 'Tigers' (1946-68)

The opening meeting at White City took place on 29 June 1928, under the promotion of Glasgow Nelson Dirt-track Motorcycle Club, and saw Jimmy Pinkerton triumph in the 350cc class. The only other event that year was a motorcycle gymkhana on 11 August, which amounted to little more than a demonstration event. After a full season of fifty-one open licence meetings (plus two rain-offs) in 1929, Glasgow joined the Northern League in 1930. On the eve of the Northern League match versus Leeds, scheduled for 13 July 1931, a meeting of the speedway directors was held, with the outcome that no more events would take place until further notice. Two rained-off fixtures (v. Wembley on 2 June, and v. Leeds on 9 June) had led to financial problems. What turned out to be the final meeting had already gone ahead against Sheffield on 7 July, when the homesters lost 25-28 in a league match. Midget-car racing was staged at the venue in 1937 and 1938. The first such meeting was a shambles though, with numerous breakdowns, and re-admission tickets had to be issued for the next event. In another meeting versus Belle Vue in 1937, the visiting drivers complained about the organisation and rough tactics, after three of their drivers had gone through the fence during the course of the match. The cinder-sport returned to the White City on 6 May 1939, when Glasgow lost 23-31 to Second Division Newcastle in an Inter-City Challenge match. Later in 1939, Glasgow Lions partook in the Northern section of the Union Cup, which also included Edinburgh, Newcastle, Sheffield and Belle Vue Seconds. The outbreak of the Second World War halted the competition though, with Glasgow propping up the group, having won just one match out of the five they had ridden. Despite the war, six open licence meetings were staged in 1940, the first on 8 May, when Glasgow Lions lost 40-43 to Belle Vue in a challenge match. The final meeting of the six was staged on 12 June, when Glasgow beat Harringay 51-39 in another challenge. Promoted by Johnnie Hoskins, speedway resumed to White City on 15 August 1945, when Glasgow defeated a London Select side 61-47 in a challenge match. The 1946 season kicked off at White City on 10 April when Bill Kitchen won the Glasgow Cup, but it wasn't until 22 April that Glasgow first used the nickname Tigers – in a challenge match at Newcastle. It was a winning start too, by a 43-40 score-line. The Tigers competed in the Northern League that season, with Ian Hoskins taking over the promoter's role from his father. The Northern League disappeared in 1947, with Glasgow joining the National League Division Two. In 1954, with an under-strength team, Glasgow resigned from the National League, prior to riding any league matches. At the time of their withdrawal, the Tigers had ridden two home fixtures in the Northern Shield, losing both. What turned out to be the last meeting at the venue for over two years was staged on 21 April,

when the Tigers lost 38-45 to Edinburgh. Speedway returned in 1956, under the promotion of Junior Bainbridge and Tommy Miller. The first meeting was held on 16 May, when Scotland lost 49-57 to an England Select side. Attendances were poor though, and the venture closed down following a meeting versus Norwich (won 54-41) on 11 July, after staging just five meetings. Under the promotion of Trevor Redmond, speedway returned to White City after a seven-year gap in 1964. The reopening fixture was held on 1 April, when a crowd of 10,000 saw the Tigers defeat Middlesbrough 44-34 in a Northern League fixture. Glasgow subsequently took their place in the Provincial League, but with the big shake-up of speedway in 1965, the Tigers became founder members of the British League. Danny Taylor took over as promoter in 1967, before Les Whaley took up the reigns in 1968. The last meeting ever staged at White City took place on 27 September 1968, when Nigel Boocock won the Glasgow Open Championship. Glasgow Tigers then moved to Hampden Park for the start of the 1969 season, while the White City Stadium was demolished shortly afterwards, to make way for the M8 motorway.

GLASGOW
ADDRESS: Helen Street, Govan, Glasgow
YEARS OF OPERATION: 1930 Training

The training track was run by a company called C&A Motors Ltd, on a site beside their works. The works provided the riders with changing rooms, while four Rudge machines were available for hire. The track was available every day of the week, except Sunday, with the loan of a machine available at a cost of half-a-crown.

GLASGOW

ADDRESS: Ashfield Stadium, Saracen Park, Hawthorn Street, Possilpark, Glasgow

YEARS OF OPERATION: 1949-52 National League Division Two; 1953 Open; 1999 British Premier League; 2000 British Premier League and British Conference League

FIRST MEETING: 19 April 1949

TRACK LENGTH: 355 yards (1949-53) ; 330 yards (1999-2000)

NICKNAME: 'Giants' (1949-53); 'Tigers' (1999-2000); (The Conference League team of 2000 were known as 'Lightning Ashfield Giants')

The original speedway track was created from the terracing at the home of Ashfield Juniors Football Club, with promoters Norrie Isbister and Johnnie Hoskins the men behind the venture. The opening meeting was held on 19 April 1949, when Ashfield beat Walthamstow 48-36 in a National League Division Two encounter. Ashfield Giants withdrew from the National League Division Two at the end of 1952, having completed four full seasons. The death of star rider Ken Le Breton (known as the 'White Ghost') in an Australian track crash in 1951 has often been cited as the primary cause for the demise of the club, with many supporters being unable to come to terms with the sad news. However, a change of race night was also a big contributory factor. Open licence challenge matches and individual meetings were staged at the venue in 1953, with the final meeting taking place on 29 September when Tommy Miller won the

Ashfield Stadium, Saracen Park, Glasgow.

Ken Le Breton Trophy. Two midget-car meetings were held after the 1953 season had ended, but there was to be a gap of over forty-five years before the speedway roar would again be heard at the stadium. After facing opposition from local churches, greyhound racing was first staged at Ashfield on 21 April 1956. The former speedway track had been grassed over in order to create the new greyhound circuit. Having left their Shawfield home at the end of 1998, Glasgow (promoted by Brian Sands) reached an agreement with the Ashfield Juniors Football Club to stage speedway at Saracen Park. After a tremendous amount of work to construct a new track, the reopening meeting took place on 25 April 1999, when the Tigers lost 41-50 to Newcastle in a Premier National Trophy encounter. With Brian Sands running Glasgow in the Premier League, the circuit also staged Conference League action in 2000, with the former Linlithgow side stationed at the stadium. The renamed Lightning Ashfield Giants completed their fixtures at the venue under the promotion of John Campbell, although they became better known as simply Ashfield Giants as the season went on. The Giants staged their opening Conference League meeting at the venue on 21 May, when they originally beat Mildenhall 49-40 on track, only for the result to become a 44-45 defeat, following the visitors' appeal against the use of an ineligible rider on the home side. A management change in February 2001 saw Alan Dick and Stewart Dickson reach an agreement to take over Brian Sands' controlling shareholding in Glasgow Speedway.

GLASGOW

ADDRESS: Cathkin Park, Cross Hill, Glasgow
YEARS OF OPERATION: 1968 Training

The stadium was originally called Hampden Park and was home to Queens Park Football Club. It was, in fact, the second ground to be called Hampden Park, but Queens Park FC eventually moved to Hampden Park (third version) in 1903, which is the place we all know today as the home of Scottish football. When Queens Park vacated the stadium, Third Lanark Football Club (who had originally been founder members of the Scottish League in 1890) moved in and renamed it New Cathkin Park. Third Lanark FC subsequently used the stadium for Scottish League Football from 1903/04 to 1966/67 inclusive. Due to a desperate financial situation, Third Lanark closed down in April 1967, and the stadium was left deserted. It was reported that Bert Harkins used the narrow shale perimeter track for practice in 1968. The site of the former stadium was subsequently redeveloped as a landscape park.

GLASGOW

ADDRESS: Hampden Park, Mount Florida, Glasgow
YEARS OF OPERATION: 1969-72 British League Division One
FIRST MEETING: 11 April 1969
TRACK LENGTH: 420 yards
NICKNAME: 'Tigers'

The stadium was constructed on twelve acres of land bought from Henry Erskine Gordon of Aikenhead House, at a cost of £800 per acre. The venue was named after John Hampden, an English

Parliamentarian who died while fighting in the English Civil War. New Hampden Park was officially opened by Sir John Ure Primrose, the Lord Provost of Glasgow, on 31 October 1903, prior to Queens Park beating Celtic 1-0 in a Scottish League football match. The speedway track was constructed on the foundations of an old cinder running circuit around the perimeter of the Queens Park soccer pitch. Having lost their White City home, Glasgow Tigers (under the promotion of Les Whaley) moved into Hampden Park in time for the 1969 British League Division One campaign. The opening meeting on the huge 420-yard circuit took place on 11 April 1969, when the Tigers defeated King's Lynn 49-29 in a Division One encounter. A change on the promoting front saw Johnnie Hoskins, Ian Hoskins and James Beaton link up with Les Whaley in 1971. Further changes to the promotional team in 1972 saw James Beaton, Les Whaley and Neil MacFarlane running the show, with Whaley subsequently being replaced in mid-season by James Wallace. The 1972 season was marred when young Norwegian Svein Kaasa was killed in a track crash at Hampden Park on 20 September. As if that wasn't enough, up-and-coming junior George Beaton lost his life in a car crash as the season drew to a close. It came as a shock when it was subsequently announced that Glasgow would be leaving Hampden Park, however. The move was described as being financially necessary in order to secure the future of British League racing in Scotland. What turned out to be the final meeting at Hampden Park had already been staged on 6 October 1972, when Glasgow defeated Oxford 43-35 in the first part of a British League Division One double-header before losing 28-50 to Sheffield.

Hampden Park, Glasgow.

Glasgow then moved their operation to Cliftonhill Stadium, Coatbridge, in time for the start of the 1973 season.

GLASGOW

ADDRESS: Blantyre Sports Stadium, Glasgow Road, Blantyre, Nr Glasgow
YEARS OF OPERATION: 1977-81 National League
FIRST MEETING: 8 July 1977
TRACK LENGTH: 340 yards (1977); 310 yards (1978-81)
NICKNAME: 'Tigers'

A first greyhound meeting was staged at the venue on 6 October 1933. Under the promotion of Dave Thomson and James Beaton, a speedway track was constructed and subsequently used by Glasgow upon their leaving Coatbridge in June 1977. The opening meeting at Blantyre went ahead on 8 July that year, when Glasgow beat Crayford 39-37 in a National League fixture. Due to its shape, the circuit was often affectionately referred to as 'The Pencil'. In 1981, the track was also used by the homeless Berwick side for five National League matches, between 1 August and 29 August. The final speedway meeting at the site was staged on 18 October 1981, when Glasgow defeated Bobby Beaton's Buccaneers 44-27 in a challenge match. The last greyhound meeting took place at the stadium on 22 April 1982. The stadium was completely demolished later in 1982, to make way for the East Kilbride Expressway.

GLASGOW

ADDRESS: Craighead Park, Forrest Street, Blantyre, Nr Glasgow
YEARS OF OPERATION: 1982-86 National League
FIRST MEETING: 30 April 1982
TRACK LENGTH: 263 metres (1982-83);

Craighead Park, Blantyre.

275 metres (1983-86)
NICKNAME: 'Tigers'

Craighead Park was the home of Blantyre Celtic Football Club, as indeed it still is to this day. The Forrest Street venue was literally a stone's throw from Blantyre Sports Stadium. Glasgow were forced to move into Craighead Park when it became known that Blantyre Sports Stadium was to be demolished to make way for a motorway, with the construction of the speedway track being undertaken by Alistair Craig. The track opened on 30 April 1982, when Glasgow defeated Rye House 60-36 in a challenge match. Promoted by Dave Thomson and James Beaton, the Tigers subsequently took their place in the National League. Twenty-eight-year-old Mike Walsh died four days after crashing at the track on 26 August 1983. With Blantyre Celtic FC revamping their pitch towards the end of the 1986 season and swallowing up some of the track, there was no long-term future for speedway at the venue and the final meeting took place on 17 October that year, when Glasgow beat Milton Keynes 47-31 in a National League fixture. Without a home track, Glasgow found themselves based at Workington in 1987.

GLASGOW
ADDRESS: Shawfield Stadium, Glasgow Road, Rutherglen, Glasgow
YEARS OF OPERATION: 1988-90 National League; 1991-94 British League Division Two; 1995-98 British Premier League
FIRST MEETING: 15 April 1988
TRACK LENGTH: 332 metres (1988-92); 302 metres (1993-95); 311 metres (1996-98)
NICKNAME: 'Tigers' (1988-95 and 1997-98) 'Scottish Monarchs' (1996)
LEAGUE CHAMPIONS: 1993, 1994
KNOCK-OUT CUP WINNERS: 1993, 1994
NATIONAL SERIES WINNERS: 1990

Shawfield was the former home of Clyde Football Club, who initially moved in during 1898. Prior to that, it is known that Thistle FC used the ground sometime around 1880. Greyhound racing was first staged at the stadium on 14 November 1932. A crowd of 7,916 is reported to have turned out to see the first-ever speedway meeting at Shawfield on 15 April 1988, when the Tigers beat their old rivals from Edinburgh 50-46 in the Convener's Trophy. Speedway in 1988 was promoted by James and Elizabeth Beaton, with Neil MacFarlane joining the management team in 1989. A change on the promoting side in 1990 saw meetings held under the auspices of Glasgow Tigers Management Ltd (Peter McBride, Anne Logan and Neil MacFarlane). With the amalgamation of the British League and National League in 1991, Glasgow found themselves in the revamped British League Division Two. Trading as Glasgow Tigers Promotions Ltd, Douglas Hopes and Neil MacFarlane became co-promoters in 1992. Neil MacFarlane quit as co-promoter in September 1994, leaving Douglas Hopes in sole control of the track. Glasgow became founder members of the British Premier League in 1995, when all the teams in British League joined forces to form one big league. However, amid financial difficulties, Glasgow closed down at the end of the 1995 campaign, with a final meeting on 15 October resulting in a 53.5-42.5 league victory over Bradford. In 1996, Shawfield was used by Edinburgh (who had lost

Shawfield Stadium, Glasgow.

their Powderhall home), under the name Scottish Monarchs. Meetings that season were promoted by John Campbell and Alex Harkess, under the banner of Edinburgh Speedway (1986) Ltd. Their opening meeting was held on 24 April, when the Scottish Monarchs beat Reading 61-35 in a British Premier League match. The final meeting of the one-season venture was staged on 13 October, when the Scottish Monarchs defeated Poole 59-37, again in a league fixture. Promoted by Neil MacFarlane on behalf of SGRL, Glasgow returned to the venue in 1997, opening on 30 March, when they defeated Edinburgh 53-35 in the Spring Trophy. The Tigers subsequently took their place in the revamped Premier League, which had become the equivalent of the second British league, following the formation of the British Elite League at the start of that season. A change on the

promotional front saw Brian Sands take up the reigns in 1998. A final meeting at Shawfield was staged on 18 October 1998, when Glasgow beat the Isle of Wight 51-39 in a semi-final leg of the Young Shield. Glasgow subsequently left the stadium, to move back into one of speedway's former homes at Ashfield in 1999.

GLOUCESTER
ADDRESS: The Stadium, Horton Road, Gloucester
YEARS OF OPERATION: 1967 Demonstration

The stadium was built in 1964 and was home to Gloucester City Football Club from 1965. Mike Parker, Charles Foot and Bill Bridgett proposed the idea of constructing a 420-yard speedway track around the perimeter of the football pitch, but the idea never got past the drawing board. In 1967, for the benefit of local dignitaries, Reg Fearman and Ron Wilson organised a speedway demonstration on the grass surrounding the soccer pitch, with Vic White, Barry Bostock, Peter Wrathall and Norman Storer all going through the motions for the occasion. That, however, was the one and only time that the speedway roar was heard at the Horton Road venue. The stadium was home to Gloucester City FC until 1986, when the club moved to their new Sudmeadow Road Stadium.

GRANGEMOUTH

ADDRESS: Speed Track Centre, Grangemouth, West Lothian
YEARS OF OPERATION: 1971
Demonstration

This was a derelict 500-yard concrete cycle track, where trials were held behind closed doors in order to establish noise levels. For the sake of the noise tests, Alan Mackie and Walter Robertson went through their paces at the venue in 1971, but nothing further was ever heard regarding speedway at the venue.

GREENFORD

ADDRESS: Greenford Driving Park, Birbeck Avenue, Perivale, Nr Ealing, Middlesex
YEARS OF OPERATION: 1928-29 Open; 1931 Open
FIRST MEETING: 7 April 1928
TRACK LENGTH: 930 yards

Greyhound racing was first staged at the stadium on 31 October 1927. The initial promoter of dirt-track racing at Greenford was Frank Longman of TT fame. An article described Greenford's

261 TIGERS v EDINBURGH NOVAFONE MONARCHS Friday, 15th April, 1988

The opening night programme from Shawfield Stadium, 1988.

opening meeting thus: 'The track is a genuine cinder track, nowhere less than 60-feet wide, consisting of two straights and two curves to form over a half-mile lap. It is the property of the London Trotting Club Ltd, so that there was excellent accommodation for the 6,000 or so spectators, while provision was made for their safety by special wire fencing round the outer edge.' The very first race at the opening meeting on 7 April 1928 saw A. Weston crash, with his machine subsequently bursting into flames. The main event at the first meeting was the Greenford Cup, which was won by Billy Galloway. Races in 1928 were staged over five laps, giving a total distance of nearly three miles. A meeting on 26 May 1928 saw sandbags placed on the straights in order to produce sharper bends. Britain's first authorised dirt-track car racing took

117

place at Greenford on 23 June 1928, with the event organised by the Junior Car Club. Greenford continued to host open licence meetings in 1929, but remained free of dirt-track racing throughout 1930. The cinder sport returned to Greenford on 22 August 1931, when a Track Championship was held. Meetings that year were promoted by Greenford Motorcycle Racing Club, whose secretary was a T.J. Strangwayes. However, racing ceased at the end of that season, mainly because of complaints about dust and noise from local residents. The last meeting staged at the venue was possibly held on 10 October – but no result or heat-details have been unearthed. Shortly before the Second World War, the area became a housing development.

H

HACKNEY

ADDRESS: Hackney Wick Greyhound Stadium, Waterden Road, London
YEARS OF OPERATION: 1935-37 National League; 1938-39 National League Division Two; 1963-64 Provincial League; 1965-67 British League; 1968-74 British League Division One; 1975-83 British League; 1984-86 National League; 1987 British League; 1988-90 National League; 1991 British League Division Two; 1995 Open; 1996 British Premier League
FIRST MEETING: 26 April 1935
TRACK LENGTH: 340 yards (1935-39); 345 yards (1963-83); 320 yards (1984-91); 329 yards (1995-96)
NICKNAME: 'Wolves' (1935-39); 'Hawks' (1963-83 & 1991); 'Kestrels' (1984-90);

'Lions' (1996)
LEAGUE CHAMPIONS: 1938, 1988
KNOCK-OUT CUP WINNERS: 1971, 1984, 1988

Greyhound racing was first staged at Hackney Stadium on 8 April 1932, when the opening ceremony took place in front of 13,000 fans. Promoted by Fred Whitehead, with Fred Evans installed as speedway manager, dirt-track racing arrived at the stadium on 26 April 1935, when a dress rehearsal was held prior to the official opening. This saw Dusty Haigh's team defeat Squib Burton's Team 19-14. The first meeting proper went ahead a week later on 3 May, when Hackney Wolves lost 29-43 to New Cross in a National League encounter. Thirty-year-old Dusty Haigh subsequently lost his life following a track crash at the stadium on 15 May 1936. Crowd levels at the venue were never that good for the top-flight action of the National League, and in 1938 Hackney opted for the cheaper running costs of the National League Division Two. The Wolves management exchanged their licence with Bristol in order to step down, with the Bulldogs heading the other way into the top division. In 1939, Hackney also partook in the Southern Section of the Union Cup, along with Bristol and Norwich. Having completed thirteen league fixtures, the war brought the season to a premature close and it was to be another twenty-three years before speedway returned to Waterden Road. The final pre-war meeting was staged on 19 August, when the homesters beat Bristol 51-33 in the Union Cup. Mike Parker brought speedway back to Waterden Road on 10 April 1963, when the renamed Hawks drew

Hackney Wick Greyhound Stadium.

38-38 with New Cross in a challenge match. The Hackney side subsequently joined the Provincial League. Having joined the club as a rider in 1964, Len Silver subsequently took over as promoter in 1965, when Hackney became founder members of the British League, following the merging of the Provincial and National Leagues. Tragedy struck three times at the stadium between 1972 and 1982 – twenty-two-year-old Alan Clegg died after crashing during a practice session on 7 January 1972, Vic Harding died the day after a track smash on 8 June 1979 and popular American Denny Pyeatt died after crashing at the track on 16 July 1982. With so many other attractions in London, Hackney actually closed down at the end of the 1983 campaign. However, Terry Russell transferred his Crayford operation to Waterden Road, with the renamed Hackney Kestrels

competing in the 1984 National League. Terry Russell was joined by Dave Pavitt as co-promoter in 1985. The latter became sole promoter in 1987, with Hackney rejoining the British League. The Kestrels dropped back into the National League in 1988, with Dave Pavitt, Jane Pavitt, Mike Western and Garry Muckley promoting. In 1989, a further change on the promotional side saw Dave Pavitt taking charge on behalf of Hackney Speedway Promotions Ltd. The year was filled with sadness though, when twenty-three-year-old Paul Muchene died on 4 July, after crashing at the track on 30 June. Upon the amalgamation of the British League and the National League, Hackney elected to run in the British League Division Two in 1991, under their old Hawks nickname. The year also heralded another change on the management side, with Derek Howes in charge. After running continuously since 1963, financial problems brought the track to premature closure when Hackney withdrew from the Second Division later that year. The last meeting was staged on 5 July, when Hackney beat Newcastle 46-44 in a Knock-out Cup fixture. A vast amount of money was spent on the stadium and it reopened to stage the first-ever British Grand Prix on 30 September 1995, when Greg Hancock won the 'A final' from Sam Ermolenko, Mark Loram and Henrik Gustafsson. Regular speedway resumed at Hackney in 1996, the renamed London Lions taking their place in the British Premier League under the promotion of Terry Russell and Ivan Henry. The reopening meeting took place on 28 March, when the Lions defeated Peterborough 51-45 in a challenge match. A second British Grand Prix was staged at Hackney on 31 August 1996, when Jason Crump took the 'A final' from Hans Nielsen, Billy Hamill and Greg Hancock. The new London venture never really caught on with the public, however, and lasted just one full season. The last meeting ever staged at Hackney went ahead on 3 October 1996, when the Lions beat Oxford 40-32 in a Premier League encounter that was abandoned after twelve heats, with the result being allowed to stand.

HALIFAX

ADDRESS: Thrum Hall Cricket Ground, Spring Hall Lane, Halifax, West Yorkshire
YEARS OF OPERATION: 1928 Open; 1929 English Dirt-track League; 1930 Open
FIRST MEETING: 2 May 1928
TRACK LENGTH: 465 yards (1928-29); 462 yards (1930)

Thrum Hall Cricket Ground, Halifax.

Covering a large area of land, Thrum Hall was the venue for both cricket and rugby, with the latter being the first staged on 18 September 1886. The cinder track (described as round, with a few straight pieces) ran around the perimeter of the pitch belonging to Halifax Cricket Club, which had actually played host to County Championship Cricket when Yorkshire entertained Kent in 1897. For the opening dirt-track meeting on 2 May 1928, when A.E. Wood won the 350cc novice solo event, the track was illuminated with acetylene flares positioned on the inside of the circuit, making it the first British meeting to be held under artificial lighting. Initially, races were run over only two laps, with everything depending on the start as the track was so narrow. However, by June 1928, the track had been much improved and a safety fence erected. During meetings, the cricket scoreboard was protected by sand-bags and straw bales. A total of fourteen meetings were staged in 1928, promoted by Halifax and District Motor Club. There were talks regarding the transfer of dirt-track racing to The Shay in the winter of 1928/29, but it would be some twenty years before such a move was made. Halifax joined the English Dirt-track League in 1929, with Halifax Speedway Company taking over on the promoting side of the venture. An experiment of car racing on the cinders was tried on 9 May 1929, but it was disappointing and lacked the anticipated thrills. There was change of promotion in August 1930, when meetings were staged under the management of Leeds Stadium. Due to falling attendances, what turned out to be the last dirt-track meeting at Thrum Hall was held on 4 September 1930, when

England defeated Australia 31-23. Greyhound racing was first held at the venue on 5 November 1931. Grass speedway was run at the venue in 1936, on the turf immediately inside the cinder track. These events were promoted jointly by Halifax and District Motor Club and Bradford and District Motor Club. Greyhound racing ceased at the stadium in December 1978.

HALIFAX
ADDRESS: The Shay Grounds, Shaw Hill, Halifax, West Yorkshire
YEARS OF OPERATION: 1949 National League Division Three; 1950-51 National League Division Two; 1965-67 British League; 1968-74 British League Division One; 1975-85 British League; 1986 Training
FIRST MEETING: 6 April 1949
TRACK LENGTH: 402 yards (1949-51); 378 yards (1965-70); 400 yards (1971-85)
NICKNAME: 'Dukes'
NATIONAL TROPHY (DIVISION TWO) WINNERS: 1950
LEAGUE CHAMPIONS: 1966
KNOCK-OUT CUP WINNERS: 1966

The Shay was first used by Halifax Town FC, when they gained Football League status in the 1921/22 season. The stadium was fashioned from a Council rubbish tip, and boasted a grandstand which had been obtained from Manchester City FC. There were talks about the introduction of dirt-track racing way back in the winter of 1928/29, but nothing came of it at that time. Plans were also afoot to stage speedway at the Shay in 1948, but this had to be abandoned when the Football League refused to permit the removal of turf from the corners of the

The Shay Grounds, Halifax.

soccer pitch. The team did ride in away challenge matches during 1948, however, using the name Halifax Nomads. Work to build the track commenced on 8 February 1949, and included the removal of 3,000 cubic yards of earth, plus the laying down of more than 200 tons of cinders to create a steeply banked 402-yard circuit around the outside of Halifax Town's soccer pitch. The track was opened by Major R.E. Austin from the Duke of Wellington's Regiment on 6 April 1949, when a crowd of over 7,000 witnessed Halifax lose 37-45 to Yarmouth in a National League Division Three encounter. The nickname 'Dukes' was the local term used for the Duke of Wellington's Regiment, who were stationed in the town, and their insignia included an elephant (to celebrate the great general's successful campaigns in India) – hence the use of an elephant on the Halifax race-jacket. Under promoter

Bruce Booth, Halifax enjoyed good support in their first year at the Shay, with a record crowd of 18,000 turning up for a challenge match versus Sheffield on 9 September. At the end of the 1949 campaign, Halifax were selected for promotion to Division Two. However, within two years the average crowd figures had dropped to less than 5,000, with the result that the stadium was to remain speedway free until 1965. The final meeting of the initial period of track action was held on 3 October 1951, when the Dukes beat Cradley Heath 50-34 in a Second Division match. Under the promotion of Reg Fearman, the reopening meeting at the Shay took place on 17 April 1965, when Halifax lost 36-41 to Long Eaton in a British League match. Former rider Eric Boothroyd linked with Reg Fearman as co-promoter in 1969. Boothroyd took up the reigns as sole promoter in 1980. A three-team tournament entitled the

Northern Threes was the last meeting ever held at the venue, on 26 October 1985. The result was: Halifax 25, Belle Vue 29, Sheffield 24. Following the final meeting, the management and riders of Halifax transferred to Bradford's Odsal Stadium in readiness for the 1986 season. Eric Monaghan held a regular training school at the Shay in early 1986. Halifax Town FC lost their League status after finishing bottom of Division Three in 1992/93. The Shaymen subsequently regained their place in the Football League and resumed in Division Three in the 1998/99 season. The stadium has undergone a major overhaul during 1999/2000, with new stands erected and the pitch being fully enclosed, with the terracing squared off to preclude any thoughts of a further return for speedway.

HAMBLE

ADDRESS: Hamble, Nr Southampton, Hampshire
YEARS OF OPERATION: 1947-50 Training
TRACK LENGTH: 355 yards

The track was marked out in a field and was apparently loosely based on Wimbledon's Plough Lane circuit. Prior to the 1947 season at Southampton's Banister Court, several Saints riders, including Jimmy Squibb, Bert Croucher, Bob Oakley, Matt Hall, Ron Lemon and Alf Boyce, held practice sessions at the Hamble track. The surface of the training circuit was described as being 'rough'. Bob Oakley ran a school at the track in the winter of 1949/50, with the pick of the trainees being local taxi driver Bill Holden. The novices paid £2 per lesson, which was all-inclusive.

HAMILTON

ADDRESS: Hamilton Showgrounds, Motherwell Road, Hamilton, Nr Glasgow
YEARS OF OPERATION: 1948-51 Open; 1953-55 Open
FIRST MEETING: 15 May 1948

Situated near the ice rink, the Duke of Hamilton's estate staged the annual Lanarkshire Farmers' Society Agricultural Show, which featured a speedway event in the evening. The dressing room was a large tent, while the pits were located in a sheep pen. The track was bladed out of a grass-less football pitch and looked comparatively smooth; the length is not recorded, as the size probably varied from year to year. A safety fence was constructed of wire netting pinned on to stakes, but there was no starting gate, with car headlights used to begin the races. The Duke of Hamilton was an interested spectator at the first speedway event at the showground on 15 May 1948, when Norman Lindsay won the Hamilton Speedway Cup. The 1949 meeting was held on 21 May and saw Glasgow defeat Hamilton in a challenge match. The team captains were Frank Boyle and Gordon McGregor. On 13 May 1950, Bothwell defeated a Glasgow Select 48-35, before the Glasgow skipper, Tommy Miller, went on to win the second-half event, the Hamilton Speedway Cup, from Willie Gordon and Ken McKinlay. In 1951, a Glasgow Select beat a Hamilton Select 46-38 on 12 May, with Ken McKinlay taking the Hamilton Cup. The scheduled 1952 meeting on 10 May between Hamilton and Glasgow was cancelled due to a foot and mouth epidemic. On 9 May 1953, the Scottish All Stars beat Bothwell 42-39, prior to

Doug Templeton lifting the Hamilton Cup. The 1954 meeting was held on 8 May and saw Willie Templeton triumphant in the Hamilton Cup, after a Glasgow Select had defeated Tannock's Eagles 45.5-37.5. The final meeting at the showground was staged on 14 May 1955, when Lanarkshire Eagles defeated Glasgow Tigers 52-30. After this meeting, Doug Templeton won the Hamilton Cup for a second time. Meetings were referred to as grass speedway in the programmes, although the riders who partook in the meetings described the surface as being of shale. Crowds of up to 6,000 were recorded at Hamilton for these annual evening speedway events.

HAMMERSMITH

ADDRESS: Hammersmith Ice Drome, Hammersmith, London
YEARS OF OPERATION: 1930 Indoor Ice Demonstration

On 16 January 1930, Wal Phillips gave a demonstration of dirt-track racing on ice at the Hammersmith Ice Drome. He used his original Scott-JAP machine for the event, with his rear wheel covered with coconut matting. After sliding around in 'doughnut' fashion circles, he proceeded to broadside around the ice, reaching speeds of 18-20 mph.

HARRINGAY

ADDRESS: Harringay Greyhound Stadium, Green Lanes, Harringay, London
YEARS OF OPERATION: 1928 Open; 1929-31 Southern League; 1934 National League and Reserve League; 1935-37 National League; 1938-39 National League Division One; 1940-42 Open; 1947-54 National League Division One; 1958-59 Open; 1961 Open
FIRST MEETING: 29 May 1928
TRACK LENGTH: 339 yards (1928); 336 yards (1929-42); 333 yards (1947-61)
NICKNAME: 'Canaries' (1929-31); 'Tigers' (1934-39); 'Racers' (1947-54)
ANNIVERSARY CUP WINNERS: 1948
NATIONAL TROPHY WINNERS: 1952
CORONATION CUP WINNERS: 1953

Greyhound racing was first staged at Harringay on 13 September 1927. The construction of the track presented a number of difficulties, as the stadium was built on the site of a former refuse tip – although as a consequence of this it had excellent drainage. International Speedway Ltd (A.J. Hunting), introduced dirt-track racing to Harringay on 29 May 1928, when Frank Arthur won the Silver Helmet and Scratch Race events. Having joined the Southern League in 1929, Harringay subsequently resigned during 1931, with Belle Vue taking over their fixtures. The final meeting at the Green Lanes venue was an Open Championship, staged on 2 June. A further meeting scheduled for 9 June (v. Stamford Bridge in the National Trophy), was cancelled and never took place. After a gap of two full years, promoters North London Speedways Ltd (Tom Bradbury-Pratt and Charles Knott) revived the sport at the venue on 31 March 1934, when the newly-named Tigers lost 20-32 to The Rest in a challenge match. Harringay partook in the National League, but also ran a team in Division Two (otherwise known as the Reserve League) that year. In 1939, Charles Knott took full control at the track, following the death of Tom Bradbury-Pratt. After completing fifteen league matches in 1939, the season was brought to an abrupt halt by the outbreak

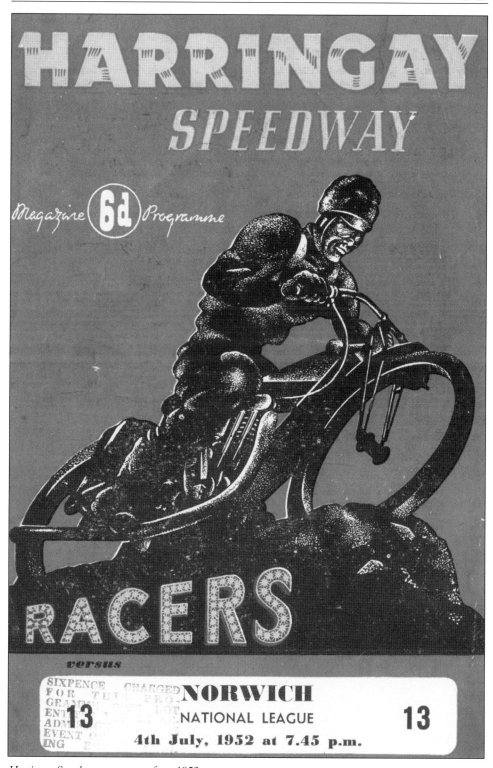

Harringay Speedway programme from 1952.

Harringay Greyhound Stadium.

of the Second World War. The final home meeting prior to the war was a Supporters Trophy event on 26 August, which was won by the great Jack Parker. In spite of the conflict, Harringay did stage a few open licence meetings between 1940 and 1942. The track reopened on 4 April 1947, when Ron Johnson and Eric French won a Best Pairs competition. Harringay subsequently resumed in the National League Division One, under the promotion of Fred Whitehead on behalf of the Greyhound Racing Association Ltd. The season was marred by the death of twenty-two-year-old Bronco Wilson, following a track accident at the stadium on 15 August. A change on the management side in 1950 saw George Kay take over as promoter on behalf of the GRA Ltd. In 1954, due to falling attendance figures, the management ran many double-headers in order to complete their fixtures by mid-August. The final meeting went ahead on 18 August, when Split Waterman won a World Championship qualifying round. Sadly, that was the end of regular racing at the venue, although four one-off meetings were staged before the track finally became another ex-speedway venue in 1961. A Cavalcade of Speed meeting was staged at Harringay on 29 October 1958, which featured just two heats of speedway, plus a final. The programme of events also included greyhound racing, stock-car racing and trotting races. Another Cavalcade of Speed was held on 28 October 1959, when Harringay beat New Cross 28-26 in a nine-heat challenge match. This meeting, and the one in the previous year, were organised by P.B. Lucas and the directors of the GRA Ltd. Finally, two meetings were held at the venue in 1961 – firstly, the Internationale on

1 July which was won by Ove Fundin. The last-ever meeting took place on 16 September, when Reg Reeves was triumphant in the Provincial League Riders' Championship. The latter meeting was run by the Provincial Speedway League Promoters' Association. Greyhound racing ceased at Harringay after a final meeting on 25 September 1987.

HARTLEPOOL
ADDRESS: Hartlepool Greyhound Stadium, Hartlepool, Cleveland
YEARS OF OPERATION: 1993
Demonstration

Paul Pickering took part in noise level tests at Hartlepool Greyhound Stadium in early 1993. It was hoped that the stadium, which also staged stock-car racing, would be given the green light for speedway. However, Hartlepool Borough Council officials considered the noise loud enough to qualify as a nuisance and that was the end of that!

HASTINGS
ADDRESS: Pilot Field Stadium, Elphinstone Road, Hastings, Sussex
YEARS OF OPERATION: 1948-49
National League Division Three
FIRST MEETING: 21 April 1948
TRACK LENGTH: 412 yards (1948); 388 yards (1949)
NICKNAME: 'Saxons'

Pilot Field Stadium was first used for football in 1923, and boasted a 1,000-seat stand that cost £8,000. Council approval for a speedway track at the stadium was obtained in December 1947. The track was constructed around the

Pilot Field Stadium, Hastings.

HASTINGS
SPEEDWAY

WEDNESDAY, JULY 7th, 1948

9.

WEATHER PERMITTING

Should it be necessary through any cause to abandon the meeting prior to the sixth race in the programme, tickets for a subsequent meeting will be issued at the exits. In no circumstances will any money be returned.

6^{D.} RIGHT OF ADMISSION RESERVED

BETTING STRICTLY PROHIBITED

★ OFFICIAL PROGRAMME ★

Meeting No. 13.   *1948 SEASON*

Rare Hastings Speedway programme from 1948.

pitch belonging to Hastings Football Club, and was opened by Alderman F. Chambers, the mayor of Hastings. Eastbourne promoter Charlie Dugard moved his Division Three champions of 1947 to Hastings, with the opening meeting held on 21 April 1948. The track was described as being the shape of a box, with very sharp corners and banked bends. That first meeting featured a National League Division Three match between Hastings Saxons and Hanley, with the homesters winning 44-39. Led by a man named Arthur Parsons, thirteen local residents complained about the noise created by speedway, and employed Attorney General Sir Hartley Shawcross to put a stop to the racing. He successfully applied for a High Court injunction preventing any further track action after the end of the 1949 season. In concluding his summing up, Mr Justice Humphreys stated: 'I will add that no attack has been made in this case upon speedway racing. It is completely untrue to say that this is a test case. My decision is not intended to be a decision that speedway racing should be stopped. What I hold is that it is proved to my satisfaction that speedway racing in this particular residential neighbourhood must stop, unless it can be carried on without that noise, without which, according to evidence, it cannot be carried on.' The final meeting at the venue was staged on 5 October 1949, when the Saxons lost 39.5-44.5, to Tamworth in a National League Division Three fixture. Charlie Dugard appealed against the High Court ruling, but this was dismissed by Lord Justice Tucker and an application for leave to appeal to the House of Lords was refused. Although Charlie Dugard felt further meetings would be permissible with

silencers fitted, an agreement could not be reached with other league clubs. Charlie was finally forced to call it a day with regard to speedway at Hastings, in March 1950. A cycle speedway meeting was held at the venue on 17 June 1950, in aid of the Hastings Carnival week. On 9 January 1954, a record attendance was established for the stadium, when 12,727 people paid to watch an FA Cup tie versus Norwich City. The former speedway track and safety fence were still in position at Pilot Field in the mid-1970s.

HEDNESFORD
ADDRESS: Hednesford Training Track, Hednesford, Nr Cannock, Staffordshire
YEARS OF OPERATION: 1955 Training; 1958-60 Training

It was reported in August 1954, that 'Les Marshall and Claude Roe, a Walsall restaurant proprietor, have been waiting since 1947 to begin work at the site, which is a disused reservoir at one of the highest points of the famous Cannock Chase. The first major event to be staged there will be a stock-car meeting on 29 August 1954. The idea is for the new stadium to be used mainly for training purposes and enable a team to be fielded in the Southern Area League.' Wilf Wilstead described the track as affording a smooth ride, and had some twenty youngsters lined up for a training school in 1955. Prior to riding in second-half events at Coventry, Rick France first rode at Hednesford in 1958. John Hart is known to have gone practising at Hednesford in both 1959 and 1960.

HEVINGHAM
ADDRESS: Norwich Raceway, Holt Road, Hevingham, Nr Norwich, Norfolk
YEARS OF OPERATION: 1976 Open

FIRST MEETING: 5 December 1976
TRACK LENGTH: 350 yards

This 33-acre site in Hevingham had been owned by Cyril Crane and Violet Littlechild since 1970. Cyril Crane had successfully staged mini- and midget-car racing at the site, prior to his plans to introduce speedway in 1976. Riding as Norwich, the proposed track had been accepted as members of the 1977 National League, so long as planning permission was granted to run meetings with motor-bikes by Broadlands District Council. The Speedway Control Board turned down permission to run a trial meeting but a track was constructed, with spectator banking, dressing rooms and a slot-in safety fence. The one and only (pirate) meeting to be staged at the venue went ahead on 5 December 1976, when a crowd of 2,000 people watched the Norwich Supporters' Trophy, which was won by Andrew Buck. The competitors partaking in the meeting were mainly juniors and non-contracted riders. As planning permission had not been granted, the raceway was subsequently served with an enforcement order to demolish all that had been constructed.

HIGH BEECH

ADDRESS: King's Oak Hotel, High
 Beech, Loughton, Essex
YEARS OF OPERATION: 1928-29 Open; 1930-31 Southern League; 1932 Open; 1935-36 Training; 1937-39 Open; 1948-50 Open; 1967 Training
FIRST MEETING: 19 February 1928
TRACK LENGTH: 361 yards (1928-29); 370 yards (1930-39); 340 yards (1948-49); 310 yards (1950)
NICKNAME: 'Foresters' (1930-39); 'Rabbits' (1948-50)

The track was situated in the grounds of the King's Oak public house, close to Epping Forest, on a former cycling and athletics cinder circuit. An open licence had been refused for a proposed meeting on 9 November 1927. High Beech was long thought to have staged the first dirt-track meeting in Britain, though this has since been contested by Camberley and Droylsden, which both hosted meetings in 1927. A crowd of 30,000 witnessed the first meeting at High Beech on 19 February 1928, which lasted from 10.30 a.m. until 5 p.m. The first final, run over five laps, was the Ilford Novice event, which was won by Fred Ralph in a time of 2 minutes 10 seconds. There was no safety fence and the spectators were gathered both inside and outside the track, which was said to consist of four straights with sharp turns. Other competitors in the opening meeting included Fred Ralph, Billy Galloway, Alf Medcalf, Reg Pointer, Ivor Creek, Keith McKay, Hugh Smythe, Sonny Wilson and Alf Foulds. The original promotion of dirt-track racing at the venue was under the direction of Jack Hill-Bailey, secretary of the Ilford Motorcycle Club. The track was altered to a 'D' shape with a conventional safety fence in time for the second meeting, on Easter Monday 9 April 1928. The reconstruction was presided over and paid for by W.J. Cearns. The track suffered from high dust problems, and a watering system was introduced in 1929 to combat this. Three stands were erected in time for the 1930 season. When High Beech closed during the 1932 season, the reason given was that Charrington's Brewary had increased the rent to £300 per meeting. The final meeting had been staged on 6 August, when London defeated the Old Boys 41-36 in a challenge match. During

High Beech, Loughton, Essex.

the winters of 1935 and 1936, the track was leased by New Cross for the purpose of coaching junior riders. Roger Frogley is known to have trained novices at the venue in 1936. The High Beech circuit staged open events during 1937, with the opening meeting probably taking place on 2 May. Open style meetings continued throughout 1938 and '39, with a final pre-war event going ahead in the form of a championship meeting on 27 August 1939. During the war, High Beech was used by the Army as a petrol dump. High Beech reopened in 1948, with S.G. Drummond and C.A.F. Pade, and other ex-servicemen, staging amateur fixtures. This was after a planned reopening in June 1947, under the direction of ex-jockey G. Byers, failed to materialise. A training school was run at High Beech during the 1948/49 winter. The track shape was again altered in 1949, giving two straights instead of the old 'D' shape.

The track staged its final meeting sometime in 1950, although the exact date remains unknown. Jimmy Gooch is known to have given private lessons at the track in 1967. The pub at this time, was under new management, and the landlord was an old time dirt-track supporter. Tommy Sweetman is also known to have practised at the track in 1967. A fortieth anniversary gathering was held at the track on 18 February 1968. A Forestry Conservation Centre was opened at the site on 23 June 1971. Regular commemorative events have been staged at High Beech in recent years, including a sixtieth anniversary gathering in 1988. Today, a visitor centre is sited on what was the first bend, close to the hotel.

HIGHBRIDGE
ADDRESS: Oak Tree Arena, Highbridge, Somerset
YEARS OF OPERATION: 2000 British

Conference League
FIRST MEETING: 2 June 2000
TRACK LENGTH: 300 metres
NICKNAME: 'Rebels'

Having searched for a suitable site for several years, promoter Andy Hewlett eventually came across land in Highbridge, which had staged banger racing some years previously. Somerset Rebels actually completed two away challenge matches in 1999 (at Buxton and St Austell), but efforts to open at Highbridge were thwarted over road access to the site. With a suitable road entrance constructed, and a superb track designed by Glyn Taylor, Britain's newest circuit was ready for the start of the 2000 Conference League season. The opening meeting, a Conference League Cup encounter with Buxton, was scheduled for 26 May, but fell foul of inclement weather. The track opened the following week though, when the Rebels beat St Austell 55-35 in a Conference League Cup fixture. The new track enjoyed good support throughout 2000; however, despite strong rumours, the club resisted the temptation to join the Premier League, with Andy Hewlett announcing that the side would remain in the Conference League in 2001.

HODDESDON
ADDRESS: Hoddesdon, Hertfordshire
YEARS OF OPERATION: 1928 Training

Buster and Roger Frogley were fortunate enough to possess a homemade track on their father's farm, which they used for training in 1928.

HOLBEACH
ADDRESS: Bell End Speedway, Whaplode St. Catherine, Holbeach, Nr Spalding, Lincolnshire

Oak Tree Arena, Highbridge.

YEARS OF OPERATION: 1936-39 Open;
1945-48 Open
TRACK LENGTH: 350 yards (1936-38);
370 yards (1939-46); 380 yards (1947-48)
NICKNAME: 'Tulips'

Bell End was so called as locals reckoned it was the furthest place you could actually hear the church bells from. Originally this was predominantly a grass-track speedway venue, but with cinders on the bends. There are, however, various conflicting reports about not only the track surface, but also the shape of the track over the years. Meetings were promoted by Holbeach and Spalding Motorcycle and Light Car Club, who issued speedway-style programmes. The date of the first meeting at Bell End is not known, with the earliest definite meeting being recorded as 18 April 1938, when Holbeach & Spalding lost 53-54 to Birmingham. There were meetings prior to this, in 1936, and eleven meetings were held in 1937, when attendances totalled 36,000. Ten meetings were staged in 1938, and these were witnessed by a total of 42,000 spectators, with mobile stands sometimes being hired to cater for them. During that 1938 season, it was decided to keep the track on the same site, rather than continue with the old policy of using about five different circuits. At least nine meetings were held in 1939, the last of which saw Wilf Jay win the Bell End Laurels on 20 August. After the war, the promoting company had a slightly different name, being known as Holbeach and District Light Car and Motorcycle Club, while programme covers were titled Bell End Speedway. A report on a 1946 meeting stated: 'The track is laid out in the middle of a field in the shape of a ring, there are no straights, the grass being replaced with a surface of sand and earth. The meeting is run on a speedway lines points system, and a starting gate, with green and red flags replacing the usual lights. The organisation, under the direction of Mr A.W. Taylor, compares with any first class speedway.' At least two meetings are confirmed to have been staged that season. On 20 July 1947 England defeated Tiger Hart's Team 61-46 in a challenge match. That was one of at least four meetings that were definitely held at the venue that year. Midget-car racing is known to have taken place at the venue on 24 August 1947. There are suggestions that the track finally closed sometime during 1948, because of increasing demands from the farmer who owned the field it was situated in.

HUDDERSFIELD
ADDRESS: Quarmby Stadium, Longwood Edge, Huddersfield, Yorkshire
YEARS OF OPERATION: 1928-29 Open
FIRST MEETING: 4 August 1928
TRACK LENGTH: 440 yards

The Quarmby Stadium track was run by the Huddersfield and District Motor Sports Club, who held a pre-opening practice session on 2 August 1928. The official opening meeting on 4 August 1928 saw Skid Skinner win the Yorkshire Championship Belt before an attendance of 6,000. The track was described as 'egg-shaped', with one particularly awkward corner. Tommy Allott took his first novice rides at Quarmby in 1929. This was a short-lived venue, which only staged four open licence events in 1928, and just one meeting in 1929, when Dusty Haigh won the scratch race on 6 April.

HULL

ADDRESS: White City Stadium, Anlaby Road, Kingston-upon-Hull, Yorkshire
YEARS OF OPERATION: 1930 Open
FIRST MEETING: 3 May 1930

Prior to dirt-track racing at White City, grass-track events were staged at the stadium throughout 1928 and 1929. A motorcycle football match between teams representing Hull and Grimsby took place at the stadium in 1928. A crowd of 7,000 were in attendance at the opening dirt-track meeting on 3 May 1930, when E. Johnston won the Hall Cross Trophy. Meetings were promoted by a London-based syndicate. Following a meeting on 16 August 1930, dirt-track racing ceased for the year in order to avoid clashing with football and rugby matches. The stadium was destroyed by fire in 1938, and subsequently rebuilt – although it collapsed under the weight of snow in the bad winter of 1947! In 1965, the site was redeveloped and high-rise flats were built, known locally as the White City flats.

HULL

ADDRESS: Hedon Stadium, Hedon, Nr Hull, East Yorkshire
YEARS OF OPERATION: 1948-49 National League Division Three
FIRST MEETING: 27 March 1948
TRACK LENGTH: 459 yards (1948); 443 yards (1949)
NICKNAME: 'Angels'

Hedon Stadium was built on the site of the former Hedon Racecourse, which was later converted into a municipal aerodrome by the Hull Corporation. It had been mooted to stage speedway at Hedon in 1947, but the application was received too late for that season. The opening speedway meeting took place on 27 March 1948, when a crowd of some 6,600 witnessed Hull lose 30-52 to Hanley in a challenge match, with the original flying club hanger used as a temporary stand. Meetings were promoted by a team led by Captain Fred Archer, and included Brigadier Carberry and Captain Aylett. The track was described as having five bends, due to the effect of a substantial bulge on the back straight. This extra bend was subsequently removed by the start of the 1949 season. The stadium was situated some distance from Hull town centre, and the speedway suffered from a lack of support as a result. The local bus company were unable to provide a special service but, as the railway ran right alongside the stadium, a train was put into operation for speedway supporters. Opened in August 1948, a new platform was provided and named Hedon Halt Station. In May 1949, an attempt was made to move the speedway to the Boulevard Stadium in Hull, but it came to nothing – although, of course, speedway was eventually staged at the venue in 1971. Following a directors' meeting on 2 September, Hull resigned from Division Three in 1949, citing falling attendance figures, with Swindon taking over their remaining fixtures. The final meeting at Hedon had already been staged, on 27 August 1949, when the Angels defeated Liverpool 54-29 in a National League Division Three encounter.

HULL

ADDRESS: The Boulevard Stadium, Airlie Street, Kingston-upon-Hull, East Yorkshire
YEARS OF OPERATION: 1971-73 British

League Division Two; 1974 British League Division One; 1975-81 British League

FIRST MEETING: 7 April 1971
TRACK LENGTH: 415 yards
NICKNAME: 'Vikings'
INTER-LEAGUE KNOCK-OUT CUP WINNERS: 1976

Hull Kingston Rovers Rugby League Club moved to the site in February 1892, but when their lease ran out, Hull Rugby League Club moved in and subsequently named it The Boulevard. Prior to Hull Rugby League Club's opening match on 21 September 1895, joiners W. Vickerman and G.W. Stephenson, under the supervision of architect James Adamson, transformed the ground into one of the best in the country, and in so doing, created the famous Threepenny Stand. It stood at seventy-five yards in length, its eleven wooden terraces and roof being made from Russian pine.

Greyhound racing was first staged at the venue on 2 July 1927, and continued until a final meeting on 11 December 1948. Initial plans to transfer speedway from Hedon to the Boulevard for the 1950 season never came to fruition. In 1971, promoters Ian Thomas and Wally Mawdsley brought the shale sport to the stadium, with the opening meeting being held on 7 April, when Hull defeated Sunderland 47-25 in a challenge match. Prior to the start of the 1974 campaign, Hull exchanged their Division Two licence with Coatbridge, so enabling the Vikings to move up to top-flight racing in the British League Division One. A change on the promoting side in 1976 saw Brian Larner replace Wally Mawdsley as co-promoter alongside Ian Thomas. Aside from 1978, when Ernie Park joined the promotional team for a season, Messrs Thomas and Larner stayed at the helm until the track's closure. Speedway brought in much-needed revenue for the

The Boulevard Stadium, Kingston-upon-Hull.

New Craven Park Stadium, Kingston-upon-Hull.

rugby club, but it was eventually dispensed with, due to its effect on the drainage and the damage it caused to the pitch. The final meeting at the venue took place on 7 October 1981, when Hull defeated Halifax 46-32 in the Yorkshire Cup. The Threepenny Stand was finally demolished in July 1990, with a new structure erected in its place. The Boulevard continues to be home to Hull Rugby League Club to this day.

HULL
ADDRESS: Humberside Ice Arena, Kingston-upon-Hull
YEARS OF OPERATION: 1994 Indoor Ice Speedway
FIRST MEETING: 6 December 1994

Ice speedway events were staged at the Humberside Arena on Tuesday 6 and Wednesday 7 December 1994. On 6 December, a Hull Select side defeated a British League Select 42-35, while the following evening saw Nigel Crabtree win the Ice Masters title, after defeating Jan Staechmann in a run-off. The events were promoted by Grenville Dicken, Dave McCoy and Glyn Taylor.

HULL
ADDRESS: New Craven Park Stadium, Preston Road, Kingston-upon-Hull, Humberside
YEARS OF OPERATION: 1995-98 British Premier League; 1999 British Elite League; 2000 British Premier League
FIRST MEETING: 5 April 1995
TRACK LENGTH: 346 metres
NICKNAME: 'Vikings'
PREMIER TROPHY WINNERS: 2000

New Craven Park is the home of Hull Kingston Rovers Rugby League Club. Speedway was introduced to the venue in

1995, by the promotional team of Grenville Dicken and Dave McCoy. The opening meeting was staged on 5 April that year, when Hull defeated Sheffield 60-36 in a challenge match. During the 1996 campaign, Dave McCoy stepped down as co-promoter in order to concentrate on his business interests, with Mike Barber and Alex Lilley joining the promotion. A further change on the promoting side saw Grenville Dicken leave the club in September 1997. In November 1997, it was announced that the club would not be running in 1998; however, Tony Mole stepped in to keep the track going in the British Premier League, having purchased the licence and assets. Another change on the promotional front saw Graham Jones, Allan Walker and Malcolm Wright take Hull into the Elite League in 1999. After just one full season of top-flight racing, the Vikings dropped back into the Premier League for the 2000 campaign, under the promotion of Malcolm Wright and Eric Boocock.

The programme from Hull's opening meeting at Craven Park in 1995.

I

IPSWICH

ADDRESS: Foxhall Heath Stadium, Foxhall Road, Ipswich, Suffolk

YEARS OF OPERATION: 1950-51 Open; 1952-53 Southern League; 1954-56 National League Division Two; 1957-58 National League; 1959 Southern Area League; 1960-62 National League; 1964 Metropolitan League; 1965 Open; 1969-71 British League Division Two; 1972-74 British League Division One; 1975-88 British League; 1989-90 National League; 1991-94 British League Division One;

1995-96 British Premier League; 1997 British Elite League and British Amateur League; 1998-2000 British Elite League

FIRST MEETING: 25 October 1950

TRACK LENGTH: 410 yards (1950-65): 328 yards (1969-2000)

NICKNAME: 'Witches' (The Amateur League team of 1997, were known as 'Anglian Angels')

KNOCK-OUT CUP WINNERS: 1970, 1971, 1976, 1978, 1981, 1984, 1998

LEAGUE CHAMPIONS: 1975, 1976, 1984, 1998

INTER-LEAGUE KNOCK-OUT CUP WINNERS: 1977

CRAVEN SHIELD WINNERS: 1998

Original proposals for the introduction of speedway were turned down by the stadium owners in the winter of 1948, with the interested parties turning their attentions to Hull instead. During the winter

Foxhall Heath Stadium, Ipswich.

of 1948/49, East Suffolk Police decided to experiment at Foxhall. They raced around the stadium on machines stripped of silencers at maximum revs, while colleagues in a loudspeaker van made all the noise they possibly could. The nearby hospital inmates didn't hear a sound and when the planning committee heard of this, they approved the plans for a speedway track. A company called Ipswich Speedway Ltd was formed, with Arthur Franklyn, Douglas Bostock and R.W. Fison the main men behind the plan to bring the shale sport to Foxhall Heath. Speedway eventually made its entrance at the venue on 25 October 1950, when Norwich riders held a mini practice meeting, featuring two heats and a final, with Phil Clarke emerging as the winner. A single sheet programme was issued for this and it shows that track record attempts and practising by local riders also took place. The first full-blown meet-

ing at the stadium was scheduled for 24 March 1951, when Norwich were to face Southampton in a challenge match. Unfortunately, the meeting was rained off, with 8,000 would-be spectators locked out. (However, one school of thought suggests that the meeting actually started, only to be abandoned after four heats due to adverse weather, with the teams locked together on 12 points apiece, but as yet there is no definite confirmation of this.) Several weeks later, what was billed as the opening meeting took place on 14 May when Ipswich lost 16-68 to Yarmouth in a challenge match. Due to delays occurring with building permits, the Ipswich fans had to wait until 1952 for league status, when the Witches joined the Southern League. In 1954, Ipswich found themselves in the National League Division Two, as the Southern League disappeared. With speedway suffering financially, just eleven tracks were operating in 1957, with the Witches amongst the chosen few in the National League. In 1959, Ipswich took part in the Southern Area League, riding under the name of Foxhall Heath, with meetings promoted by Aub Lawson. Under the promotion of Vic Gooden, Ipswich rejoined the National League in 1960. Eric Bason became promoter at Ipswich in 1962, with Vic Gooden staying on in an advisory capacity. However, having completed fifteen National League matches that season, Ipswich resigned, the last home match being a 40-38 victory over Oxford on 13 July. Falling attendances were cited as the reason for the closure, although the situation wasn't helped by the death of Jack Unstead in a track crash at the stadium on 13 April that year. Promoter John Pilblad reopened the track on 24 May 1964, when Clive Featherby won the Eastern Championship. The track subsequently held a series of open licence meetings, prior to the Witches partaking in the five-team Metropolitan League. Open licence events continued in 1965, but the track was to close down again that year. The final meeting of the first era on the 410-yard circuit was a challenge match versus Hackney on 5 June, which Ipswich lost 34-44. After closing to speedway in 1965, the original track was covered in tarmac and used for stock-car racing. The shale sport returned to Foxhall on 17 April 1969, when Ipswich were beaten 36-42 by Rochester in a British League Division Two encounter. A smaller 328-yard track had been constructed inside the stock-car circuit, with a moveable safety fence dividing the two. Promoters John Berry and Joe Thurley were the men responsible for the re-introduction of the sport to Foxhall. In 1972, Ipswich took over the

licence of West Ham, which allowed them to move into the top-flight racing of British League Division One. That year also saw John Berry running the track as sole promoter for the first time. Chris Shears joined John Berry as co-promoter at Foxhall Heath in 1984, prior to taking over as sole promoter in 1986. There were two major changes in 1989, as Ipswich joined the National League with new promoters John Louis and Mike Western at the helm. Upon the amalgamation of the British League and the National League, Ipswich joined the British League Division One in 1991. Ipswich were founder members of the British Premier League in 1995, when the divisions joined forces to form one big league. Magda Louis joined her husband, John, and Mike Western on the promotional side in 1997. That year also saw the Premier League split in two, with Ipswich partaking in the British Elite League. Two sides operated from Foxhall that year, as Ipswich also joined forces with King's Lynn to enter a composite team in the British Amateur League. Riding as the Anglian Angels, the first such meeting at Ipswich was staged on 28 March, when the homesters beat the Western Warriors 42-36. The meeting formed the second part of a double-header that had, ironically, first featured an Elite League Knockout Cup encounter between Ipswich and King's Lynn. The Amateur League operation lasted just the one season though, the final Foxhall meeting going ahead on 25 September when the Anglian Angels match versus Mildenhall was abandoned after ten heats, the home side losing 21-39. Again, this meeting had formed the second part of a double-header, being staged after an Elite League match between Ipswich and Poole. John and

Magda Louis remained as co-promoters in 1999, with Mike Western moving on to King's Lynn. Ipswich remains one of British speedway's best-supported venues, with the Witches amongst the higher echelons of the sport's Elite League.

IRVINE
ADDRESS: Irvine, Ayrshire

Bob Lindsay had his own training track in Irvine, situated next to the Dundonald Army barracks. The exact years of operation for this venture are not known.

IWADE
ADDRESS: Marshbank Farm, Old Ferry Road, Iwade, Sittingbourne, Kent
YEARS OF OPERATION: 1971 Training; 1972-93 Open and Training; 1994 British League Division Three; 1995 British Academy League; 1996 British Conference League; 1997-2000 Open and Training
FIRST MEETING: 5 November 1972
TRACK LENGTH: 250 yards (1970); 315 yards (1971-93); 352 yards (1994-97); 312 yards (1998-2000)
NICKNAME: 'Colts' (1972-93); 'Crusaders' (1994-2000)

The Iwade circuit was constructed and run by Ivor and Barry Thomas during 1970 and 1971, on the site of a former Second World War gunnery school. The original 250-yard track used straw bales as a safety fence and some reports suggest a dirt/shale surface. It was reported in March 1971 that Barry Thomas, in an effort to dry out the track, spread 85 gallons of used engine oil over the track, prior to setting fire to it. Following numerous training sessions throughout 1971 and 1972, the first proper meeting took place on 5 November 1972, when a Training School Championship was held. The meeting was won by Paul Dowdall, with Rocky Coutts second and Mick Camier third. In the early days, visitors to the track had to stop at a bungalow by the entrance, where the old lady who owned the land lived. All visitors had to shut the gate behind them, in order to stop the chickens and goats from wandering into the main road. Having used straw bales as a safety fence since opening, a proper fence was erected in 1974. Iwade defeated Mildenhall 41-37 in a training match on 15 September 1974. Michael Lee was track record holder at the circuit in 1975. Just prior to the start of the 1982 season, Andy Galvin broke his left ankle in a track accident at Iwade. Chris Galvin and Terry Waller took over the running of the track in 1984. Wimbledon junior Ian Hunter was killed in a crash there on 12 April 1987. Terry Whiberley took over the reigns at Iwade in 1987, replacing co-promoters Chris Galvin and Terry Waller. A training match versus Faringdon on 16 October 1988 resulted in a 65-30 victory for the homesters. Nathan Gaymer won the Autosmart Trophy at the circuit on 10 March 1991. Twenty-year-old Karl Nicholls was killed in a track crash at Iwade on 16 March 1994. Later in 1994, Iwade entered the British League Division Three, but withdrew after riding in one away match at Stoke (losing 27-50) on 30 July. Prior to closing, five home challenge matches had been staged, these being the first full-scale meetings held at the track. The first of the five was a 58-17 victory over Middlesbrough on 2 May. Having taken

Iwade, Kent.

over in November 1994, new promoters Graham Arnold and Peter Mason decided to change the team name to Sittingbourne (due to the location of the track) prior to the start of the 1995 season. The team partook in the British Academy League that season, before continuing in the renamed British Conference League in 1996, under the sole control of Graham Arnold. Due to the running costs of league racing, Sittingbourne opted out and continued with the training operation that had previously been so successful. The last full-scale meeting at the venue was the Nathan Gaymer Memorial Fours on 13 October 1996, which ended as follows: Sittingbourne 24, Peterborough 38, Eastbourne 19, Reading 14. A twenty-fifth anniversary meeting was staged at the track on 12 April 1997. Chris Harris was triumphant in the Under-16 Championship at the venue on 28 February 1999.

IWADE

ADDRESS: Marshbank Farm, Old Ferry Road, Iwade, Sittingbourne, Kent
YEARS OF OPERATION: 1987-90 Training; 1995-2000 Training
TRACK LENGTH: 110 metres

First constructed in 1987, this was a separate mini-track, situated close to the main circuit at Marshbank Farm. The circuit boasts a shale surface, green and red lights, a starting gate and a safety fence built from wood supplied by Ray Morton. Novices were encouraged to use the small track before graduating on to the main one. The first full scale meeting on the track was staged on 7 November 1998, when an Under-16s Championship was staged, the riders using 200cc machines.

K

KENDAL
ADDRESS: Kendal, Lancashire
YEARS OF OPERATION: 1972 Long-Track
TRACK LENGTH: 660 yards

Not much is known about this venue, and just one long-track meeting was staged on a limestone-surfaced trotting track in 1972.

KETTERING
ADDRESS: Red House Speedway, Hannington, Near Kettering, Northamptonshire
YEARS OF OPERATION: 1928-29 Open

Details of this venue are sketchy, but a newspaper article stated that 'a rough dirt-track, with ashes put down over the lumpy soil had been used in 1928 for a couple of meetings near the Red House, Hannington, but had floundered due to the efforts of the Lord's Day Observance people. The safety arrangements were minimal, only ropes and precious few of them kept the spectators back. One person leaning over the ropes had the sleeve of his macintosk ripped clean off by the sharp end of a handlebar brake lever, as the rider slid wide. The organiser, one Digger Pugh and the Pirates Motor-cycle Club, must have been staggered and obviously overwhelmed by the enormous crowd.' J. White is known to have won the 500cc expert class event at the venue in August 1929.

KING'S LYNN
ADDRESS: The Stadium, Saddlebow Road, King's Lynn, Norfolk
YEARS OF OPERATION: 1965 Open; 1966-67 British League; 1968 British League Division One; 1969-70 British League Division One and Division Two; 1971-74 British League Division One; 1975-90 British League; 1991-94 British League Division One; 1995 British Premier League; 1996 Training; 1997 British Elite League and British Amateur League; 1998-2000 British Elite League and British Conference League
FIRST MEETING: 23 May 1965
TRACK LENGTH: 400 yards (1965-75); 375 yards (1976-79); 374 yards (1980-2000)
NICKNAME: 'Stars' (1966-95); 'Knights' (1997-2000) (The Division Two team of 1969-70 was called 'Starlets'; the Amateur League team of 1997 were called 'Anglian Angels'; the 1998 Conference League team were known as 'Norfolk Braves'; the 1999 team was called 'King's Lynn Braves'; 2000 saw the Conference League team ride as 'Boston Barracuda-Braves')
KNOCK-OUT CUP WINNERS: 1977, 2000 (Based at King's Lynn in 2000, Boston also won the Conference League Knock-out Cup)
INTER-LEAGUE KNOCK-OUT CUP WINNERS: 1978, 1980

The venue was originally known as King's Lynn Greyhound Track, and the first dog meeting took place on 27 August 1951. In 1952, a grass speedway circuit was marked out on the inside of the dog track, with sand on the bends to aid broadsiding. Just one meeting was staged on the grass in 1952, with Barry East winning the Stadium Trophy on 7 September in front of 3,000 spectators. The meeting was run in aid of Lynmouth Flood Disaster Fund. Two meetings were held in 1953, King's Lynn defeating Long Eaton 43-39 in the first of them on 6 April. The meeting attracted an attendance of 1,507, and was run in aid of King's Lynn Flood Relief. The second meeting of 1953 saw King's Lynn slip to a 35-47 defeat at the hands of a side labelled East Midlands on 31 May. Stock-car racing was held at the venue in 1955 and 1956. No further speedway-style events took place until a proper 400-yard shale track was constructed at what had become a derelict stadium in 1965. Under the promotion of Maury Littlechild and Cyril Crane, the first meeting went ahead on 23 May that year, when Terry Betts lifted the Lynn Trophy. In 1969, King's Lynn fielded two teams, one in the British League Division One, and the other – with the nickname Starlets – in the British League Division Two. The Starlets' first home match was held on 27 April that year, when they beat Ipswich 41-35. In

1970, the Starlets side moved to the new Boston circuit, having completed twenty-two league fixtures, with the final home match being against Crayford on 25 July. The meeting resulted in a 51-27 victory to the King's Lynn II side. Following the death of Maury Littlechild on 12 July 1972, Violet Littlechild linked with Cyril Crane as co-promoter at Saddlebow Road. Eighteen-year-old Brett Alderton died on 21 April 1982, four days after crashing in the second-half of a meeting at King's Lynn. There was a change of promotion at Saddlebow Road in 1983, when Martin Rogers took over the running of the track. Following the Brett Alderton tragedy, another two riders lost their lives after crashing at King's Lynn in 1984: firstly, while riding in a junior match, twenty-two-year-old Neal Watson died on 19 May, then nineteen-year-old Leif Wahlman died on 29 July following a track accident the previous day in the

The Stadium, King's Lynn.

The programme from King's Lynn's 500th meeting in 1979.

European Junior Championship. Bill Barker and Malcolm Simmons took up the reigns as co-promoters at the Norfolk venue in 1988, prior to 'Simmo' stepping down in 1989, leaving Barker in sole charge. Following the amalgamation of the British and National Leagues in 1991, King's Lynn joined the revamped British League Division One. Another change on the management side, saw Keith and Cheryl Chapman take over as co-promoters in August 1992. This was after former promoter Bill Barker had announced falling crowd levels and then had the entire gate receipts from the King's Lynn-staged Commonwealth Final stolen from his home. The Stars became founder members of the twenty-one-team British Premier League in 1995. However, after drawing 48-48 with Swindon in a league fixture at Saddlebow

Road on 15 October 1995, the track closed to regular speedway for a year, with Keith Chapman unable to agree a new rental on the stadium. Tony Childs ran regular training sessions at the track in 1996. Under the promotion of Keith Chapman and Ivan Henry, King's Lynn returned to action in 1997, with a new Knights nickname. That year saw the Premier League split in two, with King's Lynn joining the top-flight racing of the British Elite League. The reopening meeting took place on 9 April, when the homesters defeated Eastbourne 46-44 in a Knock-out Cup encounter. Two teams ran at Saddlebow Road that season, as King's Lynn also linked with Ipswich to enter a composite side in the British Amateur League. Riding as the Anglian Angels, the stadium staged its first such meeting on 7 May when the homesters lost 37-41 to Ryde. The Amateur League venture lasted just that one season, with the final meeting at King's Lynn being a double-header on 13 September which saw the Angels lose 34-44 to St Austell, prior to beating Buxton 40-38. Keith Chapman took up the reigns as sole promoter in 1998, a year which again saw two teams using the stadium as a home base, when Skegness Braves (promoted by Alan Hodkinson, Cyril Crane, Stephen Blyth and Stephen Lambert) moved their Conference League operation from Marsh Lane. The first Braves meeting at their new home resulted in a 41-49 reverse against Mildenhall in a Knock-out Cup tie on 21 June. Later on in 1998, the Skegness team was renamed as Norfolk Braves, in time for their league match versus Mildenhall on 11 July. The stadium was re-named as Norfolk Arena in 1999, when another change of promotion saw Brian Griffin and Mike Western running the track. As well as the Elite League team, Conference League racing again took place at the stadium in 1999, this time under the name of King's Lynn Braves. The Braves' Conference League operation was promoted by Buster Chapman. The Norfolk Arena was also used by Rye House, for just one of their Conference League meetings on 19 September that year. A further change of promotion occurred in 2000, with Nigel Wagstaff and Keith Chapman joining Brian Griffin as co-promoters of King's Lynn. Conference League Speedway was again seen in 2000, with yet another team name being used. In an effort to find a stadium of his own, Stephen Lambert ran Boston Barracuda-Braves, with a view to re-establishing the sport in the Lincolnshire town. Boston's first meeting at the Norfolk Arena was a challenge match versus Mildenhall on 1 April, which resulted in a 43-45 defeat.

KING'S LYNN

ADDRESS: The Stadium, Saddlebow Road, King's Lynn, Norfolk
YEARS OF OPERATION: 1991 Training
TRACK LENGTH: 160 yards

£6,000 was spent on a mini-track for the purpose of training, situated on the centre green of the main circuit. The track has a chalk base, with 22-foot wide straights, while the first bend is 30-foot wide and the other 40-foot.

KIRKCALDY

ADDRESS: Kirkcaldy Ice Rink, Kirkcaldy, Fife
YEARS OF OPERATION: 1972 Indoor Ice Speedway
FIRST MEETING: 1 April 1972

This speedway venue was originally intended to open on 23 January 1972 with a meeting between Kirkcaldy Panthers and Edinburgh Monarchs, but this did not materialise. 1,500 people did attend when the meeting was finally staged on 1 April 1972, although the result is not known. This turned out to be the one and only meeting staged here.

L

LEA BRIDGE

ADDRESS: Lea Bridge Stadium, Lea Bridge Road, Leyton, London
YEARS OF OPERATION: 1928 Open; 1929-31 Southern League; 1932-33 National League; 1934 National League Division One; 1935 Training; 1938 National League Division Two; 1939 Training
FIRST MEETING: 14 July 1928
TRACK LENGTH: 446 yards (1928-29); 440 yards (1930-39)
NICKNAME: 'Saints' (1932-33); 'Cubs' (1938)

This purpose-built stadium was situated next to Lea Bridge Station, on what was previously described as a marshy rubbish dump. Prior to the much-anticipated opening of the cinder sport, greyhound racing first took place at the stadium on 7 April 1928. In a blazing heatwave, promoters Motor Speedways Ltd (Ernest J. Bass) opened the dirt-track on Saturday 14 July 1928, to a full house. The spectators witnessed Allen Kilfoyle become the main man on the night, when he took the final of the Lea Bridge Handicap. League racing was soon on the agenda and Lea Bridge operated in the Southern League from 1929 to 1931. Between 1930 and 1937, the stadium was also home to Leyton Orient Football Club, until they moved into their long-time Brisbane Road venue. During the time Orient occupied the Lea Bridge Stadium, it meant the laying of turf on the speedway track for the corners of the soccer pitch. On 26 March 1932, a first outlawed meeting was run by Tote Track Racing, who allowed betting to take place on a series of handicapped races. Later on in 1932, team racing returned to the stadium, when the renamed Clapton Saints joined the National League, having taken over the fixtures of Southampton. Promoter Charles Knott was the man in charge, and he decided on the change of team name in order to avoid the stigma associated with the unlicensed betting meetings that had started the year at Lea Bridge. In 1933, Lea Bridge Stadium was used for filming racing scenes for the movie *Britannia of Billingsgate*, while the team continued under the guise of Clapton Saints in the National League. Meetings were then run by Lea Bridge Speedways Ltd, which saw Tom Bradbury Pratt join forces with Charles Knott as co-promoter. The team name reverted back to Lea Bridge in 1934, but the track was closed by the Control Board on 27 July due to 'continuing irregularities'. A last home meeting went ahead versus Wembley on 20 July, when Lea Bridge lost 23-31 in a league encounter. The results and remaining fixtures of the side were then taken over by Walthamstow. Following the withdrawal of their speedway licence, Lea Bridge staged a series of midget-car meetings. Wembley hired the Lea Bridge track in 1935, so that their team could practise under the watchful eyes of Alec Jackson and Lionel Van Praag.

Midget-car racing was again staged at Lea Bridge from 1936 to 1938. Promoters Tom Bradbury Pratt and Charles Knott re-launched regular racing at the stadium on 1 August 1938, with the side partaking in the National League Division Two, under the name of Lea Bridge Cubs. The reopening meeting saw the Cubs beat Norwich 50-30 in a league fixture. Team racing ceased at the end of that season, however, with the last-ever meeting staged on 26 September when Lea Bridge defeated Leeds 50-33 in a league match. The track did see some action in 1939, with several riders reportedly seen training at the circuit prior to the commencement of the new season. A final greyhound meeting was staged at the stadium on 1 January 1974. The site was redeveloped later in the 1970s as an industrial area, known as the Speedway Estate.

LEEDS
ADDRESS: Post Hill Speedway, Pudsey, Nr Leeds, Yorkshire
YEARS OF OPERATION: 1928 Open
FIRST MEETING: 2 April 1928
TRACK LENGTH: 354 yards

Post Hill Speedway was reported to have staged the first ever dirt-track meeting in Yorkshire, when it opened on Easter Monday 2 April 1928. A. Moore was the star performer in the opening meeting, winning the Unlimited Solo Expert event. Amongst the other competitors at that first meeting was Fay Taylour. The cinder circuit was constructed at the foot of Post Hill, the famous hill climb. The track record set at the opening meeting was 97 seconds. Meetings were held under the promotion of

Leeds Motor Club. This was a short-lived venue that staged only a handful of meetings, the last of which took place on 29 July 1928.

LEEDS

ADDRESS: Leeds Stadium, Fullerton Park, Elland Road, Leeds, Yorkshire
YEARS OF OPERATION: 1928 Open; 1929 English Dirt-track League; 1930 Open; 1931 Northern League; 1932 Open; 1938 Open and National League Division Two
FIRST MEETING: 13 October 1928
TRACK LENGTH: 409 yards (1928-29); 402 yards (1930-32); 420 yards (1938)
NICKNAME: 'Lions' (1938)
LEAGUE CHAMPIONS: 1929

Leeds Stadium was situated next door to the football ground of Leeds United in Elland Road. Greyhound racing was first staged at the venue on 4 October 1927. The dirt-track circuit had a solid clay base with a foot of hard-rolled clinkers on top. This, in turn, was covered with three inches of cinders and coarse yellow sand. With its wire fence and slightly banked turns, it was described as not dissimilar to Belle Vue's Hyde Road circuit. A pre-official opening practice session was held at Fullerton Park on 8 October 1928. Five days later (13 October), the opening meeting saw Oliver Langton win the Golden Helmet. A further four meetings were staged that year, the last of which was on 26 December, when George Wigfield won the Golden Gauntlet. At the close of the 1929 season, the promoting company (Leeds Stadium Ltd), went into voluntary liquidation, but the creditors decided to take a chance and run the track the following year, under the guise of Leeds Stadium (1930) Ltd. John Hastings died after crashing at the circuit in July 1930. Having completed their Northern League fixtures in 1931, the Leeds track reputedly ran at least two 'pirate' Sunday meetings, despite ACU warnings not to. Several riders wore masks and used assumed names in order to avoid identification, although Drew McQueen is known to have received a suspension for partaking in one of the meetings. Open licence style meetings were held in 1932, but following a final one on 13 August, when Alec Hill won the Golden Gauntlet, the track was to remain closed for five years. Promoter Arthur Westwood brought speedway back to Fullerton Park on 6 June 1938. Initially, racing was held with an open licence, but following Nottingham's withdrawal from the National League Division Two, Leeds took over their record and remaining fixtures. However, having completed that season, no further speedway was ever staged at the venue. The last meeting at the venue was held on 13 October 1938, when the homesters lost 40-44 to Newcastle in the Northern Cup. After the Second World War, the stadium was used as a rubbish dump, prior to being purchased by Leeds United FC. Today, the site of the former stadium is partially covered by training pitches, while the remainder forms part of Fullerton Park Industrial Estate.

LEICESTER

ADDRESS: The Stadium, Blackbird Road, Leicester
YEARS OF OPERATION: 1928 Open; 1929 English Dirt-track League; 1930-31 Southern League; 1932 Open; 1937

Provincial League; 1949-50 National League Division Three; 1951-56 National League Division Two; 1957-61 National League; 1962 Provincial League; 1963 Open; 1968-74 British League Division One; 1975-83 British League

FIRST MEETING: 6 September 1928

TRACK LENGTH: 348 yards (1928-31); 364 yards (1932-36); 360 yards (1937); 382 yards (1949); 364 yards (1950); 380 yards (1951-83)

NICKNAME: 'Hunters' (1949-62); 'Lions' (1968-83)

This stadium was originally built on high ground, commanding an ample view of, on one side, the chimneys of Leicester, and on the other side, mile upon mile of open countryside. Greyhound racing was first held at the venue on 26 May 1928. The opening dirt-track meeting at Blackbird Road was held on 6 September 1928, when Skid Skinner won the senior scratch race. The opening meeting was a composite event that also featured greyhound racing. Leicester joined the English Dirt-track League in 1929, before subsequently joining the Southern League in 1930. A meeting of the creditors of Leicester Stadium Ltd (for whom Norman Coates was employed as speedway manager), was held on 22 April 1931, to nominate a liquidator for the purpose of winding up the company. The team was then withdrawn from the Southern League, with Coventry taking over their results and remaining fixtures. The track foundations and surface were re-laid by promoter Fred Mockford, prior to reopening with open licence meetings in 1932. Only two meetings are known to have been staged that year though,

the second of which was held on 6 July when a side called Home beat the Colonies 54-42. After that, the track was lost to the sport until 1937. The roar of speedway was again heard at Blackbird Road in 1937, when the team (promoted by Midland Speedways Ltd) joined the Provincial League, but the revival didn't last long, with the side resigning in mid-season after only a handful of meetings. Following the war, a proposed reopening in 1948 was delayed for a year by an appeal by local residents to the Town and Country Planning Committee over noise levels. The Leicester side did appear in at least one away challenge match in 1948 though, when they went down to a 38-46 defeat at High Beech on 18 September. Thankfully, the protesters proved to be ultimately unsuccessful, although the club was advised by the police to discontinue the playing of records at meetings. Speedway finally returned to the stadium on 8 April 1949, when Leicester Hunters lost 30-54 to Yarmouth in a National League Division Three encounter. The running of the track was then under the control of A.D. 'Alan' Sanderson, who employed Bob Peett as speedway manager. Cyril 'Squib' Burton replaced Bob Peett as manager at Blackbird Road in 1950. After two seasons of Division Three action, Leicester were promoted to Division Two, where they remained until the end of 1956. Numerous track closures meant there was only enough teams for one league in 1957, so Leicester then completed five seasons of National League racing. Under new promoter Mike Parker, the Hunters opted for Provincial League action in 1962. However, following a poor season, the team transferred to

The Stadium, Leicester.

Long Eaton for 1963. Alan Sanderson reopened Leicester in the summer of 1963, but just five open licence meetings were staged that year, the first of which occurred on 7 June when Ove Fundin won the Pride of the Midlands competition. The final meeting of the five that year was an International Pairs event for the Oceania Trophy on 23 August, which was won by the England pairing of Peter Craven and Dick Fisher. The crowds did not respond, however, and the track remained closed to speedway for a further four years. Under the promotion of Disofast Ltd (Reg Fearman and Ron Wilson), Leicester were reborn in 1968, taking over the Long Eaton side following the closure of Station Road at the end of the 1967 season. Riding with the new nickname of Lions, the first meeting back at Blackbird Road went ahead on 9 April 1968, when the homesters beat King's Lynn 48-30 in a British League Division One

encounter. A change on the management side in 1977 saw Vic White link with Reg Fearman as co-promoter. A final change of promoter at Blackbird Road occurred in 1980, with Martin Rogers taking up the reigns. What turned out to be the last-ever meeting at the venue was staged on 25 October 1983, when Leicester lost 38-40 to Belle Vue in a Grand Finale challenge match. Out of the blue, the site of the stadium was sold to Barratts for housing development, with the last action at the venue being a final greyhound meeting on 15 September 1984.

LEICESTER
ADDRESS: Leicester Super, Melton Road, Leicester
YEARS OF OPERATION: 1929 Open; 1930-31 Northern League
FIRST MEETING: 18 May 1929
TRACK LENGTH: 586 yards

The stadium was built in the winter of 1928/29, and took just five weeks to construct. The large 586-yard circuit was designed by Stewie St George, and was similar to the high-speed types found in Australia. Due to its length, races were held over only three laps. Under the auspices of Speedways and Sports Ltd, with Alec Jackson installed as racing manager, the track opened for business on Whit Saturday 18 May 1929, when Sprouts Elder won the Melton Handicap. Tragedy struck later that year though, when twenty-two-year-old Roy Sims-Reeves died after crashing at the track on 21 September. A first light-car meeting was staged at the venue on 16 November 1929. A team was formed which entered the Northern League in 1930, but their stay was to be brief. Having completed a full first year, Leicester Super withdrew from the league in August 1931, having completed fifteen matches of only their second term. The last confirmed meeting at the Melton Road venue was staged on 15 August, when the homesters beat Preston 34-20 in a league encounter. Greyhound racing was first staged at the Melton Road venue in 1931. The site of the track is now covered by allotments, while opposite lies the former Speedway Hotel – which was possibly the only pub to carry the picture of a speedway rider on its sign – although it has since been renamed.

LEICESTER
ADDRESS: Syston, Nr Leicester
YEARS OF OPERATION: 1952 Training

Several local Leicester novices banded together under the banner of Leicester Amateur Speedway Club and took a lease on a field at Syston, prior to constructing their own rough and ready training track. The president of the club was Norwich star Paddy Mills who, along with Wilf Plant, helped the lads out with advice and training. The juniors later changed their name to Novices Speedway Club of Leicester. At the end of 1952, the youngsters looked around for somewhere less primitive, eventually moving into Long Eaton.

LEICESTER
ADDRESS: Granby Halls, Aylestone Road, Leicester
YEARS OF OPERATION: 1972-73 Indoor Speedway
FIRST MEETING: 10 January 1972

Indoor meetings at Grandby Halls were promoted by Harry Bastable and Alan Eagles. Prior to the first meeting, the Speedway Control Board inspected the safety precautions at a practice session on 3 January 1972. The opening meeting, held on 10 January 1972, saw James Bond win the Midland Riders Championship on a tricky concrete surface. A total of seven meetings were staged at the venue in 1972, with a further six events in 1973. The last speedway meeting at the indoor venue took place on 6 March 1973, when a Four-Team Tournament finished as follows: Birmingham 32, Wolverhampton 25, Leicester 20, Midland Pirates 17.

LINLITHGOW
ADDRESS: Heathersfield Stadium, Whitecross Farm, Nr Linlithgow, West Lothian
YEARS OF OPERATION: 1989-90 Open and Training; 1991-93 Training; 1994 British League Division Three; 1995

British Academy League; 1996 British Conference League; 1997 British Amateur League; 1998 Open and Training; 1999 British Conference League
FIRST MEETING: 5 August 1989
TRACK LENGTH: 175 yards (1989-93); 241 yards (1994); 234 yards (1995-99)
NICKNAME: 'Lightning'
LEAGUE CHAMPIONS: 1996
KNOCK-OUT CUP WINNERS: 1996

In April 1988, it was reported that Alan Robertson was seeking planning permission to open a training track twenty miles outside Edinburgh, on the road to Falkirk. Construction of the track was completed in 1989, with Alan Robertson supervising several training sessions in order to test the circuit and make adjustments. An official opening took place on 5 August, when Hunter's Horrors defeated Prosser's Posers 30-25 in a training challenge match, with Lars Munkedal setting a track record of 48.4 seconds. Under the co-promotion of Alan Robertson and Bill Purnell, Linlithgow entered the British League Division Three in 1994. The first full-scale meeting at the track was staged on 26 June that year, when Linlithgow defeated Iwade 42-35 in a challenge match. The British League Division Three became the Academy League in 1995, prior to being renamed as the Conference League in 1996. The 1996 season saw Alan Robertson assume the role of sole promoter. The league was again re-titled for a fourth successive year in 1997, becoming the British Amateur League. The club name was also altered that season, to Lathallan, a move which was explained thus by Alan Robertson: 'I have felt for a while the councillors in the Falkirk district, in which the Heathersfield track is situated, aren't too keen to spend time

Heathersfield Stadium, Whitecross Farm, Linlithgow.

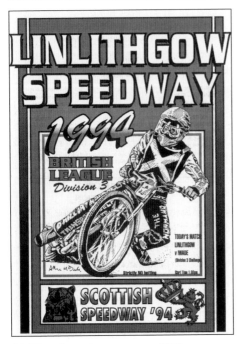

Linlithgow's opening programme, 1994.

considering any applications from a club called Linlithgow, because the town of Linlithgow is in West Lothian. That's why I've changed. Lathallan is just down the road, and it allows us to keep the Lightning nickname.' At the end of 1997, the side dropped out of league racing, with the final meeting at Heathersfield being held on 14 September, when Lathallan beat the Shuttle Cubs 38-37 in a league encounter. Training sessions and open licence individual meetings for novices were held throughout 1998, when the track ran as Heathersfield Speedway. Under the promotion of John Campbell, the track reverted back to its original name of Linlithgow in 1999, with the side competing in the British Conference League. The opening meeting of the season saw David McAllan win the Heathersfield Speedway Club

Championship on 29 May. Although the club was informed that the land the track was situated on would no longer be available to them beyond 1999, what was advertised as the Farewell to Heathersfield Four Team Tournament went ahead on 24 October and resulted as follows: Easterners 28, Midlanders 25, Borderers 22, Westerners 21. One further meeting, the Heathersfield Training Track Championship, was held on 7 November 1999, and this was billed as the real farewell to the circuit, with William Lawson triumphant. Despite not having their own track, the club took part in the 2000 Conference League under the name of Lightning Ashfield Giants, running their home matches at Ashfield Stadium in Glasgow.

LISBURN

ADDRESS: Lambeg Stadium, Lisburn, County Antrim
YEARS OF OPERATION: 1971 Open
FIRST MEETING: 28 May 1971
NICKNAME: 'Tigers'

The Lambeg Stadium was home to a trotting track, and opened to speedway in 1971. Two pirate meetings were promoted by Ginger O'Beirne, and although further events had been mooted, they didn't get off the ground due to poor crowd levels. The first meeting took place on 28 May, when Shelbourne Tigers faced a Yorkshire Select side. The second and final meeting at the stadium was the Lambeg Trophy on 11 June. Sadly, with details being so sketchy about this venue, the result of either meeting is not known. The long and wide track is known to have produced fast racing, with all heats being staged over three laps only.

LITTLE MISSENDEN
ADDRESS: Limes Farm, Little
Missenden, Nr Amersham,
Buckinghamshire
YEARS OF OPERATION: 1949 Training

Eddie, Ernie and Ron How joined
forces to purchase an old Rudge in
1949. They then marked out a track on
one of the fields on the family farm at
Little Missenden, and took it in turns to
ride. By the autumn of 1949, Ron How
had progressed enough to apply for trials at the London tracks. This was not a
shale surface and would have to be
classed as a grass speedway circuit.

LITTLE WALTHAM
ADDRESS: Montpelier Farm, Little
Waltham, Nr Chelmsford, Essex
YEARS OF OPERATION: 1969-70
Training

Former Rayleigh rider Johnny Guilfoyle
constructed his own track on land he
owned just outside Chelmsford on the
main A130. The track was comparable
to Romford, and was complete with
safety fence and shale surface. A
regular training school was held at the
circuit, with an all-inclusive charge of
£1.15/-. Johnny's younger brother,
Laurie, came to the fore as the star
pupil in 1969. The track was made
available to the Rayleigh team for
pre-season practice in 1970.

LIVERPOOL
ADDRESS: Stanley Stadium, Prescot
Road, Liverpool
YEARS OF OPERATION: 1928 Open;
1929 English Dirt-track League; 1930
Northern League; 1936-37 Provincial
League; 1949-50 National League
Division Three; 1951-53 National League
Division Two; 1957 Open; 1959 Open;
1960 Provincial League
FIRST MEETING: 25 August, 1928
TRACK LENGTH: 432 yards (1928-36);
446 yards (1937); 433 yards (1949); 440
yards (1950-51); 446 yards (1952-60)
NICKNAME: 'Merseysiders' (1936-37);
'Chads' (1949-53); 'Eagles' (1957);
'Pirates' (1960)

Stanley Stadium was built on the site of
an old brickworks, on the opposite side
of the railway line to the present Police
Athletic Ground. It boasted a stand
capable of holding 2,500, with cover on
the opposite side which was said to
hold 10,000. Greyhound racing first
took place at Stanley Stadium on
17 August 1927. Prior to the opening
dirt-track meeting, a practice was held
on 21 April, with trials the following day.
Some four months later, the opening
meeting on 25 August attracted an
attendance of 10,000, with the track
being described as having long
straights and narrow bends. Meetings
were promoted by the British Dirt-
Track Racing Association, with
Liverpool subsequently joining the
English Dirt-track League in 1929, prior
to partaking in the Northern League in
1930. During 1930, Liverpool applied to
the ACU for permission to use the tote,
which was in place for greyhound racing. They believed this would improve
attendances but, needless to say, their
request was refused. The greyhound
company turned away all applications
to run dirt-track racing in 1931, with the
result that the team transferred to
Preston. The final meeting at Stanley
Stadium had gone ahead on
10 September 1930, when the home-

A rare Liverpool programme from the reopening meeting in 1957.

sters beat Warrington 21-14 in a Northern League fixture. In 1934, John Bilsland, the chairman and owner of Electric Hare Greyhound Racing Ltd, agreed to let Highfield Rugby League Club transfer to his Stanley Stadium. Rugby was subsequently held at the venue between the 1934/35 and 1949/50 seasons inclusive. Under the promotion of Liverpool Speedways Ltd, the shale sport returned to the venue on 4 May 1936, with A.E. Atherton (Albert) installed as the front man. The reopening meeting saw Liverpool defeat Nottingham 35-34 in a National Trophy match. Liverpool subsequently joined the Provincial League, but it was a short-lived return, with E.O. Spence taking overall control during 1937, prior to transferring the Merseysiders home fixtures to Belle Vue mid-way

through the season. Prior to the move to Manchester, the final meeting at Stanley Stadium had seen Liverpool beat Birmingham 54-27 in a league encounter on 5 July. During the Second World War, the stadium was requisitioned by the RAF as the site for a barrage balloon, in order to dissuade any low-flying German bombers. With promoters Jimmy Baxter and Gordon Parkins at the helm, Liverpool Chads came into being on 11 April 1949, when Stanley Stadium reopened to speedway after an eleven-year gap. Dorothy Jollife, the 'Ballroom Queen of Great Britain', declared the track open in front of a crowd of 9,958, who saw Liverpool lose 42-66 to Hanley in a National Trophy tie. If that attendance figure was impressive, then the 16,474 gate for the next meeting versus Exeter (on 15 April) was quite staggering. The Chads took up residence in National League Division Three, but despite only finishing eighth in the final 1950 league table, they gained promotion to Division Two. However, with an unattractive side, the track again closed after the Chads had completed just sixteen league matches of the 1953 campaign. The final meeting at the track had seen Tommy Miller triumph in a World Championship qualifying round on 6 July. Despite having no track of their own, Liverpool rode in one challenge match in 1954 at Chapelizod on 20 June, which they won 44-28. With a new Eagles moniker, speedway returned in 1957, under the promotion of Reg Duval. The reopening of the track took place on 22 April, when a crowd of 11,000 witnessed the Easter Trophy, which was won by the 'Wizard of Balance', Peter Craven. However, the venture was to prove a failure after only seven meetings, with premature closure being attributed to the fact that having paid the riders the money they wanted, nothing was left in the kitty. The final meeting of this brief sojourn had gone ahead on 3 June, when Liverpool lost 44-52 to Coventry in a challenge match. Under the promotion of Mike Parker, three pirate meetings were staged in 1959, the first of which saw Liverpool lose 29-42 to Bradford on 29 July. The final meeting of the three was a Cavalcade of Speed on 23 September, which included a challenge match between Liverpool and Norwich, with the visitors winning 39-31. Promoters Mike Parker and Reg Fearman entered Liverpool in the Provincial League in 1960, with a new nickname of Pirates. It was a season of struggle though, and Liverpool gained just 8 points from their eighteen league matches. What proved to be the last-ever meeting at the stadium took place on 2 September that year, when the Pirates beat Sheffield 40-31 in a league encounter. Greyhound racing ceased at the venue following a final meeting on 11 November 1961. The site of the stadium is now covered by a fruit and vegetable market, located off Church Road.

LIVERPOOL
ADDRESS: Seaforth Greyhound Stadium, Crosby Road, Seaforth, Liverpool
YEARS OF OPERATION: 1934-35 Open
FIRST MEETING: 21 September 1934
TRACK LENGTH: 330 yards

Greyhound racing was first staged at Seaforth Stadium on 25 February 1933. Open licence dirt-track meetings were staged from 1934 to 1935, promoted by Waterloo and District Motor Club, with Hector Chipchase employed as speedway manager. The opening meeting took place on 21 September 1934, when the Seaforth Cup was raced for, although unfortunately, the result is not known. Ernie Price, Jack Gordon and Charlie Oates all took their first rides on the Seaforth cinders. The track was described as being similar to Hackney, but the turns were acute and it was a case of just rolling around them, as the slightest opening of the throttle would send a rider into the safety fence. The track closed after just two seasons, with the operation being transferred to Stanley Stadium. The final meeting at Seaforth was held on 23 September 1935, when Wimbledon were the visitors for a challenge match. Sadly, as with the track's opening event, no result is available for this meeting. Rumours of speedway's return to the venue in 1954 came to nothing. A final greyhound meeting at the stadium took place on 31 December 1965, after which the venue closed down. The site of the Seaforth Stadium is now just an open grassed area.

LIVERPOOL
ADDRESS: Stanley Stadium Car Park, Prescot Road, Liverpool
YEARS OF OPERATION: 1949-50 Training

During the winter of 1949/50, the Liverpool management received unofficial approval to construct a practice track on the Stanley Stadium car park.

LOCH RONALD
ADDRESS: Loch Ronald, Nr Wigtown, Dumfries and Galloway
YEARS OF OPERATION: 1952 Training

Glasgow novice Bill Hannah is known to have used the frozen Loch Ronald as a training track in 1952. He used a conventional speedway machine (without spikes) on a circuit marked out with stones.

LONDON

ADDRESS: White City Stadium, Wood Lane, London
YEARS OF OPERATION: 1928 Open; 1929 Southern League; 1953-58 Open; 1961 Open; 1976-78 British League; 1979-83 Open
FIRST MEETING: 19 May 1928
TRACK LENGTH: 384 yards (1928-29); 420 yards (1953-83)
NICKNAME: 'Rebels' (1976-78)
LEAGUE CHAMPIONS: 1977

White City Stadium, located in the Shepherd's Bush area of London, was originally built to stage the 1908 Olympic Games. Its name was derived from the brilliant whiteness of its ferro-concrete buildings. After the Olympics, the stadium remained derelict, until Brigadier General A.C. Critchley bought the leasehold from the Ecclesiastical Commissioners, in order to run greyhound racing, with the first such meeting going ahead on 20 June 1927. Open licence dirt-track meetings were held under the promotion of International Speedways Ltd (A.J. Hunting) in 1928 and on 19 May a crowd of some 6,000 spectators watched Lady Strathspey declare the track officially open when cutting a red, white and blue ribbon. Frank Arthur won the final of the Golden Helmet at the meeting which followed. In 1929, White City partook in the Southern League, but that was to be the end of dirt-track racing at the venue until 1953. The last known meeting, which featured scratch races, took

White City Stadium, London.

place on 4 October 1929, although no results are recorded. For one season only, 1933/34, the stadium was home to London Highfield Rugby League Club. There was then a long gap, before the shale sport formed part of a Cavalcade of Sports meeting on 20 May 1953. The riders used Vespas to save cutting up the running track, with Jack Young, Aub Lawson, Bill Kitchen, Freddie Williams, Jeff Lloyd and Split Waterman giving their services for free. Just two heats (with three riders in each) and a final were run, with Jack Young emerging with the victor's spoils. The pro-gramme of events was organised by the *Sunday Pictorial*, and was run in aid of the St John's Ambulance Brigade. The event received the full backing of Frank Gentle, chairman and managing direc-tor of the Greyhound Racing Association Ltd. The annual Cavalcade of Sports events were the only meet-ings to include speedway at the stadium between 1954 and 1958, with only three races being held in each. The 1958 meeting (organised by the *Daily Mirror*) took place on 14 May and the varied programme of events also included seven-a-side rugby, athletics, cricket, polo, show jumping, football and greyhound racing. Again, speedway was included in a Cavalcade of Sports meeting at the venue in 1961. Promoted by Danny Dunton, under the auspices of Oxspeed Ltd, speedway returned to the great venue in 1976, when a White City team was formed to partake in the British League. The first home meeting for the new side took place on 24 March that year, when the Rebels beat Wimbledon 40-38 in a challenge match. It was, however, always a problem attracting large

The programme from the last-ever meeting at White City, 1983.

enough crowds to regular team racing at the venue, and the Rebels closed at the end of only their third season. The final meeting was staged on 13 September 1978, when White City defeated Bristol 41-37 in a British League fixture. The stadium played host to big meetings between 1979 and 1983 as follows: 1979 Commonwealth Final (winner Michael Lee), Inter-Continental Final (Michael Lee), 1980 Inter-Continental Final (Chris Morton), 1981 Overseas Final (Dave Jessup), 1982 Overseas Final (Dave Jessup), World Team Cup final (USA), Embassy British Open (Dennis Sigalos), 1983 Inter-Continental Final (Hans Nielsen). That last Inter-Continental Final, staged on 7 August 1983, sadly proved to be the last meeting at the stadium. A final greyhound meeting took place at the stadium on 22 September 1984. The site of the stadium is now covered by the British Broadcasting Company's new headquarters.

LONDON

ADDRESS: London Arena, Docklands, London
YEARS OF OPERATION: 1991 Indoor Speedway
FIRST MEETING: 6 January 1991
TRACK LENGTH: 150 metres

Dave Pavitt, John Louis and Gareth Rogers, under the auspices of Arena Speedway Promotions Ltd, staged two meetings in one day on a rubberised surface at London Arena on 6 January 1991. The first event in the afternoon was a four-team tournament entitled Capital Fours, which resulted as follows: City Slickers 36, West End Wonders 30, Trafalgar Squares 18, East Enders 10. The evening Internationale individual meeting was won by Kelvin Tatum, with Andy Campbell finishing second after defeating Armando Castagna in a run-off.

LONG EATON

ADDRESS: Long Eaton Stadium, Station Road, Long Eaton, Nottinghamshire
YEARS OF OPERATION: 1929-30 Open; 1950 Open; 1951 National League Division Three; 1952 Southern League; 1953 Open and Training; 1954 Open; 1963-64 Provincial League; 1965-67 British League; 1968 Training; 1969-74 British League Division Two; 1975 Training; 1979-80 National League; 1982-90 National League; 1991-94 British League Division Two; 1995-96 British Premier League; 1997 British Premier League and British Amateur League
FIRST MEETING: 21 May 1929
TRACK LENGTH: 370 yards (1929-54);

366 yards (1963-75); 367 yards (1979-97)
NICKNAME: 'Archers' (1950-53, 1963-67 and 1974); 'Rangers' (1969-73); 'Outlaws' (1979-80); 'Invaders' (1982-97) (The Amateur League side of 1997 were called 'Shuttle Cubs')
LEAGUE CHAMPIONS: 1984

Greyhound racing was first staged at Station Road on 7 April 1928. Long Eaton were admitted to the English Dirt-track League in 1929, but never actually rode any matches in that competition. Instead, just two open licence events were staged, the first of which saw Squib Burton win the Golden Armlet on 21 May. Just one meeting is recorded for 1930, when Nottingham lost 21-29 to Leicester, the event being promoted by Leicester Stadium Ltd, the same company that promoted at Blackbird Road in Leicester. In 1949, ex-rider Arthur Sherlock, together with former Leicester Rugby player S.H. Saunders, were the directors behind a move to bring speedway back to Long Eaton. The track was ready to race by mid-July, while terracing work continued until August. The track was, however, refused a licence by the Speedway Control Board in September, even though £10,000 had been spent on improvements and renovations. Under the promotion of Long Eaton Speedway (1950) Ltd (Stan Lish, Billy Galloway, D.J. Boyer and Bob Peett), Long Eaton were given the go-ahead to run in 1950. Following a practice session on 16 May, the track staged its first meeting on 25 May, when the homesters lost 31-52 to the Third Division Stars in a challenge match. In 1951, the promoting team was reduced to three members following the departure of D.J. Boyer. Having joined the National League Division Three in

Long Eaton Stadium.

1951, Long Eaton subsequently competed in the Southern League in 1952, but they withdrew after completing twenty-one matches. Despite an average attendance of around the 4,000 mark, it was crowd levels that were cited as the main reason for the Archers' premature closure. The last meeting was a challenge match versus a Wolverhampton Select on 31 July, which Long Eaton won 52-31. In fact, that final meeting should have been a league match versus Southampton, but the visitors had broken down and failed to arrive. Luckily, some Wolverhampton riders were on hand to appear in a second-half four-team tournament, so a select side was quickly assembled in order the appease the spectators who had gathered for the meeting. Among others, Barry East, Dennis Fletcher, Ivor Brown and Vic Hall are known to have trained at the circuit in 1953.

Without a licence, Paddy Mills staged three pirate meetings in 1954, despite the participating riders facing suspension. The first of these meetings saw an East Midlands team beat a North Midlands side 44-40 on 28 August. The final meeting of the three was the Best Pairs event staged on 25 September – although a further event was advertised for 9 October, it is unlikely that this was ever held. After a gap of eight years, speedway returned on 16 April 1963, under the promotion of Disofast Ltd (Reg Fearman), with the Archers taking up residence in the Provincial League. The reopening meeting saw the home team lose 38-40 to St Austell in a league fixture. Ron Wilson joined Reg Fearman as co-promoter in 1964, prior to Long Eaton becoming founder members of the British League in 1965. The Long Eaton operation was transferred to Leicester in 1968, with only training going on at Station Road in the absence of team racing. What turned out to be the final meeting of their brief flirtation with the higher echelons of the British League had been staged on 10 October 1967, when a challenge match versus Sheffield was abandoned after nine heats with the Archers leading 32-22. In 1969, under the promotion of Ivor Brown and Vic White, Long Eaton returned to track action, with the side in the British League Division Two. It was probably at this point, with reference to Long Eaton Rangers Football Club (who had played at the venue prior to 1955), that the team was nicknamed Rangers. The first meeting of this new era was held on 10 April 1969, when the Rangers defeated Ipswich 45-33 in a league encounter. A change on the promoting side in 1970 saw Kath Brown join forces with her husband, Ivor, as co-promoter. Two changes in 1974 saw the team revert back to being known as the Archers, while Tony Allsopp joined Ivor Brown as co-promoter. At the end of the 1974 campaign, however, the track closed again for another four years. What turned out to be the final meeting of another Long Eaton era went ahead on 26 September 1974, when the Archers beat Eastbourne 40-38 in a Division Two league match. A further challenge match versus Birmingham was scheduled for 3 October, but it fell foul to the weather. An application for a licence to run in 1975 was made, although this was refused by the General Council of the National League. In spite of this, James Bond ran unlicensed training sessions at the track during the year. Promoter Dan McCormick reopened the track again in 1979, with the team riding under the name of Nottingham Outlaws. The first meeting of this venture was held on

18 April when Nottingham defeated a Daily Mirror Select 49-29. The season was marred by tragedy though, when twenty-four-year-old Nigel Wasley died on 14 September following a crash at the Station Road circuit on 29 August. A change on the promoting side in 1980 saw Bob Griffin running the show. At the end of the season, however, Station Road again closed to speedway. The last meeting of the Nottingham era was staged on 1 November, when a four-team tournament resulted as follows: Nottingham 24, Wolverhampton 30, Oxford 21, Wimbledon 20. Maurice Jones was refused a licence to run speedway at the venue in 1981. Under the promoting team of John Turner, Keith Barber and Ken McKinlay, the stadium again opened to the shale sport on 7 April 1982, and the team was then known as Long Eaton Invaders. The opening meeting resulted in a 57-39 challenge match victory over Milton Keynes. Nineteen-year-old Mick Spiers became the second rider to lose his life at the track, following a crash in a training session on 25 August 1983. The promotional side altered slightly in 1984, with John Turner and Keith Barber working in tandem as co-promoters. Mervyn Porter took over as sole promoter at Station Road in 1986. Another change of promotion occurred in 1989, with Roger Jones and Steve Yorke taking control of the track. More changes on the promotional front saw Tony Mole and Eric Boocock take over at Long Eaton in 1991. That season also saw the amalgamation of the British League and the National League, with Long Eaton taking their place in the revamped Division Two. In 1995, the Invaders took their place in the British

Premier League, as all the teams merged to form one big league. That year also saw Eric Boocock step down from the promoting side, with Graham Drury joining promoter Tony Mole as speedway manager. In 1996, there was a slight change on the promotional side, with Graham Drury becoming co-promoter alongside Tony Mole. 1997 saw the splitting of the large Premier League, with ten teams joining the Elite League, while Long Eaton and thirteen other tracks remained in a restructured Premier League set-up. The 1997 season also saw Long Eaton join forces with Wolverhampton to enter a composite team in the British Amateur League. Both tracks split the home fixtures equally, with Station Road holding its first such fixture on 23 April, when the Shuttle Cubs (as they were called) lost 29-48 to the Western Warriors. This venture lasted for only one season though, with the final Amateur League meeting being staged at Station Road on 24 September, when the Shuttle Cubs beat Oxford 39-38, prior to losing 36-41 to Buxton in a double-header. The last-ever meeting at the stadium took place on 29 October 1997, when the Invaders defeated Exeter 51-39 in the first leg of the Young Shield final. Despite much talk of speedway returning again to Station Road, nothing has materialised as yet, and in the meantime vandals have destroyed what was left of the stadium. The track is now all that remains, and it is now overgrown with weeds.

LUTON

ADDRESS: Luton Greyhound Stadium, Skimpot Lane, Dunstable Road, Luton, Bedfordshire
YEARS OF OPERATION: 1934 Open and Training; 1935 Open; 1936 Open and Training
TRACK LENGTH: 311 yards
NICKNAME: 'Hatters'

Greyhound racing was staged at the venue from the 1930s until November 1973, when the 10-acre site was sold for redevelopment. The Luton track was run primarily as a schooling centre for Wembley, with Jim Kempster and Don Durant on hand to do the coaching. In 1935, team challenge matches were staged against Wembley, West Ham, Wimbledon, Hackney, Seaforth and the Colonials, with Keith Harvey, Mike Erskine, Norman Trimnell and Jack Dalton being regular members of the Hatters side. 1935 was a very short season: having started on 6 May with a 32-21 victory over Wimbledon, the track was closed following a meeting on 13 July. Falling attendances of 2,000 or less, and the difficulty of booking suitable teams to race against were cited as the main reasons for the premature closure. The track closed in 1936, after an injunction was served over noise levels. Not too much is known about this venue, with details about first and last speedway meetings proving difficult to locate.

LYDD

ADDRESS: Lydd Speedway, Belgar Farm, Romney Road, Lydd, Kent
YEARS OF OPERATION: 1996-2000 Open and Training
FIRST MEETING: 22 September 1996
TRACK LENGTH: 201 metres
NICKNAME: 'Falcons'

A former rider at Sittingbourne, Malcolm Smith, constructed the 201-metre track on farm land set aside by a Lydd farmer. The bowl-style, sandy-surfaced track staged a demonstration meeting as its opener in order to prove to the local Council that speedway would not cause a nuisance in the area. Seventeen riders attended the opening demonstration meeting on 22 September 1996, with Ben Osborn taking the victor's spoils. The original sand surface was replaced with a conventional shale surface during the 1999 season. The track, running as Romney Falcons, has continued to stage individual and team challenge meetings as a training ground for novices, with Malcolm Smith still at the helm.

LYDDEN

ADDRESS: Lydden Hill, Lydden, Nr Folkestone, Kent
YEARS OF OPERATION: 1968-84 Long-track

FIRST MEETING: 29 September 1968

In 1959, Southern Area League side Southern Rovers were hoping to run home meetings at Lydden; however, the track was never finished and proper speedway didn't see the light of day at the venue. After many years as a grass-track circuit, Bill Chesson decided to develop the venue in 1963. An annual end-of-season meeting was held each year from 1968 to 1984, with Don Godden winning the initial one on 29 September 1968. These meetings were variously billed as international grass-track, long-track and international speedtrack events, with the surface ranging from grass to sand to shale. The final meeting at the venue was won by Martin Dugard on 14 October 1994.

Lydd Speedway, Belgar Farm, Lydd.

M

MAIDSTONE

ADDRESS: Maidstone Greyhound
Stadium, London Road, Maidstone, Kent
YEARS OF OPERATION: 1968
Demonstration

The stadium was officially opened on
22 May 1895, when it was known as
Maidstone Athletic Ground. Originally,
the venue housed a cricket pitch, with a
cinder cycling track running around the
outside. A grass-track meeting was
staged at the stadium on 10 June 1946,
when J. Colver is known to have taken
the spoils of victory. In 1968, Len Silver
applied to the local Council to stage
speedway at the stadium, but permission was refused. In preparation for an
appeal, Silver took Jack Biggs, Gary
Everett, Malcolm Brown and Graeme
Smith along to the venue for extensive
noise tests. The riders went through the
full routine of warming up, clutch starts
and flat out sprints around the perimeter of the pitch. In the mid-1970s, the
venue was given a major facelift, with
new terracing, improved floodlighting
and stand rebuilding. To commemorate
this, it was renamed as Maidstone
Stadium. Greyhound racing was also
staged at the venue, from a first meeting
on 1 October 1976 until it ceased after a
final event on 30 April 1988. Kent Invicta
Rugby League Club used the ground for
the 1983/84 season, their first home
match being staged versus Cardiff on
21 August 1983. The rugby club's last
match at the venue was against Rochdale
on 12 May 1984. The site of the stadium
is now covered by an MFI superstore.

MANCHESTER

ADDRESS: White City Greyhound
Stadium, Old Trafford, Manchester
YEARS OF OPERATION: 1928 Open;
1929 English Dirt-track League; 1930
Northern League
FIRST MEETING: 16 June 1928
TRACK LENGTH: 440 yards (1928-29);
446 yards (1930)

Like Belle Vue, the White City Stadium
had an adjoining fun fair. The British Dirt-
track Racing Association transferred its
headquarters from Audenshaw to the
White City in 1928. The track was opened
by famous TT rider Charlie Dodson on
16 June 1928, after which Sprouts Elder
performed an exhibition run on his
Douglas. The legendary Elder then went
on to win the opening Golden Helmet
event. Following that initial meeting, a
further fifty meetings were staged at the
track in 1928, the last of which went
ahead on 1 December. By all accounts,
this was one of the most difficult tracks
of all to ride. This was due to it having
very long straights and hairpin bends.
The wire safety fence was not particularly
efficient either – its height was such that,
instead of a rider hitting it and rebound-
ing, he would just about drape himself
over the top of it. As a result of this, the
lamp standards that surrounded the track
were padded to a certain distance above
the fence. Despite heading the English
Dirt-track League table in 1929, the team
resigned in September following a dispute among the promoters, although the
circuit subsequently continued on with
scratch race events. Upon closure in
1929, the running of White City was
taken over by the Belle Vue
management, who shut down the greyhound track and completely recon-

White City Greyhound Stadium, Old Trafford.

structed the dirt-track circuit. A report at the time summed this up by saying 'The Belle Vue management are occupying themselves in making a silk purse of a sow's ear, a genuinely super track is rapidly nearing completion on the site of the truly horrible thing which the White City used to be'. A team was entered in the Northern League in 1930, before the stadium was taken over by the GRA, who staged their first greyhound meeting shortly afterwards. The last dirt-track meeting at the venue was staged on 5 July that year, when the homesters lost 22-31 to Belle Vue Juniors in a challenge match. The Northern League ended in disarray, with the fixtures incomplete – although dirt-track racing had ceased in July at the White City venue, the team had still completed more matches than many of the other sides in the league! In 1972, Mike Parker transferred his stock-car

operations from Salford to the Old Trafford venue, and this was to carry on throughout the rest of the 1970s. Greyhound racing ceased at the venue following a final meeting in October 1981. Following the end of stock-car and greyhound racing, the stadium lay crumbling for ten years before being demolished, and a retail shopping park being built in its place (although the impressive archway from the original stadium is still there for all to see).

MANCHESTER
ADDRESS: G-Mex Exhibition Centre, Manchester
YEARS OF OPERATION: 1991 Indoor Speedway
FIRST MEETING: 8 December 1991

Arena Speedway Promotions Ltd, staged the one and only meeting at Manchester's impressive G-Mex Centre on 8 December 1991, when Mark Loram scooped the £1,000 first prize in the internationale event.

MANSFIELD
ADDRESS: Park Hall, Mansfield Woodhouse, Nottinghamshire
YEARS OF OPERATION: 1928-29 Open
FIRST MEETING: 19 May 1928
TRACK LENGTH: 880 yards (1928); 440 yards (1929)

This track, situated at Park Hall in Mansfield Woodhouse, was constructed on land belonging to Mr & Mrs W.B. Makings. Prior to the opening meeting, a practice session was held on 29 April 1928, when the public were allowed in free of charge, so long as they made a donation to the collection for Mansfield Hospital. Just two meetings were staged in 1928, and were promoted by Midland Motorcycle Dirt-track Racing Club. Due to torrential rain, the opening meeting on 19 May 1928 was abandoned after four heats – E. Housley was declared the winner of the Mansfield Motor Club Race, as he had been the best competitor prior to the abandonment. The half-mile, broad-based track was described as being egg-shaped, with one sweeping end, while the other provided a sharp corner. Prior to the 1929 season, the track was completely reconstructed to half the length it had been the previous year, with cinders being used as the racing surface. Sadly, it has proved impossible to find any dates or results of meetings for the 1929 season. The site of the track is now covered by a cornfield.

MARCH
ADDRESS: GER Sports Club, March, Cambridgeshire
YEARS OF OPERATION: 1945-47 Open
TRACK LENGTH: 375 yards

Meetings here were promoted by GER Sports Auto Club. The first meeting of the 1946 season is known to have taken place on 31 August, when Peterborough beat Middlesbrough 44-40 in a challenge match. The programme for the 1946 opener makes mention of a match race that took place at the venue the previous year between Tip Mills and Buster Yeomans. Not much is known about the GER Sports Club, but this is a separate venue to another one situated on Hundred Road in March, which was advertised as staging grass-track speedway racing.

MARGATE
ADDRESS: Dreamland Skating Rink, Margate, Kent
YEARS OF OPERATION: 1931 Indoor Ice Racing
FIRST MEETING: 11 February 1931

The Thanet Motor Car Club held the first of a planned series of motorcycle rink events on Tuesday 11 February 1931, when some good racing was witnessed. Eight heats of match races were held, plus two semi-finals and a final.

MARYPORT
ADDRESS: Roller-skating Rink, Maryport, Nr Workington, Cumbria
YEARS OF OPERATION: 1984 Training

Using Honda 125cc and 250cc engines, Steve Lawson, Jacko Irving, Andy Reid and Geoff Powell are known to have used the disused concrete roller-skating rink in Maryport for practice sessions. The rink was basically an outdoor concrete square that had been used for public roller-skating after the Second World War. Due to the noise, the local authority took a dim view of the practice sessions, having received several complaints from local residents. The site of the rink is now grassed over.

MARYPORT
ADDRESS: Maryport Golf Club Car Park, Maryport, Nr Workington, Cumbria
YEARS OF OPERATION: 1984-87 Training

The Council-owned car park at Maryport Golf Club had a shale-type surface, which Steve Lawson, Geoff Powell, Andy Reid and Jacko Irving sometimes used for training. With its close proximity to the main road and the risk of being spotted by the local police, plus the fact that it was nearly always in use, opportunities to practise on the car park were few and far between.

MELTON MOWBRAY
ADDRESS: Melton Mowbray, Leicestershire
YEARS OF OPERATION: 1936 Training

In 1936, Wilf Plant found a patch of land two miles from his home town of Melton Mowbray and laid out his own track. He used to practice regularly on this circuit, with Paddy Mills, Stan Williams, Don Houghton and Geoff Godwin. The Sunday practice sessions came to an end following noise complaints from a local vicar. Wilf Plant progressed on to junior races at Belle Vue in 1937, while Geoff Godwin joined the Hall Green circuit in Birmingham.

MELTON MOWBRAY
ADDRESS: Melton Greyhound Stadium, Saxby Road, Melton Mowbray, Leicestershire
YEARS OF OPERATION: 1949 Open
FIRST MEETING: 7 August 1949
TRACK LENGTH: 280 yards

Greyhound racing first took place at the stadium on 11 June 1946. A dirt-track was constructed by Wilf Plant and a band of local enthusiasts, using 200 tons of cinders on the inside of the greyhound circuit. The Control Board had banned some riders from partaking at the circuit but, despite this, the opening meeting went ahead on 7 August 1949, when a crowd of 2,000 witnessed Melton Mowbray defeat The Rest 42-41 in a challenge match. Admission was free, due to the Sunday Observance Act, although a charge of 1/- was made for the programme. A second meeting, on 4 September, featured Lions versus Tigers, with admission again free. However, for a third meeting and final meeting, held on 16 October (Lions versus Panthers), a charge of 2/3 was made. Meetings were promoted by Melton Mowbray Lion Motorcycle Club, by kind permission of The Melton Mowbray Greyhounds Ltd. Squib Burton had hoped to run a winter training school here in 1950/51, but his plans never came to fruition. Greyhound racing ceased at the stadium in 1969. The site is now an industrial estate.

MIDDLESBROUGH
ADDRESS: Cleveland Park, Stockton Road, Middlesbrough, Teesside
YEARS OF OPERATION: 1928 Open; 1929 English Dirt-track League; 1930-31 Open; 1936-38 Open; 1939 National League Division Two; 1945 Open; 1946 Northern

League; 1947-48 National League Division Two; 1953-55 Open; 1961-64 Provincial League; 1965 Open; 1966 Northern League; 1968-74 British League Division Two; 1975-90 National League; 1991-93 British League Division Two; 1994 British League Division Two and Division Three; 1995 British Premier League and British Academy League; 1996 British Premier League

FIRST MEETING: 23 August 1928

TRACK LENGTH: 410 yards (1928); 335 yards (1929-85); 330 yards (1986-92); 323 yards (1993-96)

NICKNAME: 'Bears' (1939-48; 1961-66; 1989-96); 'Teessiders' (1968-72); 'Tigers' (1973-88) (The Division 3 and Academy League sides of 1994-95 were called 'Cleveland Bays')

LEAGUE CHAMPIONS: 1946, 1947, 1981

A first greyhound meeting was held at Cleveland Park on 19 May 1928. The original 1928 dirt track was laid by the legendary Johnnie Hoskins, who promoted the venue under the name of Albion Auto Racers Ltd. The first dirt-track meeting went ahead on 23 August 1928, when a crowd of 15,000 witnessed the Stockton Handicap. Two meetings a week were staged in that inaugural season, and the crowds rolled in through the turnstiles. A team was formed, which entered the English Dirt-track League in 1929, but the fixtures were never completed and the league table ended in chaos. Tragedy struck on 12 July 1929, when nineteen-year-old Dennis Atkinson was fatally wounded in a track crash at Cleveland Park, and died the following day. Open licence events were held in 1930, only for the track to close following a meeting on 8 July when Vic Huxley won the scratch race title. However,

dirt-track racing returned to Cleveland Park later that year when National Greyhounds (Middlesbrough) Ltd staged a meeting on 4 November. Following further open licence events in 1931, the track closed down for the first of several occasions. After a gap of four years, Tom Bradbury Pratt reintroduced speedway to Cleveland Park on 28 August 1936, with the first in a series of five open licence events. Similar meetings continued throughout the next two seasons, before Middlesbrough joined the National League Division Two in 1939, only to resign having completed just nine of their fixtures. The last meeting was held on 9 June, when Middles-brough beat Norwich 47-37 in a Second Division match. Following the death of Tom Bradbury Pratt, the meetings of the 1939 season were promoted by Middlesbrough Speedway Ltd, whose managing director was Vic Wieland. After the war, the track reopened in September 1945 under the promotion of Stan Greatrex. A few open licence meetings were run, but programmes for these events were just a single sheet of paper, folded in two. This was explained by the programme notes thus: 'No more paper allowed – on with the racing'. Under the auspices of Teesside Speedway Ltd, Stan Greatrex was joined by co-promoters J.B. McCreton, Harry Whitfield and Arthur Atkinson in 1946, with Middlesbrough entering the Northern League. Two successful years of National League Division Two action then followed in 1947 and 1948. Somewhat surprisingly, the Middlesbrough team transferred to Newcastle for the 1949 season. The Middlesbrough circuit had already hosted its

Cleveland Park, Middlesbrough.

final meeting, on 21 October 1948, when the homesters beat Newcastle 56-28 in a league match. Cleveland Park was subsequently refused an open licence by the Control Board in both 1949 and 1950. Track action resumed in 1953 under an open licence, with just one meeting going ahead on 24 August. Only three open licence meetings were held at Cleveland Park in 1954. The track closed after three further meetings in 1955. The track had operated on an ACU centre permit, promoted by Middlesbrough Motor Club, with all competitors being club members from 1953 to 1955. The machines the riders used had brakes fitted, but apparently the riders never used them. The track was again closed to the shale sport until 6 April 1961, when Middlesbrough entered the Provincial League under the guidance of promoter Reg Fearman. The reopening meeting resulted in a 36-42 defeat at the hands of

Sheffield in a league fixture. Having completed four full seasons of Provincial League racing, the Middlesbrough team transferred to Halifax for 1965, leaving just three open licence events to be staged at Cleveland Park that year. The first such event took place on 22 April, when George Hunter won the Easter Trophy. Bears' captain Eric Boothroyd obtained a licence to promote in 1966, with the Bears competing in the Northern League; however, the track again closed down following a challenge match versus a Clive Hitch Select on 28 July that year. The result of that meeting was a 52-50 victory to Middlesbrough. With the formation of the British League Division Two in 1968, the track reopened on 30 May with the side renamed Teesside Teessiders (a name that was used until the end of 1978, although the nickname was changed to Tigers in 1973). The first match was a league fixture versus

Berwick, which resulted in a 43-34 win for the homesters. Meetings were held under the auspices of Allied Presentations, with Ron Wilson running the show. A change on the management side saw Wally Martin link up with Ron Wilson as co-promoter in 1976. When Ron Wilson moved on to Milton Keynes, Wally Martin was left in sole charge at Cleveland Park in 1979. Tim Swales teamed up with Wally Martin as co-promoter in 1985. That season also saw the main grandstand at the stadium lost to a fire during June. Tim Swales and his wife, Sally, took over the promoting reigns in 1986. The team went back to their original nickname of Bears in 1989 – thus completing a full circle of going from Bears, to Teessiders, to Tigers and back to Bears again. That season also saw a further change of promotion, with Stopgold Ltd (Tim Swales and Ken Knott) running the track. In 1994, a second team known as Cleveland Bays was based at Cleveland Park. The Bays competed in the British League Division Three, with their first home match in the new division taking place on 4 August, when they defeated Stoke 53-25. Malcolm Wright joined forces with Ken Knott and Tim Swales as co-promoter in 1995. The British League Division Three became the British Academy League that year, but Cleveland resigned from it having completed just four fixtures. Cleveland's one and only home match that year was staged on 9 July, when the Bays beat Mildenhall 53-43. Poor crowds for this level of racing were cited as the reason for the team's premature withdrawal. 1996 saw Tim Swales step down as co-promoter, with Malcolm Wright and Ken Knott continuing to operate the track under the auspices of Stopgold Ltd.

Cleveland Bays did complete a one-off home fixture that year, when they beat Berwick 40-36 in the Tees-Tweed Trophy on 20 June. The track closed to speedway following a final British Premier League meeting between Middlesbrough and Bradford on 19 September 1996, which resulted in a 54-42 victory to the Bears. The stadium site was subsequently sold for an extension to the neighbouring college; although, as yet, the track remains in place, the safety fence and all surrounding buildings have disappeared.

MILDENHALL

ADDRESS: West Row Fen, Mildenhall, Suffolk
YEARS OF OPERATION: 1973 Training

Originally training sessions took place on a makeshift track situated in a field adjacent to the site where Mildenhall Stadium is now situated.

MILDENHALL

ADDRESS: Mildenhall Stadium, Hayland Drove, West Row Fen, Mildenhall, Suffolk
YEARS OF OPERATION: 1973 Training; 1974 Open and Training; 1975-89 National League; 1990-91 Training; 1992 British League Division Two; 1994 British League Division Three; 1995 British Academy League; 1996 British Conference League; 1997 British Amateur League; 1998-2000 British Conference League
FIRST MEETING: 18 May 1975
TRACK LENGTH: 307 yards (1973-91); 312 yards (1992); 284 yards (1994-2000)
NICKNAME: 'Fen Tigers'
LEAGUE CHAMPIONS: 1979
LEAGUE CUP WINNERS: 2000

Local farmer Terry Waters provided the

site on which the 307-yard track was built. This new track was situated in an adjacent field to the original training circuit. The track had a base of 1,000 tons of chalk, with a red shale surface, while a wooden safety fence was gradually constructed to replace the straw bales that were used at the start of operations. Just seven riders turned up for the first-ever training session on 8 April 1973. The training school was a joint venture with Terry Waters, and sessions from 10.30 a.m. until dusk cost £2.25. Several training school team challenge matches are known to have been staged in 1974 (versus Iwade, Peterborough and Crewe). The regular training sessions at the track were to unearth one of the hottest names in the sport's history, Michael Lee. In 1975, Bernie Klatt applied for an open licence, but eventually joined forces with Colin Barber and Wally Mawdsley to enter a side in the New National League. The first full-scale meeting went ahead at the West Row venue on 18 May 1975, when Mildenhall lost 37-41 to Scunthorpe in a National League fixture. It was suggested that top-flight speedway would come to Mildenhall, firstly in 1979 and again in 1984, but nothing came to fruition on either occasion. Terry Waters and Bernie Klatt became co-promoters at West Row in 1980, prior to Bernie Klatt becoming sole promoter the following year. Following the death of Bernie Klatt, a consortium was formed to carry on the running of speedway at the stadium. Under the title of Mildenhall Speedway Promotions, the consortium included Terry and Byron Water, Theo and Barry Klatt, Brian and Gordon Palmer, Skid Parish and Bob Steward. From 1987, Skid Parish took more of a leading role in the running of speedway at the venue. Having completed fifteen seasons of National League racing, Mildenhall were expelled from the league just seven days after the official start of the 1990 season.

Mildenhall Stadium.

This was because the combined team averages of the declared line-up did not reach the 42-point limit. What had turned out to be the final meeting of that initial era of track action had been staged on 22 October 1989, when the Fen Tigers beat Ipswich 52-43 in a challenge match. Practice and training sessions, organised by Dick Partridge, were staged at the circuit in 1991, with Kevin Jolly known to have used the track at least once that year. Promoters Dick Partridge and Derek Hewitt reopened the circuit in 1992, when the initial meeting saw Tony Rickardsson win the Autovalet Trophy on 22 March. The return to track action proved short-lived, with the track closing down following a qualifying round of the HEAT Four Team Championship on 17 June 1992. The result of the final meeting was: Mildenhall 26, Rye House 30, Milton Keynes 23, Exeter 17. Financial problems were cited as the reason for the track's premature closure, with the club having completed only four league matches at the time. With the formation of the British League Division Three in 1994, Derek Hewitt again revived the club and the track reopened with a 41-37 victory over Iwade in a challenge match on 24 July. Although the league has changed names several times since, Mildenhall have continued to run in what is essentially the same division, with promoter Dingle Brown at the helm since mid-1995. The track was also used by Rye House, who staged six Conference League meetings at the venue in 1999.

MILDENHALL
ADDRESS: Mildenhall Training Track, Hayland Drove, West Row Fen, Mildenhall, Suffolk
YEARS OF OPERATION: 1987 Training; 1988 Open; 1991 Training
FIRST MEETING: 2 August 1987
TRACK LENGTH: 93 metres

Masterminded by Alan Johns, the 93-metre mini-track was constructed at a cost of £3,000 on land at the rear of the existing Mildenhall Stadium. The circuit was officially opened by Erik Gundersen on the morning of 2 August 1987. Training sessions were run by Alan Johns on Sunday mornings. A training challenge match was staged on 12 June 1988, when Mildenhall beat Eastbourne 50-39. After a couple of years of inactivity, Dick Partridge reopened the training circuit in 1991, but there has been no recorded use of the mini-track since.

MILTON KEYNES
ADDRESS: Groveway Greyhound Stadium, Milton Keynes, Buckinghamshire
YEARS OF OPERATION: 1978-88 National League; 1993 Open
FIRST MEETING: 28 March 1978
TRACK LENGTH: 324 yards (1978-80); 307 yards (1981-88)
NICKNAME: 'Knights'

Greyhound racing first took place at the Groveway on 25 July 1963, under the direction of Robert Beckett and his son, David. Prior to the venue first staging speedway in 1978, two previous applications had been turned down, including one as early as 1974. Finally, subject to final Highway Authority sanctions, Buckingham County Council gave approval to speedway for two seasons of twenty-eight meetings in 1978 and 1979. Promoters Robert Beckett and Ron

Groveway Greyhound Stadium, Milton Keynes.

Wilson eventually opened the track on 28 March 1978, when Mike Sampson won the *Daily Mirror*-sponsored Sword of Honour Classic. A change on the promoting front in 1981 saw John Yeowell and Ted Jarvis take over the running of the track. A new promoting company was formed in 1982, which saw meetings being run under the auspices of Avlec Leisure (Ted Jarvis, Lyn Whitear, Cyril Crane, Violet Littlechild and Alan Littlechild). In 1985, the running of the track altered again, with Ted Jarvis still holding the reigns under the banner of Milton Keynes Speedway Promotions. In 1988, there was one final change of promotion at the stadium, with the Milton Keynes Speedway Management Team running the show, the organisation including Stuart Allsop, Terry Cheney, David Dunn, Derek Rance and Dr Tim Sharrock. Having completed eleven years of National League racing, the final meeting at the Groveway was staged on 25 October 1988, when Mark Loram was triumphant in the Rotary Club Charity Championship. The Milton Keynes side quickly relocated to the nearby Elfield Park Stadium in time for the 1989 season. In 1993, an experimental series of meetings were staged at the Groveway, combining speedway with moto-cross – where many former Knights fans were seen in attendance. Today, the stadium remains in place, still in use for greyhound and stock-car racing, with rumours doing the rounds from time to time about a possible return for speedway.

MILTON KEYNES
ADDRESS: Elfield Park Stadium, Elfield Park, Bleak Hall, Milton Keynes, Buckinghamshire
YEARS OF OPERATION: 1981 Training;

1982-83 Open and Training; 1984-85 Training; 1986-88 Open and Training; 1989-90 National League; 1991-92 British League Division Two
FIRST MEETING: 18 April 1989
TRACK LENGTH: 250 yards (1981-88); 290 yards (1989-92)
NICKNAME: 'Knights' (1989-92)

In 1981, Bob Humphreys obtained planning permission and a fourteen-year lease from Milton Keynes Development Association to construct a training track at the site of a swamp in Elfield Park. A red shale track was constructed, with a white board safety fence, but an unusual feature of the circuit was that the centre green area was dish-shaped in order to aid drainage. Bert Harkins is known to have joined in at the very first training session on 27 September 1981, when at least thirty trainees turned up for a spin around the new circuit. Malcolm Holloway is known to have put in several laps of practice at the track in readiness for the 1982 season. A training match between Elfield Park and Wimbledon on 11 June 1983 resulted in a 41-37 victory for the homesters. Having retired from regular speedway at the end of the 1981 season, speculation about Bob Humphreys' return to the track was fuelled by reports that he had acquired new leathers and had been testing out a bike on his own track in August 1983. Subsequently, he did indeed make a comeback, joining Arena-Essex for their inaugural season of track action in 1984. In November 1985, Humphreys announced his retirement from Arena-Essex, and that he was also selling his training track at Elfield Park. The circuit was soon up and running again though, with Mick

Opening meeting programme from Elfield Park, 1989.

Brown at the helm for regular training and practice sessions. Mid-week practice sessions at Elfield Park were free of charge in 1987. Paul Dugard won the Training Track Trophy on 11 July 1987. Jan O. Pedersen ran a two-day training school at the venue in November 1988. Having lost the use of the Groveway Stadium at the end of 1988, the town's National League side moved to Elfield Park, making numerous upgrades to the stadium and track in time for the 1989 campaign. The promoters in 1989 were Milton Keynes Speedway Promotions 1989 (Stuart Allsop, Mick Barker, Terry Cheney, Geoff Davis, Bernard Newton, Chris Rance, David Dunn and Dr Tim Sharrock). The first meeting proper at the track was set for 11 April 1989, when Peterborough were scheduled to appear in a challenge match. However, this was rained off and quickly reorganised for the following week. The meeting went ahead on 18 April with the home side succumbing to a 39-57 defeat. One change to the promotion team in 1990 saw Tom Carey taking the place of Mick Barker. The promotion changed in 1991, when Milton Keynes Speedway Promotions (1989) Ltd (Terry Cheney and Gareth Rogers) took over from the 1990 consortium. With the league set-up also changing that year, Milton Keynes took their place in the British League Division Two. However, complaints from local residents over noise, coupled with track problems, would eventually bring the venue to a premature close in 1992. The 1992 season had seen a further change of promotion, with Colin Hill and Roger Jones taking over, but what turned out to be the final meeting at the stadium took place on 26 May 1992, when the 'Knights' lost 41-49 to Peterborough in a Gold Cup

match. On 2 June 1992, Milton Keynes were due to race a Gold Cup match versus Long Eaton, but the meeting was called off twenty minutes before the scheduled start time, when the referee declared the track too dangerous for racing. That proved to be the end, with the team subsequently resigning from the league. At the time of the closure, Milton Keynes had completed just two matches from their Division Two fixture list. There has been no attempt to revive the sport at Elfield Park, and the track and stadium area is now completely overgrown with weeds.

MILTON KEYNES
ADDRESS: Blade Runner Ice Rink, Milton Keynes, Buckinghamshire
YEARS OF OPERATION: 1991 Indoor Ice Speedway
FIRST MEETING: 26 December 1991

Elfield Park Stadium, Elfield Park, Milton Keynes.

Promoted by Ian Thomas and Graham Drury, two meetings were held at the Blade Runner Ice Rink on Boxing Day 1991. The afternoon session saw Graham Jones win The Ice Masters event, while the evening Euro Pairs International saw Andy Campbell and Joe Screen triumphant.

MIRFIELD

ADDRESS: Mirfield, Nr Huddersfield, Yorkshire
YEARS OF OPERATION: 1948 Training

In 1948, Jack Hughes rigged up a training track on farmland owned by his father in Mirfield. Jack Hughes and Arthur Forrest are known to have used the rough and ready circuit several times, prior to joining in with the Monday night Odsal practice sessions later on that year.

MOTHERWELL

ADDRESS: Paragon Speedway, Clyde Valley Sports Ground, Airbles Road, Motherwell, Lanarkshire
YEARS OF OPERATION: 1930-32 Open
FIRST MEETING: 27 September 1930
TRACK LENGTH: 587 yards

It was long-considered that a training track had been constructed at Wishaw Greyhound Stadium. However, extensive research has turned up evidence to prove that dirt-track racing actually took place at a former whippet-racing track called the Clyde Valley Sports Ground. The stadium was situated opposite the Tramway Power Station and was known as Paragon Speedway, staging its first meeting on 27 September 1930. Andy Nichol is known to have won at least three of the Saturday afternoon meetings held at

the venue in that year. A meeting on 25 October 1930, between Blantyre and Glasgow, was advertised on the front page of the *Motherwell Times*. The newspaper boldly stated that 'The meeting is on irrespective of the weather'. Amongst the riders listed as participating were Jimmy Pinkerton, Alfie Williams, Bill Barclay and Peter Coia for Glasgow, whilst Jack White, Bill Naismith and Andy Nichol were members of the Blantyre side. Admission was priced at 6d, with a programme costing 2d. A scratch race event is known to have been held at the venue on 4 May 1932. Greyhound racing was first staged at this venue on 22 July 1932 and went on until a final meeting in December 1959.

MOTHERWELL

ADDRESS: The Stadium, Milton Street, Motherwell, Lanarkshire
YEARS OF OPERATION: 1950 Open; 1951-54 National League Division Two; 1957 Training; 1958 Open; 1972 Open
FIRST MEETING: 14 July 1950
TRACK LENGTH: 430 yards (1950-58); 340 yards (1972)
NICKNAME: 'Eagles'

Prior to opening, John Robertson spent £100,000 on the building of the stadium, which was situated on the site of an old colliery. Thousands of tons of waste material, which had overshadowed the site, were moved and used to fill the old pit shafts. A 2,000-seat grandstand was constructed, and the stadium became home to greyhound racing and a local junior football team. The opening greyhound meeting took place on 15 October 1949. Under the auspices of Lanarkshire Speedway and Sports

Stadium Co. Ltd (Tom Reid), speedway was first staged on 14 July 1950, when the Lanarkshire Eagles beat Newcastle 48-36 in a challenge match. Motherwell joined the National League Division Two in 1951, and remained there for four complete seasons, before closing in the face of falling attendances. The final meeting before the track's closure went ahead on 8 October 1954, when the Eagles defeated Ipswich 45-39 in a league fixture. A proposed junior meeting in 1955 was never staged, due to the lack of interest from riders. Following a few training sessions in 1957, Ian Hoskins reopened the track to team speedway on 16 May 1958, when Motherwell thrashed the Belle Vue Babes 50-27 in a challenge match. 'The Ladybank Express', George Hunter, made his debut in that meeting to start a career that would run until

1984! Four further meetings were held in 1958, with the last one taking place on 11 July, when the Eagles beat Ipswich 43-34 in a challenge match. In 1972, a long track was constructed on the outside of a tarmac-covered stock-car circuit at the venue, with a scaled-down speedway circuit in the centre. A planned first speedway meeting versus Barrow on 15 May 1972 was cancelled as the track had no licence. When the licence arrived, the challenge match versus Barrow was rearranged for 29 May 1972, but was abandoned just prior to the first heat because of pouring rain. The match was again rescheduled for 5 June but was called off due to further adverse weather conditions. On 12 June a challenge match versus Teesside did go ahead, but the Eagles lost 33-42 in front of a sparse crowd and no further meetings

The Stadium, Motherwell.

were ever staged at the venue as a result.

MOTHERWELL

ADDRESS: The Stadium, Milton Street, Motherwell, Lanarkshire
YEARS OF OPERATION: 1971 Long-track Training; 1972 Long-track
TRACK LENGTH: 680 yards
FIRST MEETING: 2 January 1972

Stadium owner Bobby Kennedy had permitted training sessions on the 680-yard trotting track. Sessions were run by Allan Robertson, from noon until dusk, and cost £1 per day. Bobby Beaton is known to have ridden at the first training event in 1971. In 1972, three long-track meetings were staged on the adapted trotting track as follows: Golden Eagle Trophy on 2 January (won by Ivan Mauger), Duckhams Silver Cup on 12 April (Garry Middleton), Cham-pion of Champions Trophy on 7 May (Jim McMillan). In February 1972, Garry Middleton ran a week-long training school for Danish visitors, which culminated in a school championship that saw Carl Korneliussen take the victor's spoils.

MOTHERWELL

ADDRESS: Motherwell FC, Fir Park, Motherwell, Lanarkshire
YEARS OF OPERATION: 1996 Demonstration

In May 1996, Mick Powell and Scott Lamb appeared before 8,500 spectators in a demonstration at Motherwell Football Club. The public relations exercise was arranged by speedway fan and secretary of the soccer club, Alan Dick.

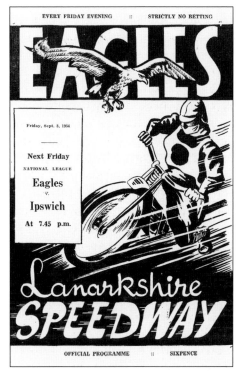

EVERY FRIDAY EVENING :: STRICTLY NO BETTING

EAGLES

Friday, Sept. 3, 1954

Next Friday
NATIONAL LEAGUE
Eagles
v.
Ipswich
At 7.45 p.m.

Lanarkshire SPEEDWAY

OFFICIAL PROGRAMME :: SIXPENCE

Motherwell programme illustration, 1954.

N

NEATH

ADDRESS: Neath Abbey Stadium, Neath, West Glamorgan
YEARS OF OPERATION: 1962 Provincial League
FIRST MEETING: 28 April 1962
TRACK LENGTH: 375 yards
NICKNAME: 'Welsh Dragons'

Situated on what had once been an iron ore slag heap, Trevor Redmond thought Neath Abbey Stadium was an ideal spot to launch a Provincial League side in 1962. Prior to Redmond's interest, plans had previously been submitted to the local Council by Leslie Maidment in March 1952. Work actually started on the track, and Freddie Williams had planned to run a training school at the venue. Reports in 1953 stated that Randolph Turpin had been approached for financial backing, with a view towards proposed operations in 1954. Nothing more was heard about this proposed venture, however, and the track was subsequently covered in tarmac for a season of stock-car racing in 1955. The stadium had been disused for several years, until Trevor Redmond came along and secured the lease to run speedway. An opening challenge match versus Wolverhampton had been scheduled for 21 April 1962, but was rained off, so what turned out to be the opener went ahead on 28 April when the Neath Dragons beat Sheffield 41-37 in a challenge match in front of a crowd of 3,000. Trevor Redmond proved to be a jack-of-all-trades, for not only was he

Opening night programme from Nelson, 1967.

the promoter, but he also rode, was club captain and team manager! Later in the season, a lack of floodlighting and a congested fixture list caused Neath to run four of their Provincial League fixtures at St Austell. The crowds didn't get behind the venture though, and what turned out to be the final meeting at the South Wales venue was staged on 1 September 1962, when the homesters beat Sheffield 41-36 in a league encounter. Within sight of the ruins of Neath Abbey, the site is now covered with an industrial estate, having been redeveloped in the late 1960s.

NELSON

ADDRESS: Seedhill Stadium, Carr Road, Nelson, Lancashire
YEARS OF OPERATION: 1967 Open; 1968-70 British League Division Two
FIRST MEETING: 5 August 1967
TRACK LENGTH: 300 yards
NICKNAME: 'Admirals'

Seedhill Stadium became the home of Nelson Football Club in 1905, when they moved a few hundred yards from the adjoining Nelson Cricket Ground, which they had previously shared. The club joined the Third Division (North) of the Football League in 1921/22, and won the divisional championship the following season to gain promotion to the Second Division. The club then constructed a new 2,000-seater stand on the Carr Road side of the ground, while the old stand was dismantled and taken to Victory Park, the home of Balnoldswick FC. Nelson did not remain in the Football League for long though, their final season being 1930/31, and they eventually folded. After the Second World War, Nelson FC reformed and joined the

Lancashire Combination League. Mike Parker introduced stock cars and then speedway to Seedhill Stadium, constructing the track around the soccer pitch. The rather square track staged its first speedway meeting on 5 August 1967, when Goog Allan won The Olympiad. A further four open licence meetings were staged that year, before a team was assembled to join the British League Division Two in 1968. With a congested fixture list due to a late start, coupled with poor crowd levels, the team resigned from the venue and moved to the Odsal Stadium to complete their fixtures as Bradford Northern in 1970. The final meeting at Seedhill Stadium took place on 20 June that year, when Nelson beat Peterborough 56-22 in a Division Two fixture. At the time of the team's withdrawal from Nelson, they had completed just eight league fixtures. After the cessation of speedway, stock-car racing continued at Seedhill right up until 1978. The stadium was demolished in 1980, to make way for the M65 Blackburn-to-Colne road, with Nelson Football Club relocating to a Council-owned pitch a few hundred yards away, in Victoria Park. The site of the former stadium remains in place today, as an open area right beside the M65 (which was completed in 1983).

NEW BRIGHTON
ADDRESS: The Tower Ground, New Brighton, Cheshire
YEARS OF OPERATION: 1933-35 Open
TRACK LENGTH: 512 yards

The Tower Ground was part of an entertainment complex, dominated by a 621-foot tower (the New Brighton Tower was actually higher than the famous Blackpool Tower, which measures 518 feet). The dirt-track was constructed between the soccer pitch of New Brighton Football Club and a banked cycling track. New Brighton Tower FC actually had a brief spell as a Football League club for three seasons between 1898/99 and 1900/01. Dirt-track racing was staged at the venue between 1933 and 1935, on an open licence, with meetings promoted by Wirral Heath Motorcycle Club, under a restricted permit. Competitors were members of the Cheshire Centre ACU Affiliated Clubs. One of the programmes from 1934 states: 'Motor-cyclists wishing to compete must give all particulars of their name etc, to the secretary at least fifteen minutes before the start of the meeting. All competitors must pay an admission fee of 1/- to the stadium only – there is no entrance fee to race.' Oliver Hart is known to have taken his first rides at New Brighton Tower in 1935. The stadium saw more Football League action between 1946/47 and 1950/51, when New Brighton FC played their Third Division (North) matches there. The autumn of 1948 saw Cheshire Town Council give approval in principle to an application by the New Brighton Tower Amusement Co. to open a speedway track at the stadium. This was despite strong protests from local residents over the noise nuisance factor, and the track was subsequently refused a licence to run speedway in 1949. In the late 1960s, the speedway track had been covered in tarmac for use as a stock-car circuit. In 1973, a further proposal to reintroduce speedway to the venue came to nothing. By the end of the 1970s, the stadium was completely derelict. Rumour suggests that

The Tower Ground, New Brighton.

the football scenes for the John Huston film *Escape to Victory* (1981), which featured Pele, Bobby Moore, Osvaldo Ardiles, Michael Caine and Sylvester Stallone among others, were filmed at New Brighton Tower.

NEW CROSS
ADDRESS: New Cross Stadium,
Hornshay Street, Old Kent Road, London
YEARS OF OPERATION: 1934 National League and Reserve League; 1935-37 National League; 1938-39 National League Division One; 1945 Open; 1946 National League; 1947-53 National League Division One; 1959 Open; 1960-61 National League; 1963 Provincial League
FIRST MEETING: 18 April 1934
TRACK LENGTH: 262 yards (1934-53); 278 yards (1959-63)
NICKNAME: 'Lambs' (1934-35); 'Tamers' (1936); 'Rangers' (1937-63)
LEAGUE CHAMPIONS: 1938, 1948

Speedway arrived at New Cross in 1934, when Fred Mockford transferred his Crystal Palace side to what would affectionately become known as the 'Frying Pan'. This name arose because it was constructed inside the existing greyhound circuit and had banking running around its entire length. The opening meeting took place before a crowd of 15,000 spectators on 18 April 1934, when New Cross defeated West Ham 32-21 in a National League fixture. New Cross also entered a team in the Reserve League in that initial season of track action. New Cross hero Tom Farndon died two days after crashing at the stadium on 28 August 1935 – he was just twenty-five years old at the time. Top-flight speedway continued at the 'Frying Pan' until war interrupted proceedings in September 1939. The final pre-war meeting saw the home side lose 34-50 to Harringay in a Division

One encounter. The sport returned to the mini-track on 27 June 1945, when Jack Parker won the aptly named Victory Cup. That was the first of only five meetings held at the track that year. League action resumed in 1946, and carried on until falling attendances in the 1950s forced Mr.Mockford to announce the track's closure. The final meeting was staged on 10 June 1953, when New Cross and Bradford drew 42-42 in a Coronation Cup match. At the time of closure, New Cross had completed just one league fixture – a 38-46 defeat at Belle Vue. New Cross Stadium staged the first-ever stock-car meeting in Britain on 16 April 1954. Johnnie Hoskins reopened the track on 19 August 1959, when the Rangers beat Wimbledon 47-43 in the first of eight open licence meetings. Two seasons of National League action followed in 1960 and 1961, before Johnnie Hoskins pulled out; the stadium was devoid of speedway throughout 1962. The track saw its last action on 21 September 1961, when Ronnie Moore won the Supporters' Trophy. Wally Mawdsley and Pete Lansdale revived the track on 12 April 1963, when New Cross defeated Hackney 45-33 in a Southern League encounter. The Rangers subsequently entered the Provincial League, although the fans did not respond to the venture and, after completing seventeen league matches, New Cross closed down for good. The last-ever meeting was held on 2 August, when New Cross lost 37-41 to Poole in a league encounter. Greyhound racing ceased at the venue following a final meeting on 3 April 1969.

NEWCASTLE

ADDRESS: Brough Park Greyhound

The first New Cross Speedway programme, 1934.

Stadium, The Fossway, Byker, Newcastle-upon-Tyne

YEARS OF OPERATION: 1929 English Dirt-track League; 1930 Open; 1938-39 National League Division Two; 1945 Open; 1946 Northern League; 1947-51 National League Division Two; 1961-64 Provincial League; 1965-67 British League; 1968-70 British League Division One; 1975-83 National League; 1984 British League; 1986-87 National League; 1989-90 National League; 1991-94 British League Division Two; 1997-2000 British Premier League

FIRST MEETING: 17 May 1929

TRACK LENGTH: 440 yards (1929-30); 359 yards (1938-51); 361 yards (1961-94); 342 yards (1997-2000)

NICKNAME: 'Diamonds' (1938-39; 1947-48; 1950-84; 1987-2000); 'Brough' (1946); 'Magpies' (1949); 'Federation Specials' (1986)

LEAGUE CHAMPIONS: 1964, 1976, 1982, 1983
KNOCK-OUT CUP WINNERS: 1976, 1982
SUPERNATIONAL WINNERS: 1982, 1983
GOLD CUP WINNERS: 1991, 1992

Brough Park Stadium was built in 1910, and was originally a horseracing course and park. Greyhound racing was first held at the stadium on 23 June 1928, with a crowd of 5,000 in attendance. Dirt-track meetings in 1929 were promoted by Newcastle Motor Racing Club Ltd, with the opening meeting going ahead on 17 May. After participating in the English Dirt-track League that season, the team dropped out of league racing in 1930, with open licence events being held instead. The track went silent following a scratch race event on 4 July 1930, and would remain that way

for seven full years. Having played two exhibition matches in February 1936, Newcastle Rugby League Club were based at Brough Park for the 1936/37 and 1937/38 seasons. Their first competitive game was against Huddersfield on 5 September 1936. Johnnie Hoskins revived speedway at the stadium in 1938, with the reopening meeting on 2 May being an English Speedway Trophy match versus Belle Vue juniors, which resulted in a 36-45 defeat. Newcastle subsequently took part in the National League Division Two, but the Second World War was to bring it all to an abrupt halt in 1939. That season had also seen the Diamonds partake in the Northern Section of the Union Cup, along with Edinburgh, Glasgow, Belle Vue II and Sheffield. The final pre-war meeting at Brough Park was in fact a Union Cup match versus Sheffield on

Brough Park Greyhound Stadium, Newcastle.

28 August, which the Diamonds won 48-35. After the war, Johnnie Hoskins (under the auspices of Brough Park Speedway Ltd) resumed with open licence fixtures in 1945, before Newcastle joined the Northern League the following year. Tragedy struck on 29 April 1946, when Bill Nichol crashed badly at Brough Park and died the following day. Later that same year, there was another fatality when Charlie Appleby died after crashing at the track on 7 October. There then followed two years of National League Division Two racing, before some surprise changes prior to the 1949 season, which saw the Newcastle team transferred to Ashfield, while the Middlesbrough side transferred to Newcastle! Those changes saw Johnnie Hoskins depart for Ashfield, with Harry Whitfield taking over the control at Brough Park, along with his fellow directors Stan Greatrex, Arthur Atkinson and J.B. McCreton. Thus Newcastle continued in National League Division Two, although their nickname was changed to Magpies – albeit for one season only. A change of management saw Archie McCulloch running the show in 1950, when the famous Magpies moniker was brought back by popular demand. A further change of promotion in 1951 saw J.S. Smith take over at Brough Park, with Roy Dook installed as technical adviser. The track closed at the end of that season and remained shut for nine years. The final meeting had gone ahead on 24 September 1951, when a Division Two double-header saw Newcastle lose 28-56 to Motherwell, before losing 37-46 to Oxford. Promoter Mike Parker resurrected the Diamonds in 1961, with Provincial League action

for the speedway-starved folk of Newcastle. Prior to any league racing, the reopening meeting saw the Diamonds beat Wolverhampton 48-30 in a challenge match. Four seasons later (in 1965), the Diamonds became founder members of the British League, upon the merger of the Provincial and National Leagues. In 1970, a change on the promoting front saw Ian Hoskins running the show on behalf of Allied Presentations Ltd, but the following year the promotion exchanged the Newcastle licence with Division Two Reading. The stadium directors, however, refused to allow lower league racing at Brough Park, with the licence subsequently being transferred to Sunderland. What turned out to have been the final meeting of Newcastle's British League era had been staged on 12 October 1970, when Ole Olsen won the Northumbrian Open Championship. Speedway returned to Brough Park in 1975, with Ian Thomas and George Graham as the new promoters. The Newcastle side took their place in the new National League, having taken the licence back from defunct Sunderland. The reopening meeting took place on 31 March, when the Diamonds beat Teesside 48-30 in the Tyne-Tees Television Trophy. With George Graham stepping down, Brian Larner linked wth Ian Thomas as co-promoter in 1976. Eighteen-year-old Chris Prime died after crashing at the track on 3 April 1978 – this being the third fatality at Brough Park. In 1980, the track was used by the homeless Berwick side for two National League matches, and one Knock-out Cup fixture. The track was again used by Berwick in 1981, for two Knock-out

Cup meetings. Robin Stannard joined Ian Thomas and Brian Larner as co-promoter in 1984, as the Diamonds rejoined the higher echelons of the British League. However, at the end of the season, the track again closed down, with the final meeting being the Spencer Oliver Farewell Trophy on 1 October, which Hans Nielsen won after beating Phil Crump in a run-off for the title. After a year's break, promoter John Turner reopened the track on 31 March 1986 with a challenge match versus Stoke. Unfortunately, the meeting was abandoned after three heats, due to heavy rain, with the Federation Specials losing 5-13 (the team was so nicknamed that year having been sponsored by the local brewery). Eric Stead took over as promoter at Brough Park in 1987, but the track again closed, following an Inter-League challenge match versus

Brough Park opening meeting programme, 1929.

Sheffield (lost 36-42) on 28 September that year. Brough Park was not closed to speedway for long, however, the shale sport returning on 26 March 1989, when Newcastle lost 43-53 to Edinburgh in a challenge match. The new promoters were Barry Wallace and Richard Bailey on behalf of Spectake Ltd. Another promotional change in 1991 saw Richard Bailey and Bill Reay heading a large management committee. Wayne Garratt had a fatal crash at Brough Park on 13 September 1992, succumbing to the injuries he had sustained two weeks later, on 28 September. Richard Bailey was joined by Trevor Barnes as co-promoter in 1994, but the track was to close once again at the end of the season. The final meeting was a British League Division Two match versus Sheffield on 25 September 1994, which the Diamonds won 52-44. A further meeting, featuring the George English Trophy and the Chris Prime Trophy, was scheduled for 2 October but was rained off. Despite efforts to restage the meeting, a suitable date could not be arranged with the stadium owner. After two more years of inactivity, promoters George English and Dave Rowland, on behalf of Newspeed Ltd, relaunched speedway at Brough Park on 30 March 1997, when Newcastle beat Berwick 51-39 in the Tyne-Tweed Trophy. Including the initial opening in 1929, this latest venture was the ninth time the track has opened. The start of the 2000 season saw Darryl Illingworth link up as a co-promoter with George English and Dave Rowland.

NEWCASTLE

ADDRESS: Gosforth Park, Great North Road, Newcastle-upon-Tyne
YEARS OF OPERATION: 1929 Open;

Gosforth Park, Newcastle-upon-Tyne.

1930 Northern League; 1931 Open
FIRST MEETING: 1 June 1929
TRACK LENGTH: 440 yards

Gosforth Park was originally home to Newcastle Rugby Union Club. In 1929, a circuit was constructed at the venue by Tyneside Speedways Ltd, to be used for dirt-track racing. The 440-yard track was banked to a height of three feet on the bends, while the stands could cater for 3,000 people, with another 15,000 on the terracing. The opening meeting was staged on 1 June 1929 but, sadly, it has not proved possible to locate any results. A side was entered in the Northern League in 1930 but, following the final meeting of the season on 3 October, Tyneside Speedways Ltd decided to go into voluntary liquidation on the advice of their solicitors – although all creditors were subsequently paid in full. Dirt-track racing was reintroduced on 29 July 1931, when an experimental meeting was held – no appearance money was paid, no times were given, no lights were used, no stars were engaged and no stunts were staged! Despite this, a crowd of some 2,500 paid 6d and 1/- for admittance, although the promoters claimed to have made only a small profit. The experiment was obviously deemed to be a failure, and was the last dirt-track meeting at the venue. There was no more of the cinder sport after 1931, with greyhound racing opening at the stadium on 21 May 1932. Greyhound racing ceased following a final meeting on 7 August 1987, after which the site was demolished and redeveloped.

NEWPORT
ADDRESS: Somerton Park, Newport
YEARS OF OPERATION: 1964 Provincial League; 1965-67 British League; 1968-74

British League Division One; 1975-76 British League; 1977 National League
FIRST MEETING: 17 April 1964
TRACK LENGTH: 376 yards (1964-71); 413 yards (1972); 390 yards (1973-76); 416 yards (1977)
NICKNAME: 'Wasps' (1964-72); 'Dragons' (1977) (Note: Newport did not use a nickname from 1973 to 1976 inclusive)
KNOCK-OUT CUP WINNERS: 1964

Newport County Football Club were formed in 1912, and played at Somerton Park from their formation. Grass-track racing, run by Newport Motor Club, was staged at Somerton Park midway through 1928, but petered out after a few months. A further grass-track meeting is known to have been staged on 14 June 1930, when Idris Jones was triumphant in the 500cc Class. Greyhound racing first arrived at the venue in 1932. Following a final greyhound meeting in 1963, the ground was sold to the Council, who then leased it to speedway promoters Charles Foot and Mike Parker. Jon Erskine constructed the track and everything was in place for the opening meeting on 17 April 1964, when a crowd of 10,000 people saw Newport Wasps lose 38-40 to Cradley Heath in a Southern League fixture. Having operated in the Provincial League in their opening season, Newport became founder members of the British League in 1965. A change of promotion saw Bill Bridgett link with Mike Parker in 1966, with Ken Sharples installed as speedway manager. Following the death of Ken in a car crash during the 1967 season, Eddie Glennon joined the promotional team of Bill Bridgett and Mike Parker at the start of the 1968 campaign. However, a terrible repeat tragedy saw Glennon die in a car crash midway through the season. Bob Radford was installed as speedway manager in 1969, prior to a change of pro-

Somerton Park, Newport.

motion in 1970, when Pete Lansdale, Pat Tapson, Wally Mawdsley and John Richards took over. 1971 saw Pete Lansdale and Pat Tapson in charge at Newport, with Maurice Morley acting as speedway manager, while Wally Mawdsley and John Richards concentrated on their operation at Exeter. A further change on the promotional side occurred in 1973, with the match programme listing Wally Mawdsley as promoter at Somerton Park on behalf of Brendon Motors, with Maurice Morley still on board as speedway manager. In 1977, Newport's team and British League licence were transferred to Bristol in time for the grand opening at Eastville Stadium. That left Newport to continue on with National League racing under the promotion of Maurice Morley, with the new nickname of Dragons. Much of the Newport fan-base disappeared to follow many of the ex-Wasps who were riding for Bristol, with the result that the shale sport was not seen again at Somerton Park after 1977. The final meeting at the venue was staged on 7 October, when Newport lost 36-42 to Eastbourne in a league encounter. The final football match at the stadium went ahead on 22 June 1993, when a large crowd witnessed a Newport County Past *v*. Present match. Newport County FC had enjoyed three spells in the Football League during their time at Somerton Park: 1920/21 to 1930/31, 1932/33 to 1938/39 and 1946/47-1987/88. By October 1993, the bulldozers had moved in and the stadium made way for a housing estate, but not before Tim Stone had acquired the grandstand seating, which he would eventually use when he relaunched the Wasps at Queensway Meadows in 1997.

NEWPORT

ADDRESS: Hayley Stadium, Plover Close, Longditch Road, Queensway Meadows, Newport

YEARS OF OPERATION: 1997 British Premier League and British Amateur League; 1998-2000 British Premier League and British Conference League

FIRST MEETING: 4 May 1997

TRACK LENGTH: 285 metres

NICKNAME: 'Wasps' (The Amateur League side of 1997 were called 'Western Warriors', while the Conference League team from 1998-2000 were known as 'Mavericks')

LEAGUE CHAMPIONS: Newport's main team has never won a league championship, although the Conference League side was triumphant in 1999.

PREMIER NATIONAL TROPHY WINNERS: 1999

Long-time supporter Tim Stone brought speedway back to Newport with a purpose-built stadium on open fields adjoining an industrial estate. The seats used in the stand were acquired from the original stadium at Somerton Park. The opening meeting was held on 4 May 1997, when the Wasps entertained Exeter in a British Premier League fixture. However, the meeting was abandoned after seven heats because of rain, with the homesters leading 24-18 at the time. Two sides operated from the track that year, Newport joining forces with Exeter to enter a team in the British Amateur League. The home fixtures were equally split between the two tracks, with the team riding as the Western Warriors. Then stadium hosted its first Amateur League fixture on 30 May, when the homesters beat Mildenhall 39-37. This

Hayley Stadium, Newport.

venture proved to be a one-year operation, with Queensway Meadows staging the last such meeting on 12 October, when the Western Warriors defeated the M4 Raven Sprockets 40-38. Apart from running a Premier League team, Newport also entered the Conference League in 1998. The Mavericks, as the second team were called, staged their opening home match on 10 April, when they beat Mildenhall 54-36. With Tim Stone still at the helm as promoter, Newport have completed four seasons of Premier League action, as well as a year as a composite side in the Amateur League, plus three seasons of Conference League racing.

NEWTON HEATH

ADDRESS: Newton Heath Training Track, Williams Road, off Dean Lane, Newton Heath, Manchester

YEARS OF OPERATION: 1950 Training; 1951 Open and Training; 1952 Training; 1953 Open and Training; 1954-55 Training; 1957 Training

TRACK LENGTH: 320 yards

NICKNAME: 'Heathens'

Situated near Newton Heath railway station, a training track was constructed on a huge disused tip by former rider Ernie Appleby in 1950. The circuit could be found by taking the Oldham Road from Manchester, before turning left down Dean Lane, where an entrance would appear after 200 yards on the right-hand side. This led to the track, which was located on top of the biggest cinder tip in the area. The track initially had no safety fence, but a solid one was constructed later on. Trainees were warned to approach the bottom bends with caution, as a particularly wide over-slide would send the rider flying down a steep slope. The circuit was used for twice-weekly training sessions at a cost of 10/- per day, with a machine also available for hire. A Newton Heath Heathens versus Ainsdale Gulls training track match took place on 17 February 1951, and resulted in a 46-34 victory to the visitors. The meeting was controlled by Bruce Booth, who also supplied helmet covers and flags. In 1952, Peter Williams was awarded a diploma at the training track, prior to signing for Belle Vue after being watched by Alice Hart. Cliff Hindle was also discovered while riding at Newton Heath, in 1952. Nigel Boocock first rode at Newton Heath in 1954 and, after three impressive practice sessions on borrowed bikes, he was instructed to purchase his own equipment. Tink Maynard used the track for practice in 1955. In 1956 the track was reconstructed, when burnt coal dust was used on the surface and topped off with a shale dressing. There is no record of activity at the circuit after training sessions in 1957.

NEWTONGRANGE
ADDRESS: Victoria Park Stadium, Newtongrange, Midlothian
YEARS OF OPERATION: 1928 Training; 1950-51 Open; 1952 Training; 1970 Open; 1973 Open
TRACK LENGTH: 430 yards
NICKNAME: 'Rockets' (1950-52); 'Saints' (1970); 'Monarchs' (1973)

Victoria Park was the home of Scottish junior football club Newtongrange Star. Full details remain sketchy, but Walter Elliott was reported to have tested a new Scott on the Newtongrange track in 1928. After reaching an agreement with the Scottish Speedway Riders

Club, the track was made available for weekday training purposes in 1950. On 2 December 1950, Newtongrange lost 24-45 to Bothwell in a challenge match. Jimmy Turner, Don Cuppleditch and Harry Darling regularly used the track for practice in 1951. On 27 October 1951, Newtongrange beat The Rest 44-38, in a challenge match. Speedway returned to Victoria Park on 27 May 1970, when Newtongrange Saints beat Berwick 39-37 in a challenge match. A total of seven meetings were staged that year (plus one other was rained off), under the promotion of Lothian Speedways, who were better known as Danny Taylor and Walter Elliot. The final match of the 1970 venture was held on 15 July, when the homesters were held to a 39-39 draw by King's Lynn Starlets. Promoted by Newtongrange Speedway

The programme from the re-opening meeting, 1970.

Victoria Park Stadium, Newtongrange.

Promotions (James Wallace and James Beaton), the shale sport returned to the venue for a series of open licence meetings in 1973. What was planned as the opener on 30 May versus Teesside fell victim to the weather, with the Diamond Jubilee Challenge Trophy versus Birmingham on 6 June becoming the first meeting. This resulted in a 38-40 reverse for the Newtongrange side, who now rode as the Monarchs. A further three meetings were staged in 1973, the last of which resulted in a 36-42 defeat at the hands of Barrow on 27 June. After the departure of speedway, Victoria Park was used for stock-car racing, although by 1994 the site of the stadium had been levelled for redevelopment.

NORTHAMPTON
ADDRESS: Northampton Greyhound Stadium, South Bridge, Northampton

YEARS OF OPERATION: 1929-30 Open
FIRST MEETING: 23 September 1929
TRACK LENGTH: 336 yards

Greyhound racing was first held at Northampton Greyhound Stadium on 7 April 1928. Dirt-track racing was introduced to the stadium by W. Ambrose and O.S. Ambrose, who constructed the track inside the greyhound circuit. On 18 September 1929, prior to the opening meeting, Nobby Kendrick gave the cinder track a trial run and it was described as very smooth, with acute turns. The track, bathed under floodlights, was declared open by W. Harvey-Reeves – in the absence of the Mayor – on 23 September 1929, when a crowd of almost 4,000 saw Billy Ellmore triumph in the Flying Sixteen event. On 18 June 1930, a meeting between Northampton and Wolverhampton was washed out by torrential rain and never re-staged. For some time before this, there had been numerous complaints about noise from the nearby general hospital and this turned out to be the last trace of the cinder sport at the venue. What had actually been the last meeting was staged the week previously, on 11 June, but the results of the scratch race event that took place have been lost in the mists of time. After the decision to abandon dirt-track activity, the stadium quickly reverted to staging three dog meetings per week. A final greyhound meeting went ahead at the stadium on 31 October 1964. A proposal to reintroduce speedway to the venue in 1965 fell through when the site was sold for industrial development.

NORWICH

ADDRESS: The Firs Stadium, Aylsham Road, Norwich, Norfolk
YEARS OF OPERATION: 1931-36 Open; 1937-39 National League Division Two; 1945 Open; 1946 Northern League; 1947-51 National League Division Two; 1952-56 National League Division One; 1957-64 National League; 1965 Training
FIRST MEETING: 13 September 1931
TRACK LENGTH: 425 yards
NICKNAME: 'Stars' (1937-64)
ACU CUP WINNERS: 1946
NORTHERN TROPHY WINNERS: 1946
LEAGUE CHAMPIONS: 1950, 1951
NATIONAL TROPHY (DIVISION TWO) WINNERS: 1951
NATIONAL TROPHY WINNERS: 1955, 1963

In 1930, the site that was to become the Firs Stadium was just a field, where local contractor Harry Pointer staged two grass-speedway meetings on 18 August and 14 September. The racing aroused so much interest that Mr Pointer had to put

up a wire fence in order to keep the crowds back! Incidentally, Geoff Pymar was a spectator at the opening meeting, but rode in the second one that was held. Cinders were put down late in 1931, turning the circuit into a dirt-track, and the first such meeting went ahead on 13 September, when Norwich beat Staines 33-26 in a challenge match. Further team meetings followed against Cambridge and Dagenham. Greyhound racing first took place at the stadium on 30 July 1932, but the sport did not last long at the venue, with the last meeting being held on 14 January 1935. Just one dirt-track meeting was staged in 1935, on Easter Monday 21 April. Only one meeting was run in 1936, on 13 September, when Putt Mossman brought his Speedway and Rodeo Circus to the track. Twenty events were staged during the meeting, including team races, match races and

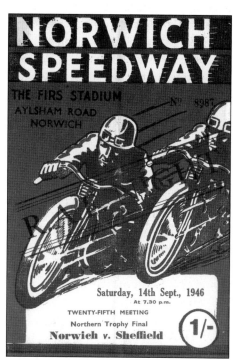

Norwich programme, 1946.

midget-car racing. Having run without an ACU permit since opening, Norwich obtained the necessary documentation in 1937, when Peter McMahon took over the running of the track under the guise of Norwich Speedways Ltd. Max Grosskreutz was installed as speedway manager, and Norwich Stars subsequently entered the National League Division Two that year, with the first official meeting at the track going ahead on 1 May. Without doubt, Arthur Reynolds was the top rider at the stadium in the grass and dirt-track days, but he had ridden under an assumed name until the track got an ACU permit, then reverted to his real name, Fred Leavis. Norwich were offered the chance of replacing Bristol in Division One in 1939, but turned it down, preferring to continue in Division Two until the outbreak of war curtailed their operation. The Stars also took part in the Southern Section of the Union Cup that season, alongside Bristol and Hackney. In 1945, the track reopened under the promotion of Ernie Howard, with Dicky Wise taking the position of speedway manager. A series of open licence meetings were run that year. The Stars rode in the Northern League in 1946, before rejoining the National League Division Two in 1947. Tragedy struck at the Norfolk circuit on 16 August 1947, when thirty-nine-year-old Cyril Anderson was killed in an accident. A change on the management front saw C.H. Sutton join Ernie Howard as co-promoter in 1948. There was another fatality at the track that season though, when Billy Wilson died two days after crashing on 3 July. In 1950, Fred Evans took over from Dicky Wise as speedway manager. A third

rider was killed at the stadium on 1 July that year, when Jock Shead of Halifax succumbed to injuries sustained in a crash. The Stars gained promotion to the top flight after winning the Division Two championship in 1951, although the shine was taken off the success when twenty-one-year-old Bob Howes died in a training crash in November. F.J. Andrews became promoter in 1954, with Gordon Parkins taking over the position of speedway manager at The Firs in 1955, replacing Fred Evans. A final change of promotion saw Harry Wharton take over in 1956, and he was to run the track along with speedway manager Gordon Parkins until its untimely closure. In 1958, Norwich also ran a team in the unfinished Junior League, which also comprised Poole II, Swindon II and Yarmouth. Twenty-eight-year-old Belle Vue rider Derek 'Tink' Maynard became the fifth racer to die after crashing at the venue on 23 July 1960. Having hurtled into the fence and split his helmet in two, 'Tink' sadly passed away in hospital the following day. The track had enjoyed good support over a thirteen-year spell in British speedway's top league, so it came as a shock when it was announced that the stadium was to be sold for housing development. The final meeting at the venue was held on 31 October 1964, when 'Tich' Read won the Supporters' Club Trophy. Prior to the cement mixers moving in, a few training sessions were held at the track in 1965.

NORWICH
ADDRESS: The Firs Stadium Car Park, Aylsham Road, Norwich, Norfolk
YEARS OF OPERATION: 1956 Training; 1959 Training
TRACK LENGTH: 300 yards

During the winter of 1956, when the main circuit was too wet for practice, several trainees marked out and used a tight 300-yard track on the stadium's cinder-based car park. Tony Clarke first rode a speedway bike at a training session in The Firs car park in 1959.

NOTTINGHAM

ADDRESS: White City Stadium, Trent Lane, Colwick Road, Nottingham
YEARS OF OPERATION: 1929 Open; 1930-31 Southern League; 1933 National League; 1934 Open; 1936-37 Provincial League; 1938 National League Division Two
FIRST MEETING: 23 March 1929
TRACK LENGTH: 440 yards (1929-31); 412 yards (1933-34); 380 yards (1936-38)
NICKNAME: 'Lacemen'

In the spring of 1927, the Nottingham Tornadoes Motor Club – of which Fred Strecker was a founder member – acquired the land on which the Olympic Grounds stood, to use for grass-track racing. At the time, the site was situated in a rural area, with nearby tennis courts providing the only company for the riders. The first grass-track meeting took place at the site on 28 July 1928, when F. Sisson won the 600cc Class event. A final grass-track meeting was held at the venue on 1 September that year, after which plans were afoot to construct a dirt-track circuit. Operating as Olympic Speedways Ltd, promoter W.M. Haslam had a dirt-track in place by February 1929, with many riders turning up to practise. The opening meeting took place on 23 March 1929, when 9,000 spectators saw George Wigfield win the senior race. Nottingham joined the Southern League in 1930, but were

suspended briefly by the ACU for having a lack of accommodation for the ambulance men. In July 1931, Nottingham resigned from the Southern League, having completed nineteen matches. The reason for their withdrawal was due to so many riders being injured, they simply could not raise a team. The season had also been marred by tragedy, with New Zealander John Garmson killed in a crash at the venue. Greyhound enthusiast Frank Parker, a Chesterfield land owner, took over the running of Olympic Speedway in 1931, staging the first dog meeting on 21 December 1931. Following a greyhound meeting on 7 September 1932, Frank Parker pulled down the original stadium and rebuilt it as the White City, before entering a Nottingham team in the National League of 1933. Greyhound racing also resumed in 1933, with the reopening meeting going ahead on 24 June. Nottingham entered the Provincial League in 1936, under the same management as Cardiff. The failure of the Welsh track put the company into difficulties, although Nottingham were saved when the bosses at Hackney took over the running at Trent Lane. A series of open events were also run in 1936, including visits from teams entitled Warwickshire (on 12 August) and South London (19 September). In 1938, the running of the track was taken over by Sheffield Speedways Ltd, with Arthur Atkinson in the driving seat. However, the last-ever meeting at the stadium took place on 31 May that year, after which Leeds took over the Lacemen's remaining National League Division Two fixtures. The speedway track was later covered in concrete and used as a parade ring for greyhounds in wet weather. In 1970, the stadium was sold for redevelopment, with a final greyhound meeting going ahead on 12 September that year.

OXFORD

ADDRESS: Cowley Stadium, Sandy Lane, Cowley, Oxford
YEARS OF OPERATION: 1939-41 Open; 1949-50 National League Division Three; 1951-52 National League Division Two; 1953 Southern League; 1954-56 National League Division Two; 1957-64 National League; 1965-67 British League; 1968-74 British League Division One; 1975 British League; 1976-83 National League; 1984-90 British League; 1991-92 British League Division One; 1993-94 British League Division Two; 1995-96 British Premier League; 1997 British Premier League and Amateur League; 1998-2000 British Elite League
FIRST MEETING: 8 April 1939
TRACK LENGTH: 370 yards (1939-41); 354 yards (1949-73); 350 yards (1974-83); 325 yards (1984-2000)
NICKNAME: 'Cheetahs' (1949-71 and 1976-2000); 'Rebels' (1972-75); 'Cubs' (The Amateur League team of 1997)
LEAGUE CHAMPIONS: 1950, 1964, 1985, 1986, 1989
NATIONAL TROPHY (DIVISION THREE) WINNERS: 1950
NATIONAL TROPHY WINNERS: 1964
BRITANNIA SHIELD WINNERS: 1964
KNOCK-OUT CUP WINNERS: 1985, 1986 (shared with Cradley Heath)
LEAGUE CUP WINNERS: 1986 (shared with Cradley Heath)
PREMIERSHIP WINNERS: 1987
GOLD CUP WINNERS: 1989

Prior to becoming Cowley Stadium, the site had been used for scrambles and side-car events during the preceding two years. Greyhound racing was first held at the stadium's opening on 31 March 1939. Dirt-track racing also arrived at the venue in 1939, and was promoted by Oxford Motorcycle Speedway Club, who moved their operation from their previous circuit at Sandford-on-Thames. The first meeting at the venue was staged on 8 April 1939, when Roy Duke was triumphant in the Oxford Motorcycle Speedway Club Championship. The circuit in those days was described as having a sandy-soil surface. George Bason later recalled that he rode at Oxford in 1939, for half-a-crown per point. A challenge match in that first year saw Oxford beat Wisbech 50-34 on 27 May. Five war-time meetings are known to have been staged at Cowley in 1940, the last of which was on 23 June. Two meetings were staged in 1941, on 4 May and 1 June. After the war, the track was reconstructed, and had banking added to a height of 9 inches on the bends, although the reopening meeting did not take place until 21 April 1949, when Oxford lost 37-47 to Hastings in a National League Division Three encounter. This meeting signified the birth of the Cheetahs, and their promoter at the time was a local man, Les Calcutt. Oxford moved into the National League Division Two in 1951, but sadly the man who pioneered the Cheetahs, Les Calcutt, died in August the following year. The Cheetahs dropped into the Southern League for one season in 1953, but were back in the National League Division Two in 1954, under the guidance of general manager John Deeley. Dickie Worth became promoter at Oxford in 1955.

Cowley Stadium, Oxford.

With the lack of tracks running throughout the country, Oxford became members of the eleven-team National League in 1957, with new man Ted Flanagan at the helm. A period of stability followed, the club remaining in the National League until a change of promotion in 1964 saw Cyril Melville and Rodney Rycroft take up the reigns. It was all change in 1965 as well, as Oxford became founder members of the British League, while there was a further alteration on the management set-up, with Danny Dunton installed as promoter. Bob Dugard became co-promoter in 1972, when the team nickname changed to Rebels. In 1975, the stadium owners were offered a large sum by Oxford City Council to sell the site for redevelopment. The team was subsequently transferred to White City for the opening of team racing at

the London venue in 1976, taking the Rebels moniker with them. Eventually, a campaign by Oxford fans saw a change of heart at Cowley and speedway continued, but in the new National League. Under the banner of Five Star (Speedway) Promotions, Tony Allsopp and Harry Bastable reintroduced the Cheetahs nickname in 1976, with Oxford remaining in the National League until the end of 1983. During that time there were several changes on the promotional side as follows: Chris Van Straaten (1978), Dan McCormick (1979), Bob Wasley (1980 to 1982) and Bernard Crapper alongside John Payne on behalf of Northern Sports (1983). In 1984, Messrs Crapper and Payne took Oxford back into the British League, when the club enjoyed a run of unsurpassed success. The stadium underwent major changes, with a super new grandstand and sports centre complex being opened in 1986. With the introduction of a riders' pay structure to British speedway in 1993, Oxford were unable to agree terms with star-man Hans Nielsen and dropped down to British League Division Two. Tony Mole became promoter at the track during the two years of Division Two racing, although Crapper and Payne remained on board as co-promoters. Upon the formation of the British Premier League in 1995, Chris Shears linked with Bernard Crapper and John Payne on the promotional side. Latterly, the club was promoted by Dave Pavitt and Keith Chapman in 1996, with Pavitt in sole control the following year, before Steve and Vanessa Purchase took the Cheetahs into the British Elite League in 1998, for what was the fiftieth consecutive year of track action at Cowley. A second team was stationed at Cowley in 1997, when Oxford Cubs competed in the British Amateur League. Their first meeting took place at the stadium on 25 May, when the Cubs defeated Berwick 42-36 in a league match that was staged as the second part of a double-header, which had earlier seen the Cheetahs entertain Edinburgh in a Premier League encounter. The Cubs venture only lasted for one season, ending with a double-header on 17 October which resulted in victories over the Anglian Angels (51-27) and the Western Warriors (48-30). To this day, Oxford Cheetahs remain in the top flight of British speedway, having now completed fifty-two successive seasons of racing at Cowley Stadium – which, with its tremendous grandstand, is one of the finest speedway venues in the country.

P

PAISLEY

ADDRESS: St Mirren Football Club, Love Street, Paisley, Renfrewshire
YEARS OF OPERATION: 1975-76 National League
FIRST MEETING: 5 April 1975
TRACK LENGTH: 391 metres
NICKNAME: 'Lions'

The stadium has been home to St Mirren Football Club since 1895. Greyhound racing was first staged at the venue on 14 October 1932. Promoters Neil MacFarlane and Joe Thurley introduced speedway to the stadium in 1975, with a very long and narrow track running around the football pitch. The opening meeting took place on 5 April 1975, when a crowd of 6,000 spectators saw the Paisley Lions defeat Birmingham 41-37 in a challenge match. Due to the combination of poor racing and an unsuccessful team, the crowds drifted away and before the end of the club's second season it was revealed that the track was in financial difficulty. What turned out to be the final meeting at Love Street was staged on 25 September 1976, when Paisley beat Boston 52-25 in a National League encounter.

PETERBOROUGH

ADDRESS: Eastfield Speed Track, Eastfield Road, Peterborough, Huntingdonshire
YEARS OF OPERATION: 1947-50 Open

Details for this track are sketchy, but it is believed to have had grass straights with

St Mirren Football Club, home of Paisley Speedway during 1975-76.

dirt on the bends, although grass speedway is known to have taken place at Eastfield Road in 1945 and 1946, when presumably it was an all-grass circuit. Peterborough riders are known to have worn a yellow race-jacket featuring a green 'P'. A challenge match was run on Sunday 3 August 1947, between Kitchen's Team and Hart's Team. A combined Norwich and Birmingham team rode against Middlesbrough on Sunday 17 August 1947, with the Middlesbrough team winning 57-27 – the meeting was apparently run with the approval of the Bishop of Peterborough! A match between Norwich and Yarmouth was run at the venue on 4 July 1948.

PETERBOROUGH

ADDRESS: East of England Showground, Alwalton, Peterborough, Huntingdonshire

YEARS OF OPERATION: 1970-74 British League Division Two; 1975-90 National League; 1991-94 British League Division Two; 1995 British Premier League; 1996 British Premier League and Conference League; 1997 British Elite League and Amateur League; 1998 British Premier League; 1999 British Elite League; 2000 British Elite League and Conference League

FIRST MEETING: 12 June 1970

TRACK LENGTH: 380 yards (1970-84); 388 yards (1995-2000)

NICKNAME: 'Panthers'; (The Conference /Amateur League teams of 1996-97 were known as 'Thundercats', while the Conference League side of 2000 were known as 'Pumas')

LEAGUE CHAMPIONS: 1992, 1998, 1999 (the Amateur League side also won their league in 1997)

KNOCK-OUT CUP WINNERS: 1992, 1999

PREMIERSHIP WINNERS: 1993

CRAVEN SHIELD WINNERS: 1999

East of England Showground, Peterborough.

Prior to speedway arriving at the impressive East of England Showground, planning permission had actually been approved to stage the sport at the nearby Fengate Greyhound Stadium. This plan never came to fruition, however, after complaints about possible noise nuisance from local residents. The sport eventually came to Peterborough in 1970, at the 100-acre East of England Showground, home of many huge agricultural shows and horse events throughout the year. The multi-track promotional group Allied Presentations Ltd (Len Silver, Reg Fearman, Ron Wilson, Danny Dunton and Maurice Littlechild), exchanged their open licence with the Division Two licence of Fred Osborn at Plymouth, and Peterborough Panthers was born. In front of over 3,000 people, the opening meeting at Alwalton was staged on 12 June 1970, when Peterborough beat Rayleigh

51-27 in a British League Division Two match. Peterborough continued in the British League Division Two until it became the new National League in 1975. Also that year there was a change of promotion, which saw Cowley Speedway Promotion Ltd take charge – although still with Danny Dunton running the show, as he had done on behalf of Allied Presentations Ltd since the start in 1970. Tragedy struck at the Showground when eighteen-year-old Stephen Defew died four days after an accident on 9 July 1977. There was further bad news when Craig Featherby was killed in a track crash at the stadium on 16 September 1983. Former Leicester promoter Martin Rogers took over the reigns at Peterborough in the winter of 1984. Rogers, along with his wife, Lin, were to run the club until the middle of 1988, when David Hawkins took over as promoter. The club ran into financial problems in the early 1990s, culminating in David Hawkins having his promoting licence suspended in 1991. The following season saw new promoters in the shape of Ramsden Sports Promotions Ltd (James Easter and Peter Oakes). Later on, in 1993, Peter Oakes was in sole charge of the club, following the departure of James Easter. The Panthers became members of the British Premier League in 1995, with the supporters enjoying their first taste of the world's top riders on a regular basis, prior to becoming founder members of the Elite League in 1997. During 1996 and 1997, two teams operated at the track, with Peterborough Thundercats also competing in the British Conference League. The first meeting for the new side was a double-header on 5 July 1996, which resulted in a 39-39 draw with Ryde, prior to a 48-29 victory over Reading Ravens. The Thundercats had actually been due to open against Ryde on 24 May, but the meeting fell foul to inclement weather. With a change of name to the British Amateur League in 1997, the Thundercats completed their second and final season, with their last meeting, another double-header, going ahead on 3 October. Both meetings resulted in wins for the homesters: 45-32 over the Western Warriors and 51-27 against Belle Vue Colts. In 1998, Jim Lynch joined the promoting team of Peter Oakes and Sarah Gudgeon, with the club dropping back into the Premier League due to the problems of trying to fit in home matches around the Grand Prix series. Having purchased Peter Oakes' share in Ramsden Sports Promotion Ltd, Ian Jarvis joined up with Jim Lynch as the promoting team in 1999, with the Panthers returning to the top

flight of Elite League racing. The 2000 season saw Peterborough enter a second team in the British Conference League. Riding with the nickname of Pumas, their opening meeting was a challenge match versus Boston on 21 April, which ended as a 40-50 defeat for the home side.

PETERBOROUGH
ADDRESS: Vicarage Farm Road, Peterborough, Huntingdonshire
YEARS OF OPERATION: 1976-77 Training
FIRST MEETING: 12 December 1976

This was a training track prepared by Peterborough Amateur Motorcycle Club in 1976. The Mayor of Peterborough officially opened the track on 12 December that year, when a demonstration event was held. The highlight of the day was a match race between Richard Greer and Tony Featherstone. Other riders known to have trained at the circuit included Trevor Charley, Andrew Buck and Paul Cooper.

PINEWOOD
ADDRESS: Pinewood Studios, Iver Heath, Nr Slough, Berkshire
YEARS OF OPERATION: 1948 Speedway Scene Filming
TRACK LENGTH: 200 yards

For the shooting of the Jack Lee film *Once a Jolly Swagman*, starring Dirk Bogarde, Bonar Colleano and Renee Asherson, most scenes were filmed at New Cross Stadium. Owing to other commitments, however, it was not always possible to use the Old Kent Road venue, so a speedway track based on the New Cross circuit was laid on a lot at Pinewood Studios. The makeshift cinder track was 600 ft long and 30 ft wide, with one bend having a 190 ft curve, while the other had a smaller radius of 85 ft. The New Cross pits were also reconstructed to the last detail. Alongside the track, a concrete roadway was laid for the camera car to follow the riders when filming was in progress. An aerial photograph of Pinewood Studios clearly shows the speedway track on a rear lot.

PLYMOUTH

ADDRESS: Pennycross Stadium, Pennycross, Plymouth, Devon
YEARS OF OPERATION: 1931 Open; 1932-34 National League; 1935 Open; 1936 Provincial League; 1937 Open; 1947-49 National League Division Three; 1950 National League Division Two; 1951 National League Division Three; 1952-53 Southern League; 1954 National League Division Two; 1959-60 Open; 1961-62 Provincial League; 1968-69 British League Division Two; 1970 Open
FIRST MEETING: 13 June 1931
TRACK LENGTH: 410 yards (1931-37); 400 yards (1947-51 and 1968); 413 yards (1952-54 and 1961-62 and 1969-70); 417 yards (1959-60)
NICKNAME: 'Panthers' (1936); 'Devils' (1947-54, 1962 and 1968-70); 'Drakes' (1960); 'Bulldogs' (1961)
NATIONAL TROPHY (SOUTHERN LEAGUE) WINNERS: 1952

Greyhound racing was first staged at Pennycross Stadium on 28 May 1928. After talk of dirt-track racing arriving in Plymouth as early as 1929, it was not until 1931 that Western Speedways Ltd (H.F. Hore) finally opened the track at Pennycross Stadium. Open licence meetings were staged in that initial year, the first of which saw Plymouth beat Exeter 32-21, in an inter-track challenge match on 13 June. In 1932, Plymouth also took part in the National Speedway Association Trophy, which was a league-style competition that preceded the National League Championship. Following three years of league action, Jack Coleback took over as promoter in 1935, staging open licence meetings to an average gate of 4,000 people. The first meeting under his control was held on 16 July, when Tiger Lewis won the Raven Trophy. A season of Provincial League racing followed in 1936, only for open licence events to return in 1937, although dates and details of this are sketchy. Following the war, Plymouth Devils were born, with the team partaking in the National League Division Three, under the management of Plymouth Sports Stadium Ltd. The reopening meeting took place on 24 April 1947, when George Bason won the Mayor Trophy. The team subsequently went from Division Three to Division Two and back again in 1951, but tragedy struck that year, when thirty-six-year-old Dick Jenkins crashed and died at the track on 3 May. After two years of Southern League action, the Devils were back in the National League Division Two, only to withdraw after only completing two league fixtures. The final meeting before closure was a qualifying round of the World Championship on 8 July 1954, which was won by Brian McKeown. The track remained shut until 27 March 1959, when Plymouth lost 47-49 to a Midlands Select'side. A further four open licence meetings were staged that year. These meetings were held under Western Promotions Ltd (Trevor Redmond and E. Netcott). A Cavalcade of Speed meeting was held at Pennycross Stadium on 6 June 1960, and although the programme did not feature speedway, some sidecar races were held. Two speedway meetings were staged by promoter Eric Salmon in 1960: versus Bristol in a Western Cup match on 8 September (36-36), and a qualifying round of the Provincial Riders' Championship on 15 September (won by Eric Hockaday). A further meeting against Exeter was mooted for 22 September, but it was never staged. It appeared from the programme of the first meeting versus Bristol, that there was some dilemma regarding the team nickname at the time, with the choice being between Drakes and Drummers. This was somewhat odd, as a drake's head was clearly depicted on the programme cover! Reopening on 31 March 1961, Plymouth lost 33-40 to Poole in the Easter Cup, prior to entering the Provincial League with a new Bulldogs moniker. Reverting back to the Devils nickname in 1962, promoter Bernard Curtiss continued with Provincial League racing, but at the end of the year the track was to close again. Presented by Westward Television, the final meeting went ahead on 4 October when Jimmy Squibb won the Champion of Champions Trophy, after beating Chris Blewett in a run-off for the title. Following a break of five years, promoter Fred Osborn reintroduced speedway to the stadium once again, making Plymouth founder members of British League Division Two. Their opening match was a league fixture against Weymouth on 31 May 1968, which the Devils won 41-36. The meeting had originally been scheduled for 24 May, but had to be rescheduled after falling victim to rain. Rather interestingly, the track had been covered in tarmac prior to 1968, and in order to stage speedway a top dressing of silver sand had to be applied to provide a suitable surface. During the

Plymouth Speedway programme, 1953.

1969/70 winter, the tarmac was ripped up and a proper shale surface was laid for the 1970 season; however, the track was to only stage eleven open licence events, as promoter Fed Osborn had exchanged his Division Two licence with the newly opening Peterborough. Attendances dropped off badly in 1970, and the last-ever meeting at the venue was staged on 17 July that year, when Mac Woolford won the Bromley Bowl. Greyhound racing ceased at Pennycross Stadium in 1972, after which the area was redeveloped; it is today covered by a factory.

PONTYPRIDD
ADDRESS: Taff Vale Park, Pontypridd, Mid Glamorgan
YEARS OF OPERATION: 1929 Open

P

FIRST MEETING: 20 May 1929
TRACK LENGTH: 440 yards

Pontypridd were admitted to the Rugby League in the summer of 1926, and played at Taff Vale Park from 1926/27 to 1927/28. Pontypridd's last match at the venue took place versus Oldham on 22 October 1928. Prior to that, two international rugby matches had taken place at the stadium – Wales *v*. Australia on 10 December 1921, and Wales *v*. England on 12 April 1926. Frank Moody, a cruiserweight Lonsdale belt holder, together with J.E. Brooks, the chairman of the Welsh Boxing Association, were the men who showed great enterprise in bringing the cinder sport to Taff Vale Park in 1929. The opening dirt-track meeting took place on 20 May 1929, when Cardiff drew 26-26, with The Valleys in a challenge match. Incidentally, that opening meeting went ahead immediately after a Glamorgan County Cricket Club match, which had taken place at Pontypridd on the same day. Nineteen open licence meetings are known to have been staged in that initial year of dirt-track racing at the venue. There are rumours that dirt-track racing may have been staged at the venue in 1930, but as yet nothing definite has come to light. Grass-track racing was staged at the venue before and after the Second World War (1934-35 and 1945-48), with the meetings being promoted by Pontypridd and District Motorcycle Club. The stadium site is now used as a school rugby ground.

POOLE
ADDRESS: Poole Stadium, Wimborne Road, Poole, Dorset

YEARS OF OPERATION: 1948-51 National League Division Three; 1952-55 National League Division Two; 1956 National League Division One; 1957 Open; 1958-59 National League; 1960-63 Provincial League; 1964 Provincial League and Metropolitan League; 1965-67 British League; 1968-74 British League Division One; 1975-84 British League; 1985-90 National League; 1991-94 British League Division One; 1995-96 British Premier League; 1997-2000 British Elite League
FIRST MEETING: 26 April 1948
TRACK LENGTH: 420 yards (1948-59); 380 yards (1960-89); 406 yards (1990-94); 396 yards (1995); 328 yards (1996-2000)
NICKNAME: 'Pirates' (1948-84 and 1987-2000); 'Wildcats' (1985-86)
LEAGUE CHAMPIONS: 1951, 1952, 1955, 1961, 1962, 1969, 1989, 1990, 1994
NATIONAL TROPHY (DIVISION TWO) WINNERS: 1952, 1955
KNOCK-OUT CUP WINNERS: 1990

The stadium, which was home to Poole Town Football Club, originally opened on 26 August 1933, for a Western League match versus Wells City. Speedway was first proposed at the stadium as early as 1937, and then again in 1947, when Poole Borough Council turned down an offer of £1,000 from Poole Motor Club to run the sport. Prior to speedway finally being introduced in 1948, the stadium had contained a tarmac cycle track. In 1948, Herby Hayden, Cliff Brewer and Jack Crutcher were successful in finally bringing the shale sport to Poole when the Council accepted £1,000 per year rent for a ten-year lease. The deal also meant that the promoters were responsible for all repairs, plus the rates, while the Council also got 2.5 per cent of the total gross takings. The original safety fence was constructed from the tops of Morrison shelters, but the promoters were not allowed to employ labour to paint it, so it was done in one day by 200 volunteer schoolboys. The track was opened by the Mayor of Poole in front of 6,000 spectators on 26 April 1948, when Poole took on Yarmouth in a National Trophy match. Poole won the meeting 74-32, but the meeting was marred by a crash on the first bend of the very first heat, when Reg Craven suffered severe head injuries. He sadly died eight days later, on 4 May. The stadium subsequently staged its first floodlit meeting on 27 September 1948, when the Pirates faced Exeter in a National League Division Three fixture. The running of the track was taken over in 1951 by Len Matchan and Geoffrey

Bravery, after Cliff Brewer had unsuccessfully tried to get the rent reduced. Having gained promotion, Poole raced in Division Two from 1952. On 9 May 1955, twenty-seven-year-old Johnny Thomson crashed and fractured his left femur at the track. Tragically, four days later he suffered an embolism and died in Poole Hospital. Poole were again promoted in 1956, when the Wimborne Road circuit staged top-flight racing for the first time. The year was again filled with sadness however, when Malcolm Flood died the day after a track crash at the stadium on 2 April. Having operated in all three divisions of the National League since opening, it was a surprise when Poole withdrew altogether in March 1957. Petrol rationing was cited as the reason for the track's closure, although Jack Crutcher subsequently

Poole Stadium, Dorset.

reopened the track in July to run seven open licence meetings, having purchased the share capital of Poole Speedway Ltd from Geoffrey Bravery and Len Matchan. The first of the seven meetings went ahead on 29 July, when Poole lost 45-51 to Rayleigh in a challenge match. Also that year, Rayleigh ran two of their home National League matches at the stadium – on 2 September (versus Norwich) and 23 September (versus Belle Vue). Rather interestingly, they chose to use the name Rayleigh Pirates for these two meetings. Rayleigh promoter Vic Gooden and R. Dixey reached an agreement to take over at Poole in 1958, with the Pirates rejoining the National League. Poole also had a team participating in the unfinished Junior League that year. The Poole licence was transferred to Ipswich in 1960, and that heralded the arrival of legendary promoter Charles Knott, who took the Pirates into the Provincial League. Mr Knott set about modernising the stadium, and this included two new grandstands, as well as the laying of a new speedway track inside a greyhound circuit. At the same time, the starting gate was moved, from the west to the east side of the stadium, while the pits were relocated on the second bend. Greyhound racing was introduced to the venue in 1961, with the first such meeting being run on 8 May. A new 1,400-seater grandstand was opened by Sir Stanley Rous on 19 August 1961, prior to a Southern League football match between Poole and Hastings United. In 1964, a team called Newpool – a composite side made up of the juniors of Newport and Poole – entered the Metropolitan. However, the motley side failed to com-

plete any matches at Poole Stadium, and the league table ended in disarray, with none of the competing sides finishing their fixtures. After four years of Provincial League racing, Poole became founder members of the British League in 1965. Aged eighty-four, Charles Knott died at the end of the 1974 campaign, with Charles Foot continuing on with the running of the circuit. Twenty-six-year-old Kevin Holden died after crashing at the track on 27 April 1977. Promotional changes in 1979 saw Reg Fearman and Terry Chandler take charge of the Pirates, on behalf of Poole Stadium Ltd. After twenty years of top-flight British speedway at the venue, the future of the track was put in jeopardy when Poole Stadium Ltd went into liquidation in January 1985. In March 1985, however, promoters Mervyn Stewkesbury and Pete Ansell moved their Weymouth operation to Wimborne Road, and Poole took over the Wildcats moniker. What followed was six successful years of National League racing, although the Wildcats nickname reverted back to Pirates in 1987. In July 1990, the track was completely reconstructed, making it longer and wider to encompass the area that had formed the greyhound circuit. With the amalgamation of the leagues in 1991, Poole went back into top-flight racing, joining the new British League Division One, with the duo of Mervyn Stewkesbury and Pete Ansell still promoting under the guise of Betterment Properties (Leisure Activities) Ltd. Poole Town FC played their last-ever game at the stadium on 23 April 1994, before moving to ground-share with Hamworthy United. The track completed its fiftieth consecutive year of speedway in 1997, having become founder members of the new British Elite League. Later that year, further stadium changes culminated in the opening of a superb new glass-fronted grandstand on the back straight side of the circuit, while the track itself was upgraded to gain FIM approval. A new promotional team of Matthew Ford and Michael Golding joined forces with Pete Ansell in 1999, as Poole continued to go from strength to strength with some of the biggest crowds in modern-day British speedway.

PORTMARNOCK

ADDRESS: Portmarnock Raceway, Dublin
YEARS OF OPERATION: 1970 Training; 1986 Long-track
TRACK LENGTH: 800 yards

In preparation for the reopening of speedway at Shelbourne Park in 1970, a training track was constructed at Portmarnock Raceway by the Irish Speedway Racing Club. The track opened on 23 March that year, and was used regularly thereafter by Irish riders. An American-style long-track meeting was staged at the venue on 30 August 1986, when Tim Brown won the Chester Point of Ayre Club event.

PORTSMOUTH

ADDRESS: Wessex Stadium, Copnor Gardens, Portsmouth, Hampshire
YEARS OF OPERATION: 1929-30 Open
FIRST MEETING: 10 August 1929
TRACK LENGTH: 382 yards

A track had originally been laid at the Wessex Stadium by A.J. Hunting of International Speedways Ltd for a planned opening in September 1928, but for one

reason or another no meetings ever took place that year. Greyhound racing was first staged at Copnor on 30 June 1928, but its existence was short-lived and it ceased after a final meeting on 29 November 1930. Prior to the opening meeting in 1929, the promoters (Dirt-Track Speedways Ltd) publicised the fact with a parading circus and large billboards. The first meeting at the stadium was held on 10 August 1929, when the legendary Sprouts Elder was triumphant in the Golden Gauntlet. Dirt-track racing ceased after only four meetings in that initial year, apparently due to the bumpy track and a lack of covered accommodation for spectators. All four meetings were run in August, the last of which was run on the final day of the month. After the track was re-laid and covered stands erected, trials were held on three occasions in early April (on 5, 9 and 12). Racing subsequently resumed on Easter Monday 21 April 1930, with a scratch race event. Proposals to enter the Southern League in 1931 ended abruptly in October 1930, when the City Council bought the stadium and announced plans to build housing on the site, although they never actually did. The last dirt-track meeting was held on 2 October 1930, when Portsmouth and West Ham drew 26-26 in a challenge match.

PORTSMOUTH

ADDRESS: Portsmouth Greyhound and Sports Stadium, Target Road, Tipnor, Portsmouth, Hampshire
YEARS OF OPERATION: 1935 Open; 1937 Open
FIRST MEETING: 2 October 1935
TRACK LENGTH: 300 yards

Greyhound racing was first staged at the venue on 25 May 1931. Grass-track racing is known to have been staged at the stadium in 1933. In 1935, promoter Tom Bradbury-Pratt and a team of fifty men constructed a speedway track inside the existing greyhound circuit, but it was to only hold one neutral meeting, when Harringay staged their National League match versus Hackney on 2 October. Due to a successful year, Harringay had run short of fixture space, hence the reason for holding the match at Portsmouth – which resulted in a 32-35 defeat for the 'home' side. One further meeting was scheduled in 1935, a challenge match between Wembley and Wimbledon on 9 October, but it was rained off. There were no further meetings at the stadium until 1937, when they were promoted by Albatross Motorcycle Club as open-to-centre events. Just two meetings were staged that year, the first of which was held on 14 July, when Portsmouth beat Basingstoke 28-25 in a challenge match. The other meeting in 1937, and the last to be staged at the stadium, went ahead on 29 September when Portsmouth beat Reading 36-26 in a challenge match. Stock-car racing was held at the stadium in 1955. Plans to reintroduce speedway in the early 1970s came to nothing following objections from local residents, fearful of excessive noise levels and traffic problems. Today, the stadium is still in operation, running regular greyhound meetings.

PRESTATYN
ADDRESS: Prestatyn Raceway, Nr Rhyl
YEARS OF OPERATION: 1967-69 Long-track
TRACK LENGTH: 800 yards

Howard Cole raced at the initial meeting on the Prestatyn trotting track, which was organised by the Point of Ayre Club in 1967. Don Godden won

Portsmouth Greyhound and Sports Stadium.

the event on the 800-yard limestone granite and coral surface. Another event, held on 30 August 1967, saw Malcolm Simmons emerge victorious on the track, which had been constructed by then Motherwell owner George Kennedy. Mike Parker took over the running of meetings in 1969, with Council approval to stage seven events. A Court injunction was taken out by local residents later in 1969, on the grounds of nuisance created by noise, dust and fumes. The injunction was defeated, but the playing of music was prohibited. Racing was finally curtailed when a further injunction from a nearby hotel was upheld.

PRESTON
ADDRESS: Farringdon Park, New Hall Lane, Preston, Lancashire
YEARS OF OPERATION: 1929 English Dirt-track League; 1930-31 Northern League; 1932 Open
FIRST MEETING: 29 March 1929
TRACK LENGTH: 440 yards (1929); 413 yards (1930-32)
KNOCK-OUT CUP WINNERS: 1929

Farringdon Park originally featured a cinder-surfaced cycling track that had been in operation for twenty-five years, before the arrival of dirt-track racing in 1929. In 1925, the owners, Horrockses Cotton, had accepted a lease on the ground, at £25 per year, by a rugby club called Preston Grasshoppers. In 1929, W.D. Meagher (chairman of the Northern Dirt-track Owners Association) teamed up with J.C.H. Hollins and Captain H. Sharples (directors of Preston North End Football Club) to form a company called Preston Speedway Ltd, and quickly reached an agreement to hold meetings at the venue. A 440-yard track was constructed, along with pits and a riders' room, complete with canteen. Hot and cold showers were also available in the rugby club's pavilion. The opening Golden Helmet meeting went ahead on Good Friday 29 March that year, and the public responded in large numbers, witnessing Arthur Jervis triumph in the final. Soon, Preston had become founder members of the English Dirt-track League, riding their first home league match versus Leeds on 27 April. However, not long after opening, tragedy struck, when twenty-two-year-old John Stockdale was killed in an accident on 11 May. Sadly, there was another death at the track in that initial year of action, when Jack Smith crashed on 10 August. Following these deaths, the Preston circuit came in for a certain amount of criticism, being described as 'a billiard table with peas on it' and therefore very difficult to ride. Alterations had been made to the track prior to the 1930 season, but it didn't stop a third rider from being killed on 24 July, when twenty-three-year-old Jim Carnie succumbed to the injuries he had suffered in an accident while racing for the Golden Helmet. A meeting of creditors took place on 11 September 1930 to consider an offer by the directors to pay 5/- in the pound in preference to going into liquidation. Bad weather and high rider demands were alleged to be responsible for the situation. After much discussion, the creditors decided to accept the offer from Preston Speedway Ltd – several of the creditors were in fact riders. Northern League racing continued in 1931, with Liverpool moving into Preston, having been forced out of their

Stanley Stadium by the greyhound company's non-interest in dirt-track racing that year. Under the banner of Preston Speedways (1932) Ltd, William Jones took over the running of the track in 1932, but just a few open licence meetings were staged before the track closed down for good. The demise of the textile industry was blamed for the fact that local folk could not afford the 1/- admission, never mind the 3d for a programme. The last known meeting was held on 14 April, when the Golden Armlet was raced for. A further meeting was almost held versus Sheffield on 19 May, but this was cancelled due to the small attendance.

R

RAINHAM

ADDRESS: Chadwell St Mary, Nr Grays, Essex
YEARS OF OPERATION: 1950-53 Training
TRACK LENGTH: 280 yards

Although referred to as Rainham, this training track was actually situated much closer to Grays (sometimes the venue was even mistakenly called Chelmsford, which was some eighteen miles away). The track was constructed using red shale, on the site of a disused sand-pit, by Johnny Guilfoyle and the Powell brothers, Ivor and Dick, in 1950. The track was opened with the backing of the local Council, and ran every day except Sunday. Both Pat Clarke and Jack Hillard took their first speedway rides on the training track in 1950 and 1951 respectively. Ray Terry and John Lalley were the best of the novices at the

venue in 1952. The track closed at the end of a three-year lease in 1953. The safety fence was subsequently reconstructed at Rye House in 1971.

RAHENY

ADDRESS: Raheny Pony Trotting Track, Raheny, Dublin
YEARS OF OPERATION: 1946-47 Long-track

Little is known about this venue, other than the fact that long-track meetings were promoted by the Leinster Club in 1946 and 1947.

RAYLEIGH

ADDRESS: Rayleigh Stadium, South Arterial Road, Laindon, Nr Basildon, Essex
YEARS OF OPERATION: 1933 Open; 1936 Open

Details of this venue, which could possibly have been known as Central Speedway or even Laindon Stadium, are sketchy. A dirt-track meeting is known to have been staged on 5 June 1933, organised by Hadleigh and District Motorcycle and Light Car Club. Vic Gooden took his first rides at the stadium in 1936.

RAYLEIGH

ADDRESS: Rayleigh Weir Stadium, Southend Arterial Road, Rayleigh, Essex
YEARS OF OPERATION: 1948 Open; 1949-51 National League Division Three; 1952-53 Southern League; 1954-56 National League Division Two; 1957 National League and Southern Area League; 1958 Training; 1959 Open; 1960-61 Provincial League; 1962 Training;

1963 Provincial League; 1964 Metropolitan League; 1965 Open; 1966 Training; 1968-73 British League Division Two

FIRST MEETING: 17 July 1948

TRACK LENGTH: 385 yards (1948-52); 365 yards (1953-73)

NICKNAME: 'Rockets'; (The Southern Area League team of 1957 were known as 'Rovers')

LEAGUE CHAMPIONS: 1952, 1953, 1960 (The Southern Area League side also won the championship in 1957)

Rayleigh Weir Stadium was built in 1948, with greyhound racing being staged right from the off. Speedway wasn't long in arriving at the venue, with stadium owners F.B. McGreavey and F.L. Rundle employing Frank Arnold as their general manager. The black cinder track staged its first action on 17 July 1948, when a Possibles versus Probables meeting took place. The following week, on 24 July, the official opening saw Rayleigh beat Leicester 51-32 in a challenge match. Guests of honour at the grand opening were Patricia Roc and Bill Owen, stars of the speedway-based film *Once A Jolly Swagman*. After a successful year of open licence events, Rayleigh entered the National League Division Three in 1949, but midway through the year there was a change of promotion R.M. & R. (Holdings) Ltd, who employed Roy Dook as their speedway manager. A further change of promotion saw Arthur and Tippy Atkinson running the show in 1950, and they were to remain in the hot-seat until the end of 1956, as the team went from Division Three to the Southern League, prior to joining Division Two. In 1957, Vic Gooden became promoter, as the team ended up in the eleven-team National League. Interestingly that year, Vic Gooden's list of staff included future multi-track promoter Wally Mawdsley as track manager. Due to falling attendances that year, Vic Gooden ran two of Rayleigh's home league matches at Poole (on 2 and 23 September). Also in 1957, a second side was based at the Weir, with Rayleigh Rovers competing in the Southern Area League, along with Eastbourne, Aldershot and Rye House. The track was used for training sessions in 1958, under the instruction of Ray Jones and Peter Arnold. Just one meeting was held at the venue in 1959, when an unlicensed Cavalcade of Sport meeting took place on 27 March. Regular team racing resumed in 1960 (promoted by Pete Lansdale), with Rayleigh entering the Provincial League,

Rayleigh's twenty-first anniversary programme, 1969.

209

but the track was to close early the following year, although they did complete their league programme. The last home match was staged on 7 August 1961, when Rayleigh beat Edinburgh 40-38 in a Provincial League fixture. Sunday practice sessions were held in 1962, when between twenty to thirty riders turned up each week to receive tuition from Alec Lilley. Promoted by Gordon Cox, the track reopened on 12 April 1963, when Rayleigh lost 30-48 to Exeter in a challenge match. The Rockets subsequently partook in the Provincial League that year, before a short-season of only a few open licence meetings in 1964, which included Rayleigh's participation in the unfinished Metropolitan League. Incidentally, Gordon Cox had been joined by Stan Clark and Maurice McDermott on the promoting front for that 1964 season. Just two meetings were run in 1965, with Jimmy Heard winning the Easter Trophy on 16 April and Tommy Sweetman victorious in a World Championship qualifier on 15 May. In 1968, Allied Presentations Ltd (with Len Silver at the helm), reopened the circuit, making the Rockets founder members of British League Division Two. The first meeting of that era went ahead on 11 May 1968, when Rayleigh defeated Plymouth 40-34 in a league encounter. The last-ever meeting at the stadium took place on 20 October 1973, when the Rockets beat Eastbourne 48-47 in a challenge match. Due to its location on the main London-to-Southend road, rumours were rife of redevelopment at the site, with Len Silver moving the Rayleigh team to Rye House in time for the 1974 campaign. A final greyhound meeting at

Rayleigh Weir took place on 8 March 1974. The stadium was subsequently demolished and redeveloped, and is now the site of a supermarket.

READING
ADDRESS: Reading Greyhound Stadium, Oxford Road, Tilehurst, Reading, Berkshire
YEARS OF OPERATION: 1968-70 British League Division Two; 1971-73 British League Division One
FIRST MEETING: 17 June 1968
TRACK LENGTH: 360 yards
NICKNAME: 'Racers'
LEAGUE CHAMPIONS: 1973

A first grass-speedway meeting is known to have been staged at Tilehurst Stadium on 16 May 1932, promoted by South Reading Motorcycle Club. A second such meeting was held on 11 June that year, this time promoted by Reading and District Motor Cycle Club. Tilehurst was refused an open licence to stage speedway in both 1947 and 1948. The stadium was subsequently proposed as a speedway venue in 1949, and again in 1965, but nothing came to fruition on either occasion. Finally, under the promotion of Allied Presentations Ltd, fronted by Reg Fearman, Reading Greyhound Stadium staged its first-ever speedway meeting on 17 June 1968, when the newly-formed Racers beat Nelson 41-37 in a British League Division Two encounter. Admission prices for the opening meeting were 5/- for adults, and 3/- for children, with an attendance of some 5,000 people being recorded. In 1971, following three seasons of Division Two racing, Reading exchanged their licence with Newcastle, which allowed the Racers to move into Division One. The stadium closed at the end of the 1973 season, due to road development plans. The final speedway meeting at the venue was held on 8 October that year, when Reading defeated Ole Olsen's United Seven 45-33 in a challenge match. The search for a new home began, with the Racers eventually moving to Smallmead Stadium in 1975. A final greyhound meeting was held at Tilehurst on 1 January 1974.

READING

ADDRESS: Smallmead Stadium, Bennet Road, Smallmead, Reading, Berkshire

YEARS OF OPERATION: 1975-90 British League; 1991-94 British League Division One; 1995 British Premier League; 1996 British Premier League and British Conference League; 1997 British Premier League and British Amateur League; 1998-2000 British Premier League

FIRST MEETING: 28 April 1975

TRACK LENGTH: 307 metres

NICKNAME: 'Racers' (The 1996 Conference League side were known as 'Ravens', while the 1997 Amateur League team side were known as 'M4 Raven Sprockets')

LEAGUE CHAMPIONS: 1980, 1990, 1992, 1997

KNOCK-OUT CUP WINNERS: 1990, 1998

PREMIERSHIP WINNERS: 1991, 1993

BSPA CUP WINNERS: 1992

When the Racers lost the use of Tilehurst, Reg Fearman, along with Bill Dore, Frank Higley and Len Silver, never gave up, and with the help of the local council a suitable location for a new track was eventually found. Smallmead Stadium was built on a site that was previously a Corporation rubbish tip. It was

Reading's opening meeting programme, 1968.

originally proposed to stage British League Division One speedway at the stadium in 1974, but construction work was not completed in time. Having had to sit out the 1974 season, the Racers were back in action the following year, Smallmead opening on 28 April 1975, when 10,000 shale- starved fans crammed into the new stadium to witness the Racers beat Hull 48-30 in a British League fixture. An opening greyhound meeting was staged at Smallmead on 10 June 1975. Changes on the administration side in 1980 saw Dave Lanning take the role of speedway executive, while Bill Dore's daughter, Pat Bliss, also joined the promotional team. Dave Lanning moved on in 1981, with co-promoters Bill Dore, Frank Higley and Pat Bliss taking more of an active role.

Smallmead Stadium, Reading.

Further changes in 1987 saw Brian Leonard join the promotional team of Bliss and Dore. By 1988, however, Brian Leonard had moved on, and the track was under the control of the father and daughter team of Bill Dore and Pat Bliss. With the amalgamation of the leagues in 1991, Reading became members of the new British League Division One. All the teams from Divisions One and Two joined forces in 1995, to form the twenty-one-team British Premier League, with the Racers taking their place in the new set-up. In 1996, Reading also entered a team in the British Conference League. Riding as the Ravens, the new side took to the track for their opening Smallmead meeting on 22 July, when they lost 37-40 to Linlithgow. This venture was a one-season operation, however, and the last meeting was held at Smallmead on 21 October when the Ravens beat Arena-Essex 44-34. British speedway changed direction again in 1997, when the huge Premier League split into two, with the formation of a ten-team Elite League and a fourteen-team Premier League. Due to falling attendances at Smallmead, Reading opted to go into the revamped version of the Premier League. A second team was also based at Smallmead that season, when Reading joined forces with Swindon to enter a composite side in the British Amateur League. The home fixtures were equally split between the two tracks, with the team operating under the name of M4 Raven Sprockets. Reading staged its opening Amateur League meeting on 27 April, when the M4 Raven Sprockets lost 34-43 to Ryde. The venture lasted only the one season, and the final Smallmead meeting went ahead on 8 September, when the homesters lost 36-40 to Buxton. The

1998 season ended on a very sad note in early December when co-promoter Bill Dore died in Radcliffe Hospital, Oxford, at the age of seventy-six. In November 1999, Channel 4 screened a fly-on-the-wall look at Reading speedway, with much of the programme having been filmed at Smallmead. Pat Bliss remains as sole-promoter of the track, having already seen the Racers through the last twenty years.

READING

ADDRESS: Reading Training Track, Bennet Road, Smallmead, Reading, Berkshire

YEARS OF OPERATION: 1992-93 Training; 1994 Open and Training; 1995-96 Training; 1997 Open and Training; 1998-2000 Training

FIRST MEETING: 26 April 1992

TRACK LENGTH: 250 metres

In 1991, Jeff Sealey set about constructing a training track on land adjacent to Smallmead Stadium. The well-appointed 250-metre circuit boasted a cushion-style safety fence, and was actually located behind the first and second bend of the main Smallmead track. Prior to opening, the track was passed by the Control Board, who thought it was better than several National League circuits operating at the time. The mini-track was also given the thumbs up by Mitch Shirra, Hans Nielsen and Kelvin Tatum. Since opening on 26 April 1992, the track has been used regularly for training and practice sessions, with the odd team training match thrown in for good measure. One training session didn't have too favourable an outcome though, when Gary Chessell broke his collarbone in a crash on 20 March. The track is still in use today.

Reading Training Track, Smallmead, Reading.

Matchams Park, Ringwood.

RINGWOOD

ADDRESS: Matchams Park, Hurn Road, Ringwood, Hampshire
YEARS OF OPERATION: 1937-39 Open; 1946-47 Open and Training

It seems likely that the pre-war Ringwood track was situated at the rear of the existing stadium. It was reported that Crasher Warren scored full points for Holbeach in a visit to Ringwood in 1938. A meeting is known to have been staged on 18 June 1939, when Bournemouth lost 40-62 to Holbeach. After the war, further open licence events and training sessions were held at the venue during 1946 and 1947.

RINGWOOD

ADDRESS: Matchams Park, Hurn Road, Ringwood, Hampshire
YEARS OF OPERATION: 1950 Training; 1951-53 Open; 1954-55 Southern Area League; 1972 Training; 1973 Open and Training; 1989-90 Training; 1993 Training
FIRST MEETING: 5 May 1951
TRACK LENGTH: 385 yards (1950); 375 yards (1951-55)
NICKNAME: 'Turfs' (1953-55)

The original speedway operations at this venue were under the control of John Crutcher. The red shale track was laid by Alf Elliott, and featured a concrete grid and modern starting gate. A training session was held on Boxing Day 1950, at which Brian Crutcher took his first speedway ride. A sign at the end of the long, bush-lined drive bore the words 'St Leonard's Training School'. The first actual meeting at the track took place on 5 May 1951, when Ron Goulding won the St Leonard's Novices Championship. Training and open licence events were staged from the start of 1951 until 1953, before Ringwood entered the Southern Area League in 1954. Theirs was a short stay in the

Southern Area League however, for, having completed the 1954 season, the Turfs withdrew from the league in 1955, after eight matches. The last meeting at the venue was held on 22 May that year, when the homesters beat Eastbourne 55-27 in a league match. The speedway track was subsequently covered in tarmac and used for stock-car racing. The training track of the 1970s was constructed inside the stock-car track, with school sessions run by Mike Broadbanks. The reopening took place on 14 May 1972, and regular sessions were held throughout 1972 and 1973. The final meeting of 1973 saw Russell Foot win the open training track championship meeting with a 15-point maximum. The track was all set to reopen in 1974, but these plans were precluded by stadium redevelopment. Representatives from Poole rebuilt the track during 1988, and used it for training purposes in 1989 and 1990. Kevin Smart became the first rider to try out the relaid track in July 1989, prior to the construction of the safety fence. Jeremy Doncaster ran a training school at the track in 1990. A training session is known to have taken place at the track on 7 February 1993.

RINGWOOD

ADDRESS: Matchams Park, Hurn Road, Ringwood, Hampshire
YEARS OF OPERATION: 1988-93 Mini Long-track
FIRST MEETING: 23 June 1988

In 1988, a mini long-track with a sand surface was constructed outside the stock-car circuit at Matchams Park. An opening meeting was staged on 23 June that year, and meetings continued into 1989. Further long-track meetings were staged at the venue from 1990 until 1992. The opening meeting of the 1993 season, scheduled for 13 March between Matchams and Rye House, was cancelled after sidecar passenger Peter Lain was killed in a pre-meeting practice accident.

ROCHDALE

ADDRESS: The Athletic Grounds, Milnrow Road, Rochdale, Lancashire
YEARS OF OPERATION: 1928 Open; 1929 English Dirt-track League; 1930 Northern League; 1970-71 British League Division Two
FIRST MEETING: 18 August 1928
TRACK LENGTH: 441 yards (1928-30); 418 yards (1970-71)
NICKNAME: 'Hornets' (1970-71)

Rochdale Hornets Rugby League Club first played at Milnrow Road in 1894. Prior to dirt-track racing's arrival in 1928, the venue was famous for its cycle and running track, which had been laid some thirty-three years previously. The outer banked cycling track was 502 yards long, while inside was the quarter-mile ash circuit on which the Northern Counties AAA held their 1924 Olympic trials. Grass-track racing took place at the stadium on 17 July 1928, followed by a gymkhana on 4 August. Managed by Alec Dovener, the opening dirt-track meeting took place before an audience of 7,000 on 18 August 1928, when Eric Langton was triumphant in the scratch race event. Although booked to ride in the meeting, Sprouts Elder failed to appear. Twenty-five-year-old Cliff Mawson lost his life after crashing at the track on 20 October 1928. Open licence events were the order of the day in 1928, before a Rochdale team competed in the English Dirt-track

The Athletics Grounds, Rochdale.

League (1929) and Northern League (1930). The lease of the stadium expired on 11 August, 1930, with the track being taken over by Manchester Motor Sports. The new promoters introduced betting at their first meeting on 16 August 1930, but it was a failure, with one Manchester bookmaker claiming his takings did not even cover the rail fare to Rochdale. The riders in that meeting were all imported from the banned Audenshaw track and, along with all the officials, were subsequently suspended by the ACU. This could well have been the final meeting of that era, as a following meeting planned for 23 August was abandoned without a race being run, due to the lack of a crowd. Greyhound racing was first held at the stadium on 18 June 1932, and continued until December 1969, when stock-car racing was introduced. Speedway returned to Rochdale

in 1970, under the control of Dent Oliver, when Belle Vue transferred their successful Division Two side to the track, opening with a 46-32 challenge match victory over Crewe on 29 March. Running speedway on narrow square-shaped tracks around rugby pitches has never been popular with supporters, and the track closed for good at the end of the 1971 season. The final meeting was held on 22 October that year, when the homesters lost 37-40 to Rayleigh in a British League Division Two fixture. The track licence was subsequently transferred to Ellesmere Port in 1972. The 190-foot grandstand, which served the speedway organisers throughout 1970 and 1971, had originally been built in 1936 by Fletcher Bolton of Rochdale, and boasted seating for 1,300. There was a proposal to reintroduce speedway at Rochdale in 1973, but this fell flat when both British League Division Two and open licences were refused. Following complaints from local residents about noise, stock-car racing ceased in 1987. Rochdale Hornets' final rugby league match at the venue went ahead on 16 April 1988, and it was reported that they took the original scoreboard with them when they left. Since then, the rugby club has ground-shared at Spotland, the home of Rochdale Football Club. In April 1989, planning consent was given for a Morrisons supermarket and petrol station, which now occupy the site.

ROCHESTER

ADDRESS: City Way Stadium, Rochester, Kent
YEARS OF OPERATION: 1931 Training; 1932 Open; 1969 Demonstration
FIRST MEETING: 1 August, 1932
TRACK LENGTH: 355 yards

In 1931, it was announced that a dirt track was being constructed at the City Way Stadium, and that trial meetings were to be staged on 9, 16 and 23 December that year. A further trial event was later advertised for Boxing Day. The first actual meeting went ahead on 1 August 1932, when Alf Foulds won the Chatham Scratch event. Just one further meeting was held on 9 August 1932, after which the sport ceased at the stadium. Greyhound racing was first staged at the venue on 1 June 1936. Wally Mawdsley and Pete Lansdale proposed to reintroduce speedway to the stadium in 1969, so a trial was held for the benefit of Council officials on 14 March that year. Reg Luckhurst, Martyn Piddock, Judd Drew and Rob Stewart took part in a demonstration race, which was won by

Piddock. Rochester Bombers were originally given planning permission by the City Council to race at the stadium, but having ridden their first two away British League Division Two matches, they then found that Kent County Council had refused to approve the planning application. The Bombers raced a further two away league matches, prior to moving into Brooklands Stadium at Romford – where they completed their 1969 fixtures as Romford Bombers. A final greyhound meeting was held at City Way Stadium on 4 October 1979. The stadium was demolished in 1980, and the site redeveloped.

ROMAN CAMP

ADDRESS: Roman Camp, Nr Broxburn, West Lothian
YEARS OF OPERATION: 1982 Training

This was a trotting track, which was used for just one training session in 1982 – the owner claimed that the speedway machines cut up the track too much, and ruled out any further use.

ROMFORD

ADDRESS: Brooklands Stadium, Brooklands Road, Mawneys, Romford, Essex
YEARS OF OPERATION: 1969-71 British League Division Two
FIRST MEETING: 29 May 1969
TRACK LENGTH: 375 yards
NICKNAME: 'Bombers'

Brooklands Stadium was originally part of a much larger sports complex that included facilities for hockey, tennis and cricket. In 1929, Romford Football Club moved in and built a small double-sided stand, with one side facing the football pitch, while the other faced the cricket field. The highest recorded attendance at the stadium was 18,237 for a 1951 FA Amateur Cup match between Romford and Southall. Speedway arrived at the stadium quite unexpectedly, thanks to the demise of another track. Rochester Bombers had originally been given planning permission by the City Council to race at the City Way Stadium, but found that Kent County Council had refused to approve the planning application. Promoters Wally Mawdsley and Pete Lansdale reaching an agreement to move the team into Brooklands Stadium, where they completed their 1969 fixtures as Romford Bombers. The opening meeting at the stadium was staged on 29 May that year, when Romford beat Crewe 45-33 in a challenge match. Attendances for meetings were always good, despite the track being constructed around the football pitch, with a stone wall safety fence in parts. After three seasons of British League Division Two racing, the track was forced to close after local residents got a High Court judge to side in their favour over noise nuisance. The final meeting at the track was held on 30 September 1971, when Romford lost 36-41 to Rayleigh in the Essex Gold Cup. Prior to the closure of West Ham's Custom House Stadium, Romford moved their operation to the London circuit for a handful of fixtures in 1972. Brooklands Stadium was redeveloped as a housing estate, work commencing on 30 April 1977.

ROTHERHAM
ADDRESS: Greyhound Stadium, Hellaby, Rotherham, South Yorkshire

YEARS OF OPERATION: 1929-30 Open
FIRST MEETING: 18 May 1929

Greyhound racing was first staged at the stadium on 7 April 1928. The dirt track, which was also sometimes referred to as Bramley, was situated behind the workshops of 'Skid' Skinner, the Manchester (White City) rider. The first meeting at the venue was held on 18 May 1929, when 'Broadside' Hall won the Bramley Scratch event in front of an audience of some 3,000. 'Skid' Skinner originally ran the track, regularly putting up a silver helmet award to be contested for. During August 1929, the track was taken over by a new syndicate led by Percy Carnelley and William Hunt, although 'Skid' Skinner was still on board as a director. Thirty-five meetings were run in that opening season, with regular action on a Thursday and Saturday each week. The operation was scaled down in 1930, with just five meetings being staged, the last of which saw 'Broadside' Hall win the Silver Helmet on 9 June.

RYDE
ADDRESS: Smallbrook Stadium, Ashey Road, Ryde, Isle of Wight
YEARS OF OPERATION: 1995 Demonstration; 1996 British Conference League; 1997 British Premier League and British Amateur League; 1998-2000 British Premier League
FIRST MEETING: 13 May 1996
TRACK LENGTH: 396 metres (1996); 392 metres (1997); 382 metres (1998-99); 380 metres (2000)
NICKNAME: 'Wight Wizards' (Conference /Amateur League team); 'Islanders' (Premier League side)
YOUNG SHIELD WINNERS: 1998

Martin Willis and Justin Elkins participated in noise level tests at Smallbrook Stadium in December 1995. Newport Isle of Wight Council were satisfied with the outcome and gave planning permission for five years of speedway at the venue. A track was subsequently laid around the football pitch, on a disused athletics track, with the first meeting going ahead on 13 May 1996, when Martin Willis won the Island Individual Championship. Promoters at the venue in the first two years of Conference League/Amateur League racing (1996 and 1997) were Mark Firmin and Gareth Rogers. British Premier League racing also arrived in 1997, when Skegness promoters Peter Oakes and Sarah Gudgeon transferred their operation to the island. Their first meeting, ridden as Skegness Braves, was a qualifying round of the Four Team Championship on 7 July, which finished thus: Long Eaton 28, Hull 25, Skegness 22, Stoke 21. The team were subsequently renamed as Isle of Wight Islanders. What turned out to be the last Amateur League fixture was staged on 6 October 1997, when the Wight Wizards drew 39-39 with the M4 Raven Sprockets. Since 1998, the track has continued with just the Premier League side, running under the promotion of Martin Newnham and Dave Pavitt.

RYE HOUSE

ADDRESS: Hoddesdon Stadium, Rye Road, Hoddesdon, Hertfordshire
YEARS OF OPERATION: 1935 Open and Training; 1936-37 Open; 1938 Sunday Dirt-track League; 1939-43 Open; 1945-53 Open; 1954-57 Southern Area League
TRACK LENGTH: 440 yards
LEAGUE CHAMPIONS: 1954, 1955, 1956
NICKNAME: 'Roosters' (1955)

The first known activity at Hoddesdon was a grass-track meeting organised by

Smallbrook Stadium, Ryde, Isle of Wight.

the Hertford and District Motorcycle and Car Club on 17 June 1934. The original Rye House dirt-track operation opened in 1935, quickly becoming renowned for unearthing talented prospects – as it continued to do throughout its history. Sadly, the dates and results of the first meetings at the venue have thus far proved impossible to trace. Greyhound racing was first staged at the venue in 1935. Training and open licence meetings were held throughout the 1930s, before Rye House partook in the Sunday Dirt-track League in 1938, under the promotion of Hackney Wick Speedway Motor Club. Six meetings were run in 1940, under the title of Dick Case's Speedway, organised by Harringay Speedway Motorcycle and Light Car Club. Fourteen meetings were staged in 1941, again under the heading of Dick

Case's Speedway, while another six were held in 1942. The Harringay Speedway MC & LCC organised and ran four meetings in 1943, with the gate receipts going towards the British Red Cross Prisoners of War Parcels Fund. The track was rented to West Ham on Wednesdays in 1946, for the purpose of giving the Hammers riders plenty of extra practice. Dick Case continued to run the track after the war, being handily placed for the job as he was the manager of the public house right next to the circuit. George Kay subsequently took over the running of the track in 1949. Tragedy struck at Rye House in July 1950, when Robert Stocker was killed in a track accident. Aside from the usual open licence events and training at the track, Rye House also participated in the Southern Area League from 1954 to 1957. The final

Hoddesdon Stadium.

meeting at the venue took place on 22 September 1957, when the homesters beat Rayleigh 51-32 in a Southern Area League fixture. In 1958, Rye House moved to the current track, which was built on an adjoining site. The original Rye House track later became a go-kart circuit, which it still is to this day.

RYE HOUSE

ADDRESS: Rye House Stadium, Rye Road, Hoddesdon, Hertfordshire
YEARS OF OPERATION: 1958 Open; 1959 Southern Area League; 1960-66 Open and Training; 1967 Training; 1969-73 Open and Training; 1974 British League Division Two; 1975-90 National League; 1991-93 British League Division Two; 2000 British Conference League
FIRST MEETING: 3 August 1958
TRACK LENGTH: 325 yards (1958-64); 284 yards (1965-85); 281 yards (1986-93); 263 yards (2000)
KNOCK-OUT CUP WINNERS: 1979
LEAGUE CHAMPIONS: 1980
NICKNAME: 'Red Devils' (1960-73); 'Rockets' (1974-2000)

The new Rye House track was built in the summer of 1958, on a former stock-car circuit adjoining the original site. The circuit hosted six open licence meetings in its initial year, with the opener being staged on 3 August, when Brian Meredith won the August Trophy. As they had done at their previous home, Rye House graced the Southern Area League in 1959, before reverting back to an open licence in 1960. Rye House became known as 'The Acknowledged Training Track', bringing through many youngsters during the 1960s, latterly under the auspices of WBS Promotions (Bill Wainwright, John

Bailey and Tommy Sweetman). A change on the promoting front saw Jack Carter link with John Bailey at the tail-end of the decade. Interestingly, from 1971 to 1973, Carter and Bailey were listed in the programme as proprietors at Rye House, with Johnny Guilfoyle and Bill Mathieson as promoters. In 1971, a new safety fence was brought in from Johnny Guilfoyle's former training track at Chadwell St Mary. Under the banner of Allied Presentations Ltd, Len Silver moved his Rayleigh side to Hoddesdon in time for the start of the 1974 British League Division Two campaign. The opening meeting of this new venture was held on Sunday 21 April, when the renamed Rockets defeated Canterbury 41-36 in the Johnnie Hoskins Birthday Cup. In 1975, the Rockets became founder members of the new National League (which was basically the British League Division Two under a different title). Len Silver still ran the show in 1975, but under the banner of Rye House Speedway Ltd. Another slight change in 1976 saw the track promoted by Rye House Speedway Ltd, under the direction of Colin Pratt and Len Silver. That remained the case until 1980, when Len Silver continued on as sole promoter of the track. Having completed twelve years at the helm, Len Silver bowed out at the end of the 1985 campaign, in order to concentrate on his Silver-Ski holidays business. Ronnie Russell became the new promoter of the Rockets in 1986, and remained in sole charge until 1989, when Barry Klatt joined him as co-promoter. With the amalgamation of the leagues in 1991, Rye House found themselves back in the British League Division Two. A

Rye House Stadium, Hoddesdon.

change on the promoting front in 1993 saw Roger Shute and Peter Redfern link up with Ronnie Russell as co-promoters. Falling crowd levels had become a major cause for concern in 1993, however, and, despite the efforts of the promotion, a solution could not be found. After the 1993 season had ended, both Roger Shute and Peter Redfern left the promotion due to ill health, and Ronnie Russell had little alternative than to inform the BSPA that the Rockets would not be running in 1994. What turned out to be the final meeting of a twenty-year stint in Division Two racing had been held on 24 October 1993, when Rye House lost 34-43 to Arena-Essex in the Herts-Essex Cup. The track was subsequently covered in tarmac and used for stock-car racing, with the likelihood of any further speedway looking remote. In 1999, a group of Rockets enthusiasts, headed

by John Stoneman and Steve Ribbons, with Len Silver as president, got together to form the Rye House Speedway Club and assembled a side to compete in the British Conference League. The new Rockets staged their home meetings at Eastbourne, Mildenhall and King's Lynn during the year, the first of which was held at Eastbourne on 9 May, when Rye House defeated King's Lynn Braves 44-43. The ultimate aim was to try and get back to their old stadium of course, but, even so, it was still a major surprise to most people when they succeeded in securing a rental agreement with the Rye House Stadium bosses in 2000. This was achieved through the increased financial support of Len Silver, who adopted a more traditional promoter's role. The only problem of being back at Hoddesdon was that the track (and safety fence) had to be constructed every week on top of the stock-car circuit. A reopening challenge match versus Southampton was scheduled for 1 May but fell victim to inclement weather. The meeting eventually went ahead on 15 May, when the Rockets ran out 48-42 winners. The future of Rye House Speedway was secured later in the 2000 season, when, after detailed negotiations, Len Silver acquired the master lease on the stadium, which meant that a new and permanent track could be constructed at the end of the season.

S

ST AUSTELL

ADDRESS: Cornish Stadium, Par Moor, St Austell, Cornwall

YEARS OF OPERATION: 1949 Open; 1950-51 National League Division Three; 1952-53 Southern League; 1954 Training; 1958-61 Open; 1962-63 Provincial League; 1964 Training; 1969 Demonstration; 1978 Training

FIRST MEETING: 14 June 1949

TRACK LENGTH: 360 yards

NICKNAME: 'Pixies' (1949); 'Badgers' (1949); 'Gulls' (1949-61 and 1963); 'Dragons' (1962)

The building of the Cornish Stadium was financed by A.D. Richards and R.H. Luke in 1949. Speedway arrived at the venue that year and, following the construction of a copper-sand dressed circuit, St Austell were originally granted a probationary licence. The promoters were Cornish Stadium Ltd (the aforementioned Richards and Luke). An opening meeting was staged on 14 June, when a crowd of over 12,000 people saw a Peter Robinson Select beat a Cyril Quick Select 46-37. Following the opening meeting in 1949, challenge matches continued to be run, initially using 'Pixies' as a moniker, but on 12 July this was changed to 'Badgers', before the name 'Gulls' was first used a week later. The renamed Gulls joined National League Division Three in 1950. On 4 August 1951, a sheepdog trials event was promoted and the programme was indentical to the normal speedway issue and even included several photographs of riders in action. With new promoter John Selleck at the helm, St Austell joined the Southern League in 1952. Sadly though, just one further season of action followed before the track was taken over by car racing events. The final season of regular team racing at the stadium was marred when twenty-

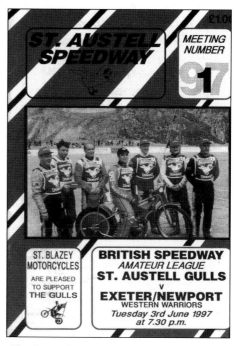

Clay Country Moto Parc's opening programme, 1997.

Cornish Stadium, St Austell.

six-year-old Australian Ted Stevens died following a crash on 14 April 1953. What turned out to be the last meeting for five years was held on 13 October that year, when the Gulls lost 39-46 to Norwich in a challenge match. One August day in 1954, with the track lying empty, Jack Gates took a ride around, prior to leaving for Australia. Afterwards he stated: 'There was no one to cheer, no one to watch, but I got the biggest thrill I've had in England this year!' Promoter Trevor Redmond brought speedway back to the venue in 1958, opening on 30 July with a Best Pairs event that was won by Jack Geran and Gerry Hussey. Including the Gulls participation in the regional Western League in 1960 and 1961, open licence events continued until Neath (another of Trevor Redmond's tracks), used the stadium to complete their fixtures in 1962, starting with a Provincial League match versus Edinburgh on 10 July

which the Dragons won 42-36. The Welsh side completed their run of four league matches at the venue on 5 September with a 44-34 victory over Newcastle in a league match. Trevor Redmond continued to run the show in 1963, with the return of the Gulls in Provincial League action, but that year was to be the final one of team action for St Austell until Brian Annear resurrected the side at Claycountry Moto Parc in 1997. The last meeting proper at the Cornish Stadium was held on 1 October 1963, when Cornwall defeated Devon 33-21 in a challenge match. In 1964 the Cornish Stadium was used for training purposes, with Chris Blewett known to have used the circuit following an arm injury. Trevor Redmond and Chris Julian gave a speedway demonstration at the venue in 1969. Although the track had been covered in tarmac, a thin covering of shale had been spread on the bends, enabling them to slide their machines. Several juniors are known to have practised on the tarmac-covered circuit in 1978. A final stock-car meeting was staged at the venue by Trevor Redmond in 1987, after which the site was sold for redevelopment as a supermarket.

ST AUSTELL

ADDRESS: Claycountry Moto Parc, Longstone Pit, Nr Nanpean, St Austell, Cornwall
YEARS OF OPERATION: 1997 British Amateur League; 1998-2000 British Conference League
FIRST MEETING: 3 June 1997
TRACK LENGTH: 230 metres
NICKNAME: 'Gulls'
LEAGUE CHAMPIONS: 1998
KNOCK-OUT CUP WINNERS: 1998, 1999

Promoter Brian Annear (a former track worker at the Cornish Stadium in the 1960s) constructed this track in the pic-turesque setting of the English China Clays International pits at Longstone, on the outskirts of St Austell. The track opened with a British Amateur League match versus the Western Warriors on 3 June 1997, which resulted in a 34-41 defeat for the Gulls. St Austell continued with the change of the Amateur League into the Conference League in 1998, where they successfully remained until the close of the 2000 season, when Brian Annear's lease ran out. The final meeting held at Claycountry Moto Parc took place on 5 September 2000, when Shane Colvin won the Cornish Grand National. A further meeting (a four-team tournament) was mooted for 12 September, but nothing ever came of it. There were rumours that the owners of the site wanted to reopen the pit, although it was later announced that promoters Godfrey Spargo, Peter Dearing, Shirley Stephens and Ray Purvis had reached an agreement to

Clay Country Moto Parc, St Austell.

stage a season of Premier League racing at the venue in 2001. They proposed to change several things at the venue, not least of which was the team name – which became Trelawny Tigers.

SALFORD

ADDRESS: Salford Albion Stadium, Cromwell Road, Salford
YEARS OF OPERATION: 1928 Open; 1929 English Dirt-track League
FIRST MEETING: 15 August 1928

The stadium, situated across the road from the now defunct Manchester Racecourse, was originally built for greyhounds and staged its first such meeting on 7 April 1928. Dirt-track racing opened under the auspices of Albion Auto Racers Ltd – the promoting company of the forefather of speedway, Johnnie Hoskins. The first meeting was staged on 15 August 1928, when Eric Langton won the scratch race event. The directors closed the track down in September 1929, but the riders attached to the club took over and ran their own meetings. However, only a handful of meetings were staged, as by the last one on 18 October, the track was in such a poor state that Squib Burton walked out after his first ride. The meetings made a loss and that was the end of Salford speedway. In 1970 the former dirt-track was uncovered and restored to use by reinforcing the bends and coating the surface with granite dust, for the purpose of stock-car racing. However, the stock-car meetings were later to become the subject of Court action by Salford Council. Greyhound racing continued at the stadium right up to a final meeting on 30 September 1976. The venue

Salford Albion Stadium.

226

Quibell Park, Scunthorpe.

was subsequently demolished and the site is now covered by the Albion Casino, so named after the former st adium.

SCUNTHORPE

ADDRESS: Quibell Park, Brumby Wood Lane, Scunthorpe, Lincolnshire
YEARS OF OPERATION: 1971 Open; 1972-74 British League Division Two; 1975-78 National League
FIRST MEETING: 3 May 1971
TRACK LENGTH: 440 yards
NICKNAME: 'Saints'

Quibell Park was a cycling and athletics stadium, situated on the western side of Scunthorpe. Promoters Vic White and Ivor Brown introduced the shale sport to the venue in 1971, operating with an open licence in that initial year. Permission was obtained to share the athletics track, which was to cause problems in later years. The first meeting at the new track, situated within the banked cycling circuit, was staged on 3 May 1971, when 4,000 spectators witnessed Scunthorpe beat Hull 39-38 in the Humberside Trophy. In 1972, Scunthorpe joined British League Division Two, but after finishing bottom of the league there was a change of promotion for 1973, with Brian Osborn taking over. By 1974, the athletics club had begun to complain about the damage speedway bikes were doing to the track they both used. With a change of league title in 1975, Scunthorpe became founder members of the New National League. The Saints continued on in the National League until 1978, when Brian Osborn was finally ordered to take his team away from Quibell Park, following numerous disputes over the athletics track. The final meeting at the venue

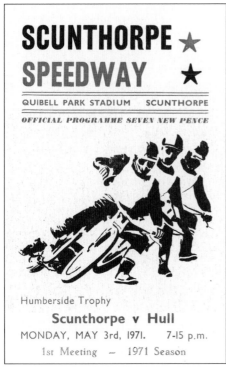

SCUNTHORPE ★ SPEEDWAY ★

QUIBELL PARK STADIUM   SCUNTHORPE

OFFICIAL PROGRAMME SEVEN NEW PENCE

Humberside Trophy
Scunthorpe v Hull
MONDAY, MAY 3rd, 1971.   7-15 p.m.
1st Meeting — 1971 Season

The first Scunthorpe Speedway programme, 1971.

went ahead on 16 October 1978, when Scunthorpe lost 37-41 to Eastbourne in a National League encounter. The Council subsequently offered Brian Osborn a site at Ashby Ville, and work began on the construction of a new track. Quibell Park remains in place today, still holding regular cycling and athletics events.

SCUNTHORPE

ADDRESS: Ashby Ville Stadium, off Queensway, Ashby, Scunthorpe
YEARS OF OPERATION: 1979-85 National League
FIRST MEETING: 6 May 1979
TRACK LENGTH: 315 metres
NICKNAME: 'Stags'

Having lost the use of Quibell Park, Scunthorpe promoter Brian Osborn set about building a new home for his team at Ashby Ville in December 1978. A couple of changes saw a new Stags nickname for the team, while Ted Hornsby became co-promoter alongside Osborn. The new track opened on 6 May 1979, when the homesters lost 38-40 to Middlesbrough in a challenge match. Having started the National League season late, due to the construction of the track, there were further problems when the Speedway Control Board temporarily suspended Scunthorpe's licence while improvements were made to the stadium. This eventually meant a congested fixture list at the tail-end of the year, but somehow the club completed their league matches with the aid of three double-headers. There was a change on the promoting front in mid-1981, when Brian Osborn sold his share in the club to Ted Hornsby and Richard Judge. By 1984, Richard Judge had assumed sole control of the track. The club then became wrapped up in a dispute with the local Council over unpaid rent and the future looked bleak. Tony and Betty Nicholls then stepped in to keep the track going, taking over as promoters in 1985. The track didn't stay open for much longer though, as after completing just nine National League fixtures, Scunthorpe officially withdrew from the league on 22 May 1985. Falling attendance figures were cited as the reason for the track's premature closure. The last-ever meeting at Ashby Ville Stadium had already been staged nine days previously on 13 May, when the Stags defeated Peterborough 40-37 in a league encounter. The stadium was subsequently used for stock-car racing, but has since been demolished and is now the site of a shopping complex.

Ashby Ville Stadium, Scunthorpe.

SHEFFIELD

ADDRESS: Owlerton Sports Stadium, Penistone Road, Owlerton, Sheffield, South Yorkshire

YEARS OF OPERATION: 1929 English Dirt-track League; 1930-31 Northern League; 1932 Speedway National Association Trophy; 1933 National League; 1938-39 National League Division Two; 1945 Open; 1946 Northern League; 1947-50 National League Division Two; 1951-52 Open; 1960-64 Provincial League; 1965-67 British League; 1968-74 British League Division One; 1975-88 British League; 1991-94 British League Division Two; 1995 British Premier League; 1996 British Premier League and British Conference League; 1997-99 British Premier League; 2000 British Premier League and British Conference League

FIRST MEETING: 30 March 1929

TRACK LENGTH: 442 yards (1929-31); 400 yards (1932-35); 390 yards (1938-48); 400 yards (1949-73); 395 yards (1974-2000)

NICKNAME: 'Tigers' (1938-49 and 1951-2000); 'Tars' (1950) (The Conference League side of 1996 were known as 'Owlerton Prowlers', while the 2000 version of the second side were called 'Sheffield Prowlers')

BRITISH SPEEDWAY CUP (DIVISION TWO) WINNERS: 1947

KNOCK-OUT CUP WINNERS: 1974

LEAGUE CHAMPIONS: 1999 (The Conference League side won their championship in 2000)

YOUNG SHIELD WINNERS: 1999

PREMIERSHIP WINNERS: 2000

Dirt-track racing first arrived at Owlerton under the auspices of Provincial Dirt-Tracks Ltd, which was the company name of Spencer Stratton, Clem Beckett and Jimmy Hindle. The three had acquired

Owlerton Sports Stadium, Sheffield.

open land at Owlerton Meadows, and began constructing the original track in 1928. With a track and stadium complete by 1929, the first dirt-track meeting went ahead on Easter Saturday 30 March that year, when Clem Beckett won the Golden Helmet in front of a crowd of 15,000 spectators. Sheffield entered the English Dirt-track League, but ended the season with their fixtures incomplete and the league table in chaos. In 1930, Sheffield rode in the Northern League, but at the end of the 1931 campaign the promotion went bankrupt. The final meeting, a charity event, had been staged on 24 September when Frank Burgess won the Golden Helmet. Crowds had tailed off and the official receiver accepted an offer of £1,000 for the stadium from Michael Gleeson and Bernard Meggitt. The new owners shortened the dirt-track and installed a greyhound circuit, staging

their first such meeting on 12 January 1932 in front of some 10,000 spectators. Arthur Westwood (trading as Sheffield Speedway Ltd) stepped in to promote the speedway side in 1932, when Sheffield partook in the National Speedway Association Trophy, opening with a 15-37 defeat at the hands of Belle Vue on 13 April. The track closed after just nine meetings though, with the side not entering the National League Championship. The final meeting of the nine was held on 22 June and saw Sheffield slump to a 22-32 defeat to Stamford Bridge. Sheffield did enter the National League in 1933, opening on 10 May against Clapton with an 18-45 defeat but, following a match against Wembley on 4 October (won 33-30), the track closed and lay empty for four years. Arthur Westwood reopened the track in 1938, and changed it to the 'D' shape it has since become famous for. The reopening meeting was versus West Ham Hawks on 5 April and it was a winning start for the homesters, with a 39-32 scoreline. Sheffield subsequently joined the National League Division Two, but initially promising crowds tailed off and the promotion again went bankrupt at the end of the season. The track carried on in 1939 however, under the control of Bluey Wilkinson, with the team again in Division Two. Sheffield also rode in the Northern Section of the Union Cup that year, along with Edinburgh, Glasgow, Newcastle and Belle Vue II. The season was brought to a premature close with the declaration of war on 3 September, and Sheffield closed down for another five years. The final pre-war meeting had gone ahead on 24 August, when the Tigers beat Belle Vue II 42.5-40.5, in a Union Cup encounter. Sheffield reopened on 13 September 1945, when Bill Pitcher won the Bluey Wilkinson Cup. Under the control of Frank Varey and Alice Hart, just two meetings were run that year, with the second featuring a challenge match between Yorkshire and Lancashire. The following year, Sheffield entered the Northern League, which then became the National League Division Two in 1947. The Tigers remained in Division Two for the rest of the decade, with Frank Varey and Alice Hart promoting them until the end of 1949, when Varey departed in order to spend more time running the sport at Edinburgh. Alice Hart then took sole charge and changed the team nickname to Tars. In 1951, however, Frank Varey returned as promoter, linking up with Eric Langton for a season of open licence racing, having restored

Sheffield's Golden Jubilee programme, 1979.

the Tigers nickname. The venture didn't last long, and after a sixth meeting on 3 May versus Halifax in the Midland Shield (42-42), the promoters closed the track due to a lack of support. Varey reopened the track on 26 June 1952, when Len Williams won the Fifty Guineas Trophy. However, after running open licence events for the rest of the season, the track was to close down again until 1960. The last meeting had seen Len Williams win the Cussens Trophy on 11 September 1952. Varey once more reopened the track on 21 April 1960, when the homesters suffered a 26-46 reverse at the hands of Belle Vue Reserves in a challenge match. The team subsequently entered the Provincial League, where they remained until the formation of the British League in 1965. After his long association with the club, Frank Varey retired at the end of the 1972 campaign. County Speedways Ltd took over in 1973, with Terry Thornhill installed as the speedway manager. John Dews subsequently replaced Terry Thornhill as speedway manager in 1977. A further promotional change saw Ray Glover take over at Sheffield in 1980. More management changes in 1984 saw Ray Glover sell the promotional rights on to Maurice Ducker. The stadium was also used by Sheffield Eagles Rugby League Club from 2 September 1984 to 23 April 1989. This was never a satisfactory arrangement as, due to the speedway track, the corners of the pitch and the in-goal area had to be laid on rubber mats. After running continuously since 1960, the Tigers were to close at the end of the 1988 season, with the final Owlerton meeting being held on 13 October that year, when Sheffield beat Reading 48-41 in a British League encounter. A further league match versus Cradley Heath was rained off on 20 October but never re-staged. In the wake of the nearby Hillsborough disaster, Owlerton Stadium was closed to all sports on 14 September 1989, on safety grounds. The stadium subsequently reopened with the capacity limited to 2,400 people at any one time. Under the promotion of Cliff Carr, speedway returned to the venue in 1991, with the Tigers entering the British League Division Two. The reopening meeting was held on 7 April, when Sheffield and Belle Vue drew 45-45 in a challenge match. Falling attendances had seen the club fall into financial difficulties, with Neil Machin and Tim Lucking (trading as Class Trend Ltd) coming to the rescue and taking over from Cliff Carr in July 1992. Along with all the remaining sides in British speedway, Sheffield became members of the British Premier League in 1995. Sadly, Tim Lucking died in July 1996, with Malcolm Wright eventually buying the late co-promoter's shares to join Neil

Machin in the running of the club. The 1996 season also saw Sheffield enter a side in the British Conference League. Riding as Owlerton Prowlers, the new side rode their first home match on 25 April, beating Peterborough Thundercats 43-34. This proved to be a one-year venture, with the final meeting going ahead on 10 October, when the Prowlers beat Berwick 40-38. At the end of 1996 the large Premier League was split in two, with the formation of an Elite League, but Sheffield opted to stay where they were, in the revamped Premier League. Former rider Louis Carr joined forces with the promotional team of Neil Machin and Malcolm Wright in 1997, with the fortunes of the club going from strength to strength on a sound footing, right up to the present day. Two teams operated from the stadium in 2000, with Sheffield entering a second team in the British Conference League. Riding as Sheffield Prowlers, the team completed their opening home match on 9 April, defeating Buxton 50-40.

SHEFFIELD

ADDRESS: Sheffield Training Track, Penistone Road, Owlerton, Sheffield, South Yorkshire

YEARS OF OPERATION: 1978-79 Training; 1980 Open and Training; 1981 Training; 1982 Open and Training; 1983 Training; 1992-2000 Training

TRACK LENGTH: 200 metres

The original idea to construct a training track came from John Dews, the circuit being laid in early 1978 on land previously used as a training pitch by Sheffield Wednesday Football Club at the rear of the existing Owlerton Stadium. Ian M. Stead took his first-ever

Sheffield Training Track, Owlerton.

speedway rides at the circuit in 1980, when only twelve years of age. Ray and Carl Glover ran fortnightly training sessions at the track in 1981. Paul Bentley won the Senior A Final of a training track championship on 3 July 1982. Having not been used since 1983, the track fell into a state of disrepair, until Graham Trollope began reconstruction work late in 1991. The track reopened on 4 January 1992, after several previous attempts to start had been thwarted by the weather. Louis Carr ran a training school at the circuit in 1994. A two-day USA School of Excellence was run at the venue by Charles Ermolenko in 1996. A training school was run by Greg Hancock and Billy Hamill on the 'D'- shaped mini-track in October 1997. The mini-circuit has been used regularly by team riders and juniors during its two periods of activity (1978-83 and 1992-2000).

SKEGNESS
ADDRESS: Skegness Stadium, Marsh Lane, Orby, Skegness, Lincolnshire
YEARS OF OPERATION: 1997 British Premier League; 1998 British Conference League
FIRST MEETING: 13 April 1997
TRACK LENGTH: 300 metres
NICKNAME: 'Braves'

Speedway arrived at the Skegness Stadium in 1997, with the tarmac stock-car track being replaced by a shale surface. The speedway safety fence had to be erected prior to meetings, and then taken down afterwards to enable the stock cars to run. Promoters of the 1997 Premier League venture were Peter Oakes and Sarah Gudgeon, with the opening meeting going ahead on 13 April when Brent Werner was victorious in the Central Engineering Lincolnshire Trophy. Crowd levels were never brilliant at the venue

Skegness Stadium.

and three rained-off meetings certainly did not help matters, so due to financial reasons the promoters were forced to look elsewhere to fulfil their fixtures. The team eventually relocated to Ryde, bringing Premier League racing to the Isle of Wight for the very first time. At the time of their move from Skegness, just five meetings (including a double-header) had been held at the Marsh Lane venue, the last of which was on 29 May 1997, when the homesters lost 31-59 to Arena-Essex in a Knock-out Cup tie. In 1998, Stephen Lambert decided to reintroduce speedway to the venue, and entered Skegness in the British Conference League, along with co-promoters Alan Hodkinson, Cyril Crane and Stephen Blyth. The track opened again on 24 May 1998, when the Braves lost 40-48 to Mildenhall in the Fen Trophy. The venture at Skegness didn't last for long, however, due to problems created by track-sharing with stock cars. Having run just three meetings at the venue, the team moved to King's Lynn in order to complete fixtures, eventually becoming known as Norfolk Braves. The last-ever meeting at Skegness was staged on 7 June 1998, when the homesters lost 38-51 to St Austell in a league fixture. One further meeting, a qualifying round of the Conference League Riders' Championship, was scheduled for 13 June, but this fell foul of inclement weather and was eventually run at King's Lynn.

SMALLFORD
ADDRESS: Smallford Speedway, Hatfield Road, Nr St Albans, Hertfordshire
YEARS OF OPERATION: 1936 Open and Training; 1937 Open; 1938 Sunday Dirt-track League; 1939 Open
NICKNAME: 'Stags'

The Smallford track was situated on the Hatfield Road, approximately two miles from St Albans. In 1936, open-style meetings were promoted by Hertford and District Motorcycle and Car Club, although dates and results remain unknown. This was a drive-in speedway, where spectators could watch the action from the comfort of their vehicle. In 1938, Smallford entered the Sunday Dirt-track League, with matches versus Dagenham, Eastbourne, Romford and Rye House. Changes were made in 1939, which saw the track smoothed out and a covered stand installed near the pits for spectators. Nothing more was heard of the venue following the outbreak of the Second World War. The site of the former track is now covered by a potato field.

SOLIHULL
ADDRESS: Solihull Ice Rink, Solihull, Nr Birmingham, Warwickshire
YEARS OF OPERATION: 1972 Indoor Ice Speedway
FIRST MEETING: 13 March 1972

Indoor ice speedway was popular in 1972, with meetings being held at Aviemore, Kirkcaldy and Murrayfield, so it was no surprise to see a similar event staged at Solihull Ice Rink. The one and only meeting staged at the venue went ahead on 13 March that year, when Birmingham entertained a Midland Select in a challenge match.

SOUTHAMPTON
ADDRESS: The Stadium, Banister Court, Southampton, Hampshire
YEARS OF OPERATION: 1928 Open, 1929-31 Southern League; 1932 Speedway National Association Trophy; 1935 Open;

1936-37 Provincial League; 1938 National League Division Two; 1939 National League Division One; 1940 Open; 1947-48 National League Division Three; 1949-51 National League Division Two; 1952-53 Southern League; 1954-56 National League Division Two; 1957-63 National League
FIRST MEETING: 6 October 1928
TRACK LENGTH: 440 yards (1928-29); 378 yards (1930-40); 333 yards (1947-63)
NICKNAME: 'Saints'
PROVINCIAL TROPHY WINNERS: 1936
LEAGUE CHAMPIONS: 1936, 1962
ANNIVERSARY CUP (DIVISION THREE) WINNERS: 1948
NATIONAL TROPHY (DIVISION TWO) WINNERS: 1956
NATIONAL TROPHY WINNERS: 1961
KNOCK-OUT CUP WINNERS: 1961, 1963

The site occupied by Banister Court Stadium was previously covered by a school, which had relocated to Shirley in 1927. Charles Knott purchased the site that year, and set about the construction of a greyhound stadium right next door to the County Cricket ground. Upon completion, the venue also included a dirt track and an inner circuit for roller-skating, plus an area for tennis and roller-hockey. Greyhound racing was first held at the stadium on 6 August 1928. Originally the dog circuit was inside the dirt-track, although the positions were reversed prior to the 1930 season. Promoter G.E. Baxter (known as Jimmy), under the auspices of Dirt-Track Speedways Ltd, introduced the cinder sport to the stadium in 1928, with a trial being the first action on 29 September that year. The track officially opened the follow-

S

Southampton Speedway programme, 1952.

ing week on 6 October, when Sprouts Elder won the Golden Gauntlet. Southampton entered the Southern League in 1929, and completed three years in that sphere, before partaking in the Speedway National Association Trophy in 1932. Having completed eleven matches, Southampton moved their operation to Lea Bridge, where they rode as Clapton Saints for the rest of the competition, and in the National League that followed. The final meeting at Banister Court had been staged on 25 May, when the homesters beat West Ham 27-26. After two seasons without dirt-track racing at Banister Court, two neutral meetings were held in 1935, the first of which saw Belle Vue defeat

Wembley 57-51 in a challenge match on 1 October. The Saints reformed in 1936, joining the Provincial League prior to it becoming the National League Division Two in 1938. In 1939, Southampton joined Division One, following an exchange of licence with Bristol, after the Knowle-based side had endured a disastrous year of top-flight racing in the previous year. However, having completed seventeen matches of the league campaign, the Saints were forced to close early, due to the outbreak of war. Two meetings were staged at Easter in 1940, including a 46-62 defeat at the hands of Harringay in a challenge match on 25 March. Banister Court then remained closed to the cinder sport until 1947, when Jimmy Baxter brought the Saints back to life in the National League Division Three. The reopening meeting went ahead on 29 April, when George Bason won the Southampton Trophy. The season was marred by tragedy when Peter Jackson lost his life after crashing at Banister Court on 8 July. Another season of Division Three racing followed in 1948, before the Saints were promoted to Division Two in 1949. After just seven league matches of the 1951 campaign, promoter Jimmy Baxter withdrew Southampton from the league and closed the track down, following a World Championship qualifying round on 10 July, which was won by Bob Oakley. The crippling effects of the ludicrous entertainment tax that speedway was saddled with could be cited as the reason for the track's premature closure. A composite Gala of Sport event was subsequently held on 21 July and the indications are that some speedway was held during the programme.

Midget-car racing was first staged at the stadium later that year, on 4 September. Charles Knott resurrected speedway at the venue on 24 March 1952, when the Possibles took on the Probables in a trial match. The meeting was abandoned after eighteen heats, with the Possibles leading 61.5-43.5 at the time. Southampton subsequently took part in the Southern League that season, and again in 1953. Upon the Southern League's merger into the National League in 1954, the Saints found themselves back in Division Two. Stock-car racing was first held at Banister Court that year, on 14 September. Bantam-car racing first appeared at the stadium on 11 April 1955. The Saints' 1956 campaign was to end in great sadness, when club captain Ernie Rawlins was killed at Banister Court on 18 September in an inter-league match versus Birmingham. With so few teams left running, Southampton found themselves in the eleven-team National League in 1957, where they would remain until the track's closure at the end of the 1963 season. A third rider lost his life at the venue, when Alan Pearce died following an accident on 27 March 1959. The last speedway meeting at Banister Court was held on 3 October 1963, when the Saints defeated Wimbledon 43-35 in a challenge match. A final greyhound meeting was staged at the venue three weeks later, on 22 October. The stadium was subsequently demolished and the site used for housing.

SOUTHAMPTON
ADDRESS: Southampton Ice Rink, Southampton, Hampshire
YEARS OF OPERATION: 1967 Indoor Ice Speedway Demonstration

Barry Briggs gave a demonstration of speedway racing at Southampton Ice Rink in 1967. 'Briggo' completed a few test laps, prior to rink officials calling a halt when the ice began to cut up badly.

STAINFORTH
ADDRESS: Stainforth Greyhound Stadium, Stainforth, Nr Doncaster, South Yorkshire
YEARS OF OPERATION: 1930 Open
FIRST MEETING: 21 April 1930
TRACK LENGTH: 440 yards

The cinder sport arrived at Stainforth in 1930, promoted by Stainforth Dirt-track (Doncaster) Ltd. The opening meeting was held on 21 April 1930, when George Wigfield won the Broadway Handicap. A total of nine meetings were staged in that initial period, including a final one on 9 June, when Tommy Allott won the Gray & Raynes Cup. Following this meeting, the promotion went into liquidation and the track closed down. A rider co-operative reopened the track two months later on 8 August, with a further meeting being staged a week later on 16 August, when Tommy Allott was triumphant in the Broadway Handicap. There is no record of any subsequent track action at the short-lived venue.

STAINES
ADDRESS: Staines Greyhound Stadium, Wraysbury Road, Staines, Middlesex
YEARS OF OPERATION: 1938-39 Open

Greyhound racing was first staged at the stadium on 21 January 1928. Hawks Speedways were refused an ACU licence to run dirt-track meetings at Staines in 1934. Putt Mossmann held one of his famous motor-cycle rodeos at Staines Stadium in 1938. Another application for an ACU licence was refused in 1947, although midget-car racing was held at the Middlesex venue that year. A further application for a licence was again refused in 1948, after an objection from the local Town Planning Committee. However, following an appeal in 1949, permission was granted to run speedway on one day a week, although no meetings were ever held. Many prominent grass-track exponents took part in a meeting organised by the South Midland Centre of the ACU on 19 August 1950. Stock-car racing was first held at the venue on 8 April 1955, on a newly-installed shale surface. Sidecar speedway took place at the track in 1956. Greyhound racing ceased at the venue in 1960, and stock-car racing also finished that year, following a final meeting on 17 June. The stadium was subsequently demolished to make way for a bypass and bridge.

STAMFORD BRIDGE

ADDRESS: Stamford Bridge Stadium, Fulham Road, London
YEARS OF OPERATION: 1928 Open; 1929-31 Southern League; 1932 National League
FIRST MEETING: 5 May 1928
TRACK LENGTH: 445 yards
NICKNAME: 'Pensioners'
LEAGUE CHAMPIONS: 1929
NATIONAL ASSOCIATION TROPHY WINNERS: 1932

Stamford Bridge had been owned by H.A. Mears since 1904, and he initially offered the facilities to Fulham Football Club, who turned down the opportunity. In 1905, Chelsea Football Club were formed and took up residence at the stadium – where they have been ever since of course. Dirt-track racing came to Stamford Bridge in 1928, under the promotion of Claude Langdon. The track was constructed around the soccer pitch of Chelsea Football Club, and as such was very narrow, with long straights and almost square corners. Push starts were used, due to the narrowness of the circuit, as it was considered too dangerous to have all the riders going into the first turn together. The opening meeting, held under floodlights, was staged on 5 May 1928, when Roger Frogley was triumphant in the Senior Handicap event. This is a challenger for the first floodlit meeting in Britain, but comes a close second to Thrum Hall in Halifax, which ran under artificial lighting just three nights previously. Prior to the first meeting at The Bridge, the crowd of 25,000 spectators witnessed the track declared open by Queenie Thomas, who led a parade of riders round in formation. Shortly after opening, tragedy struck at the track in May when nineteen-year-old Charlie Biddle was killed in a racing accident. International Speedways Ltd (A.J. Hunting), took over the running of the track in 1929, with Stamford Bridge entering the Southern League. A change of promotion in 1930 saw the Motor Track Racing Association Ltd take charge. Other changes that year saw the track widened by 5ft (to the ACU minimum width of 25ft), with the boarding at the base of the safety fence being heightened and painted white, while the floodlighting was also augmented. The widened track allowed scratch races with four riders, whereas previously a maximum of only three men per race had been

Stamford Bridge Stadium, London.

allowed. In 1931, black cinders were laid on the circuit, so that it could be used for the dual purpose of dirt-track racing and athletics events. Stamford Bridge competed in the National Speedway Association Trophy, prior to competing in the National League Championship in 1932, but the end of the season brought the curtain down on dirt-track racing at the London venue. The last-ever meeting was held on 1 October that year, when the homesters beat Wembley 29-25 in a league fixture. Greyhound racing was first staged at the stadium on 31 July 1937, and continued on until a final meeting on 1 August, 1968. A crowd of 50,000 people reportedly watched an opening midget-car meeting on 13 May 1948. Today, the stadium is part of a multi-complex, which includes a hotel, shops and leisure facilities.

STEPPS
ADDRESS: Trotting Stadium, Marshall Park, Stepps, Nr Glasgow
YEARS OF OPERATION: 1961 Training

In September 1948, the Speedway Control Board decided to visit the Trotting Stadium at Stepps, before deciding to refuse an application to run speedway there. In 1949, Billy Galloway again tried to get permission to run speedway at the venue, but this was turned down once more. Midget-car racing was staged at the stadium in 1952. A further application was made in 1953, while a team sponsor had actually gone so far as to purchase a batch of new machines, with the ultimate aim of deploying an all-Scottish team. Unfortunately, once again the application was refused by the Control Board. Despite the objections to speedway, both midget car and trotting events were held at the stadium in 1953. Both Bert Harkins and Brian Black are known to

239

have practised at the stadium in 1961, but no actual meetings were ever staged at the venue.

STOCKPORT

ADDRESS: Hazel Grove Greyhound Stadium, Hazel Grove, Nr Stockport, Cheshire
YEARS OF OPERATION: 1937 Open
FIRST MEETING: 5 May 1937

Hazel Grove Stadium was situated in between two huge brick railway bridges, three miles on the Macclesfield side of Stockport. Greyhound racing was first staged at the stadium on 23 December 1932. Manchester Sports Motor Club, a group of local enthusiasts, built their own track with a safety fence, and rough terracing was erected before their funds ran out. The promoters decided to run some meetings anyway, in an effort to raise money for the purchase of cinders in order to ultimately run genuine speedway. A badly-organised opening meeting took place on 5 May 1937, taking three hours to run, having started half an hour late, on a track that was described as rough and bumpy. Less than a month after the opening meeting, it was farewell to the speedway-cum-grass-track at Hazel Grove, when the track was closed by the Council following complaints of noise irritation. Greyhound racing ceased at the venue in June 1960.

STOKE

ADDRESS: Hanley Stadium, Sun Street, Hanley, Staffordshire
YEARS OF OPERATION: 1929 English Dirt-track League and Open; 1939 National League Division Two; 1947-49 National League Division Three; 1950-53 National League Division Two; 1960-63 Provincial League
FIRST MEETING: 11 April 1929
TRACK LENGTH: 350 yards (1929-53); 347 yards (1960-63)
NICKNAME: 'Potters'
LEAGUE CHAMPIONS: 1949

Greyhound racing was first held at the Sun Street venue on 31 March 1928. Promoted by British Speedways Ltd (Jack Cunliffe, Captain Lingard, F.K. Wilkie and R. Greer), Hanley Stadium staged its first dirt-track meeting on 11 April 1929, when 7,000 people witnessed Arthur Jervis win the Golden Helmet. Hanley, as the team was called, entered the English Dirt-track League upon Bolton's withdrawal in that opening season. After only a handful of meetings, however, they themselves pulled out of the league. At the time of their withdrawal, just one league match had been held at Sun Street, versus Burnley on 18 May. Dirt-track racing did continue at the venue, however, with scratch race and handicap events being staged. Following the final meeting that season, on 5 September when Larry Boulton won the Golden Helmet, dirt-track racing ceased at the venue until 1939 – although midget-car racing took place in 1938. In 1939, the renamed Stoke side partook in National League Division Two, under the promotion of J. France, having opened with a 45-38 challenge match victory over Belle Vue Reserves on 20 April. However, having staged just eleven meetings, the track again closed following a 45-38 league victory against Hackney on 29 June. A lack of support was cited as the reason for the premature closure, with Belle

Vue Reserves taking over the Stoke licence and remaining fixtures. Following the war, the track was back in action in 1947, under the promotion of Tiger Stevenson, who entered Hanley in the National League Division Three. The reopening meeting at Sun Street took place on 8 May that year, when the homesters beat Cradley Heath 48-33 in a challenge match. The Potters were promoted to Division Two in 1950, having won the Division Three championship the previous year. During 1951, the running of the track was taken over by Les Gregory, following the departure of Tiger Stevenson. After riding under the name of Hanley since 1947, the team name reverted back to Stoke in 1952, at the behest of Les Gregory. Having completed four years of National League Division Two racing, the track again closed at the end of the 1953 campaign, due to the fact that attendance figures had fallen to the 5,000 mark. The last meeting of that era was a Division Two double-header on 26 September, which saw the Potters lose 41-43 to Poole before defeating Wolverhampton 58-26. Mike Parker and Reg Fearman brought speedway back to Sun Street in 1960, with the Potters running in the Provincial League. In front of 12,000 fans, the Potters opened with a 44-26 Provincial League victory over Liverpool on 15 April. After four seasons in the Provincial League, the Potters were again forced to close, this time because the stadium had been sold for redevelopment. The final meeting at the venue was staged on 26 October 1963, when a Three Team Tournament was held for the Harjacmor Trophy. The result of Sun Street's last-ever meeting was: Stoke 34, Wolverhampton 19, Long

Stoke Speedway programme, 1949.

Eaton 19. A final greyhound meeting took place at the stadium on 18 October 1963. The stadium was subsequently demolished late in 1963, and is now covered by a firm of car dealers.

STOKE

ADDRESS: Newcastle-under-Lyme Stadium, Loomer Road, Chesterton, Stoke, Staffordshire

YEARS OF OPERATION: 1972 Training; 1973-74 British League Division Two; 1975-90 National League; 1991-92 British League Division Two; 1994 British League Division Three; 1995 British Academy League; 1996-2000 British Premier League

FIRST MEETING: 12 April 1973

TRACK LENGTH: 380 yards (1973); 348 yards (1974); 395 yards (1975-78); 368 yards (1979-92); 341 yards (1994-2000)

NICKNAME: 'Potters'

Russ Bragg was the leader of a consortium behind the construction of the Newcastle-under-Lyme Stadium in 1972. In an effort to bring speedway back to the Stoke area, a track was laid, and tested out by Ole Olsen, Pete Jarman and Roy Trigg on 23 October 1972. Along with co-promoter Pete Lansdale, Russ Bragg entered Chesterton (as they were then called) into the 1973 British League Division Two. The opening meeting at the new circuit took place on 12 April 1973, when Chesterton beat Birmingham 43-35 in a challenge match. The team name was changed to Stoke in 1974, when Russ Bragg became sole promoter of the track. In 1975, Stoke were founder members of the New National League, with a slight change of promotion to Five Star Presentations. Russ Bragg was still on board, but was joined by both Tony Allsopp and Harry Bastable in the run-

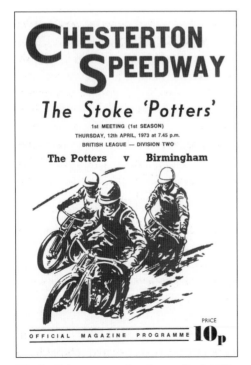

The first Stoke programme from Loomer Road, 1973.

ning of the club. A first greyhound meeting was held at the stadium on 11 April 1975. There was a further change at the top in 1976, when Mike Parker Promotions Ltd took over at the track. Another change of promotion in 1977 saw Les Jenkins, Joe Thurley and Chris Harrison assume control. Yet another change in 1978 saw Joe Thurley joined by Dai Evans and Ray Sant as co-promoters, under the banner of Stoke Speedway Ltd. Chris Van Straaten joined the promotion in 1979, replacing Joe Thurley. The annual merry-go-round of promoters continued in 1980, when Trent Speedway Promotions took over. This was the trading name used by John Dews and Ray Sant. With Stoke continuing in the National League, John Dews and Ray Sant were joined at the helm by Fred Collier in 1982. The promotion changed again in 1987, when Paul Gray joined Ray Sant in the hot seat. In March 1988, the former promoter and the man responsible for the rebirth of Stoke speedway, Russ Bragg, died after being badly burnt in an accident while at work. There was yet another change of promoter in 1989, when Eric Stead took up the reigns of the club. Following the sad death of Eric Stead at the tail-end of 1990, Dave Tattum became promoter at Loomer Road in time for the Potters' opening meeting in the re-titled British League Division Two (following the amalgamation of the British League and the National League). Former promoter Paul Gray linked up with Dave Tattum to run the track in 1992, but at the end of that season the track closed down due to falling attendances. The final meeting had been held on 31 October that year, when the Potters beat Rye House 57-33 in a Division Two encounter. After a year of

Newcastle-under-Lyme Stadium, Loomer Road, Chesterton.

inactivity at Loomer Road, save for midget-car racing, the Potters returned in 1994, entering the new British League Division Three under the promotion of Graham Wright. The reopening meeting was staged on 2 July that year, when Stoke were defeated 43-52 by Peterborough in a challenge match. The British League Division Three became the Academy League in 1995, when another change of promotion at Loomer Road saw Ray Sant return as co-promoter with Alan Wilde. More changes in 1996 saw the homeless Cradley team move to the stadium for British Premier League action, under the guise of Cradley Heath & Stoke Heathens, promoted by Les Pottinger, Sven Heiding and Jan O. Pedersen. With the formation of the Elite League in 1997, the Potters returned to the track, but elected to stay in the Premier League. As had become usual, there was a change on the promotion front, with John Woolridge at the head of a new

consortium that also included Dave Beresford and Bernard Loftus. In 1998, Steve Rees became co-promoter with John Woolridge, but a series of postponed fixtures, coupled with poor crowd levels, saw the track in crisis by June. However, the Potters survived following the umpteenth change on the promotional side when Dave Tattum replaced Steve Rees. Dave Tattum has remained in control up to the present day, initially alongside John Woolridge in 1999, but latterly as sole promoter into 2000 and beyond.

STREATHAM
ADDRESS: Streatham Ice Rink, Streatham, London
YEARS OF OPERATION: 1933 Indoor Ice Racing

Not much is known about this venue, but indoor ice racing was staged at Streatham in 1933.

SUNDERLAND

ADDRESS: Sunderland Greyhound Stadium, Newcastle Road, East Boldon, County Durham
YEARS OF OPERATION: 1964 Provincial League; 1971-74 British League Division Two
FIRST MEETING: 21 April 1964
TRACK LENGTH: 310 yards
NICKNAME: 'Saints' (1964); 'Stars' (1971-73); 'Gladiators' (1974)

Greyhound racing was first held at Sunderland Stadium on 23 March 1940. Speedway was first introduced to the venue by Mike Parker and Bill Bridgett in 1964, when Sunderland Saints joined the Provincial League. Opening the season on 21 April, the homesters lost 32-44 to Newcastle in a challenge match. The track had closed down by June, when the Saints had completed a total of just three league fixtures. Poor weather had seen crowds fall from 6,500 to around 1,000, and this was cited as the reason for the track's premature closure. The final meeting of this period at the East Boldon venue was held on 9 June, when Ivan Mauger won the Cock o' the North Trophy. This was the last of just eight meetings held at the stadium in that abortive first season. After a six-year gap, the track was reopened by Allied Presentations Ltd on 2 May 1971, when the renamed Stars beat Teesside 40-38 in the North-East Trophy. Competing in the British League Division Two, Allied Presentations Ltd ran the show until Elizabeth and Ken Taylor took over in 1973. In 1974, the track was promoted by Derek Fell and Alan Chorlton under the guise of Felton Speedway Promotions Ltd, with the team nickname again altered to Gladiators. There was a change of promotion in June, when the Taylor family returned, but speedway never

Sunderland Greyhound Stadium, East Boldon.

really caught on at this venue, and the track closed at the completion of the 1974 fixture list. The last-ever meeting was staged on 13 September that year, when Sunderland beat Stoke 41-37 in a league match. Sunderland's track licence was subsequently transferred to Newcastle in 1975.

SWINDON

ADDRESS: Swindon Autodrome, Cricklade Road, Gorse Hill, Swindon, Wiltshire
YEARS OF OPERATION: 1928-30 Open
FIRST MEETING: 4 August 1928
TRACK LENGTH: 356 yards

In the summer of 1928, with a view to staging dirt-track racing, the Swindon Sports Club Ltd purchased a large piece of meadowland at the rear of the Duke of Edinburgh Hotel on the Cricklade Road in the Gorse Hill area of Swindon. Walter Hobbs, the chairman of the Swindon Sports Club Ltd, was the main driving force behind the track, which staged meetings in conjunction with the North Wiltshire Motorcycle and Light Car Club. Over 5,000 tons of ash, chalk and earth were utilised in making the racing strip, which was encircled by mounds of earth to provide crude terracing for spectators. The track opened on 4 August 1928, when C. Harman won both the Swindon Scratch Race and Gorse Hill Scratch Race. The track was managed by J.E. Whittington, who doubled as the publican at the adjacent hotel. Twelve open licence meetings were staged at the venue in 1928, with similar events again in 1929 and 1930, after which the track closed for good. The 1930 meetings were held under the promotion of Swindon Speedways Stadiums Ltd. The Duke of Edinburgh Hotel

A very rare Swindon Speedway programme, 1930.

remains in place today, while most of the land behind it is now covered with houses and garages.

SWINDON

ADDRESS: Abbey Stadium, Blunsdon, Nr Swindon, Wiltshire
YEARS OF OPERATION: 1949 Open and National League Division Three; 1950-51 National League Division Three; 1952-53 Southern League; 1954-56 National League Division Two; 1957-64 National League; 1965-67 British League; 1968-74 British League Division One; 1975-90 British League; 1991-92 British League Division One; 1993-94 British League Division Two; 1995 British Premier League; 1996 British Premier League and Conference League; 1997 British Elite League and Amateur League; 1998 British

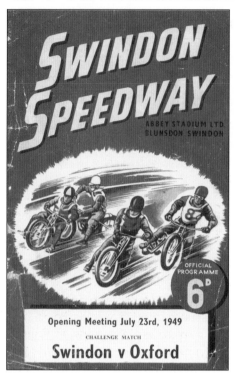

Swindon's first meeting at Blunsden Stadium, 1949.

Elite League; 1999-2000 British Premier League

FIRST MEETING: 23 July 1949
TRACK LENGTH: 410 yards (1949-59); 395 yards (1960-2000)
NICKNAME: 'Robins' (The Conference League team of 1996 were known as 'Sprockets', while the Amateur League side of 1997 were called 'M4 Raven Sprockets')
LEAGUE CHAMPIONS: 1956, 1957, 1967
KNOCK-OUT CUP WINNERS: 2000
YOUNG SHIELD WINNERS: 2000

The original promoters of Swindon were Bert Hearse and Reg Witcomb, who constructed a 410-yard cinder track at Blunsdon. Banking was built up around the circuit, with earth taken from the car park area, which was dug out to a depth of 18 inches. The opening meeting took place on 23 July 1949, when Swindon lost 39-45 to Oxford in a challenge match in front of a crowd of 8,000 people. Later in 1949, Hull were forced to close down, having completed thirty-five fixtures of their National League Division Three programme. Swindon took their place in the division, and completed the Hull side's remaining fixtures. The Robins remained in Division Three until it became the Southern League in 1952. A first midget-car meeting was held at Blunsdon on 11 October 1952. Greyhound racing was also first staged at the Abbey Stadium three weeks later, on 1 November 1952. Bill Dutton replaced Reg Witcomb in 1953, teaming up with Bert Hearse in the running of the track. In 1954, Swindon reverted to National League Division Two action, with Norman Parker replacing Bill Dutton on the management side. That year also saw a first stock-car meeting at Blunsdon, on 25 September. A further change in 1955 saw Vic Scales join Bert Hearse at Swindon, following the departure of Norman Parker due to the pressure of business. In 1956, Bert Hearse was back in sole charge, and that was to remain the case until the end of 1964. 1957 saw Swindon compete in the eleven-team National League, following the gradual decline of the sport and closure of many tracks. Two teams operated at Blunsdon in 1958, with Swindon also entering a side in the Junior League. Although the junior competition only had four teams, the fixtures were never completed and the league table ended in disarray. Swindon became founder members of the British League in 1965, with Ted Nelson taking over as promoter on behalf of the stadium owners – he was to run the show right up until the end of the 1978 campaign. Wally Mawdsley became promoter at Blunsdon in 1979, and remained in place until Richard Vowles took up the reigns in 1983. Tragedy struck at Swindon on 11 September 1982, when twenty-year-old Martin Hewlett collapsed after a meeting against Birmingham, and died a few days later. Richard Vowles' tenure as promoter ended in 1986, when he was unable to carry on due to a combination of falling attendances and the terms of his agreement with the then stadium owners, British Car Auctions. For a brief and worrying time the track actually closed down in August, but was resurrected when Ted Nelson and Bill Chandler were put in charge of speedway affairs by the stadium owners. Soon after the track had resumed in 1986, Blunsdon staged its 1,000th meeting on 20 September, when Cradley Heath were the visitors for a British League match. With the amalga-

mation of the British and National Leagues, Swindon became members of the British League Division One in 1991. However, having finished bottom of their division that year, the rules meant the Robins should have been relegated. However, they were reprieved by events at two other tracks. Under the constitution of the BSPA, Division Two had to have an equal number of tracks to Division One. Swindon's top-flight status was therefore preserved when Division One Berwick dropped back into Division Two, while Mildenhall also entered the lower division. Swindon finished bottom again in 1992, and there was to be no escape from relegation a second time, with Mervyn Stewkesbury and Pete Ansell taking over as promoters of British League Division Two racing at the track in 1993. The British Premier League was formed in 1995, and this saw a further change of promotion at Blunsdon, with

Abbey Stadium, Swindon.

Martin Yeates and Peter Toogood taking control. Peter Toogood took sole control in 1996, when Swindon also entered a team in the British Conference League. Blunsdon hosted its first such meeting on 12 May that year, when Swindon Sprockets beat Arena-Essex 48-30. The Conference League venture only lasted for one season, with a final Blunsdon meeting going ahead on 21 September 1996, when the Sprockets defeated Eastbourne Starlets 46½-31½. 1997 saw the formation of the British Elite League, with Swindon taking their place in the new ten-team higher division. Swindon also joined forces with Reading to enter a composite side, made up mainly from juniors, in the British Amateur League that year. The home fixtures were equally split between the two tracks, with the team riding under the name of M4 Raven Sprockets. The opening British Amateur League fixture at Blunsdon was staged on 17 May that year, when the Raven Sprockets beat Belle Vue Colts 41-32. The final Amateur League match at Blunsdon was held on 20 September 1997, when the Raven Sprockets combination side defeated the Anglian Angels 44-34. Also in 1997, the Abbey Stadium was purchased for £1.2 million by the Bristol-based BS Group. In 1998, Peter Toogood was joined by co-promoter Richard Evans in the running of the track, with the regular Saturday night racing slot being lost to greyhound racing. Racing on Thursdays proved unpopular with supporters and a riders' pay policy was introduced at the end of the season. The top Elite League boys could not accept the pay on offer and eventually Swindon applied to race in the Premier League in 1999, with Peter Toogood back at the helm as sole promoter. Along with team

manager Jed Stone and promoting manager Mick Bell, Peter Toogood took Swindon through a remarkable year in 2000, which saw an upsurge in support as Thursday night racing was finally accepted. The club's future is now assured, having completed fifty-two consecutive seasons. There was sadness amongst the good times of 2000 though, with the death of former stadium supremo Ted Nelson in August.

SWINDON
ADDRESS: Abbey Stadium Car Park, Blunsdon, Nr Swindon, Wiltshire
YEARS OF OPERATION: 1950 Training
TRACK LENGTH: 260 yards

In February 1950, a practice track was laid in the car park at Blunsdon. Members of the Swindon team, along with selected novices, used the track for training. This was a temporary measure, due to the fact that the riders were not permitted to use the proper Swindon track until the first week in March that year.

SWINDON
ADDRESS: Swindon Training Track, Abbey Stadium, Blunsdon, Nr Swindon, Wiltshire
YEARS OF OPERATION: 1991-95 Training

The Swindon training track was built on the centre green of the main track during the winter of 1990/91. Regular schooling sessions were held under the guidance of Malcolm Holloway in 1991. The track continued to be used until 1995, when Alun Rossiter ran a training school at a cost of £10 for riders aged under sixteen, and £20 for those over sixteen.

T

TAMWORTH

ADDRESS: Mile Oak Speedway, Sutton Road, Mile Oak, Tamworth, Staffordshire
YEARS OF OPERATION: 1932-34 Open
FIRST MEETING: 17 July 1932
TRACK LENGTH: 275 yards

The opening scratch race meeting at Mile Oak took place on 17 July 1932, with a further three meetings being staged that year under the promotion of G.B. Mountford and Harold Trimnell. Three meetings were held at the venue in 1933, with a further three in 1934, prior to the track closing for good. This, unfortunately, is another of those venues of which details are vague, with dates and details of meetings remaining difficult to detect.

TAMWORTH

ADDRESS: Deer Park, Watling Street, Fazeley, Tamworth, Staffordshire
YEARS OF OPERATION: 1947-50 National League Division Three
FIRST MEETING: 30 April 1947
TRACK LENGTH: 352 yards
NICKNAME: 'Hounds' (1947-49); 'Tammies' (1950)
BRITISH SPEEDWAY CUP (DIVISION THREE) WINNERS: 1947

The stadium was constructed on a former cricket ground (on which W.G. Grace is said to have once played) in the grounds of Sir Robert Peel's estate, after promoter Arthur Westwood had spent many months searching Army dumps all over the country for a suitable venue. Having employed ex-servicemen, he succeeded

Tamworth Speedway programme, 1947.

in building a fine stadium, which boasted covered stands for 5,000 spectators. Prior to opening with a Best Pairs meeting on 30 April 1947 (which was won by Len Tupling and Harwood Pike), the track was officially declared open by entertainer George Formby. Tamworth Hounds subsequently took their place in the National League Division Three, where they would stay throughout their four-year existence. In May of that initial year of speedway action, 10,000 tons of clinker were added to the terracing, in order to give the supporters a better view. The bends were banked in readiness for the 1948 season, as inexperienced Division Three riders had been inclined to drift outwards on the turns throughout the opening season. A change on the management side in 1949 saw Arthur Westwood resign as promoter, with Phil Hart taking over as speedway manager. Les Marshall, under the auspices of Auto Speedways Ltd, became promoter in 1950, but falling attendances saw the track close down prior to the completion of the side's fixtures. That year had also seen a change of nickname to Tammies. The final meeting at the venue was staged on 27 September, when Tamworth beat Aldershot 45-38 in a Division Three fixture. Tamworth subsequently completed their league fixtures with a double-header at Birmingham's Alexander Sports Stadium on 18 October, which saw them defeat Rayleigh 51-32, before losing 37-47 to Leicester. The track had also been used for training during that final season of activity. Stock-car racing was first held at the stadium on 30 June 1960, promoted by Harry Twigg and Syd Farndon. The site of the stadium is now covered by Deer Park housing estate.

TELFORD

ADDRESS: Telford Ice Rink, Telford, Shropshire
YEARS OF OPERATION: 1985 Demonstration; 1986 Indoor Ice Speedway; 1988-2001 Indoor Ice Speedway
FIRST MEETING: 16 February 1986
TRACK LENGTH: 110 metres

In October 1985, Jan Andersson, Chris Morton and Phil Collins gave a demonstration of indoor speedway on ice at the Telford rink. Promoted by Graham Drury and Ian Thomas, a first meeting was staged at the venue on the afternoon of Sunday 16 February 1986, when Hans Nielsen won the Skoal Bandit Ice International event. A further meeting was held in the evening, when the Rest of the World defeated England 52-25 in an International Challenge match. Two more events were held at the venue on 30 November 1986, when Jan Andersson won the Ice International Individual Trophy, prior to the Rest of the World beating England 40-37. After a year's break in 1987, the Telford Ice Show has become an annual event in the speedway calendar, with an afternoon and evening meeting on the middle Sunday of each February. Dates of subsequent meetings, and winners of the British Open Championship – as it has become known – are as follows: 14/2/88 Jan Andersson, 19/2/89 Andy Campbell, 18/2/90 Andy Campbell, 17/2/91 Andy Campbell, 16/2/92 Graham Jones, 14/2/93 Per Jonsson, 13/2/94 Hans Nielsen, 19/2/95 Hans Nielsen, 18/2/96 Wayne Broadhurst, 16/2/97 Ronnie Correy, 15/2/98 Mario Jirout, 14/2/99 Paul Hurry, 13/2/00 Wayne Broadhurst, 18/2/01 Jan Staechmann.

THORNE

ADDRESS: Thorne Stadium, Woodhouse Road, Thorne, South Yorkshire
YEARS OF OPERATION: 1929-30 Open

The exact date of the opening meeting at Thorne is not known, but a meeting is confirmed to have been staged on 25 August 1929. Thorne hosted its first meeting of the 1930 season on 22 March, when Skid Fenton was triumphant in the Flying Nine Race. At least fifteen meetings were held that year, the last known event taking place on 1 July 1930, when Tommy Bateman won the Curtiss Cup. The site of the track is now covered by a farm and its ancillary buildings.

Tonbridge Stadium, Collier Street, Kent.

TONBRIDGE

ADDRESS: Collier Street, Yalding, Nr Tonbridge, Kent
YEARS OF OPERATION: 1984-2000 Long-track

This is a boarded circuit, most famous for holding the annual Bonfire Burnup meeting (promoted by Tonbridge Motorcycle Club), which was staged every year from 1984 to 1999 inclusive, with the 2000 event being washed out by heavy rain. The track surface consists of a mixture of grass, sand and shale.

TRAGO

ADDRESS: Trago Stadium, Bodmin, Cornwall
YEARS OF OPERATION: 1980 Indoor Demonstration; 1982 Indoor Speedway
FIRST MEETING: 31 December 1980

On 31 December 1980, Tony Sanford, Bill Bowden, Phil Bealey and Benji Bealey attended an indoor meeting at Trago Stadium. This was primarily an arena for horse riding, but was sometimes used for schoolboy trials and grass-track demonstrations, as was the case on this day. After watching a huge total of seventy-seven races, it was nearing 5 p.m. before Tony Sanford and his friends gave a speedway demonstration on the circuit. Ideally suited for horse events, the riders found the track to be too deep for speedway, with Tony Sanford crashing out during his first ride, and having to spend the New Year celebrations in hospital with concussion. Bill Bowden also crashed first time out, while the Bealey brothers decided not to ride after all. Over the course of two days in 1982 (27 and 28 November), the Castrol-sponsored British Indoor Championship was held at Trago Stadium. The non-stop action saw the riders complete an arduous programme of moto-cross and speedway. Mark Roberts emerged as the winner of the speedway event, finishing ahead of Jason Thomas. As with the demonstration in 1980, however, it appears that the riders had problems staying in contact with their machines, due to the deepness of the track.

TREDEGAR
ADDRESS: Recreation Ground, Tredegar, Monmouthshire
YEARS OF OPERATION: 1929-30 Open
FIRST MEETING: 6 August 1929
TRACK LENGTH: 432 yards

Dirt-track racing was brought to Tredegar by Edgar Jones, who received great assistance from Cardiff director Jimmy Hindle. The Recreation Ground boasted a grandstand and enclosure, which were also used by spectators at rugby matches. The dirt-track was constructed around the rugby pitch, using 6 inches of clinker ballast, with a 3-inch facing of coke breeze. The track length on the outer edge was measured at 504 yards, while the inside was 432 yards – which gives some idea of just how wide the sweeping circuit was. The opening meeting took place on 6 August 1929, when an attendance of 6,800 saw Nick Carter triumphant in the Recreation Ground Handicap. Prior to the meeting, Jimmy Hindle became the first rider to take to the track, completing four demonstration laps. Seven meetings were staged in that initial season of racing, with open licence events continuing into 1930. The last known meeting at the venue was a scratch race event on 10 June 1930. The stadium was also used for greyhound racing, but for only for short periods. The site is now used as a local football ground, under Council ownership.

WAKEFIELD
ADDRESS: Wakefield Greyhound Stadium, Wakefield, Yorkshire
YEARS OF OPERATION: 1972 Demonstration

Greyhound racing was first staged at the venue in 1933, on what was described as a triangular-shaped track. Ivor Brown proposed using this venue for speedway, with the track to be constructed inside the greyhound circuit. For the benefit of Council representatives and noise level tests, a simulated meeting was held in 1972, when Peter Jarvis, Peter Taylor, Barry Holdsworth and Peter Wrathall warmed up their machines and rode around the centre green. In 1973, Ivor Brown gained permission from the local Council and duly received a track licence, only for the stadium owner to sell the site for redevelopment. A final greyhound meeting was held at the venue on 14 November 1973.

WALTHAMSTOW
ADDRESS: Walthamstow Stadium, Chingford Road, East London
YEARS OF OPERATION: 1934 National League; 1949-51 National League Division Two
FIRST MEETING: 16 August 1934
TRACK LENGTH: 306 yards (1934); 282 yards (1949-51)
NICKNAME: 'Wolves'

Walthamstow greyhound circuit began life on a site on Chingford Road, which was originally used as a rubbish dump by local residents. The track was constructed by William Chandler, with the first greyhound meeting taking place on 15 April 1931. Using granite chippings for the track surface, speedway arrived at the stadium in 1934, under the promotion of Fred Mockford and Dicky Maybrook. The opening meeting saw Walthamstow defeat Wimbledon 29-25 in a National League encounter on 16 August. This was after the premature closure of Lea Bridge, Walthamstow taking over the former Leyton-based team's remaining fixtures. However, at the end of the season, the team was forced to move again, following a court injunction against the noise. The side eventually relocated to Hackney, in readiness for the opening of the Waterden Road track in 1935. The

last of only eight meetings at the Chingford Road venue had seen Walthamstow race against Wembley in a league fixture on 3 October 1934. In 1936, a magnificent ballroom was added to the Walthamstow Stadium complex. Two midget-car meetings were held at Walthamstow Stadium in May 1948. Promoted by Walthamstow Speedway Ltd, under the direction of Charles Chandler, speedway returned to the venue in 1949, with the Wolves taking their place in the National League Division Two. The reopening meeting took place on 4 April when Walthamstow and Southampton drew 41-41 in a league match. A manager was employed to run the speedway – in that initial year back on track this responsibility fell on the shoulders of Wally Lloyd. A change of speedway manager saw John Deeley at the helm in 1950 and 1951. The Wolves venture came to

Walthamstow Stadium.

a premature close after only three seasons of racing, as it was always a problem to attract a crowd to a Division Two track that was situated between more illustrious teams at Harringay and West Ham. The last-ever meeting at the venue took place on 8 October 1951, when Walthamstow beat Edinburgh 51-33 in a league match. Stadium owner Bill Chandler died in 1950, but his seven sons have continued to run the venue ever since. A new glass-fronted stand was built in 1971, running along the entire length of the enclosure.

WARRINGTON

ADDRESS: Arpley Motordrome, Slutchers Lane, Warrington, Cheshire
YEARS OF OPERATION: 1929 English Dirt-track League; 1930 Northern League; 1949 Demonstration
FIRST MEETING: 29 March 1929
TRACK LENGTH: 396 yards

Dirt-track racing arrived at the Arpley Motordrome in 1929, when the track was officially opened by H. Horrocks, whose firm was responsible for the installation of the electric floodlights. Following the opening ceremony on 29 March, the first meeting was held before a crowd of 10,000 spectators, who witnessed Squib Burton race to victory in the Golden Helmet. The track was alleged to be the only 'D'-shaped circuit in the North of England at the time. Meetings were promoted by Warrington Dirt-track Racing Association, whose directors included Tommy Hatch and the brothers S.A. and L.C. Crabtree. Warrington became founder members of the English Dirt-track League, but found themselves expelled late on in the season, with the league table falling into disarray due to the premature closure of several tracks throughout the year. In 1930, Warrington entered the Northern League, but at the close of the season the Warrington Dirt-track Racing Association went into the hands of the liquidators. The final meeting had been held on 12 September, when England beat The Rest 33-20 in a challenge match. One further scratch race meeting had been scheduled for 19 September, but this was rained off. The track was subsequently taken over by General Speedways for a possible 1931 opening, but this did not come to fruition. A proposed speedway venture at the stadium in 1950 hinged around being able to increase the ground capacity by 3,000 – with the capacity at the time said to be only 8,000-9,000. A Liverpool company was behind the venture, and work was originally planned for completion by January 1950. It was hoped to hold trials and train a side for entry into league racing. The track would be 350 yards, with long straights and narrow bends and a regular Friday race night. In 1949, six Liverpool novices, under the guidance of Charlie Oates, raced their machines around the inside of the dog track as Council officials walked around the immediate neighbourhood judging the effects of noise – no objections were raised. However, the closure of Hastings had an effect on the Warrington backers, who then withdrew their financial support. Greyhound racing was first staged at the venue on 23 May 1931, with a final such meeting being held on 21 May 1956.

WELWYN GARDEN CITY
ADDRESS: Welwyn Garden City Stadium, Welwyn Garden City, Hertfordshire
YEARS OF OPERATION: 1971 Demonstration
TRACK LENGTH: 550 yards

In 1971, Reg Luckhurst was accompanied by some Kent grass-track racers to the Welwyn Garden City Stadium, in order to give a demonstration to local Council officials and the stadium owners. The man behind the idea was Ian Hoskins, with the venture to be known as Speedbowl Racing. Two meetings were planned for the 550-yard tarmac-covered cycle track, on 29 August and 26 September, but the project was curtailed due to opposition from local residents.

WEMBLEY

ADDRESS: Empire Stadium, Wembley, Middlesex

YEARS OF OPERATION: 1929-31 Southern League; 1932-33 National League; 1934 National League and Reserve League; 1935-36 National League; 1937-39 National League Division One; 1946 National League; 1947-56 National League Division One; 1957-69 Open; 1970-71 British League Division One; 1972-76 Open; 1978 Open; 1981 Open

FIRST MEETING: 16 May 1929

TRACK LENGTH: 378 yards (1929-76); 376 yards (1978-81)

NICKNAME: 'Lions'

LEAGUE CHAMPIONS: 1930, 1931, 1932, 1946, 1947, 1949, 1950, 1951, 1952, 1953

NATIONAL TROPHY WINNERS: 1931, 1932, 1948, 1954

BRITISH SPEEDWAY CUP WINNERS: 1947

The stadium was originally constructed as the centrepiece for the British Empire Exhibition, which was staged at a cost of £12 million soon after the end of the First World War, on a site covering some 220 acres. The stadium was built to the design of Sir Owen Williams, and was completed in exactly 300 days.

The last speedway programme from Wembley, 1981.

The innovative structure was finished in time to stage the famous 1923 FA Cup final. However, despite getting 100,000 visitors every hour from the day it opened, the British Empire Exhibition lost money and the stadium closed down in October 1925. Arthur Elvin quickly raised £120,000 and purchased the stadium from the official receiver, before subsequently reselling it for £150,000, and becoming managing director of Wembley Stadium Ltd. Under Elvin's guidance, greyhound racing was first staged at Wembley on 10 December 1927, in front of a crowd of 70,000 people. Elvin then wanted to stage dirt-track racing at the super stadium and appointed Johnnie Hoskins as manager, with the first meeting going ahead on 16 May 1929. A crowd of 19,456 were in attendance to see Roger Frogley win the Empire Stadium

Wembley Stadium.

Shield on that opening night. Wembley subsequently joined the Southern League and were credited with setting up the first supporters' club later that same season. Wembley staged the Star Championship Final from 1930 to 1935 – this being the forerunner of the World Championship. In 1932, Wembley also took part in the National Speedway Association Trophy, which was held prior to the National League Championship. In 1934, Wembley operated two teams, one in the National League, and the other in the Reserve League. Johnnie Hoskins departed to run West Ham in 1935, with Alec Jackson taking over the reigns at Wembley as speedway manager. The first-ever World Championship Final was held at Wembley on 10 September 1936, when Lionel Van Praag emerged victorious. Subsequent World Finals were held in 1937 (won by Jack Milne) and 1938 (won by Bluey Wilkinson), while the Lions con-

tinued to run in the National League Division One, prior to the Second World War bringing everything to a premature close in September 1939. The final pre-war meeting at the venue had seen Wembley beat Southampton 74-33 in a National Trophy match on 31 August. After the war, Wembley resumed in the National League, starting on 9 May with a 50-32 home victory over Belle Vue. Later on, a temporary replacement for the World Final was held in the form of the British Riders' Championship, which was run from 1946 to 1948. The winners of these events were: Tommy Price (1946), Jack Parker (1947) and Vic Duggan (1948). Wembley were forced to ride most of their home meetings at Wimbledon in 1948, due to the Olympic Games being held at the Empire Stadium. World Finals resumed at Wembley on 22 September 1949, when Tommy Price was triumphant. Wembley continued to hold the major tournament every year until 1960 inclusive, with the winners being: Freddie Williams (1950 and 1953), Jack Young (1951 and 1952), Ronnie Moore (1954 and 1959), Peter Craven (1955), Ove Fundin (1956 and 1960), Barry Briggs (1957 and 1958). Meanwhile, the Lions continued in the National League until the end of the 1956 campaign, and would have participated in 1957, although they withdrew shortly after the death of Sir Arthur Elvin, the chairman of Wembley Stadium and a strong supporter of speedway. The final league match at the great venue had been held on 13 September 1956, when Wembley beat Wimbledon 44-40. World Finals continued on an intermittent basis, producing champions as follows: Peter Craven (1962), Ove Fundin (1963 and 1967), Bjorn Knutsson (1965), Ivan Mauger (1969). The World Team Cup Final was also staged at the stadium on 21 September 1968, when Ivan Mauger led Great Britain to victory. Out of the blue, team racing returned in 1970, with Wembley joining the British League Division One, having taken over the licence of Edinburgh. Promoted by Trevor Redmond and Bernard Cottrell, the first meeting of the new era was held on 30 May that year, when the reformed Lions beat Hackney 41-37 in a league fixture. The venture only lasted for two seasons, however, as the stadium was unable to guarantee regular use to the sport because of its many other commitments. What turned out to be the final meeting of the two-year stint was staged on 2 October 1971, when Bert Harkins and Brian Collins won the Simpson Motors Invitation Pairs. Big meetings continued at Wembley, however, as follows: 1971

European Final (won by Ivan Mauger), 1972 World Final (Ivan Mauger), 1973 Daily Mirror International Tournament Final (England, after Peter Collins had defeated Sweden's Anders Michanek in a run-off following a 39-39 draw), World Team Cup Final (Great Britain), 1974 European Final (Peter Collins), 1975 World Final (Ole Olsen), 1976 Inter-Continental Final (Peter Collins), 1978 World Final (Ole Olsen). The last-ever meeting at the stadium took place on 5 September 1981, when Bruce Penhall won the World Championship Final. The stadium has continued to stage major football matches as well as pop concerts, and is due to be knocked down and rebuilt minus the famous twin towers.

WEMBLEY
ADDRESS: Empire Stadium Car Park, Wembley, Middlesex
YEARS OF OPERATION: 1934 Training; 1936-37 Training; 1951-52 Training

In 1934, it was reported that as the Wembley track would not be ready for use until the start of the season, cinders had been laid in front of the stadium in order to allow the riders some practice. An article in 1936 stated that 'The car park at Wembley has to be rolled every other day, because George Greenwood uses it to practice clutch starts'. In 1937, it was reported that the Wembley management had erected the original starting gate in the spacious car park, for the purpose of allowing riders to practice their starting techniques. Prior to the war, Malcolm Craven received coaching from Colin Watson on the rough surface of the car park. In 1951, Bruce Abernethy also practised in the car park, watched by young ladies from the American roller-skating musical *Skating Vanities*. Having injured his knee, Freddie Williams spent some time testing it out in a trial in 1952.

WEMBLEY

ADDRESS: Wembley Arena, Wembley, Middlesex
YEARS OF OPERATION: 1979-83 Indoor Speedway
FIRST MEETING: 2 December 1979
TRACK LENGTH: 118 yards

Promoted by Ivan Mauger, Barry Briggs, Ian Thomas and Brian Larner, indoor speedway was first staged on a cement surface at Wembley Arena on Sunday 2 December 1979. The winner of the opening Lada Indoor International was Ivan Mauger. A second meeting was held on 14 December 1980, when Great Britain defeated the Rest of the World 40-38. The venue hosted three further meetings as follows: 29.11.1981 Peter Collins' Lions 32 Bruce Penhall's Select 45, 28.11.1982 Lions 37 World Select 40, 27.11.1983 Kenny Carter's Lions 38 World Select 40.

WEST HAM

ADDRESS: Custom House Stadium, Prince Regent Lane, London
YEARS OF OPERATION: 1928 Open; 1929-31 Southern League; 1932-33 National League; 1934 National League and Reserve League; 1935-37 National League; 1938-39 National League Division One; 1940-42 Open; 1946 National League; 1947-55 National League Division One; 1964 National League; 1965-67 British League; 1968-71 British League Division One; 1972 British League Division Two

FIRST MEETING: 28 July 1928
TRACK LENGTH: 440 yards (1928-53); 415 yards (1954-72)
NICKNAME: 'Hammers' (1930-71); 'Bombers' (1972)
LEAGUE CHAMPIONS: 1937, 1965
A.C.U. CUP WINNERS: 1938
KNOCK-OUT CUP WINNERS: 1965

Having transferred his operation from Celtic Park at Glasgow, Jimmy Baxter (under the banner of Dirt-Track Speedways Ltd) promoted the first meeting at Custom House on 28 July 1928, when Sprouts Elder won the Golden Gauntlet. Prior to that initial meeting, the track was officially opened by Alderman Jack Jones MP. Greyhound racing was first held at the stadium on 4 August 1928. Following a season of open licence meetings in 1928, West Ham spent three seasons (1929 to 1931) in the Southern League. Jimmy Baxter was still pulling the strings at Custom House in 1930, although by that time he was under the auspices of West Ham Stadium Ltd. A change of promotion occurred in 1931, when West Ham was run under the banner of Wembley Stadium Ltd, with Arthur Elvin as promoter and Alec Jackson as speedway manager. In 1932, West Ham also took part in the National Speedway Association Trophy, which was a league-style competition that preceded the National League Championship. There was a further change of promotion in 1933, when Fred Fearnley took over under the banner of West Ham (1933) Ltd. In 1934, Fred Fearnley was joined by Stanley Greening as co-promoter at Custom House. Also that season, West Ham operated a side in the Reserve League (or Second Division as it is sometimes referred to), as well as the National League. Another change on the management side in 1935 saw Johnnie Hoskins and Victor Martin link up as co-promoters of the Hammers. A second team, known as West Ham Hawks, competed in the National Provincial Trophy in 1936, riding their home matches at Southampton. West Ham Hawks again operated in 1938, riding their home National League Division Two fixtures at Dagenham. With the outbreak of war, the 1939 season was brought to a premature close, although Johnnie Hoskins ran four wartime meetings in 1940, the first of which saw the Hammers defeat a combined New Cross and Wembley side 47-37 on 22 March. The last of the four events that year saw Bill Longley triumph in the London Cup Trophy. Further wartime meetings were staged in 1941 and 1942. After the war, the reopening meeting at Custom House took place on Good Friday 19 April 1946, when a huge crowd of 57,000 spectators witnessed the Hammers go down to a 41-42 defeat at the hands of Wembley in a challenge match. West Ham subsequently rejoined the National League, under the management of Arthur Atkinson and Stan Greatrex. Throughout 1946, West Ham rented Hoddesdon Stadium (Rye House) every Wednesday, in order to give their riders extra practice. A new tarmac starting area was laid at Custom House in May 1947. There was a change on the management side in 1950, when Alan Sanderson acquired the licence and installed the returning Johnnie Hoskins as promoter. Twenty-five-year-old American rider Ernie Roccio died the day after crashing at Custom House

on 22 July 1952. With Johnnie Hoskins departing for Belle Vue in 1953, Ken Brett became speedway manager for a short time, until Tiger Stevenson took over later in the season. Twenty-four-year-old Harry Eyre died after crashing at the track on 6 July 1953. West Ham closed at the end of the 1955 campaign, amid the general demise of speedway in during the mid-1950s. The final meeting was staged on 6 September that year, when Barry Briggs won the Stadium Cup. In 1964, West Ham was reopened by a consortium of National League promoters (headed by Charles Ochiltree), with Tommy Price installed as promoter. The speedway roar returned to Custom House on Tuesday 7 April that year, when the Hammers defeated Wimbledon 46-38 in a challenge match witnessed by a crowd of 15,000. The reopening season was marred though, when thirty-three-year-old Swindon rider Tadeusz Teodorowicz crashed at Custom House on Tuesday 1 September, being knocked out in the process. After a fight for life that lasted 142 days, 'Teo' died without regaining consciousness in January 1965. With the National League joining forces with the Provincial League, West Ham became founder members of the British League in 1965. Twenty-six-year-old Australian Dave Wills lost his life after crashing at the West Ham track on 22 June 1965. Dave Lanning became speedway manager at Custom House in 1966, and remained in place until Gordon Parkins took over in 1970. With the stadium being sold for redevelopment, West Ham withdrew from the British League Division One after the 1971 season, with their licence being transferred to Ipswich. Prior to the closure of the stadium, Wally Mawdsley and Pete Lansdale moved their Second Division operation from Romford to Custom House for a handful of fixtures in 1972. What turned out to be the last-ever meeting at the venue was staged on 23 May that year, when West Ham Bombers lost 38-40 to Hull in a Division Two league match. The licence was subsequently transferred to Barrow, in order to allow the Holker Street side to join Division Two of the British League. Custom House hosted a final greyhound meeting on 26 May 1972. The former stadium site is now covered by a housing estate.

WEST HAM
ADDRESS: Custom House Stadium Car Park, Prince Regent Lane, London
YEARS OF OPERATION: 1948 Training
TRACK LENGTH: 300 yards

In 1948, a practice circuit was used in the spacious Custom House car park, in order to help the Hammers riders prepare for their visits to smaller tracks. The track was also used by novices, with large numbers of youngsters seen careering around the circuit. In May 1948, Reg Fearman received coaching on the makeshift track from Cliff Watson and Aub Lawson.

WEST HAM
ADDRESS: Becton & Welling Amateur Speedway Club, rear Custom House Stadium, Prince Regent Lane, London
YEARS OF OPERATION: 1954 Training

The Becton & Welling Amateur Speedway Club was formed by Vic Duffy and Harry Hassan in 1954. The members of the club came from the West Essex, Kent, Woolwich and Bexley Cycle Speedway League. A large cinder track was constructed at the rear of the Custom House stadium, and was also used for cycle speedway. An arrangement was made with West Ham's reserves, whereby they stored the Becton & Welling Club machines and helped with the maintenance of them.

WEST WELLOW
ADDRESS: West Wellow, Nr Southampton, Hampshire
YEARS OF OPERATION: 1961 Training
TRACK LENGTH: 350 yards

A local farmer allowed one of his fields to be used for the construction of a training track at West Wellow in 1961. Alby Golden was in charge of the training school at the venue, with sessions held on Sunday afternoons.

WESTON-SUPER-MARE
ADDRESS: Rugby Ground, Drove Road, Weston-Super-Mare, Somerset
YEARS OF OPERATION: 1971 Demonstration

Prior to 1970, when Robin Martakies was refused a licence to run speedway at Weston, the proposed site had been used for go-kart racing. Promoters John Richards and Wally Mawdsley planned to stage speedway at the Rugby Ground in 1972, and to this end a noise demonstration was staged late in 1971. Maurice Morley, Pete Smith, Pete Lansdale and Ted Laessing spent two and a half hours going through the motions on all four corners of the stadium, but it was to no avail and speedway was never staged at the venue.

WEYMOUTH

ADDRESS: Wessex Stadium, Radipole Lane, Weymouth, Dorset

YEARS OF OPERATION: 1954 Open; 1955 National League Division Two; 1962-63 Open; 1964 Metropolitan League; 1965 Open; 1966-67 Training; 1968 British League Division Two; 1969-70 Training; 1971-73 Open and Training; 1974 British League Division Two; 1975-84 National League; 1985 Open and Training

FIRST MEETING: 4 August 1954

TRACK LENGTH: 379 yards (1954-73); 380 yards (1974-85)

NICKNAME: 'Scorchers' (1954-55); 'Royals' (1962-65); 'Eagles' (1968); 'Wizards' (1974-77); 'Wildcats' (1978-84)

In May 1951, J.W. Coates, along with his wife, and S.F. Crew, attempted to gain possession of 17 acres of land in Weymouth, for the purpose of building a speedway and sports stadium. In November 1952 it was reported that work on the stadium would commence the following September, when the land became available. Greyhound racing was first staged at the Wessex Stadium during 1954. Under the promotion of Wessex Stadiums Ltd (J.W. Coates, R. Barzilay and Bill Dutton), the track was opened by then World Champion Freddie Williams on 4 August 1954, prior to a meeting which saw Young England defeat Young Overseas 48-35. Open licence events were held throughout August and September 1954, before Weymouth Scorchers entered the National League Division Two in 1955. However, having completed just five home league matches, plus a National Trophy fixture, Weymouth resigned from the league. The final meeting was held on 20 May, when the Scorchers lost 39-57 to

Wessex Stadium, Weymouth.

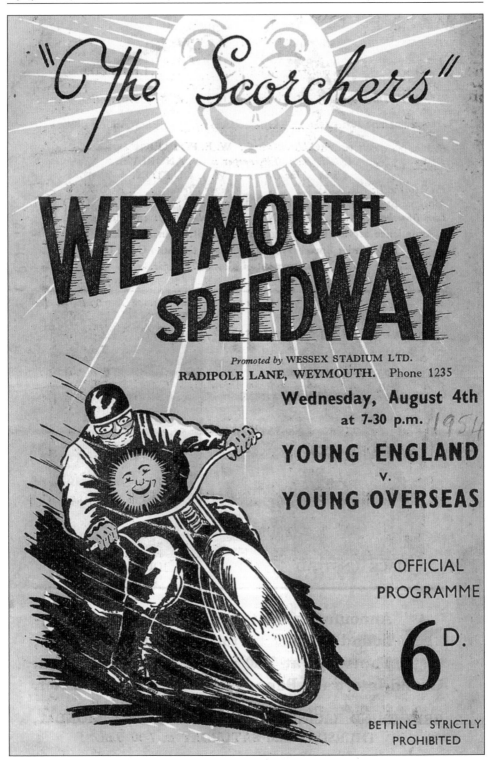

Weymouth Speedway programme from the first-ever meeting, 4 August 1954.

Rayleigh in a league fixture. Having remained closed to speedway for six years, the track reopened on 20 July 1962, when Buster Brown was victorious in the Wessex Championship. Under the promotion of John Pilblad, the renamed Weymouth Royals continued to run in open licence fixtures throughout 1962 and 1963, prior to linking up with the Metropolitan League in 1964, with just two open licence fixtures being run in 1965. Organised by the Southern Centre Grass-track Riders Association, Lew Coffin and Jimmy Squibb ran training sessions at Radipole Lane throughout the winter of 1966/67. Among the riders that came through the ranks from those schools were Colin Sanders and Mike Cake. In 1968, promoted by Wally Mawdsley and Pete Lansdale, Weymouth were founder members of the British League Division Two, with a new Eagles moniker. The stadium hosted the first meeting of the new era on 2 June that year, when the homesters defeated Plymouth 42-36 in a league encounter. That meeting had originally been scheduled for 26 May, but had fallen victim to inclement weather. Having completed their fixtures early in 1968, the track closed after a final meeting on 4 August – the result of that last meeting being a 48-28 league victory over Berwick. Low attendance levels were cited as the reason for not continuing with league racing at the venue. The track was used for training from 1969 to 1973 inclusive, again under the instruction of Lew Coffin. On top of the training sessions, a total of six training school matches and individual championships were staged during 1971 to 1973, and an away

training school match was ridden at Wolverhampton on 27 February 1972. The stadium and its site were purchased by Harry Davis in 1971. Under the auspices of Wessex Speedway Promotions (Harry Davis, Ted Holding, Cyril Crane and Gordon Parkins), and with yet another new nickname of 'Wizards', Weymouth rejoined the National League Division Two in 1974. The track again reopened on 2 April, when Weymouth beat Boston 43-35 in a challenge match. The British League Division Two became the New National League in 1975, and subsequently the National League in 1977, as Weymouth enjoyed their longest run of continuous league racing. Between those years, the track was run under the sole promotion of Harry Davis, although still operating as Wessex Speedway Promotions. A fifth nickname was employed from 1978 onwards, when Len Silver and Dave Erskine, trading as Weymouth Speedway Ltd, took over as promoters, with the side becoming known as Weymouth Wildcats. A change on the management side in 1979 saw Brian Constable installed as promoter on behalf of Allied Presentations Ltd. There was a further change of promoter in 1980, when Mervyn Stewkesbury took over under the banner of Betterment Properties (Leisure Activities) Ltd. In 1984, Alan Hodder and Pete Ansell linked up alongside Mervyn Stewkesbury as co-promoters. Future redevelopment at the stadium was mooted, but it was still a surprise in early 1985 when it was announced that Weymouth would be switching their operation to Poole. What turned out to be the final meeting at the stadium had already been held on 11 September 1984, when Weymouth beat Rye House 50-28 in a National League encounter. In 1985, a three-day John Davis training school was held at the stadium, from 28 February to 2 March. The last known speedway activity at the stadium probably took place on 2 November 1985, when Weymouth lost 29-47 to Wimbledon in a training track match. In 1986, it was announced that the venue would cease to be a motor sport venue from 1 June. A new stadium, costing £1 million, was subsequently constructed on the site to house Weymouth Football Club. The new stadium was built to Alliance League standards and boasted a 10,000 capacity. The first match at the new ground was played on 26 August 1987, when Weymouth beat Lincoln City 3-0 in a Conference League fixture.

WHALLEY
ADDRESS: Dean's Pleasure Ground, Whalley, Lancashire
YEARS OF OPERATION: 1929-30 Amateur Open and Training
TRACK LENGTH: 150 yards

The small 150-yard track, described as being circular and unbanked, was run by Whalley Dirt Track Club. It was a facility for members only – with membership restricted to just thirty in total – with a ten-mile radius qualification. Only two riders were permitted to use the track at any one time, due to its width and the smallness of the circuit. Claude Rye and Joe Abbott were amongst the tutors at the mini-track. A rally was held at the track on 30 March 1930, when several top riders went through their paces in front of a crowd of 4,000. The riders included Ham Burrill, Joe Abbott,

Claude Rye, Jim Carnie, Tony Golding and Jack Tye. Admission was free, but a collection was made in order to assist club funds, while refreshments were made available at the Assembly Rooms, situated close to the track.

WHITLEY BAY
ADDRESS: Hillheads, Whitley Bay, Tyne and Wear
YEARS OF OPERATION: 1929 Open
FIRST MEETING: 20 April 1929
TRACK LENGTH: 440 yards

Situated at Hillheads, on the outskirts of Whitley Bay, a dirt-track was laid in 1929, around the perimeter of the pitch used by Rockcliffe Rugby Football Club. Open licence events were staged at the venue that year, with meetings promoted by Tyneside Speedways Ltd. The first meeting took place on 20 April 1929, when Harry Whitfield was triumphant in the Golden Helmet. This was a short-lived venue, with the final meeting, a scratch race event, going ahead on 26 June 1929.

WIGAN
ADDRESS: Poolstock Stadium, Wigan, Lancashire
YEARS OF OPERATION: 1947 National League Division Two; 1960 Open
FIRST MEETING: 4 April 1947
TRACK LENGTH: 321 yards (1947); 294 yards (1960)
NICKNAME: 'Warriors'

Greyhound racing was first staged at Poolstock Stadium on 9 March 1932. Promoted by Joe Waxman and Jimmy Wolfenden, speedway arrived at Poolstock Stadium in 1947, with the first meeting going ahead on 4 April when Phil Clarke won the Easter Cup. Wigan Warriors sub-

Greyhound and Sports Stadium, Wigan.

sequently took their place in the National League Division Two. The Wigan team transferred to Fleetwood in 1948, following a difference of opinion between the greyhound and speedway parties. The dispute was soon resolved, but the Control Board then refused an application for a licence to run open meetings at the venue. The final meeting at Poolstock had been held on 18 October 1947, when the homesters lost 41-43 to Bristol in a league match. The track reopened in 1960, under the direction of Don Potter and Percy Frith, with the first meeting going ahead on 10 June, when Wigan Warriors beat Norwich 38-34 in a challenge match witnessed by 2,000 spectators. Just eight open licence meetings were staged in 1960, with the final one being held on 1 August, when the Warriors defeated Bradford 52-20. Speedway was not staged at the venue again, and a final greyhound meeting was

held on 28 February 1973, after which the site was redeveloped with housing.

WIGAN

ADDRESS: Greyhound and Sports Stadium, Woodhouse Lane, Wigan, Lancashire
YEARS OF OPERATION: 1952-53 Open
FIRST MEETING: 2 May 1952
TRACK LENGTH: 294 yards
NICKNAME: 'Panthers'

The stadium hosted its first greyhound meeting on 17 March 1928. Speedway arrived at Woodhouse Lane in 1952, with the opening meeting being staged on 2 May, when Wigan Panthers beat Stoke 50-33 in a challenge match. Under the promotion of Peggy Waxman, open licence meetings continued throughout 1952, until the Control Board suspended the track's licence in August. The last meeting was

Scarce Wigan Speedway programme from Poolstock Stadium, 1947.

held on 1 August, when Wigan defeated a team dubbed Overseas 45-38 in a challenge match. Promoted by L. Coates, amateur meetings were held at the venue in 1953; however, these only drew attendances in the region of 600 people. The track subsequently closed after a handful of meetings, due to the ill health suffered by Mr Coates. In 1953, a training school was run at Woodhouse Lane by Bill Griffiths, Ernie Appleby and Oliver Hart. For the purpose of the school, the track was covered by full insurance, having been passed by insurance inspectors. Oliver and Ron Hart planned to hold novice meetings at the venue in 1954, but discussions broke down over outstanding payments from the 1952 promotion for the safety fence, starting gate and lighting. Wigan did, however, partake in one meeting in 1954, losing 30-41 at Chapelizod on 23 May. A final greyhound meeting was held at the stadium in April 1961. Both the speedway and greyhound circuits were lost in 1970, when the venue was completely rebuilt as a municipally-controlled athletics stadium.

WIMBLEDON

ADDRESS: Wimbledon Stadium, Plough Lane, London
YEARS OF OPERATION: 1928 Open; 1929-31 Southern League; 1932-33 National League; 1934 National League and Reserve League; 1935-36 National League; 1937-39 National League Division One; 1946 National League; 1947-56 National League Division One; 1957-64 National League; 1965-67 British League; 1968-74 British League Division One; 1975-84 British League; 1985-90 National League; 1991 British League Division One
FIRST MEETING: 28 May 1928

TRACK LENGTH: 330 yards (1928); 343 yards (1929-56); 355 yards (1957-67); 1239 yards (4 laps, 1968-79); 1275 yards (4 laps, 1980); 1234 yards (4 laps, 1981-82); 1275 yards (4 laps, 1983-91)
NICKNAME: 'Dons'
NATIONAL TROPHY WINNERS: 1938, 1950, 1951, 1953, 1956, 1959, 1960, 1962
R.A.C. CUP WINNERS: 1954
LEAGUE CHAMPIONS: 1954, 1955, 1956, 1958, 1959, 1960, 1961
BRITANNIA SHIELD WINNERS: 1959
KNOCK-OUT CUP WINNERS: 1962, 1968, 1969, 1970

The site that the stadium was constructed on was marshy and caused considerable building problems, and by the time the venue was ready to open, South London Greyhound Racecourses Ltd, the consortium which had purchased the site, were in financial difficulties. W.J. Cearns, whose firm had constructed the stadium, put in a large sum of money to take the place on and save the venture, which first opened for greyhound racing on 20 June 1927. In association with A.J. Hunting of International Speedways, Cearns introduced dirt-track racing to the Greyhound Racing Association Stadium in 1928. The opening meeting took place on 28 May when Frank Arthur won the Golden Helmet. Wimbledon were pioneers of the Southern League in 1929, along with Stamford Bridge, Southampton, Coventry, Crystal Palace, Wembley, West Ham, White City (London), Harringay, Perry Barr (Birmingham), Lea Bridge and Hall Green (Birmingham). Wimbledon remained in the Southern League until the formation of the National League in 1932. In that that season, Wimbledon also competed in the National Speedway Association Trophy, which was a league-

Wimbledon Stadium.

style competition that preceded the National League Championship. Wimbledon operated two teams in 1934, one in the National League and the other in the Reserve League. Ronnie Greene took over as promoter in 1937 – he was, of course, to go on and become a legend in the history of Wimbledon speedway. Tragedy struck on 27 September 1937, when twenty-two-year-old Reg Vigor died following a crash at the track. The accident happened in heat two of a National League match versus Harringay, when the young Dons rider caught his footrest in the wire fence and was somersaulted down the track. Although no bones were broken, the youngster remained unconscious, dying three days later at Nelson Hospital in Merton. The Dons remained in top-flight National League speedway right up to the closure of the sport at the outbreak of war in September 1939. The Plough Lane circuit hosted its final pre-war meeting on 28 August, when the Dons defeated Southampton 56-28 in a National League encounter. In 1944, the grandstand and offices were blitzed, and all the stadium records were destroyed. The track reopened on 19 April 1946, with the Dons losing 31-47 to New Cross in a challenge match. The attendance for that meeting was an amazing 42,000, with a further 10,000 locked out. The Dons subsequently took their place back in the National League. Wimbledon were founder members of the British League in 1965, with their first meeting of the new era being a challenge match versus Coventry on 3 April, which the they won 42-35. Having promoted the Dons since 1937, Ronnie Greene retired at the end of the 1971 season. John Cearns subsequently took up the promoting reigns and installed Cyril Maidment as speedway manager. Legendary former promoter Ronnie

Greene sadly died in November 1978. The financial problems created by running a track in London, with all its rival public attractions, saw the Dons join the National League in 1985. In 1987, a new promoting company was formed entitled Wimbledon Speedway (1987) Ltd (David Pickles, Don Scarff, John Powell, Bob Burchett and John Smart). During the intervening years, there were several changes to the members of the company, but meetings continued to be run under the joint direction of this organisation and John Cearns, right up until the track's closure in 1991. Having said that, the track was run by promoters in 1988 (Russell Lanning and John Berry) and 1989 (Don Scarff and Russell Lanning), although still under the direction of Wimbledon Speedway (1987) Ltd and John Cearns. For 1990 and 1991, the running of meetings saw Don Scarff acting as speedway manager, with considerable help from Peter Brown. When the two leagues amalgamated in 1991, Wimbledon opted to join the British League Division One, but without a team sponsor the track lost money on a weekly basis and the promoters had little option but to close the track. The final meeting at the well-appointed stadium took place on 5 June that year, when a qualifying round of the Four Team Championship was staged. With rain falling throughout, the meeting was eventually abandoned after eight heats with the scores at the time being: Reading 17, Wimbledon 14, Poole 9, Swindon 8. The team subsequently transferred to Eastbourne in order to complete their fixtures. The start and finish line were some 23 yards apart at Wimbledon, hence the track length

Wimbledon's first meeting after the war, 1946.

being measured over a four-lap distance since 1968. At the close of the circuit in 1991, the actual length of the track was 313 yards. There has been the odd rumour of speedway returning to Plough Lane during the intervening years, but as yet nothing has come to fruition.

WOLVERHAMPTON
ADDRESS: Monmore Green Stadium, Sutherland Avenue, Monmore Green, Wolverhampton, West Midlands
YEARS OF OPERATION: 1928-30 Open; 1950 Open; 1951 National League Division Three; 1952 Southern League; 1953-54 National League Division Two; 1961-64 Provincial League; 1965-67 British League; 1968-74 British League Division One; 1975-80 British League;

1981 National League; 1984-90 British League; 1991-94 British League Division One; 1995-96 British Premier League; 1997 British Elite League and British Amateur League; 1998-2000 British Elite League

FIRST MEETING: 30 May 1928

TRACK LENGTH: 329 yards (1928-81); 312 yards (1984-85); 306 yards (1986-96); 288 yards (1997-2000)

NICKNAME: 'Wasps' (1951-54); 'Wolves' (1961-2000) (The Amateur League side of 1997 were known as 'Shuttle Cubs')

LEAGUE CHAMPIONS: 1963, 1991, 1996

PREMIERSHIP WINNERS: 1992, 1997

GOLD CUP WINNERS: 1992

KNOCK-OUT CUP WINNERS: 1996

Greyhound racing was first staged at Monmore Green on 1 January 1928, in front of a crowd of 1,000 spectators. Constructed inside the greyhound circuit, Monmore Green hosted its first-ever dirt-track meeting on 30 May 1928, under the auspices of Wolverhampton Dirt-track Motorcycle Club. They were the first of no fewer than six different organisations who promoted dirt-track racing at the venue in that initial year, the others being: Walsall Motorcycle Club, Wolverhampton Motorcycle and Car Club, Monmore Motorcycle Sports Club, Birmingham Motorcycle Club and finally the British Dirt-track Racing Association Ltd. In 1929, a further change of promotion saw Midland Speedways Ltd running the show as Monmore Green continued to stage open licence events. Yet another change on the management side saw Midland Greyhound Racing Co. Ltd promoting dirt-track racing later on in 1929. Wolverhampton ran a third season of open events in 1930, but after Billy Dallison had won both the scratch and handicap events on 24 June, no further meetings were held until 1950. Norman

Monmore Green Stadium, Wolverhampton.

Pritchard reopened the track late in 1950, with just one meeting being staged on 14 October, when Wolverhampton Wulfrunians beat Sheffield 58-26 in a challenge match. Under the promotion of Arthur Simcock (trading as Parkside Speedways Ltd), Wolverhampton Wasps joined the National League Division Three in 1951, prior to taking part in the Southern League in 1952, when Len Matchan became co-promoter with Arthur Simcock. In 1953, Wolverhampton amalgamated with Cradley Heath, with the side running in the National League Division Two. Under the new set-up, Parkside Speedways Ltd were still the promoters, with John Deeley as speedway manager in partnership with Les Gregory. Tragedy struck when twenty-one-year-old Mike Rogers died after crashing at Monmore Green on 5 June 1953. Jack Cunningham became speedway manager in 1954, but Wolverhampton resigned from Division Two in May prior to the completion of a single league match. Their closure was due to an inability to be able to sign a team that was strong enough to compete. Prior to the closure, Monmore Green had staged just three Northern Shield fixtures, one league match (*v.* Coventry) and a challenge match (*v.* Wimbledon). The final match at the stadium was a Northern Shield fixture versus Motherwell on 14 May, when the under-strength Wasps lost 28-56. A further National Trophy fixture against Swindon was scheduled for 21 May, but the meeting was cancelled and never staged. Again, the track reopened in 1961, with the renamed Wolves joining the Provincial League under the promotion of Bill Bridgett and Mike Parker. The opening fixture of

Wolverhampton Speedway programme, 1951.

this new era was held on 7 April, when Wolverhampton beat Stoke 40-35 in a challenge match. Wolverhampton subsequently became founder members of the British League in 1965. A magnificent new stand, with a plate-glass frontage and a tiered restaurant, was opened at Monmore Green in 1969. Twenty-seven-year-old New Zealander Gary Peterson lost his life following a crash in heat eleven of the Midland Cup Final versus Oxford at Monmore Green on 17 October 1975. Following a season of National League racing in 1981 (under the promotion of Dan McCormick), the track closed amidst poor crowd levels. The final meeting was staged on 30 August that year, when Wolves lost 28-50 to Middlesbrough in a league match. After two years of closure, promoter Peter Adams brought speed-

271

way back to Monmore Green on 19 March 1984, when Wolverhampton lost 30-48 to Belle Vue in a challenge match. Due to a combination of health and personal reasons, Peter Adams quit as promoter in July 1986. Under the auspices of Powar Ltd, Chris Van Straaten subsequently took over the running of the track. With the amalgamation of the British League and the National League, Wolverhampton were automatic members of the British League Division One in 1991. Wolves then became founder members of the British Premier League in 1995. With the split of the large Premier League, Wolves joined the British Elite League in 1997. Wolverhampton also joined forces with Long Eaton in 1997, to enter a composite side in the British Amateur League. The home fixtures were split equally between the two tracks, with Monmore Green staging its first such fixture on 2 June, when the Shuttle Cubs beat the M4 Raven Sprockets 43-32. The meeting did, in fact, form the second part of a double-header, following an Elite League match between Wolverhampton and Swindon. This proved to be a one-season venture, with the final Amateur League match at Monmore Green going ahead on 25 August, when a fixture versus Belle Vue Colts was abandoned after eight heats, with the homesters leading 26-19. This meeting also formed the second part of a double-header, which had previously featured Wolverhampton against Belle Vue in an Elite League encounter. Having promoted at Monmore Green since 1986, Chris Van Straaten was joined by co-promoter John Woolridge in 2000, as Wolverhampton continued to be one of the most professionally-run tracks in British speedway.

WOLVERHAMPTON
ADDRESS: Whispering Wheels, Temple Street, Wolverhampton
YEARS OF OPERATION: 1971-72 Indoor Speedway
FIRST MEETING: 14 December 1971

This was an indoor speedway venue, with meetings on a wooden surfaced track promoted by Harry Bastable and Alan Eagles. The track length was under 100 yards in length, accommodation limited to just 300 spectators. The machines used were 175cc, with the racing described as motorised cycle speedway. The first meeting at the venue was staged on 14 December 1971, when Arthur Browning and Andy Hunt won the Best Pairs event. Further meetings were staged on 22 December 1971 and 5 January 1972, before a final event a week later on 12 January which saw The Rest defeat Birmingham 42-36.

WOMBWELL
ADDRESS: Ings Road Stadium, New Scarbro, Low Valley, Wombwell, South Yorkshire
YEARS OF OPERATION: 1929 Open
FIRST MEETING: 14 April 1929

A dirt-track was laid at the Ings Road Stadium by Darfield Motorcycle Club, who staged the opening meeting on Sunday 14 April 1929, when E. Davies won the handicap event. Little else is known about this venue, apart from the fact that dirt-track racing was only staged there in 1929. The site of the stadium was directly opposite a sewage treatment plant and is now covered by a large private house and grounds.

WOMBWELL

ADDRESS: South Yorkshire Sports Stadium, Station Road, Wombwell, South Yorkshire

YEARS OF OPERATION: 1929 Open; 1930 Northern League; 1931 Open; 1947-48 National League Division Three; 1964-65 Training

FIRST MEETING: 9 May 1929

TRACK LENGTH: 424 yards (1929-31); 443 yards (1947-48)

NICKNAME: Colliers (1947-48)

The stadium first hosted greyhound racing on 21 April 1928. Darfield and District Motorcycle and Light Car Club promoted meetings at Wombwell in June 1928 and, although they referred to it as a dirt-track meeting, it was almost certainly a grass-track event. In April 1929, the South Yorkshire Sports Stadium changed hands at auction, and the new manager, F. Broadbent, set about the construction of a proper dirt track. The first meeting of an open licence season subsequently went ahead on 9 May that year, when Bert Round was triumphant in the scratch race event. Following the success of the open licence events of 1929, Wombwell subsequently joined the Northern League in 1930. The track reverted back to holding open licence meetings in 1931, but following a track championship meeting on 31 August (won by George Wigfield), there was no further dirt-track racing at the venue until 1947. Promoted by Barnsley Motorcycle and Car Club, a restricted grass-track meeting was staged at the stadium on 2 June 1946. Speedway returned in 1947, when, with the nickname of 'Colliers', Wombwell entered a team in the National League Division Three,

promoted by Will Bednash. The reopening meeting at the track was held on Friday 9 May that year, when Wombwell defeated Tamworth 54-39 in a challenge match. After completing just two seasons, the track again closed following a final meeting on Friday 22 October 1948, when the homesters defeated Yarmouth 50-34 in a Division Three encounter. Stock-car racing was held at the venue in 1954. A final greyhound meeting was held at Station Road in 1957. Wombwell was used as a Sunday training track during 1964, with Frank Varey apparently building a bike to be loaned out at the circuit. The promoters of the training venture were J.C. Ward and P.A. Hattersley, who charged 25/- per session, inclusive of insurance. For riders who wished to hire a machine, the charge was 50/-. The first session went ahead on 7 June that year, with a final one being held on 1 November. The track reopened for training on 7 March 1965, with the same charges applying as in the previous season. Visitors to the track that year were known to have included Ray Wilson, Eric Boocock, Stan Holey and Alan Jay. The track was still visible in 1968, but the site has subsequently been covered by industrial units.

WORKINGTON

ADDRESS: Lonsdale Park, Workington, Cumberland

YEARS OF OPERATION: 1931-32 Open; 1937-38 Open

FIRST MEETING: 15 August 1931

TRACK LENGTH: 439 yards (1931-32); 459 yards (1937)

The first Workington Rugby League Club (known as Zebras) used Lonsdale Park

Lonsdale Park, Workington.

from 1898 to 1909. The stadium was subsequently used for county and representative fixtures from the early part of the century, until after the Second World War. Workington Reds Football Club used the ground before 1913, and again after reforming, from 1921 to 1937. In 1926, the stadium was purchased by Harry Hurrell from Lord Lonsdale, with Alex Moffatt of the Cumberland Greyhound Company later becoming the sole lessee. Promoted by West Cumberland Motor Club, a gymkhana-style cinder-track race was staged at the venue in 1929, in conjunction with the Shareholders Committee of Workington FC Ltd. The event was staged with the object of assisting the funds of the football club. The idea of dirt-track racing in Workington was first mooted by Rol Stobbart at the AGM of the West Cumberland Motor Club on 23 March 1931. A crowd of some 2,000 spectators

turned out for the first meeting on Saturday 15 August that year, when G.B. Mortimer won both the scratch and handicap events. The meeting proved to be a financial disaster for the organisers and no further meetings were staged that year. Border Sports Club reopened the track in 1932, staging the first of eight meetings on 14 May, when Rol Stobbart won the scratch race. The final meeting of the 1932 season was held on 27 August, when Vic Ctercteko was victorious in the track championship. There was no further speedway until 24 April 1937, when the cinder sport ran throughout the summer months, under the promotion of Rol and Maurice Stobbart. Later in 1937, with the help of the Council, Workington FC moved to Brough Park, a new ground adjacent to Lonsdale Park, playing the first game at their new home on 25 September that year. Further open licence dirt-track meetings were held at

Lonsdale Park in 1938, although dates and details remain vague. Lonsdale Park still remains in place to this very day, and is located some 300 yards behind the back straight stand of Derwent Park.

WORKINGTON

ADDRESS: Derwent Park Stadium, Workington, Cumberland
YEARS OF OPERATION: 1970-74 British League Division Two; 1975-81 National League; 1985 Open; 1987 National League; 1994 Demonstration; 1999-2000 British Premier League
FIRST MEETING: 3 April 1970
TRACK LENGTH: 398 yards (1970-77 and 1999-2000); 390 yards (1978-80 and 1985); 394 yards (1981 and 1987)
NICKNAME: 'Comets' ('Tigers' was the nickname used when Glasgow occupied the track in 1987)

Derwent Park was constructed on 11ft of ash and rubble, the site being a former Council rubbish tip. The Council granted Workington Town Rugby League Club a 199-year lease at a peppercorn rent on the 18-acre site, which comprised the ground and former training pitch. All the work on the ground was carried out at cost price (including the erection of the stand), with help from the Supporters' Club. The 'A' team played at Derwent Park in the 1947/48 season; however, scarcity of building permits and the cost of materials delayed the senior side's opening fixture until 27 August 1956. The grandstand at Derwent Park is built on what was once a tidal estuary known as The Saltings. Fishing boats are known to have tied up there prior to the First World War. Work on the steel-framed, brick-faced 1,700-seater stand started in March 1956. It was

Derwent Park Stadium, Workington.

Workington Speedway programme from the first-ever meeting at Derwent Park, 1970.

designed and built by Tom Mitchell, utilising a £13,000 Rugby League loan. The ends of the stand are set at an angle of 45 degrees, to enable full viewing of the corner areas. Under the auspices of Premier Sporting Promotions, Ian Thomas and Jeff Brownhut introduced speedway to the Cumberland venue on 3 April 1970, when the newly-formed Comets lost 37-39 to Berwick in the Border Trophy. Almost 5,000 fans flocked to that opening meeting, after which the team settled into the regular team racing in British League Division Two. By 1972, the promotion had changed slightly, with Ian Thomas and Workington Town Rugby League Club listed as co-promoters in the matchday programme. In 1975, Workington became founder members of the New National League, with George Graham taking over as promoter. A further change of promotion occurred in 1978, which saw Ron Cooper and Eddy Thornborrow take over at the helm. Eddy Thornborrow became sole promoter of the Comets' affairs in 1980, but by 1981 Ron Bagley had taken over at Derwent Park. The track was also used by Berwick in 1981, for one of their 'home' Knock-out Cup matches, versus Weymouth on 17 July. Sadly though, due to falling attendances, Derwent Park closed at the end of that season, with the final meeting being held on 25 September, when Jackson's Jackals beat Kelly's Comets 40-38 in a challenge match. Speedway returned to Derwent Park in 1985, when Dave Younghusband promoted a series of open licence events, starting with the Jim Bowen Trophy on 28 April, which saw Garry Clegg emerge victorious from a meeting that was curtailed after twelve heats due to inclement weather. The last meeting of the twelve staged during the one-year venture was held on 13 October, when Jacko Irving won the Supporters' Trophy. Under the promotion of Dave Thomson and James Beaton, Glasgow used Derwent Park for their 'home' meetings in 1987, opening on 1 May with a 55-23 National League victory over Boston. The team rode as Glasgow Tigers until 27 July, but from 7 August they became known as Workington Tigers. Just over a month later, however, Workington were expelled from the National League on 15 September for failing to promote the track in a satisfactory manner. The final meeting of an unhappy year had been staged two days previously, when the homesters lost 37-41 to Wimbledon in a league fixture. In 1994, Steve Lawson completed over twenty laps for the benefit of a Border Television news item on the twenty-fifth anniversary reunion, which took place at the stadium on 22 October. The track again reopened in 1999, under the promotion of Tony Mole and Ian Thomas, with the Comets taking their place in the British Premier League. The new era began on 20 March, when Workington beat Newcastle 47-41 in a challenge match. Since then, the track has gone from strength to strength, enjoying tremendous support into the year 2000 and beyond. On 14 December 2000, Channel 5 screened an hour-long programme documenting a year in the life of Workington speedway – much of the film having been shot at Derwent Park.

Y

YARMOUTH

ADDRESS: Yarmouth Stadium, Caister Road, Caister-on-Sea, Great Yarmouth, Norfolk

YEARS OF OPERATION: 1948-49 National League Division Three; 1950-53 National League Division Two; 1957-58 Open; 1959 Southern Area League; 1960 Provincial League; 1961 Open

FIRST MEETING: 20 April 1948

TRACK LENGTH: 327 yards (1948-52); 325 yards (1953-61)

NICKNAME: 'Bloaters'

There was originally another stadium in Caister Road, which first held grey-

Yarmouth Speedway programme, 1948.

hound racing on 25 March 1932. That same year, two grass-speedway meetings were also held at the venue. Later on, that particular site was redeveloped as a heliport, which remains to this day. Greyhound racing was first staged at the real Yarmouth Stadium on 11 May 1940, the venue having been built by Len Franklin. Speedway arrived at the stadium in 1948, under the directorship of Len Franklin, Ernie Wedon and C.G. Yaxley, in cooperation with the directors of Norwich Speedway, who entered a Yarmouth team in the National League Division Three. The front man employed as speedway manager in 1948 was Dick Wise. The opening meeting at the stadium was staged on 20 April 1948, when Bert Rawlinson won the East Coast Trophy in front of 3,000 spectators. The track was described as having bends that were so acute it looked as if the two straights had been squeezed together by a giant hand! The initial year of speedway was marred when Australian Max Pearce died the day after crashing at Caister Road on 13 July. After two seasons of National League Division Three racing, the Bloaters were promoted to Division Two in 1950. That same season saw the directors run the track on their own for the first time, without the assistance of the Norwich management. Ernie Wedon took over as speedway manager, replacing Dick Wise, who had run the track since 1948. Wedon would remain in that position until the track's untimely closure at the end of 1953. Having completed four years of Division Two racing, Yarmouth applied to open later than usual in 1954 – as a seaside town, crowds were poor in the early part of the season. However, their

Yarmouth Stadium, Caister-on-Sea.

request to open in June was turned down by the Control Board, and Yarmouth withdrew from the league. What turned out to be the final meeting of the first period of track action at the stadium had already taken place on 22 September 1953, when the Bloaters beat Poole 50-34 in a National League Division Two encounter. Riding as East Anglia, the track reopened in 1957, under the promotion of Alf Weedon, Percy Leighton and Ted Courtnell, with the latter acting as speedway manager. Nine open licence fixtures were staged that year, the first of which saw Ove Fundin win the East Anglia Trophy on 2 July. A further series of open licence fixtures were held in 1958, when Yarmouth also entered the ill-fated Junior League. The Bloaters never actually rode a home match in the Junior League, fulfilling just two away engagements, with the final league table ending in a shambles amid the chaos of several unridden fixtures. In 1959, Yarmouth entered the Southern Area League, competing against Eastbourne, Aldershot, Rye House and Foxhall Heath (Ipswich). Following a year of Provincial League racing in 1960, open licence meetings were staged in 1961, when Yarmouth also took part in the East Anglian League, which included Rayleigh, Ipswich 'B' and Norwich 'B'. The last-ever speedway meeting at the venue was staged on 8 August that year, when Pete Jarman won the Kings of Oxford Trophy.

YORK

ADDRESS: Burnholme Estate, Beck Lane, Heworth, York

Y

YEARS OF OPERATION: 1930
Demonstration; 1931 Open
FIRST MEETING: 25 October 1930
TRACK LENGTH: 442 yards

The track was probably better known as Burnholme, as it was situated on the Burnholme Estate, near Beck Lane in York. The estate was comprised of a fine country house, along with coach-house and stables, with land totalling forty-three acres. The track was first opened to the public, free of charge, on 25 October 1930, for a demonstration by Tommy Gamble. However, spectators had to wait until the following year for the first meeting proper, which was held on Good Friday 3 April. Unfortunately, the opening meeting was affected by light rain, and as a result only 1,000 people were in attendance. A further twenty-two meetings were scheduled at the venue in 1931, but the track was forced to close prematurely, due to bad the weather which had seen five meetings postponed and another one abandoned. The final meeting at the track went ahead on 12 August that year, but there were no subsequent meetings at the venue. Much of the Burnholme Estate is today covered in mews-style living accommodation.

YORK
ADDRESS: York Stadium, Green Hammerton, Nr York, North Yorkshire
YEARS OF OPERATION: 1980-82 Long-Track
FIRST MEETING: 14 September 1980
TRACK LENGTH: 880 yards
York Stadium boasted two grandstands and was well served with bars and parking facilities. Long-track meetings were promoted by the Auto 66 Club on a shale-surfaced trotting track. The first meeting at the stadium was won by Trevor Banks on 14 September 1980. The last known meeting at the venue took place on 19 July 1982, when Ivan Mauger was triumphant.

BEACH VENUES

At one time or another since the birth of dirt-track racing in Britain, there probably aren't many beaches which have not been used for the purpose of practising. The following is a general guide of the known sand/beach venues.

ABERAVON

ADDRESS: Aberavon Beach, Port Talbot, Glamorgan
YEARS OF OPERATION: 1982

Ian Sizer used the beach at Aberavon for practice, prior to Christmas in 1982.

ABERDOVEY

ADDRESS: Borth Sands, Aberdovey, North Wales
YEARS OF OPERATION: 1971 Training

Archie Wilkinson is known to have made regular trips to the sands at Borth, for the purpose of training in 1971.

AINSDALE

ADDRESS: Ainsdale Sands, Ainsdale, Lancashire
YEARS OF OPERATION: 1948-49 Training; 1950-53 Open; 1954-58 Training; 1959 Open; 1960-66 Training; 1968 Training; 1970-74 Training; 1977 Training; 1980 Training
TRACK LENGTH: 380 yards
NICKNAME: 'Gulls'

In 1948, Liverpool novices sought out Charlie Oates and asked his advice about training. Before the beach could be used for practice, much hard work had to be done in digging up anti-invasion posts, which sprinkled the smooth stretches of sand. After several weeks, an area was cleared and levelled for a track. Training from 1948 until 1951 was organised by the aforementioned Charlie Oates, when roughly ten to twenty novices found their way to Ainsdale each week, using old machines for the initial rides, before moving on to better equipment as their riding improved. Training for the opening phase was done solo, then in pairs, until such time as the novices were considered capable of actual racing. Crowds were seated on the sand dunes to watch the afternoon training sessions. The spot used for training was exactly between Freshfield and Ainsdale, thus avoiding noise problems. As time went by, a regular track was marked out, plus an alternative one to defeat the tides. The riders were given numbered jackets for identification. There was also an elastic starting gate and coloured flags also made an appearance. Handicap racing was introduced in 1950, which attracted regular team riders, who wanted to keep fit with proper racing. A helpful leaflet was issued stating: 'For the benefit of those who travel by train, alight at Ainsdale Station, walk down to the beach, turn left towards Formby and walk for two miles. Cars may be taken along the beach and parked alongside the track'. A Winter Trainee's Trophy, staged on 19 February 1950, was won by Bill Bridgett. The track was measured to be 380 yards and was marked out with sandbags. The following week, 2,000 people attended the Ainsdale Supporters Trophy, which was won by Brian Craven. In March 1950, it was reported that the Ainsdale training season had closed. The article went on to say that it was perhaps for the better, as riders using the sands had been warned that they would be regarded as trespassing by Ince Blundell Estate, to whom the particular part of the foreshore belonged. However, if any prospective riders came to an agreement with Southport Corporation regarding noise levels, the estate would then continue to allow racing! On 18 February 1951, Ainsdale beat Newton Heath 47-37 in a training-track challenge match. Later that month, it was reported that 'Ainsdale practice track will be rented for four-pence per annum by Liverpool rider Charlie Oates. Owners of the sands, Ince Blundell Estates, have sportingly agreed to the use of the track for peppercorn rent.' In March 1952, Peter Craven took part in a series of special match races at Ainsdale. On 30 March 1952, Ainsdale again beat Newton Heath (37-31) in a training-track challenge match. In December 1955, it was reported that the sands were being used by midget cars, which could have spelt an end to speedway racing, due to the excessive noise, but thankfully this was averted. Peter and Brian Craven were among the riders training at Ainsdale in March 1956. There were complaints about the noise in 1960, due to some riders not keeping to the original site between Freshfield and Ainsdale. Mr M. Dormer held training school sessions at the venue throughout 1961. In 1962, the site was used by novices from Bradford and Sheffield. Stan Holey was known to have practised there in 1963. Norman Pugh, Bob Gandy and Mike Hawkins practised on the sands throughout the winter of 1965/66, but in so doing, clashed with the local National Nature Reserve controllers and nearby councils. Some novices used the Ainsdale sands over Christmas 1968, before switching to Belle Vue. Colin Meredith took his first rides on a speedway machine at Ainsdale sands in 1970. Keith White had training outings at Ainsdale in 1971 and 1972. Alan Grimshaw is known to have ridden on the sands in 1973. Michael Nesbitt, the son of the Ellesmere Port track manager, died after a fall at the close of a practice session at Ainsdale on Sunday 27 October 1974. Robert Craven began riding speedway bikes at Ainsdale in 1977. In 1993, a group of young riders attempted to practise at Ainsdale in spite of complaints from local residents.

ASKAM
ADDRESS: Askam Sands, Askam-in-Furness, Cumbria
YEARS OF OPERATION: 1972-73
Training

Tom Owen, Cliff Hindle and Alan Wilkinson put on a demonstration as part of the Duddon Inshore Rescue Team's Gala Day in July 1972. Cliff Hindle, along with his son, Ian, used the sands at Askam to train youngsters throughout the winter of 1972/73.

BARROW
ADDRESS: Walney Sands, Barrow-in-Furness
YEARS OF OPERATION: 1970

Ian Hindle used the sands at Walney for training in 1970.

BRASSA
ADDRESS: Brassa Sands, Ayrshire
YEARS OF OPERATION: 1976 Training

The sands at Brassa were used for training by local Ayrshire riders in 1976.

COCKLAW
ADDRESS: Cocklaw Beach, Nr Berwick-upon-Tweed, Northumberland
YEARS OF OPERATION: 1988-90 Sand Racing
FIRST MEETING: 7 February 1988

On 7 February 1988, the second leg of a challenge match between a side led by Mark Courtney and one led by Steve Lawson took place on Cocklaw Beach. Lawson's Louts had won the first-leg in Cumbria 41-37, but Courtney's team produced a solid display to win the return match 46-30, and gain an aggregate triumph of 83-71. Straw bales marked the track, while a piece of long elastic was used as the starting gate. Points scorers were: (Crusaders) Martin Dixon 12, Ian Rae 9, Mark Courtney 7, Mark Crang 6, Sean Courtney 5, Nig Allan 4, Mick Morning 3; (Louts) Geoff Powell 12, Steve Lawson 10, Mick Bewley 5, Shaun Bickley 1, Carl Foulder 1, Paul MacCarten 1. A year later, Mark Courtney organised a full-scale individual meeting on the sands at Cocklaw Beach, to raise money for Cancer Research. The proposal got the go-ahead from the Council, and although admission couldn't be charged, donations were asked for. The meeting went ahead on Sunday 26 February 1989, with the track marked out with bales of straw. The spectators, who were kept behind a roped-off area, saw a twenty-one-race presentation, which raised £500 for the charity. The meeting was sponsored by Mitsubishi, with Ian Atkinson taking first place. A third and final meeting (the Beach Classic, sponsored by Redpath Cars) was staged on 4 March 1990, and was won by Martin Dixon.

DAWLISH WARREN
ADDRESS: Dawlish Warren Beach, Devon
YEARS OF OPERATION: 1952-55 Training

The beach at Dawlish Warren was used by several Exeter riders prior to the 1952 season. The riders marked out tracks of different sizes for practice purposes. Cyril Lock, a promising young Exeter novice, was known to have trained on the beach during the winter of 1953/54. Among others, Goog Hoskin used the sands for training before the 1955 season got underway.

DIRLETON
ADDRESS: Dirleton Broad Sands, Nr North Berwick, Lothian
YEARS OF OPERATION: 1953 Training

A track was marked out on the sands, with Harry Darling, Artie Fisher and Jack Jones known to have used the site frequently. Dick Campbell, Roy Bester and mechanic Jimmy White are also known to have assisted with coaching, often providing helpful hints.

DRURIDGE BAY
ADDRESS: Druridge Bay, Nr Lynemouth, Northumberland
YEARS OF OPERATION: 1946-47 Training; 1962 Training; 1968 Training

Johnnie Hoskins took a dozen novices down to the beach in early 1946 for training – his best finds were Alec 'Farmer' Grant and Doug Gray. Newcastle novices are known to have regularly practised on the fine stretch of sands at Druridge Bay throughout 1947. In 1962, Dave Younghusband is known to have attended a Don Wilkinson training school that was held on the beach. Mike Hiftle used the bay for training in 1968.

DUBLIN
ADDRESS: Dollymount Strand, Dublin
YEARS OF OPERATION: 1952 Training; 1968-69 Training

The sands at Dollymount are known to have been used for training by novices in January, February and March 1952. The shape of the track was based on Shelbourne Park, and was marked out by Paddy Cullen using string and beach debris. The beach was again used for winter training in 1968/69.

EDINBURGH
ADDRESS: Seafield Beach, Edinburgh
YEARS OF OPERATION: 1949-50 Training

Don Cuppleditch and Bob Mark used Seafield beach for practice during the winter of 1949/50. The area is now built over with a sewage works.

GUERNSEY
ADDRESS: Guernsey Sands, Channel Islands
YEARS OF OPERATION: 1969
Hughie Saunders was known to have practised on the sands at Guernsey during the summer of 1969.

IRVINE
ADDRESS: Irvine Bay, Strathclyde
YEARS OF OPERATION: 1948-49 Training

Willie Wilson and Bill Bates are known to have trained at Irvine Bay during the winter of 1948/49.

MABLETHORPE
ADDRESS: Mablethorpe Sands, Lincolnshire
YEARS OF OPERATION: 1970

Carl Glover first rode a speedway bike on the sands at Mablethorpe in 1970.

MARYPORT
ADDRESS: Allonby Sands, Maryport, Nr

Workington, Cumbria
YEARS OF OPERATION: 1971-2000
Training

Maurice Stobbart originally held training sessions on the sands at Allonby Bay in 1971. Prior to riding for Workington, Steve Watson took his first rides on the sands in 1971. Steve Lawson regularly used the sands that adjoin the family farm for practice from 1972 to 1992. Andy Reid, Steve McDermott, Jacko Irving, Des Wilson and Geoff Powell have all trained on the sands throughout their careers in speedway. In 1988, a challenge match took place between Lawson's Louts and the Courtney Crusaders, which resulted in a 41-37 victory to Steve Lawson's side. Other riders partaking in the meeting included Mark Courtney, Sean Courtney, Geoff Powell and Martin Dixon. Craig Branney and Lee Smethills are known to have practised on the sands after the end of the 2000 season. Barry Briggs gave tuition to upcoming hopeful Robert Brown on the sands in 2000.

MORPETH
ADDRESS: Morpeth Sands, Northumberland
YEARS OF OPERATION: 1948 Training

Alan Nicholson spent much of 1948 training at Morpeth Sands, prior to applying for a trial at Hull.

NEWQUAY
ADDRESS: Newquay Beach, Cornwall
YEARS OF OPERATION: 1937 Training

Bill Collins used the beach at Newquay for training in 1937, under the guidance of Bert Jones.

SCREMERSTON

ADDRESS: Scremerston Sands, Berwick-upon-Tweed
YEARS OF OPERATION: 1985-86 Training

Sean Courtney used the beach at Scremerston for training during the winter of 1985/86.

SOUTHPORT

ADDRESS: Southport Sands, Lancashire
YEARS OF OPERATION: 1956 Training; 1993 Training

Among other riders, Stan Holey, Vic Lonsdale and Tommy Roper used Southport Sands for practising in 1956. Chris Cobby was reported to have used the sands for training in 1993.

TROON

ADDRESS: Ayrshire Sands, Troon
YEARS OF OPERATION: 1973 Training; 1982 Training; 1988 Training

It was reported in 1973 that a number of young hopefuls had regularly used the deserted sands between Troon and Prestwick for practice. Among those known to have trained on the sands were John and Jim Beresford, Johnny Rodger and Calum MacAulay. Glasgow rider Martin McKinna is known to have used the sands for practice sessions in 1982. During the Christmas break in 1988, Kenny McKinna, along with Colin and Fred Caffrey, were seen racing on the sands, using speedway bikes and 125cc machines.

WESTON-SUPER-MARE

ADDRESS: Brean Sands, Weston-Super-Mare
YEARS OF OPERATION: 1958 Training; 1974 Training

Ron Tuck used the sands for practice in 1958. Barry Duke is known to have trained on the Brean Sands in 1974.

WHITLEY BAY

ADDRESS: Whitley Bay, Tyne and Wear
YEARS OF OPERATION: 1946

Newcastle novices are known to have trained at Whitley Bay during the winter of 1946.

GRASS SPEEDWAY TRACKS

For the sake of completeness, the following is a list of 137 grass speedway circuits, with their known years of operation as speedways shown in brackets. Many of these venues have caused great confusion to speedway historians over the years, due to inclusion of the word 'speedway' in their advertising, reports or programmes.

Abridge Speedway (1932-37 and 1946-50)
Acklam Speedway (1932)
Addington Speedway, Carshalton (1931)
Aero Speedway, Folkestone (1930)
Aintree Grass Speedway (1928-30)
Albion Speedway, Edenbridge (1930; 1934)
Ashford Grass Speedway (1928-39; 1947-48) Sometimes also known as Blind Lane Speedway
Ashton Grass Speedway (1947-51)
Avebury Speedway (1939)
Aylestone Lane Speedway, Wigston Magna (1933-38)
Belmont Grass Speedway (1931)
Blandford Speedway (1946)
Boxmoor Speedway (1932)
Brambletye Speedway (1930-31)

Brands Hatch Speedway (1932-39; 1946-49)

Bridge Speedway, Basingstoke (1936-39)

Brimsdown Dirt-Track (1928)

Broome Park Speedway, Barham (1938-39; 1946-47)

Bugle Speedway (1930-31)

Calmore Grass Speedway (1938-39)

Cannards Grave Speedway, Shepton Mallet (1937-39)

Cannfield Speedway (1932-39; 1951)

Carnegie Speedway, Wigan (1932)

Castle Speedway, Hickstead (1938)

Catherington Speedway, Hordean (1936)

Chaddesley Corbett Speedway (1939)

Chard Speedway (1942-43)

Chingford Speedway (1929)

Cleethorpes Speedway (1932)

Corfe Mullen Speedway (1937-39)

Cromford Speedway, Matlock (1930)

Crookhorn Grass Speedway, Portsmouth (1973-74)

Crowhurst Grass Speedway (1928-31)

Crown Speedway, Tolldown (1939)

Denmead Speedway (1936)

Dodd's Weir Speedway (1932)

Downend Speedway, Bristol (1937)

Dundridge Speedway, Bishop's Waltham (1938)

Dunstable Speedway (1929-30)

Ely Grass Speedway (1948)

Fakenham Speedway (1932)

Farleigh Castle Speedway (1938-40; 1946-54; 1991-92)

Filton Speedway, Bristol (1944-45)

Flying Mile Circuit, Biggin Hill (1936)

Folkestone Grass Speedway (1929)

Folkestone Heights Speedway (1946-47)

Folkington Speedway (1932)

Fordham Speedway (1928-29)

Four Green Pillars Speedway, Wrotham Heath (1930)

Grassmore Speedway (1929)

Great North Road Grass Speedway,

Southgate (1929)

Griestling Speedway, Hastings (1932)

Grimsby Road Speedway, Waltham (1932)

Gunton Hall Speedway, Lowestoft (1934)

Hall Field Speedway, Northwich (1930)

Hallfield Speedway, Lostock (1930)

Handforth Speedway (1928-30)

Hanworth Speedway (1930)

Hardy Speedway, Grimsby (1944-45)

Hastings Speedway, Stonestile Lane (1936)

Hastings Speedway, Westfield (1937-38)

Hearts Delight Speedway, Canterbury (1935-38)

Hempstead Sports Club Speedway, Gillingham (1938)

Henfield Speedway (1938)

High Lane Speedway, Woodford (1930-31)

Hill Top Speedway, Amesbury (1934)

Humberstone Speedway, Grimsby (1931)

Hundred Road Grass Speedway, March (1946)

Ivy House Speedway, Chalfont (1934-37)

Iwade Grass Speedway (1932)

Kessingland Speedway, Lowestoft (1933-35)

Keyworth Speedway, Nottingham (1932-34)

King's Head Speedway, Horsebridge (1931)

Kingsdown Speedway (1947-51)

Klondyke Speedway, Elwick (1937-39)

Krooner Park Speedway, Camberley (1933)

Limes Speedway, Wisbech (1938-39)

Lindops Speedway, Chester (1933)

Linwood Road Speedway, Market Rasen (1931)

Matts Hill Speedway, Rainham (1935-36)

Middlewich Speedway (1931)

Midgham Speedway (1936)

Miers Court Speedway, Rainham (1936-37)

Mill Lane Speedway, Barnetby (1929; 1931-32; 1934)

Monks Pool Speedway, West Molesey (1930)

Mountnessing Speedway (1931-34)

Murrell Green Speedway, Hartley Wintney (1938)

New Rayleigh Speedway, Rayleigh (1939)

Newmarket Grass Speedway (1939)

North Hant's Speedway, Murrel Green (1936-38; 1946-47)

Ormskirk Speedway (1931-33)

Oxford Speedway Club, Sandford (1936-38)

Pakefield East Coast Speedway, Lowestoft (1935-36)

Panfield Grass Speedway (1931)

Popham Speedway, Winchester (1937)

Quarry Hill Speedway, Scotch Corner (1930)

Ramper Speedway, Gainsborough (1933)

Randalls Park Speedway, Leatherhead (1929-39)

Rettendon Speedway (1946-47)

Reeves Farm Speedway, Chalfont (1946-49)

Rocky Park Speedway, St. Austell (1932-35; 1947-48)

Roke Down Speedway, Bournemouth (1947-50)

Ropersole Speedway (1934)

Salisbury Speedway (1935-39)

Seale Hall Speedway, Lancaster (1931-32)

Sewardstone Grass Speedway (1930-31; 1938)

Shepperton Speedway (1938-39)

Sherborne Grass Speedway, Dorset (1946)

Sunnyhill Speedway, Sittingbourne (1929-31)

Station Speedway, Builth Wells (1932)

Stonehouse Speedway, Streatham (1931)

Swainswick Speedway (1939)

Swineshead Speedway, Boston (1930)

Tamworth Speedway, Fazeley (1932-33)

Taunton Speedway (1937-39; 1945-46)

The Speedway, Birkdale (1946-47)

The Speedway, Bishop's Watham (1936-38)

The Speedway, Sandbach (1929)

The Speedway, Sedlescombe Road, Hastings (1931)

Thornwell Speedway (1929)

Treviscoe Speedway (1946)

Underwood Speedway, Loughborough (1929-31)

Upton Down Speedway, Burford (1949-50)

Valley Speedway, Branksome, Bournemouth (1931)

Waltham Cross Speedway (1929)

Walthamstow Speedway (1929)

Watford Speedway (1938)

Waveney Speed Track, Bradwell (1932)

Westbere Butts Speedway (1930-33)

Westfield Road Speedway, Barton-upon-Humber (1933)

Weybourne Speedway, Aldershot (1935)

Whitehaven Speedway (1930-31)

Willow Bridge Speedway, Darlington (1931-33)

Wisbech Dirt-Track (1937-39; 1946-48)

Wroughton Speedway (1937-39)

Wymering Park Speedway, Portsmouth (1928-31)

Yarmouth Speedway (1932)

A small selection of other sports titles available from Tempus Publishing:

Speedway titles:

Speedway in East Anglia	Norman Jacobs	0 7524 1882 3
Speedway in London	Norman Jacobs	0 7524 2221 9
Speedway in Scotland	Jim Henry/Ian Moultray	0 7524 2229 4
Bristol Bulldogs	David Woods	0 7524 2231 6

Football titles:

Crystal Palace FC	Revd Nigel Sands	0 7524 1544 1
Devon Derbies	Mike Holgate	0 7524 1898 X
Gillingham FC	Roger Triggs	0 7524 1567 0
Hull City FC	Chris Elton	0 7524 1620 0
Leeds United FC	David Saffer/Howard Dapin	0 7524 1642 1
Millwall FC	Millwall FC Museum	0 7524 1849 1
Motherwell FC	John Swinburne	0 7524 1511 5
Oxford United FC	Jon Murray	0 7524 1183 7
Reading FC 1871-1997	David Downs	0 7524 1061 X
Rotherham United FC	Gerry Somerton	0 7524 1670 7
Sheffield United FC	Denis Clarebrough	0 7524 1059 8
Stoke City FC	Tony Matthews	0 7524 1698 7
Sunderland AFC	Alan Brett & George Hoare	0 7524 0716 3

Rugby League titles:

Halifax RLFC	Andrew Hardcastle	0 7524 1831 9
Hunslet RLFC	Les Hoole	0 7524 1641 3
Leeds RLFC	Phil Caplan & Les Hoole	0 7524 1140 3
Salford RLFC	Graham Morris	0 7524 1897 1
Sheffield Eagles RLFC	John Cornwell	0 7524 1830 0

Rugby Union titles:

Bristol RFC	Mark Hoskins & Dave Fox	0 7524 1875 0
The Five Nations Story	David Hands	0 7524 1851 3
Newcastle RFC	Alan Hedley	0 7524 2046 1
Newport RFC: 1874-1950	Steve Lewis	0 7524 1570 0

Cricket titles:

Glamorgan CCC	Andrew Hignell	0 7524 0792 9
Leicestershire CCC	Dennis Lambert	0 7524 1864 5
Somerset CCC	Somerset Cricket Museum	0 7524 1585 9
Worcestershire CCC	Les Hatton	0 7524 1834 3
Yorkshire CCC	Mick Pope	0 7524 0756 2

Please contact Tempus Publishing for a full stocklist.